Above & Beyond 🌿 Parsley

THE SIMPLEST ELEMENTS CAN SPLASH

A VIVID PORTRAIT ONTO THE CANVAS

OF ENTERTAINING.

CHAMPAGNE FANTASY ✿ *59*

Above & Beyond Parsley

Food

for the

Senses

Presented by

The Junior League of Kansas City, Missouri

Also by The Junior League of
Kansas City, Missouri:

Company's Coming (1975)
Beyond Parsley (1984)

First printing August 1992

Printed in the United States of America

ISBN 0-9607076-2-X

10 9 8 7 6 5 4 3   93 94 95 96

The purpose of the Junior League is to train
volunteers to serve the community. The profit
realized from the sale of *Above & Beyond
Parsley* will be used for community projects
sponsored by The Junior League of Kansas
City, Missouri.

For information on ordering copies of cookbooks
published by The Junior League of Kansas City,
Missouri, contact:

Cookbook Committee
Junior League of Kansas City, MO
P. O. Box 413-934
Kansas City, MO 64141

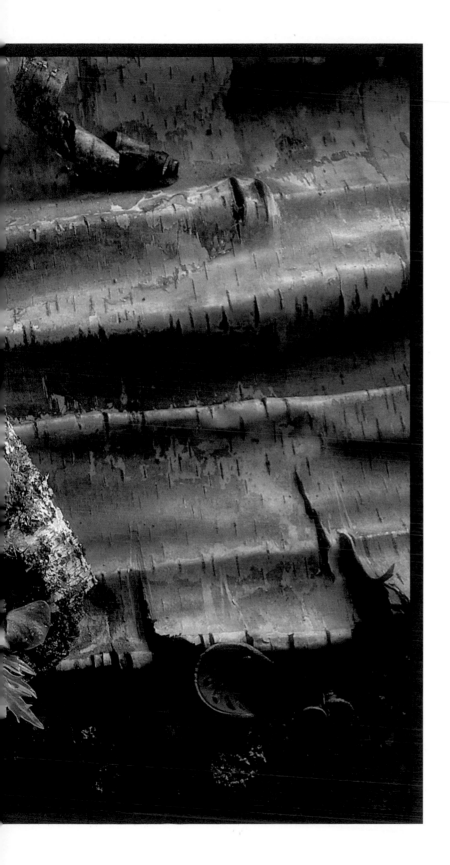

RIPPLES OF COLOR

AND TUMBLING SHAPES

CREATE STARTLING EDDIES

OF VISUAL APPEAL.

AUTUMN RIVER SALAD 🍂 97

Table of Contents

Appetizers   32

Bread & Breakfast   60

Salads   92

Soups & Stews   120

Meats   142

Poultry   164

Fish & Seafood   186

Pasta & Pizza   206

Vegetables & Grains   230

Desserts   252

Acknowledgments   286

Indexes   289

WHEN IMAGINATION

PLAYS IN THE GARDEN OF POSSIBILITIES,

PRETTY PASTRIES SPRING ALL IN A ROW.

CITRUS BLOSSOMS 🍃 278

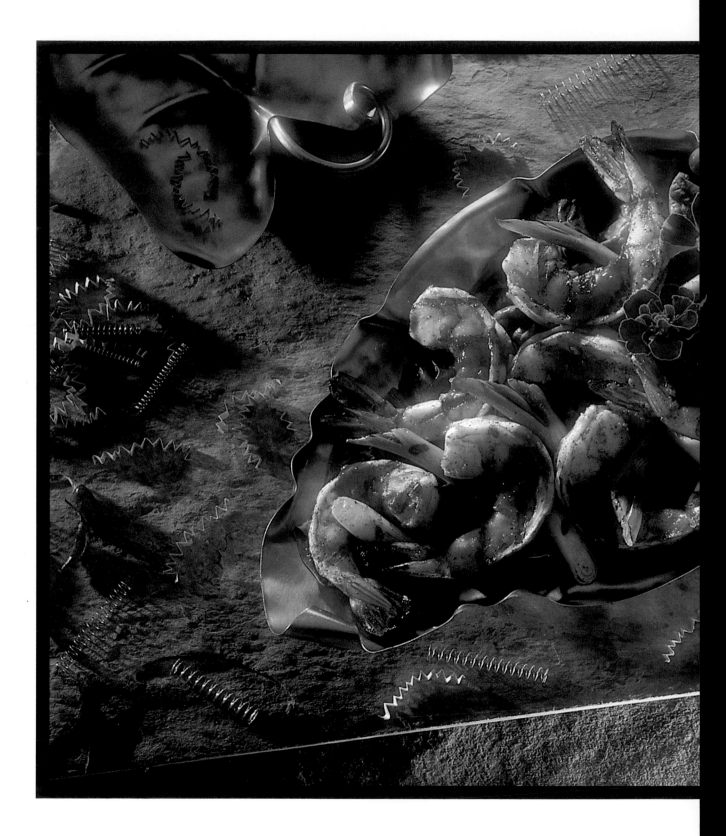

SPRINGY TEXTURES AND LIVELY CRUNCH

MAKE CERTAIN FOODS LEAP TO THE NIBBLE.

SHRIMP KABOBS AND RED PEPPER SAUCE ✒ 189

Steering Committee

Co-Chairmen
Jan Bergman Flanagan
Jane Doyle Guthrie

Business Manager
Lyn Cravens

Business Support Chairman
Debbie Ray Pope

Recipe Chairman
Martha M. Steele

Recipe Development Chairman
Siobhan McLaughlin-Lesley

Testing Co-Chairmen
Lisa Ray Curran
Merrill Dean Myers

Editors
Laura Babcock Sutherland
Karen Massman VanAsdale

Design & Production Chairman
Merrily Thomson Jackson

Production Research
Cynthia Schradle Owens

Marketing Chairman
Karen Conde Adler

Special Events Chairman
Annie Kampfe Miller

Committee Assistant
Susan Trainor Price

PROFESSIONAL CREDITS

Title
West Associates Advertising & Design

Concept, Design & Art Direction
Anne Simmons/WRK, Inc.

Food Styling
Vicki Johnson

Photography
Ernie Block/Ernie Block Studio, Inc.

Film Processing
Image Point, Inc.

Consultants
Bill Crooks/PB&J Restaurants, Inc.
Ken & Diane Crouse/Crouse Catering
Linda Zey Davis
Chuck Matney/Matney Floral Design

THE TONGUE GLIDES SMOOTHLY

OVER SILKY SURFACES LIKE THE SWEEP

OF A SHOOTING STAR.

BOURSIN BLUE CHEESECAKE 🌿 47

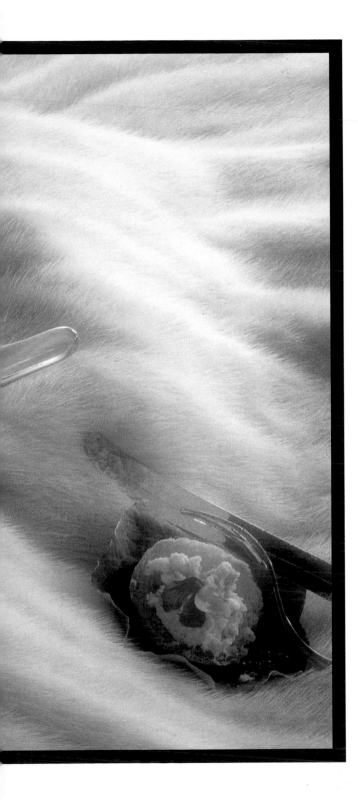

FOOD preparation and presentation, whether simple or elaborate, can easily transcend the expected and deliciously engage the imagination.
The textures of foods, alone or in appealing combinations, can invite savoring and discovery.
Colors and shapes can interact smoothly or in daring juxtaposition to create mood and lively interest.
Aromas can evoke strong, pleasurable associations, heightening the enjoyable anticipation of memorable meals.
This climb above and beyond the ordinary occurs along the stairway of the senses.

SEE *the swirl of blackberry pinwheels, the ribbon tangles of pasta, the tumble of greens and flowers in a fresh spring salad.*

FEEL *feathery mousse, springy shrimp, crunchy pepitas, juicy corn.*

SMELL *citrusy lemongrass, fruity olive oils, smoky seared tenderloins, garlicky pesto.*

TASTE *peppery arugula, pungent wild mushrooms, the tang of chutney, the nutty sweetness of marzipan.*

This is a book about the multifaceted pleasures of food, including the details and ambience of the dining environment.
These elements can add a potent dimension to the sensory play of the menu.
Our goal is to capture *your* imagination and captivate *your* senses. With the variety of recipes and tips interwoven here, we hope to whet your appetite for the finishing touches that nudge food presentation
Above & Beyond Parsley.

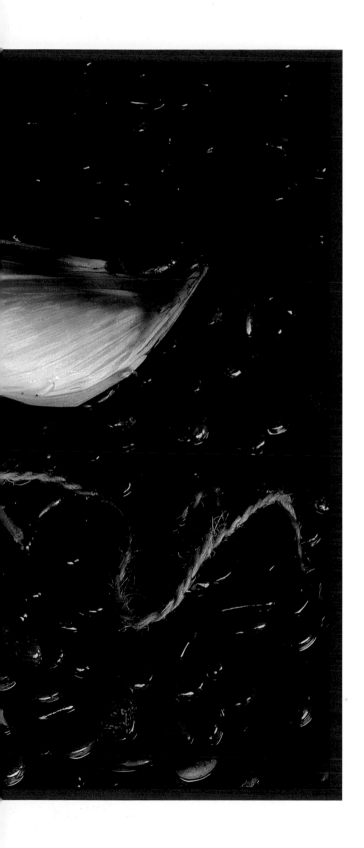

THE GIFT OF THE GRILL—

HOT RIVULETS OF FLAVOR

WAIT TO STREAM FROM

CRISP KERNELS

WHEN HUSKY WRAPPERS

FALL AWAY.

GRILLED HERB CORN ON THE COB ✿ *238*

BASKING HEAT COAXES GRAIN

INTO FRAGRANT FORMS

AND LOOSENS THE EARTHY PERFUME

OF COMPANION HERBS.

SAGE CELERY SEED BREAD  62

ROMA FENNEL BREAD 🌿 63

SAVORY OLIVE NUT BREAD 🌿 70

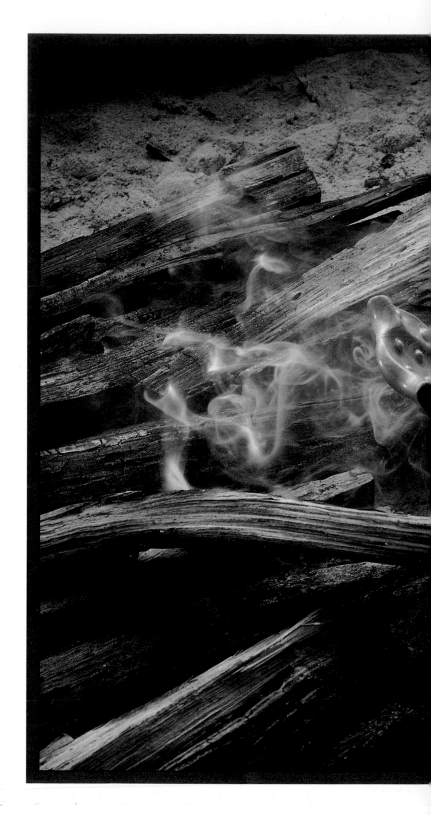

HEARTY FLAVORS

CAN REST WELL TOGETHER,

LINGERING AFTER THE MEAL

LIKE TRACES

OF SWEET SMOKE.

**HERBED BLACK BEAN SOUP
WITH SMOKED CHICKEN** 🍃 *123*

THE SOFT GRAINY TEXTURE OF FRAGILE SOUFFLÉS OFFERS A

FLEETING ENCOUNTER WITH TIMELESS EATING PLEASURE.

POLENTA PEPPER SOUFFLÉS ✑ *247*

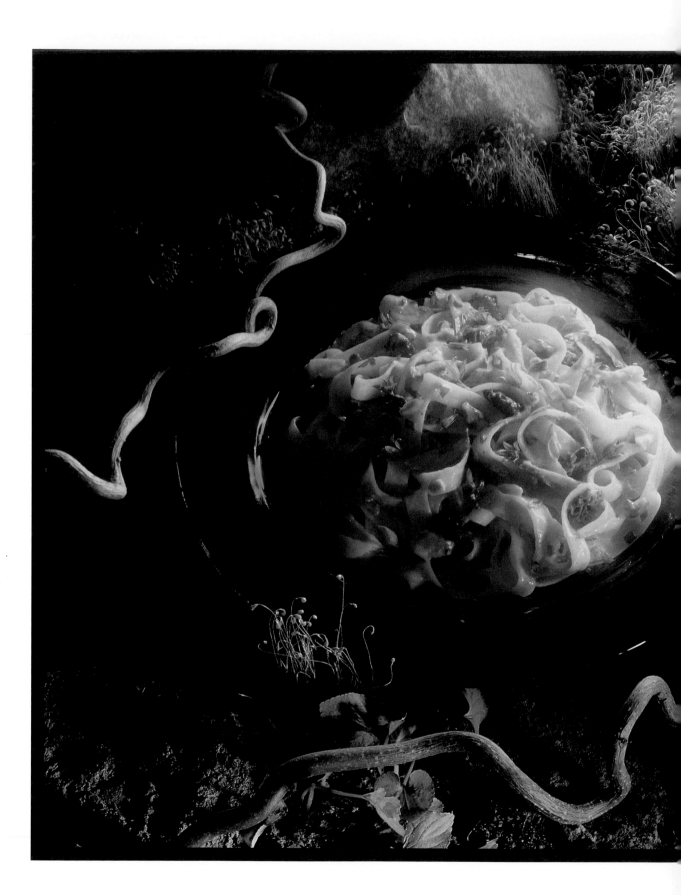

EDIBLE WILD TREASURES

REVEAL RICH HIDING PLACES

WITHIN THE PALATE'S

FAMILIAR RANGE.

RIVER COUNTRY PASTA ✿ *215*

WARM MORNING COLORS RUN LIKE SPILLED CREAM, POOLING ON

PLATES AND DAPPLING THE TABLE WITH SUNNY TOUCHES.

POACHED EGGS IN AVOCADO ✒ 89

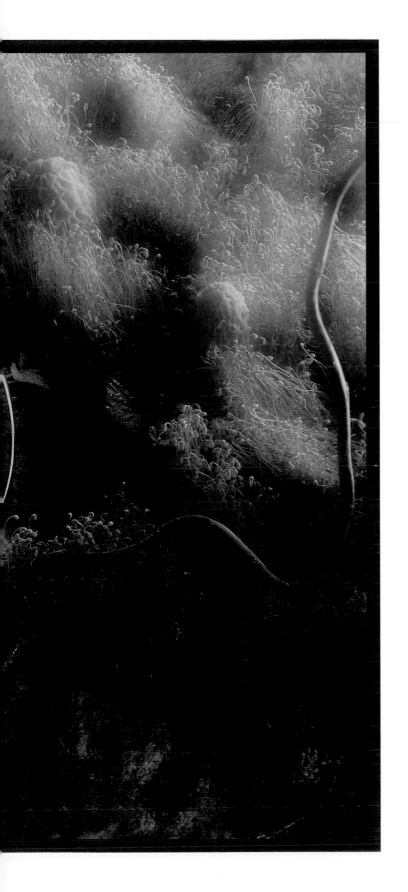

EDIBLE WILD TREASURES

REVEAL RICH HIDING PLACES

WITHIN THE PALATE'S

FAMILIAR RANGE.

RIVER COUNTRY PASTA ✽ *215*

ELEMENTAL AROMAS

SHARPLY AWAKEN THE APPETITE

AND ROUSE LAYERS OF

PLEASANT ASSOCIATIONS.

STUFFED CRANBERRY-PEPPER GAME HENS ✷ 182

WARM MORNING COLORS RUN LIKE SPILLED CREAM, POOLING ON

PLATES AND DAPPLING THE TABLE WITH SUNNY TOUCHES.

POACHED EGGS IN AVOCADO ✿ *89*

POCKETS JUST

NATURALLY COLLECT

WONDERFUL THINGS —

SAVORY MORSELS,

GLORIOUS GOODIES

AND TASTY BITS OF

THIS AND THAT.

GRILLED LAMB PITA POCKETS *161*

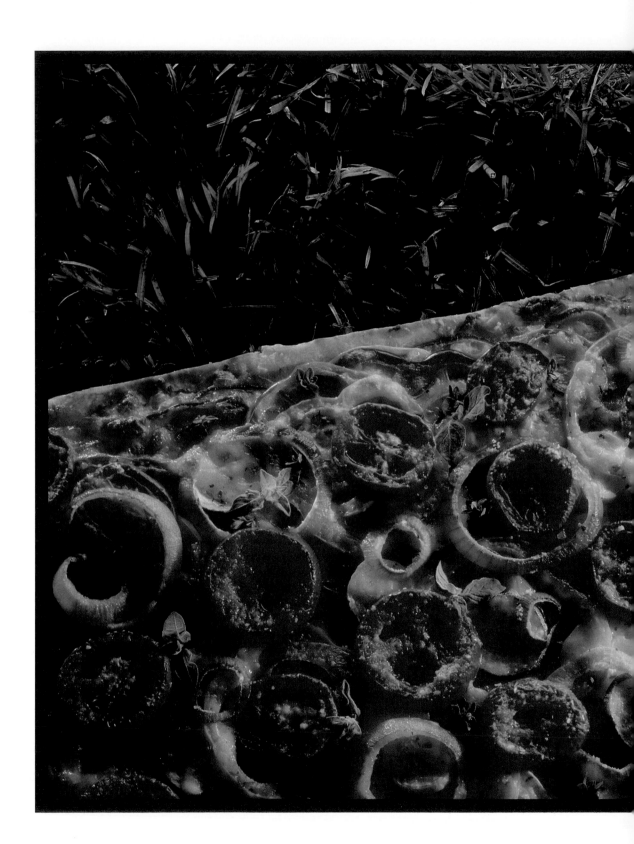

RIPE SUMMER FLAVORS

BURST IRREPRESSIBLY THROUGH THE SEASON'S

LUSH ABUNDANCE.

SUMMER PHYLLO PIZZA 🍃 *223*

SOME SWEET ENDINGS

    HOVER LIGHT AS A DREAM,

TICKLING AND TEASING

ONE MORE STIR

    FROM DROWSY TASTE BUDS.

COLD WHITE CHOCOLATE SOUFFLÉ ❧ *272*

DIPS, SPREADS & PATÉS

Artichokes Athena, 43
Avocado Mousse, 49
Black and White Spread, 54
Black-Eyed Peaco de Gallo, 52
Caesar Cream, 53
Caviar Supreme, 55
Curried Cauliflower, 54
Fresh Fruit Salsa, 53
Lemon Olive Caviar, 50
Mediterranean Mélange, 51
Olive Paste, 51
Pâté with Apricots and Pistachios, 38
Roasted Red Pepper Garlic Dip, 52
Sun-Dried Tomato Vinaigrette, 54
White Salsa Dip, 52

CHEESE & CHEESECAKES

Boursin Blue Cheesecake, 47
Brie and Pear Bundles, 44
Farmer's Market Pie, 49
Feta Cheese Parcels, 42
Fontina Grilled in Vine Leaves, 46
Fruit with Sherried Cheese, 43
Gruyère Cheesecake, 45
Herbed Mozzarella, 45
Marinated Goat Cheese, 44
Queso Grill, 47
Santa Fe Cheesecake, 46
Smoked Salmon and Onion Cheesecake, 48
Stuffed Spinach Crêpes, 42

PASTRIES & TOASTS

Basic Bruschetta, 57
Chèvre Pine Nut Toasts with Sun-Dried Tomato Pesto, 56
Jiao Z, 37
Roquefort Toasts, 56
Shrimp and Spinach Phyllo with Mustard Cream Sauce, 36
Sweet Onion Bites, 58
Thai Pies, 37

MEATS & SEAFOOD

Carpaccio Dijonnaise, 39
Shrimp Cakes, 35
Shrimp in Dijon Vinaigrette, 34
Smoked Salmon with Salmon Biscuits, 34
Tenderloin with Three Sauces, 39
Tropical Seviche, 35
Veal Meatballs with Tomato Sauce, 40

COCKTAIL PICK-UPS

Peppery Pepitas, 58
Spiced Olives, 57

MINI RECIPES

Beverages, 59
Herbed Goat Cheese, 57
Toasted Pita Triangles, 40
Tomato and Fennel Spread, 57

Appetizers

Pictured finishing touch:

FREEZING HERBS

AND

FLOWERS IN ICE CUBES, 59

SPECIAL TOPIC BOXES

BEVERAGES, 59

CHEESE BITES, 41

A TASTY BITE, 50

Shrimp in Dijon Vinaigrette

3 pounds large shrimp,
peeled and deveined

1/2 cup finely chopped fresh parsley

1/2 cup finely chopped shallots

1/2 cup tarragon vinegar

1/2 cup white wine vinegar

1 cup olive oil

8 tablespoons Dijon mustard

4 teaspoons red pepper flakes

2 teaspoons salt

Freshly ground pepper, to taste

1 tablespoon fresh lemon juice

Cook shrimp in boiling salted water until pink. Drain and transfer to a large bowl. Combine remaining ingredients and pour over warm shrimp. Toss well so that every shrimp is coated. Cover and refrigerate for at least 8 to 10 hours (overnight is best). Drain excess sauce from shrimp before serving.

Serves 8–10

Must be prepared in advance.

An easy-to-make appetizer or first course. The flavors will intensify when marinated overnight. Serve in a large bowl lined with lettuce and kale.

Smoked Salmon with Salmon Biscuits

1 cup flour

1-1/2 teaspoons baking powder

1/4 teaspoon salt

1 tablespoon cold, unsalted butter,
cut into bits

2-1/4 ounces smoked salmon, minced

3 tablespoons snipped fresh dill

6–8 tablespoons heavy cream

6 heaping tablespoons sour cream

3 ounces thinly sliced smoked salmon

Fresh dill sprigs, to garnish

Preheat oven to 400 degrees. In a medium bowl, sift together flour, baking powder and salt. Blend in butter until mixture resembles coarse meal. Stir in minced salmon, 2 tablespoons dill and enough heavy cream to make a soft dough. Form dough into a ball.

On a lightly floured surface, roll or pat out dough until 1/2-inch thick. Cut out 3 biscuits with a 2-inch cutter dipped in flour, shaping and rerolling dough as necessary. Place dough cutouts on a baking sheet 1 inch apart. Brush tops lightly with remaining cream and bake for 15 to 17 minutes or until puffed and golden and a toothpick inserted in the center comes out clean.

Mix remaining 1 tablespoon dill into sour cream. With a serrated knife, gently halve biscuits horizontally and transfer, cut-side up, to a plate or serving platter. Mound 1 teaspoon sour cream mixture onto each biscuit and top with a slice of smoked salmon. Garnish each plate or the serving platter with dill sprigs.

Serves 6

*Tender biscuits take on a salmon blush. For a first-course Valentine's treat, pair heart-shaped versions with **Red Pepper Soup**.*

Shrimp Cakes

1/4 of a medium tart apple

1 pound shrimp, peeled and deveined

3 strips bacon

1/4 cup chopped scallions (green parts only)

1 teaspoon minced fresh ginger

1/2 teaspoon salt

1/4 teaspoon sugar

Pinch of freshly ground white pepper

1 teaspoon shao-hsing wine or dry sherry

2 teaspoons cornstarch

2 eggs

1/4 cup peanut oil

2 cups shredded lettuce

Peel and finely dice apple. Cut shrimp into very small pieces. Fry bacon until crisp. Drain and crumble into fine pieces. Combine apple, shrimp, bacon, scallions and ginger. Add salt, sugar, pepper, wine and cornstarch. Mix well. Add unbeaten eggs and carefully mix again.

Heat peanut oil in a frying pan. When oil is hot, drop in heaping tablespoons of shrimp mixture. Cook for 1 minute, then turn each cake over. When lightly golden, remove with a slotted spatula and lay on a bed of shredded lettuce. Serve immediately. (May be made ahead and reheated on a baking sheet in a 400-degree oven. Watch carefully, heating no longer than 5 minutes.)

Serves 8

*These beautiful cakes are delicious with a dollop of plain yogurt, sour cream, **Fresh Fruit Salsa** or cucumber dill sauce. Try them as a light lunch as well as an appetizer.*

Tropical Seviche

1 pound bay scallops or quartered sea scallops

1/2 cup white wine

1-1/2 cups fresh lime juice

6 scallions, chopped (white parts only)

1/2 cup fresh orange juice

1/2 yellow bell pepper, chopped

1/2 red bell pepper, chopped

1 Anaheim chili, chopped

4 tablespoons cilantro, minced

1/2 cup olive oil

1/2 teaspoon oregano

1 teaspoon salt

Freshly ground pepper, to taste

Belgian endive leaves

Grated zest of 3 limes, to garnish

Poach scallops in white wine and 1/2 cup lime juice for about 2 minutes. Then marinate scallops and scallions in remaining lime juice and orange juice. Chill for at least 4 hours.

Drain well and discard marinade. Add next 8 ingredients to scallops and scallions and mix. Separate Belgian endive leaves and spoon seviche into cavity. Garnish with lime zest and serve.

Serves 6

Beautiful colors make this an elegant appetizer for a special gathering. Arrange on a glass platter or spoon into a wine or champagne goblet and insert endive leaves around the perimeter.

3/4 pound fresh spinach, stems removed

1 carrot, peeled and grated

4 cloves garlic, minced

1 egg

1/2 cup crème fraîche or 4 tablespoons heavy cream

Salt and freshly ground pepper, to taste

1/2 teaspoon ground nutmeg

1 pound medium shrimp, peeled and deveined

24–32 sheets phyllo pastry

1/2 cup (1 stick) unsalted butter, melted

1/4 cup freshly grated Parmesan cheese

Egg wash (optional)

Sauce:

2 shallots, finely chopped

1 tablespoon butter

1/2 cup dry white wine

1/4 cup clam juice

Dash of freshly ground pepper

1-1/4 cup heavy cream

2 tablespoons Dijon mustard

Wash, drain and pat spinach leaves dry. In a large bowl, toss spinach, carrot and garlic. Beat egg until frothy. Add along with crème fraîche, salt, pepper and nutmeg to spinach mixture and combine. Toss in shrimp and set mixture aside.

Brush 1 sheet of phyllo with melted butter and sprinkle with a pinch of Parmesan cheese. Repeat with 3 more sheets, layering each on top of the other. Spread 1/6 of the spinach-shrimp mixture along the short end of layered phyllo closest to you, keeping a 2-1/2 to 3-inch margin on each side. Fold right and left margins over, pressing lightly. Roll into bundles, starting with the spinach and shrimp–topped end. Repeat the process for 5 to 7 more bundles.

Preheat oven to 375 degrees. Arrange phyllo bundles on lightly greased baking sheets and brush with egg wash, if desired. Bake until golden brown, about 15 minutes. Top with warm mustard sauce and serve.

For sauce: In a heavy, medium saucepan, sauté shallots in butter for about 2 minutes. Add wine, clam juice and pepper, simmering and stirring until liquid is reduced to 1/4 cup. Stir in cream and bring to a boil. Reduce to medium heat and simmer, stirring often, until sauce thickens and will coat the back of a spoon (about 10 minutes). Reduce heat to low and whisk in mustard. Taste, adjust seasoning and add more mustard if desired.

Serves 6

A delightful, versatile prelude or even a light entree for a small group. The mustard sauce is also delicious served over fish or chicken.

Fresh ginger keeps in frozen form indefinitely. Grate as much as needed straight from the freezer—no need to peel or thaw.

Thai Pies

1/4 cup peanut oil

12 frozen white dinner rolls, defrosted

3/4 cup Szechuan peanut sauce

2 poached chicken breasts, shredded

1–2 carrots, julienned or shaved

2 scallions, sliced thin diagonally

8 ounces shredded
Monterey Jack cheese

Thai chili sauce (available in
Asian markets)

Grease baking sheets with some of peanut oil. Brush rolls with remaining peanut oil and follow package directions for rising. When rolls have risen, use hands to press each into a 4-inch circle. Place on baking sheet and spread 2 tablespoons peanut sauce on each.

Scatter shredded chicken over peanut sauce. Follow with carrots, scallions and cheese. Drizzle chili sauce over all (sauce is hot, so use sparingly). Bake in a 375-degree oven for 8 to 10 minutes. Peanut sauce will darken if overbaked.

Serves 8–12

Serve individually or cut into bite-sized squares. If pressed for time, use boboli rounds. As an alternative to the fiery chili sauce, combine 1/4 cup Hoisin sauce with 1 tablespoon each of water, sugar and sesame oil. Bring to a boil, reduce heat and simmer over low heat for 3 minutes.

Jiao Z

1/2 pound ground pork

8 ounces cooked spinach

5 scallions, chopped

2–3 tablespoons soy sauce

2 tablespoons sesame oil

2–3 tablespoons freshly chopped garlic

1-1/2 tablespoons grated fresh ginger

1-1/2 teaspoons salt

1 egg white

1 package won ton skins
(4- by 4-inch squares)

Combine all ingredients except egg white and spoon into won ton skins (about 1 teaspoon per wrapper). Fold on line to form triangles. Seal corners and edges with egg white. Bring outside corners up to meet and seal again with egg white.

Boil for about 5 to 10 minutes. Dumplings will float, then sink and then usually float again. Do not undercook, as pork will not be done; do not overcook or dumplings will be too soft.

As an alternative, heat wok with oil. Add dumplings and fry until golden.

Makes 50–60

These authentic Chinese morsels (pronounced "jouzit") are also known as potstickers. Have flavored soy sauces, sweet and sour sauce and hot mustard available for dipping. The boiled variety are also great in soup.

Pâté with Apricots and Pistachios

1 pound chicken livers

1-1/2 cups milk

1/3 cup dried apricots

1 cup dry white wine

3 tablespoons clarified butter

2 cloves garlic

2 tablespoons heavy cream

1/8 teaspoon ground cloves

1/8 teaspoon ground ginger

1/8 teaspoon ground cinnamon

1/8 teaspoon ground white pepper

1 tablespoon fresh lemon juice

1/2 cup (1 stick) unsalted butter

1/3 cup shelled pistachios

Place chicken livers in a resealable plastic bag or a medium bowl and cover with milk. Refrigerate covered overnight. In another storage bag or small covered bowl, combine apricots and white wine. Leave at room temperature overnight.

Drain apricots and reserve white wine. Drain chicken livers and pat dry. In a heavy skillet, melt clarified butter. Add chicken livers and cook, stirring frequently until firm. Remove from heat. Transfer livers to a food processor.

Add reserved white wine to skillet and stir to incorporate with juices of the livers. Pour liquid from skillet into food processor. Add garlic, cream, spices and lemon juice and puree until smooth. Add 1/2 cup butter and pulse until well mixed. Add pistachios and apricots and pulse until coarsely chopped (small but not fine), or mix by hand. Transfer mixture to a crock, plain mold or serving dish, cover tightly and refrigerate for 24 hours.

To serve, let pâté stand at room temperature for 30 minutes. Serve with toasted baguette slices or mild crackers. Garnish with additional chopped apricots and pistachios.

Serves 12

Must be started 2 days ahead.

An elegant, well-seasoned spread with a surprise apricot taste.

Serve vegetable dippers in clean clay pots as a relish centerpiece. For added visual effect, paint pots in interesting designs.

There's more than one way to "dip in"—include a variety of these in your repertoire: artichoke leaves, fried or cooked; asparagus spears; broccoli florets; carrot sticks or slices; cauliflower florets; celery sticks; cherry tomatoes; fennel sticks; green onion stalks; jícama slices; Japanese eggplant; kohlrabi spears; mushrooms, sliced or whole; purple, green, red or yellow bell pepper slices or sticks; snow pea pods; sugar snap peas; sun-dried tomatoes (dry slices); sweet potato slices (raw); zucchini or yellow squash slices or spears.

Carpaccio Dijonnaise

1 pound uncooked prime beef fillet

3–4 tablespoons fresh lemon juice

1/4 cup olive oil, plus additional to brush meat

1 medium shallot, minced

2 cloves garlic, minced

1 tablespoon Dijon mustard

1-1/2 tablespoons soy sauce

Freshly ground pepper, to taste

Capers, rinsed and drained, to garnish

Lemon slices, to garnish

Trim and thinly slice beef into 12 to 18 pieces. Gently pound meat until paper thin. Arrange 2 to 3 slices in center of each serving plate. Sprinkle generously with lemon juice, reserving 1 tablespoon. Brush meat lightly with olive oil.

In a small bowl, combine shallots, garlic, mustard, soy sauce and remaining lemon juice. Slowly pour in olive oil and whisk to incorporate. Drizzle sauce over meat. Grind pepper over the top and garnish with capers on edges of slices and lemon slice in center.

Serves 8

Try adding thin slices of Parmesan cheese or serve with baguette slices. The rich dressing is also wonderful when doubled and served over cold roast beef salad.

Tenderloin with Three Sauces

1/4 cup olive oil

1 pound beef tenderloin, trimmed

1/4 cup fresh cracked pepper

1/8 cup salt or salt crystals

1 baguette

Cilantro leaves, to garnish

Thai sauce:

1/2 cup mayonnaise

1/2 ounce Oriental chili paste, or to taste

1/4 cup chopped cilantro

Horseradish sauce:

1/4 cup prepared horseradish

1 cup sour cream

Dijon sauce:

1/2 cup heavy cream

1/4 cup Dijon mustard

In a skillet, heat oil until it begins to smoke. Combine pepper and salt. While oil heats, roll tenderloin in pepper and salt mixture, distributing evenly. Brown tenderloin in oil on each side until rare. Refrigerate until cool and ready to slice.

For Thai sauce: Mix mayonnaise, chili paste and chopped cilantro. Chill until serving time.

For horseradish sauce: Stir horseradish into sour cream. Refrigerate for 2 hours to incorporate flavors. Stir again before serving.

For Dijon sauce: Beat cream with an electric mixer until stiff, then whisk in Dijon mustard. Chill until serving.

To serve, slice tenderloin paper thin and arrange on baguette slices, topped with alternating sauces. Use cilantro leaves to garnish.

Serves 8–10

A delicious and elegant addition to a cocktail buffet. As a serving variation, offer the sauces in a trio of bowls for guests to select the topping of choice.

1 pound ground veal

1/4 pound uncooked bacon, minced

1 medium onion, minced

1 tablespoon minced fresh parsley

1 teaspoon fresh thyme or 1/2 teaspoon dried

1/2 teaspoon marjoram

1 cup fresh bread crumbs

1/2 cup cold water

Salt and freshly ground pepper, to taste

Flour to coat meatballs

Oil and butter, for frying

4 tablespoons sour cream

Black olives, to garnish

Lemon quarters, to garnish

Sauce:

---

2 tablespoons butter

1 medium onion, minced

2-1/2 tablespoons flour

2 cups canned tomatoes or fresh, peeled and seeded

1 cup chicken broth

Salt and freshly ground pepper, to taste

Pinch of sugar

Bouquet garni of 1 bay leaf, 1 clove garlic, 1 teaspoon basil, 1 teaspoon oregano, 5 peppercorns, and chopped parsley

Put veal and bacon into a bowl. Add onion, parsley, thyme, marjoram and bread crumbs. Work in the cold water, a little at a time. Knead mixture together and season with salt and pepper.

Shape meat mixture into walnut-sized balls. Roll lightly with flour and fry quickly in a small amount of hot oil and butter, a few at a time, until brown. Drain on absorbent paper.

For sauce: In a large saucepan, melt butter and sauté onions. Add flour and mix well. Add remaining ingredients and bring to a boil. Simmer for 30 to 40 minutes. Strain and adjust seasoning to taste.

Lay meatballs in a large shallow casserole. Top with sauce, cover and bake in a 350-degree oven for 30 minutes.

To serve, spoon sour cream over meatballs in sauce and shake dish gently to mix in. Garnish with black olives and lemon quarters and serve.

Serves 10–12

Present on a buffet as a pleasant departure from familiar cocktail meatballs.

Toasted Pita Triangles

2 teaspoons lemon pepper • 2 teaspoons ground cumin

6 pita bread rounds • 1/2 cup melted butter

In a saucepan, stir lemon pepper and cumin into melted butter. With the tip of a knife, halve each pita round and open each half into 2 pieces. Cut pieces into triangle shapes, dip into butter mixture and place on a broiler pan. Broil until crisp. Serve as a delicious accompaniment to dips, soups and salads.

*Inquisitive palates and helpful specialty-store proprietors
increasingly broaden cheese's reign as both staple and rarest of treats. A comfortable
knowledge of "wheys and means" permits a rewarding
range of possibilities.*

The Family Tree

Pungent *hard, grating cheeses* like Romano and Parmesan are delicious sprinkled on salads and pastas or sliced and served alongside fruit such as pears. *Cheddar and cheddar types* range from mild to sharp, depending on the aging. Look for portions that are firm and moist. *Mild cheeses* such as Muenster, Gouda, Edam, provolone and mozzarella range from firm to semisoft and offer rich oily textures and nutty flavors. *Swiss and Gruyère types* have holes caused by bacteria that also contribute to their characteristic flavors. These are favored for quiches and tarts. *Blue-veined cheeses* such as Roquefort, Stilton and Gorgonzola are crumbly, semisoft to hard, and emit a sharp salt flavor. They perform well with dried fruits and nuts as well as in dressings. *Soft ripening varieties* such as Brie and Camembert are soft-crusted with creamy interiors. Toss with hot pasta or spread on crusty bread. *Buttery/creamy cheeses* are typified by Danish white cream cheese and aged goat cheese.

Winning Combinations

*Add pizzazz and interest to the standby cheese board by taking a step
"beyond the cracker." Decorate it as well, with fresh grape, lemon, ti or fig leaves,
to add great appeal to a simple appetizer or dessert presentation.
The following partners are offered as food for thought:*

Lezay on hard slices of sun-dried tomatoes *Roquefort paired with crisp celery hearts* *Explorateur on black pepper water crackers* *Triple cream Brie with lemon curd and gingersnaps* *Huntsman spread on scones or crumpets* *Maytag blue and hearty wine crackers* *Royal Provence with French cocktail toasts* *Manchego melted over blue corn chips* *Reggiano, ripe pears and sweet grapes* *Fresh mozzarella on focaccia breadsticks* *Melted Compté on sourdough slices* *Blue Castello plus wheatmeal biscuits* *Appenzeller on Swedish crispbread* *Pyrenees on thin sesame wafers* *Mascarpone with Amaretto-flavored biscotti*

Stuffed Spinach Crêpes

1/4 pound spinach, washed and drained

1 cup flour

Pinch of salt

1 egg

2/3 cup milk

Butter or oil, for cooking

Filling:

1 (8-ounce) package cream cheese, softened to room temperature

Salt and freshly ground pepper, to taste

1/4 cup chopped chives

8 long chives, to garnish

In a saucepan, cook spinach with a little water and push through a strainer to make a thin puree. Sift flour into a bowl with salt. Beat in egg and milk. Add spinach puree. Allow batter to stand for 10 to 20 minutes.

For filling: Season cream cheese with salt and pepper and add chopped chives. Mix and set aside.

Melt butter in a crêpe pan and use batter to make 8 small, thin crêpes. Put about 2 tablespoons of cheese filling in each and roll up. Tie with chive bows and serve.

Serves 8

The secrets to creating a pretty presentation with these bundles are a very soft cream cheese filling spread lightly on very thin crêpes.

Feta Cheese Parcels

1-1/4 pounds feta cheese

1–2 tablespoons olive oil

3 tablespoons finely chopped savory or thyme

1 (8-ounce) package phyllo pastry

24 dried figs or dates, halved

1 cup melted butter

Scallion or leek strips, blanched (optional)

In a bowl, mash cheese and olive oil with a fork and season with herbs. Cut sheets of phyllo into 4-inch squares. Spoon 1 teaspoon of cheese mixture into the center of each, add a fig or date half, and draw the sides up to form a little pouch. Press edges together with water to seal.

Preheat oven to 375 degrees. Lightly brush each pouch with melted butter and bake for 10 to 15 minutes until crisp and golden. For a festive look, tie a blanched scallion or leek strip around each parcel.

Makes 48 parcels

A scrumptious bite of creamy, tangy cheese and sweet dried figs. Delicious with aperitifs!

Bring a hint of fragrance to the table by tying packets of light potpourri to the arm or back of guests' chairs.

Artichokes Athena

2 medium artichokes

Fresh lemon juice

2 tablespoons water

Vinaigrette:

3 tablespoons fresh lemon juice

2 tablespoons olive oil

1 tablespoon water

1/2 teaspoon oregano, crushed

Filling:

1/2 cup bulgur or packaged pilaf mix

1/4 teaspoon salt

1 cup hot water

1/2 cup crumbled feta cheese

1/4 cup snipped fresh parsley

1 large tomato peeled, seeded and chopped

Cut stems and outer loose leaves from artichokes. Cut 1 inch off of tops. Snip off short leaf tips. Brush cut edges with lemon juice. Place artichokes in a 1-1/2- to 2-quart microwave-safe dish. Add 2 tablespoons water. Microwave, covered, on high for 7 to 10 minutes or until a leaf peels away easily. Turn dish once while cooking. Drain and cool. Halve each artichoke lengthwise, then discard center leaves and choke.

For vinaigrette: Combine lemon juice, oil, water and oregano. Place artichokes in a resealable plastic bag. Pour dressing over artichokes and seal bag. Chill for several hours, turning the bag occasionally.

For filling: Combine bulgur, salt and hot water. Let stand for 1 hour, then drain. Add feta cheese, parsley and chopped tomato. Cover and chill.

To serve, drain artichokes, reserving vinaigrette. Stand cut-side up. Stir reserved vinaigrette into bulgur mixture and spoon into artichoke halves.

Serves 4

Serve these on a marble slab, nestled in mounds of Greek olives and grape leaves.

Fruit with Sherried Cheese

1/2 pound Gorgonzola cheese

2 tablespoons butter or margarine, softened

3 tablespoons dry sherry

1/2 teaspoon paprika

Fresh lemon juice

Apple and pear slices

Place cheese in a bowl and mash with a fork. Blend in butter, sherry and paprika. Beat until smooth and creamy. Heap into a serving bowl and chill for 1 hour or more.

Dip fruit slices in lemon juice and arrange on a platter. Place cheese mixture in a bowl or other serving container in the center of the platter.

Serves 10–12

Sherry adds a heady touch to this creamy dip. Serve with a variety of fruits, crackers or toast points.

Brie and Pear Bundles

2 ripe Anjou pears, cored and chopped

1/2 cup chopped toasted almonds

1/2 cup crushed shortbread cookies

1 tablespoon Grand Marnier

12 sheets phyllo pastry

3/4 cup melted butter

3/4 pound Brie cheese

12 long, thin strips of orange peel (softened in warm water) or long-stemmed violets, to garnish

In a medium bowl, combine pears, almonds, cookies and Grand Marnier. Brush 1 phyllo sheet with butter and fold lengthwise in half. Cut into 2 squares. Repeat with remaining phyllo.

Cut Brie into 24 equal pieces. Place 1 piece of Brie and 2 tablespoons pear mixture into center of each pastry square. Bring up opposite corners of pastry, press together and twist gently to seal. Place on baking sheet. Repeat with remaining ingredients. Preheat oven to 425 degrees.

Bake bundles for about 10 minutes or until golden. Tie top of each bundle with orange peel for a lovely effect.

Serves 12

*These tempting Brie and pear bundles may be served warm or at room temperature. In a pinch for time, substitute prepared **Pear Chutney** for the fruit filling (see "Chutney" in Meats). Bundles may be assembled in advance and baked as needed.*

Marinated Goat Cheese

8 rounds good-quality goat cheese (2–3 ounces each)

1-1/2 cups extra-virgin olive oil

4 bay leaves

1 tablespoon mixed white, black and green peppercorns

1-1/2 tablespoons thyme

3 large cloves garlic, slivered

3 tablespoons slivered fresh basil

1 tablespoon pink peppercorns or colorful peppercorn mixture

Sliced sourdough bread

Place goat cheese on an ovenproof platter or flat dish large enough to hold cheese rounds without touching each other.

In a saucepan over medium-high heat, heat oil, bay leaves, peppercorn mixture and thyme until mixture begins to sizzle and pop. Immediately remove from heat and pour over cheeses. Sprinkle garlic slivers, basil and pink peppercorns over cheeses. Cover and refrigerate overnight.

Bring to room temperature before serving. Serve with slices of sourdough bread.

Makes 8 first-course servings or cuts into 24 cocktail servings

Must be prepared in advance.

Tart goat cheese in olive oil and spices also is tasty alongside a luncheon entree or on top of a bed of greens. Goat cheese may be stored in the refrigerator for up to 2 weeks.

Gruyère Cheesecake

8 tablespoons (1 stick) butter

1-1/3 cups fine toasted bread crumbs

3 (8-ounce) packages cream cheese, softened to room temperature

1/4 cup heavy cream

1/2 teaspoon salt

1/4 teaspoon ground nutmeg

1/4 teaspoon cayenne pepper

4 eggs

1-1/4 cups shredded Gruyère cheese

1 (10-ounce) package frozen chopped spinach, thawed and squeezed dry

3 tablespoons minced scallions

3/4 pound mushrooms, finely chopped

Salt and freshly ground pepper, to taste

Sauce:

1/4 cup olive oil

2 tablespoons minced garlic

6 scallions, chopped

2 (16-ounce) cans stewed tomatoes

4 tablespoons minced fresh basil

1 teaspoon brown sugar

For sauce: In a 3-quart saucepan, heat olive oil and sauté garlic and scallions until transparent. Stir in tomatoes, basil and sugar and simmer for 1 hour.

Melt 5 tablespoons butter. In a small bowl, combine bread crumbs and melted butter. Butter a 9-inch springform pan and press crumbs onto bottom and sides. Bake at 350 degrees for 8 to 10 minutes. Set aside to cool.

In a large bowl, beat cream cheese, cream, salt, nutmeg and cayenne pepper together until smooth. Beat in eggs 1 at a time. Divide cream cheese mixture between 2 bowls. Stir Gruyère cheese into one and stir spinach and scallions into the other. Pour spinach mixture into the cooled crust.

In a medium skillet, melt remaining 3 tablespoons butter and sauté mushrooms over medium heat until all moisture evaporates. Spoon mushrooms over spinach filling, then pour Gruyère mixture over mushrooms. Set springform pan on a baking sheet and bake at 325 degrees for 1-1/4 hours. Turn oven off and cool cheesecake for 1 hour with the oven door ajar, then cool on a rack to room temperature. Serve in wedges topped with warm sauce.

Serves 12–16

*This delectable blend of Gruyère, basil and tomatoes also makes an excellent brunch entree alongside **Spicy Apple Sausage Patties**.*

Herbed Mozzarella

1 cup extra-virgin olive oil

1/8 cup chopped fresh oregano leaves

1 teaspoon red pepper flakes

1/8 cup chopped fresh basil leaves

1 teaspoon chopped garlic

1/2 teaspoon salt

1/2 teaspoon freshly ground pepper

1 (9-ounce) package fresh, small water-packed mozzarella balls, drained

In a small bowl, combine oil, oregano, red pepper flakes, basil, garlic, salt and pepper. Arrange mozzarella balls in a nonmetal, shallow pan, just large enough to hold cheese in a single layer. Pour oil mixture over cheese and coat well. Cover and refrigerate overnight to allow flavors to develop. (Marinade may be used as a base for salad dressing after cheese has been eaten.)

Serves 12

Serve on radicchio or endive leaves as an interesting first course, or with baguette slices or bruschetta. Fresh water-packed mozzarella is the key to success in this delicious recipe; any other will not absorb the marinade properly.

Santa Fe Cheesecake

1 cup finely crushed tortilla chips

3 tablespoons butter
or margarine, melted

2 (8-ounce) packages cream cheese,
softened to room temperature

2 eggs

8 ounces shredded Colby/Monterey
Jack cheese blend

1 (4-ounce) can chopped
green chilies, drained

Dash of hot pepper sauce

1 cup sour cream, room temperature

1 cup chopped orange or
yellow bell pepper, to garnish

1/2 cup sliced scallions (tops included),
to garnish

1/3 cup chopped tomatoes, to garnish

1/4 cup sliced black olives, to garnish

Preheat oven to 325 degrees. In a small bowl, combine tortilla chips and melted butter. Press onto the bottom of a 9-inch springform pan and bake for 15 minutes.

In a large bowl, beat cream cheese and eggs until well blended. Mix in shredded cheese, green chilies and hot pepper sauce. Pour over tortilla chip crust and bake for 30 minutes.

Spread sour cream evenly over warm cheesecake. Run a knife around edge of cheesecake to loosen from pan. Cool before removing rim of pan. Chill thoroughly.

Garnish with peppers, scallions, tomatoes and olives just before serving. Serve with crackers or heavy tortilla chips.

Serves 8–10

To create a Mexican blanket pattern on this cheesecake, cut three 8- by 3-inch diamond-shaped templates out of heavy paper and place side by side on top of chilled sour cream surface. Sprinkle scallion slices around paper cutouts. Remove templates and fill in spaces with chopped bell peppers. Add a stripe of chopped tomatoes passing through the centers of the pepper diamonds, and sprinkle olive slices over tomatoes.

Fontina Grilled in Vine Leaves

8 grape leaves

3 tablespoons extra-virgin olive oil

1 pound Fontina or Gruyère cheese,
cut into 1-ounce portions

1-1/2 tablespoons chopped fresh thyme

1-1/2 tablespoons
chopped fresh oregano

Freshly ground pepper, to taste

Slices of sourdough bread,
brushed with olive oil, rubbed with
garlic and grilled

Prepare a small charcoal or wood fire. Brush oil onto the underside of each grape leaf and place cheese in center. Brush cheese with a little olive oil, sprinkle with chopped herbs and season to taste. Fold grape leaf so that it overlaps cheese and turn so that folded side is down. Or fold into bundles using 2 grape leaves for each piece of cheese.

Over a medium fire, grill wrapped cheese, folded-side down, for approximately 2 minutes per side or until cheese has softened and leaf is slightly charred. Set leaf on a warm plate and open. Serve immediately with grilled sourdough bread. (Or place cheese and grape leaf bundles on top of baguette slices and bake in a 300-degree oven for 10 minutes. Serve immediately.)

Serves 8

Surprise your guests with this special first course. Grape leaves can be found in gourmet markets or Greek food stores. Enhance with Sun-Dried Tomato Vinaigrette.

Boursin Blue Cheesecake

3/4 cup cracker crumbs
(wheat thins or buttery crackers)

2 tablespoons melted butter

1 (5-ounce) package Boursin cheese

1 (8-ounce) plus 1 (3-ounce) package
cream cheese, softened to room
temperature

10 ounces Stilton (or other blue cheese)

1 cup sour cream

3 eggs

1/8 teaspoon freshly ground pepper

1/4 cup sherry

1/3 cup milk

Preheat oven to 350 degrees. Combine cracker crumbs and melted butter and press into the bottom of an 8-inch springform pan. Bake for 5 to 8 minutes or until very lightly browned.

Mix remaining ingredients in a food processor. Pour mixture onto crust in springform pan. Wrap bottom and sides of pan in a double thickness of aluminum foil and then place it inside a larger pan, adding enough hot water to the larger pan to come halfway up the sides of the springform pan. Bake at 350 degrees for 50 to 55 minutes. (Do not overbake or brown.) Done when a knife inserted in the middle comes out clean. Chill and serve.

Serves 16–20

Blue cheese lovers will delight in this creamy creation. Garnish with nasturtiums and fresh herbs and serve on a platter with fruit and nuts. Spread on bagel chips, sweet biscuits, water crackers or toasted sourdough bread.

For intimate gatherings, prepare smaller versions. Butter four to five 8-ounce soufflé dishes, omit cracker-crumb crust, and place prepared soufflés on a baking sheet in a 325-degree oven. Bake for about 45 minutes, watching carefully for browning. These freeze well.

Queso Grill

1 pound Monterey Jack cheese

4 ounces grated cheddar cheese

1 cup medium-hot chunky
picante sauce, or fresh salsa

1 cup refried beans

1/4 pound small cooked shrimp, peeled

Cut Monterey Jack cheese into 1/4-inch slices and arrange in a 10-inch iron skillet, overlapping slices to cover pan bottom. Top with cheddar cheese. Spoon picante sauce over cheese. Spread refried beans into an 8-inch circle over sauce. Place shrimp over beans.

Place pan on a prepared grill, 4 to 6 inches above coals. Close lid and let heat and smoke for approximately 10 minutes.

(Don't have coals too hot or cheese will burn. Place skillet on grill with only a few coals below.) Serve with tortilla chips.

Serves 8–10

Great to grill and serve with drinks while everyone is waiting for steaks or hamburgers.

Smoked Salmon and Onion Cheesecake

5 tablespoons freshly grated Parmesan cheese

2 tablespoons fine dry bread crumbs

3 tablespoons butter

1 cup chopped onion

1 cup chopped red bell pepper

3-1/2 (8-ounce) packages cream cheese, softened to room temperature

4 eggs

1/3 cup heavy cream

1/2 pound smoked salmon trimmings, chopped

1/2 cup freshly grated Gruyère cheese (about 2 ounces)

Salt and freshly ground pepper, to taste

1 tablespoon fresh lemon juice

Dash of hot pepper sauce

Preheat oven 300 degrees. Butter bottom and sides of an 8-inch springform pan. Mix 2 tablespoons Parmesan cheese with bread crumbs and sprinkle into prepared pan. Coat with crumb mixture by turning pan. Wrap foil around the bottom and 2 inches up outside of pan.

In a heavy medium skillet, melt butter over medium heat. Add onion and pepper and sauté until tender, about 5 minutes. Cool.

Using an electric mixer, beat cream cheese, eggs and cream in a bowl until well blended.

Fold salmon, Gruyère and remaining 3 tablespoons Parmesan cheese into onion mixture. Season with salt and pepper, lemon juice and hot pepper sauce and fold into cream cheese mixture. Pour mixture into springform pan. Prepare a water bath by placing cheesecake pan inside a larger baking pan, adding enough boiling water to the larger pan to come up 2 inches on the sides of the springform pan. Bake until firm to the touch (approximately 1 hour and 40 minutes).

Remove cheesecake from water bath and turn oven off. Return cheesecake to oven and let stand for 1 hour. Transfer cheesecake to a wire rack and cool for at least 2 hours. Serve with crackers and fruit.

Serves 30

A sophisticated savory that's perfect for cocktail buffets or as a starter. Top with a red pepper sauce and garnish with fresh dill and a red pepper cut to look like a flower. For a milder salmon taste, puree salmon rather than chopping. For smaller crowds, cut the recipe in half and use a 4-inch springform pan.

Herbed cream cheese easily steps in as a terrific last-minute appetizer. Soften 8 ounces of plain cream cheese in the microwave for 1 to 2 minutes, then combine with 1/4 cup of chopped fresh herbs. Add a splash of vinaigrette and serve.

Avocado Mousse

4 avocados

2 (8-ounce) packages cream cheese, softened to room temperature

Grated zest and juice of 2 lemons

1 envelope unflavored gelatin

1/2 cup heavy cream, whipped

Lettuce leaves

Salsa

Halve avocados, remove pits and scoop pulp into a food processor fitted with a steel blade. Process avocados, then add cream cheese and lemon zest until fully incorporated and smooth.

In a small saucepan, sprinkle gelatin over 1/4 cup cold water and lemon juice. Heat and stir until gelatin is dissolved. With food processor running, pour dissolved gelatin through the feed tube and process for 10 seconds. Remove blade from processor and fold in whipped cream. Pour filling into a 7-inch springform pan, smoothing the top. Refrigerate for 3 hours or until set.

To serve, remove ring from springform and place mousse onto a serving platter lined with a bed of greens. Slice mousse and top with fresh salsa.

Serves 16–20 (appetizer)

Garnish with flowering pineapple sage or lemon slices and serve with additional fresh salsa and baguette slices or crackers.

Farmer's Market Pie

1 (9-inch) pastry shell, uncooked

1-1/2 (8-ounce) packages cream cheese, softened to room temperature

2 ounces blue cheese

1/2 cup mayonnaise

1/2 teaspoon onion salt

1/4 teaspoon garlic salt

Topping:

Cherry tomatoes, halved

Mushrooms, sliced

Parsley leaves, whole or chopped

Green and black olives, sliced

Hard-cooked eggs, sliced or chopped

Carrots, sliced

Peppers, diced

Cucumbers, sliced

Stretch pastry shell to 11 inches. Pierce with a fork. Place on a baking sheet and bake in a 425-degree oven for 8 minutes or until golden brown. Cool, then place on a serving platter.

Beat cream cheese, blue cheese, mayonnaise and salts together until fluffy. Spread over cooled crust. Cover and chill for at least 4 hours. Top in circular patterns with a combination of suggested vegetables.

Serves 8

The blue cheese makes this vegetable hors d'oeuvre pie richly pungent. Serve in slices as a first course or cut into individual squares for bite-sized snacks. Make individual "pies" for a luncheon to serve with tuna or chicken salad.

Lemon Olive Caviar

2 cups finely chopped black olives

2 tablespoons bottled chopped garlic

1 teaspoon freshly ground black pepper

1-1/2 teaspoons finely grated lemon zest

2 tablespoons fresh lemon juice

2 tablespoons finely chopped onion

2–3 tablespoons olive oil

1-1/2 tablespoons Worcestershire sauce

Combine all ingredients. If finer texture is desired, turn mixture into a food processor and process for a few seconds, just until fine. Chill. Offer with tortilla chips, sliced fresh baguettes or assorted crackers.

Serves 6–8

For a more potent taste, use chopped fresh garlic instead of the milder bottled variety. Garnish with chopped pimientos and tendrils of lemon zest.

A Tasty Bite

Olives are the perfect finger food—easy to pick up, a cinch to serve and an attractive accompaniment to predinner cocktails. Nature offers them in a wide array of colors (green, black, purple or brown); sizes (large or small); textures (plump and juicy or slightly shriveled); and flavors (acidic, fruity and rich).

Fresh olives tend to be slightly bitter; however, much of the taste depends on how ripe the olive is when picked and by what process. Most olives are brine or salt-cured and then packed in olive oil or a vinegar marinade. A sampling follows, categorized by nationality:

California—Most of the canned black olives at your local market come from California, and a few varieties do stand out. Greek-style black (purple-black and firm); Greek-style-green (cracked with an interesting flavor); and Sicilian-style (crisp-tasting).
French—A product of the Provence, dark-brown Niçoise olives are small and tender, while the Picholine offers a crisp and salty flavor. *Greek*—Try purple-black Kalamatas for their rich flavor and dark green Naphlions for a crisp, fruity taste. *Italian*—Some of this nation's finest include the large, black Alfonso, the mellow, dull-green Calabrese, the tiny, wrinkled Gaeta, the rich-flavored, black Liguria and the bitter-tasting, green Sicilian.

Olives are appealing straight from the jar and are wonderfully versatile in a wide variety of dishes. Though cured, they respond well to marinades. Chopped, they can function as faux caviar; as a paste, they become a tantalizing alternative to butter or cream cheese. Perk up your appetizer repertoire with a bountiful assortment of these briny fruits.

Olive Paste

10 ounces ripe black olives, preferably kalamata

1 teaspoon oregano

1/2 teaspoon basil

1/2–1 teaspoon balsamic vinegar

1/4 teaspoon sugar

2 teaspoons extra-virgin olive oil

Place olives on a work surface and use a meat pounder or the side of a large knife to split flesh. Remove and discard pits.

In a food processor, combine olives, oregano, basil, vinegar and sugar. Process for several minutes, scraping down the sides frequently, until a paste forms. With the machine on, drizzle in olive oil. (Alternatively, for a slightly coarser texture, pound olives in a mortar with a pestle, then add remaining ingredients and pound to a paste.)

Transfer to a covered container and refrigerate.

Serves 6–8

Serve this rich paste over grilled polenta, crusty bread, boiled, baked or mashed potatoes, fennel or sweet red peppers, or try mixing it into pastas, risotto or mayonnaise.

Mediterranean Mélange

1 (7-ounce) jar roasted red peppers, drained

Grated zest of 2 lemons

1 tablespoon fresh lemon juice

1/2 cup Niçoise olives, pitted and halved

1 tablespoon capers

6 scallions, shredded

1 tablespoon fennel seeds

3 dashes of cayenne pepper

1 tablespoon olive oil

Dice peppers into 1/2-inch pieces. In a bowl, combine red peppers, lemon zest, lemon juice, olives, capers, scallions, fennel seeds and cayenne pepper. Add olive oil to taste and serve.

Serves 4–6

A technicolor treat of robust earthy flavors. Serve in a bowl surrounded by crackers or other dippers such as green peppers, mushrooms, zucchini, cucumbers, salami or artichoke hearts.

Capers are sun-dried and pickled flower buds of a Mediterranean bush.

Their pungent flavor lends piquancy to any dish.

White Salsa Dip

1 cup mayonnaise

1 cup sour cream

Juice of 3 limes

4 cloves garlic, crushed

1-1/2 cups finely chopped fresh cilantro

1 (6-ounce) can pitted black olives, drained and coarsely chopped

1-1/2 cups finely chopped scallions

1/2 teaspoon hot pepper sauce, or to taste

Salt and freshly ground white pepper, to taste (optional)

In a medium bowl, combine mayonnaise and sour cream. Add lime juice, garlic, cilantro, black olives, scallions, hot pepper sauce, salt and pepper. Taste and adjust seasonings if desired. Chill until serving.

Makes 4–5 cups

For an appealing color, serve this wonderfully refreshing salsa with blue corn tortilla chips. The flavor mellows when made ahead.

Roasted Red Pepper Garlic Dip

2 red bell peppers

2 cloves garlic, minced

1 (8-ounce) package cream cheese, softened to room temperature

2 tablespoons fresh lime juice

3 tablespoons finely chopped basil

1 tablespoon finely chopped parsley

1/2 teaspoon salt

1/4 teaspoon freshly ground white pepper

Roast whole peppers by broiling approximately 6 inches from heat until blackened on all sides (turn with tongs). Let rest for 10 minutes, then drain and peel off skins. Cut in half and remove stem, seeds and ribs. Place peppers in a food processor fitted with a steel blade and add remaining ingredients. Process until creamy. Serve as a dipping sauce with crudités.

Serves 8–10

This dip is lovely served in a large hollowed-out red pepper. Use an assortment of dippers: green pepper strips, mozzarella sticks, jumbo pitted black olives, pepperoni slices or small breadsticks.

Black-Eyed Peaco de Gallo

2 (15-ounce) cans black-eyed peas, rinsed and drained

1 (15-ounce) can white hominy, rinsed and drained

2 medium tomatoes, chopped and drained

2 cloves garlic, minced

1 medium red or green bell pepper, chopped

1/2 cup chopped fresh parsley

1 cup zesty Italian-style dressing

Combine all ingredients and serve with heavy tortilla chips or pita toasts.

Serves 12

Serve this colorful blend of vegetables as an appetizer or as a salad. For additional "bite," toss in chopped scallions or jalapeño peppers. Best when made a day ahead.

Fresh Fruit Salsa

2 cups finely chopped tomatillos (about 6)

2 cups finely chopped tomatoes

2 cups finely chopped melon (cantaloupe, honeydew, Crenshaw or a combination)

1 cup finely chopped kiwi (about 4)

1 cup finely chopped red onion

2 bunches cilantro, leaves only, chopped

Juice of 2 lemons

Juice of 2 limes

2 tablespoons olive oil

1/2 cup finely chopped and seeded jalapeño peppers (about 8)

Salt and freshly ground pepper, to taste

Combine all ingredients either by hand or in a food processor. Salsa will be prettier if chopped by hand, but much quicker to prepare in a food processor.

Makes 8 cups

A colorful jumble of taste and texture to serve with assorted tortilla chips. It's also a light refreshing addition to a simple portion of fish.

Caesar Cream

1/2 cup freshly grated Parmesan cheese

3 canned anchovy fillets, drained

2–3 tablespoons fresh lemon juice

1/2 cup packed fresh parsley

1 tablespoon capers

Cracked pepper, to taste

1 cup light or regular sour cream

Finely shredded Parmesan cheese, to garnish

3 heads romaine lettuce

In a blender or a food processor, combine grated Parmesan cheese, 2 anchovy fillets, lemon juice, parsley, capers and cracked pepper. Puree until smooth. Add 3 to 4 tablespoons sour cream if necessary to help mixture puree well. In a small bowl, mix puree with remaining sour cream. Add more lemon juice, if desired. Cover and chill overnight.

Select small inner leaves from heads of romaine. Rinse and crisp for dipping.

Garnish with remaining anchovy and Parmesan cheese. Place cream in a bowl on a serving platter surrounded by lettuce leaves for dipping.

Makes 1-1/4 cups

Must be prepared in advance.

Caesar salad lovers will delight in this creamy, pale green dip. Other dippers might include asparagus spears, different colored pepper strips, pea pods, or baguette slices toasted and topped with Parmesan cheese.

Curried Cauliflower

1 medium head cauliflower

2 cups mayonnaise

2 teaspoons curry powder

1 teaspoon hot pepper sauce,
or to taste

1 teaspoon Worcestershire sauce

1 teaspoon fresh lemon juice

1 tablespoon grated onion

1 tablespoon chopped
parsley, to garnish

Leaving the cauliflower whole, trim, clean and remove core. Steam for 40 minutes, until florets pierce easily with a fork.

In a bowl, combine mayonnaise, curry powder, hot pepper sauce, Worcestershire sauce, lemon juice and grated onion. After cauliflower has cooled, spread curry mixture over top and sides. Cover and refrigerate for 24 hours.

To serve, arrange cauliflower on a platter, sprinkle with parsley and surround with crackers.

Serves 12

Must be prepared in advance.

The whole head of cauliflower makes a striking presentation. For best results, choose a firm cauliflower with compact florets.

Black and White Spread

1/2 (15-ounce) can
pitted black olives, drained

1 (8-ounce) package cream cheese,
softened to room temperature

1/2 cup (1 stick) butter, softened

1/4 cup chopped scallions

In a food processor, blend all ingredients until smooth. Chill and serve with crudités or crackers.

Serves 8–10

For a checkered effect, serve with small party-style light and dark rye bread.

Sun-Dried Tomato Vinaigrette

40 oil-packed sun-dried tomato halves
(approximately 3 jars)

1/2 cup minced shallots

2 tablespoons minced garlic

2 cups chopped fresh basil

1 cup plus 3 tablespoons olive oil

1/2 cup red wine vinegar

Drain sun-dried tomatoes and reserve 1/3 cup oil. In a food processor, mince tomatoes. Add reserved oil, shallots, garlic, basil, olive oil and vinegar and blend until creamy. Transfer to a bowl, cover and refrigerate. Bring to room temperature to serve.

Makes about 6 cups

A rich, intensely flavored vinaigrette, this also halves well for smaller groups. Spoon onto bruschetta or herbed cream cheese.

1 envelope unflavored gelatin

1/4 cup cold water

1 (4-ounce) jar black or red caviar (or half of each)

Fresh lemon juice, to taste

Thinly sliced pumpernickel bread

Egg layer:

4 hard-cooked eggs, chopped

1/2 cup mayonnaise

1 large scallion, chopped

Freshly ground white pepper, to taste

1/4 cup minced fresh parsley

3/4 teaspoon salt

Dash of hot pepper sauce

Avocado layer:

1 medium avocado (9 ounces), pureed just before using

1 medium avocado (9 ounces), diced just before using

1 large shallot, minced

2 tablespoons mayonnaise

Dash of hot pepper sauce

2 tablespoons fresh lemon juice

1/2 teaspoon salt

Freshly ground pepper, to taste

Sour cream and shallot layer:

1 cup sour cream

2 shallots, minced

Line the bottom of a 1-quart soufflé dish with foil, extending 4 inches beyond the rim on 2 sides to form "handles." Oil lightly.

Soften gelatin in cold water, then liquefy by microwaving on low for 20 seconds. (Gelatin will be divided between the 3 layers.)

For egg layer: Combine all ingredients with 1 tablespoon gelatin. Taste and adjust seasoning. Spread egg mixture into prepared dish, smoothing the top. Wipe excess off foil with a paper towel.

For avocado layer: Combine all ingredients with 1 tablespoon gelatin. Taste and adjust seasoning. Gently spread mixture over egg layer.

For sour cream and shallot layer: Mix sour cream, shallot and remaining 2 tablespoons gelatin. Spread carefully over avocado layer, cover tightly with plastic wrap and refrigerate overnight.

Just before serving, rinse caviar in a fine sieve. Sprinkle with lemon juice and drain. Lift mold out of soufflé dish using foil handles. Spread caviar over the top and serve with slices of dark pumpernickel bread.

Serves 12–16

Must be prepared in advance.

This elegant appetizer combines rich caviar with a variety of textures and flavors. During the Christmas holidays, use red caviar and garnish with seasonal greenery.

Black caviar comes in several grades and price ranges.

Red caviar is a less expensive variety. Serve with classic accompaniments

of iced vodka and champagne.

Chèvre Pine Nut Toasts with Sun-Dried Tomato Pesto

1/2 (8-ounce) package cream cheese, softened to room temperature

4 ounces Chèvre (goat cheese)

1 tablespoon vodka

1 baguette, sliced

1/4 cup pine nuts, toasted

Pesto:

4 cloves garlic, minced

3 tablespoons olive oil

1 (14-ounce) can Italian plum tomatoes

1/2 cup oil-packed sun-dried tomatoes, oil reserved

1/4 cup shredded fresh basil

In a food processor, process cream cheese, goat cheese and vodka until smooth. Refrigerate until ready to use.

For pesto: Sauté garlic in olive oil until heated through. Do not brown. Coarsely chop Italian plum tomatoes and add to garlic and oil. Simmer over medium-low heat until thick, about 1 hour. Coarsely chop sun-dried tomatoes and add to mixture, stirring to incorporate.

Allow mixture to cool, then process in a blender or food processor until smooth. Add basil reserved oil from sun-dried tomatoes through the feed tube. Add additional olive oil as needed. Pulse several times to incorporate. Transfer mixture to a small bowl and refrigerate until ready to use.

Toast baguette slices, then spread with cheese mixture and sprinkle a few pine nuts on top. Place a teaspoon of tomato pesto in the center of each.

Serves 16–20

An interesting and striking blend of tart goat cheese, crisp toast and rich pesto. The cheese may also be served as a spread by placing it in ramekins and sprinkling pine nuts on top.

Roquefort Toasts

2-1/2 ounces blue cheese

1-1/2 tablespoons unsalted butter, softened

Pinch of celery salt

Dash of cayenne pepper

3-1/2 tablespoons whipped cream cheese

1/2 bunch fresh chives, chopped

18 (1/2-inch thick) baguette slices

1 clove garlic, halved

Olive oil

6 Belgian endive leaves, to garnish

In a food processor, blend cheese, butter, celery salt, cayenne pepper, whipped cream cheese and chives. Mold cheese mixture and chill.

Broil bread slices lightly on both sides. Rub one side of each with garlic and drizzle with oil.

To serve, line platter with endive leaves, top with cheese and surround with toast.

Serves 8–12

For a cocktail buffet, serve this creamy mixture on a variety of "bottoms." (For inspiration, see "Cheese Bites" box.)

Basic Bruschetta

1 pound baguette (no larger than 3 inches in diameter)

1/2 cup olive oil

2–3 cloves garlic, halved

Slice bread on the diagonal 3/4-inch thick. Place slices on a baking sheet and broil both sides until lightly toasted. Make an "X" on one side of each slice by rubbing with the garlic halves. Brush each lightly but thoroughly with olive oil.

Serves 12

Bruschetta is wonderful plain or as a base for many toppings. Try it with pesto, **Tomato and Fennel Spread** or **Herbed Goat Cheese.**

Spiced Olives

1 (7–8 ounce) jar pimiento-stuffed queen-sized green olives

4 cloves garlic, halved or quartered

2 tablespoons vinegar, preferably pepper

1 teaspoon dill

1–2 teaspoons red pepper flakes

10 whole cloves

In a saucepan, empty contents of olive jar (olives and liquid). Lightly crush garlic cloves. Add garlic, vinegar, dill, pepper flakes and whole cloves. Heat mixture just to boiling and remove from heat. Return mixture to jar or covered container and refrigerate.

Serves 6–8

Prepare ahead—the fire increases with time. These are delightful on an appetizer tray to offer with drinks. Use white wine vinegar if pepper vinegar is unavailable.

Tomato and Fennel Spread

2 large ripe tomatoes, seeded and diced • 1/2 fennel bulb, trimmed and diced • 1/2 cup olive oil • 1/4 cup chopped fresh basil • Salt and freshly ground pepper, to taste

In a bowl, toss ingredients together and season to taste. Mound on top of warm bruschetta. Makes about 3 cups.

Herbed Goat Cheese

10–12 ounces Montrachet or other mild goat cheese • 3 tablespoons milk or cream
Coarsely chopped fresh chives, to taste • Coarsely chopped fresh thyme, to taste • Freshly ground pepper, to taste • 1 teaspoon grated lemon zest • 1/2 teaspoon fresh lemon juice

In a food processor, break cheese into pieces and process, adding milk or cream to help smooth. Add remaining ingredients. Process until well mixed. Spread onto bruschetta or serve in a crock. Makes 1-1/2 cups.

Sweet Onion Bites

2 cups very thinly sliced sweet onions
(Vidalia or 1015)
Buttered pumpernickel slices

Marinade:

1/2 cup vegetable oil

1 teaspoon salt

2 tablespoons fresh lemon juice

Freshly ground pepper, to taste

1/2–1 teaspoon paprika

1/2 teaspoon sugar

1/4 cup crumbled blue cheese

Mix all marinade ingredients well. Place onion slices in a glass bowl and pour marinade over all. Cover and chill for at least 24 hours.

Drain onions and serve on thin buttered slices of pumpernickel bread. Reserve marinade for use on salads.

Serves 30–40

Must be prepared in advance.

This tangy marinade accentuates the sweet onion crunch of these unusual appetizers. Garnish your platter with an array of colorful edible blossoms.

Peppery Pepitas

4 cloves garlic, crushed

3 tablespoons olive oil

2 teaspoons cumin

1/2 teaspoon ground coriander

1 teaspoon cayenne pepper,
or more to taste

2 cups shelled pepitas (pumpkin seeds)

1 tablespoon sea salt

Preheat oven to 400 degrees. In a small skillet, heat olive oil over low heat. Add crushed garlic cloves and cook for 5 minutes. (Do not brown.) Discard garlic. Add cumin, coriander and cayenne pepper to pan and stir once. Turn off heat and stir oil, allowing spices to incorporate.

Place pepitas in a bowl and pour oil over all. Add salt and toss to coat. Spread seeds on a baking sheet in a single layer. Pour any remaining oil onto seeds and bake until seeds are slightly brown, approximately 7 to 10 minutes. Seeds may start to pop a little.

Makes 2 cups

These spicy nibbles are impossible to resist. Raw pumpkin seeds may be purchased at natural grocers and health food stores. If using fresh pumpkin seeds, first dry them on a baking sheet for at least 3 hours.

Seasonal Vidalia onions are known for their juicy sweetness.

Take advantage of these pale yellow bulbs during their May and June peak.

Most entertaining begins with an offering of potables. Whether mulled wine, spiced tea or exotic chilled summer drinks, presentation can heighten enjoyment. For example, add flavor and color to ice cubes with juice or flavored seltzers. For a visual "spike," fill ice cube trays halfway with water, then add a clean herb leaf or edible flower. When that layer is frozen, top off trays with more water (so that herbs don't float to the top). Cheers!

Champagne and Guava Nectar

3 ounces chilled guava nectar

6 ounces chilled champagne

Lime slices, to garnish

Pour guava nectar into 2 chilled wine glasses. Add champagne to each and stir once. Garnish with lime slices and serve.

Serves 2

Herbed Vodka

1 fifth vodka

1 sprig fresh rosemary, bruised

1 sprig fresh thyme, bruised

Add herbs to vodka and infuse at room temperature for 24 hours. Strain and return to bottle, leaving a bit of each herb in the bottle. Freeze until serving.

Thoroughly Warming Brew

2 tablespoons butter

1 medium onion, chopped

1 bay leaf

1 (16-ounce) can whole tomatoes, coarsely chopped

Pinch of sugar

Freshly ground pepper, to taste

6 cups chicken broth

1 cup dry white wine

In a medium saucepan, melt butter and add onion, bay leaf, chopped tomatoes, sugar and pepper. Cook and stir over low heat until mixture is very thick and almost all liquid has evaporated. In a large saucepan, heat chicken broth and stir in tomato mixture. Heat to boiling, then simmer over low heat for 30 minutes. Strain out all solids.

Ladle into mugs, adding about 2 tablespoons white wine per mug just before serving.

Serves 8

Black Tea Vodka

1 fifth vodka

2 tablespoons fruit and spice black tea, or 5 teaspoons black tea and 1/2 teaspoon whole cloves

Add tea to vodka and infuse at room temperature for 24 hours. Strain and return to bottle. Freeze until serving.

Champagne Fantasy

2 quarts champagne

1 cup sugar

1 (12-ounce) can cranberry juice concentrate, undiluted

1-1/2 cups Southern Comfort

1/2 cup lemon juice

Dash of bitters

Mix all ingredients and serve with a few whole cranberries in each glass.

Serves 8–12

Cranberry Vodka

2 cups vodka

5 cups cranberries

2-1/4 cups water

1-1/4 cups sugar

Combine cranberries, water and sugar in a large heavy saucepan. Bring to a boil, stirring often to dissolve sugar. Cool completely and mix in vodka. Cover and let stand for 2 days at room temperature. Strain mixture through a sieve. Pour over ice and serve. Refrigerate unused portions.

Anise Vodka

1 fifth vodka

2-1/2 teaspoons crushed anise seed

Add anise seeds to vodka and infuse at room temperature for 24 hours. Recap bottle and freeze until serving.

YEAST BREADS

Anise Seed Bread, 67
Cheese and Herb Wreath, 68
Citrus Bows, 77
Deli Rye Bread, 64
Focaccia, 69
Harlequin Loaves, 66
Mustard Wheat Bread, 65
Red Bell Pepper Bread, 65
Roma Fennel Bread, 63
Rosemary Breadsticks, 67
Sage Celery Seed Bread, 62
Stonehenge Bread, 62
Swedish Oatmeal Wheat Bread, 63
White Swan Rolls, 72

QUICK BREADS

Blarney Bread, 74
Caraway Bread, 71
Confetti Loaf, 74
Crescent Moon Sweet Rolls, 76
Plaza Popovers, 71
Raisin Spice Bread, 73
Savory Olive Nut Bread, 70
Sesame Zucchini Bread, 70

BREAD PUDDING & SPOONBREAD

Onion and Corn Spoonbread, 72
Parmesan Bread Pudding, 73

MUFFINS

Butterscotch Pumpkin Muffins, 80
Citrus Berry Muffins, 78
Jeweled Oat Muffins, 81
Morningside Peach Muffins, 78
Nutty Muffins, 79
Pecan Muffins, 77
Roanoke Farm Muffins, 79
Rosy Rhubarb Muffins, 80

COFFEE CAKES

Harvest Brunch Cake, 83
Honey-Almond Coffee Cake, 82
Macadamia Nut Coffee Cake, 81

BREAKFAST

Apple Jack Compote, 87
Carriage House Bake, 86
Cheese Soufflé Roll, 88
Country Manor Breakfast Tart, 91
Crab and Cheese Tarts, 87
Creamy Ham Brioches, 85
Hyde Park Waffles, 85
Italian Strata, 90
Poached Eggs in Avocado, 89
Puerto Vallarta Crêpes, 89
Rum Raisin French Toast, 83
Stuffed French Toast with Orange Sauce, 84
Swiss Custard, 86
Wild Mushroom Quiches in Acorn Squash, 90

MINI RECIPES

Fast Lane Bread Topping, 64
Flavored Butters, 75

Bread & Breakfast

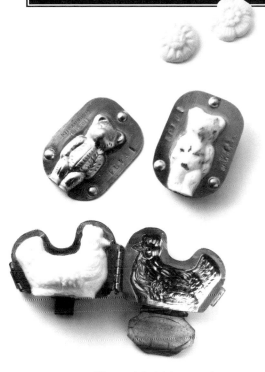

Pictured finishing touch:

USING

CHOCOLATE MOLDS

TO SHAPE BUTTER, 71

SPECIAL TOPIC BOXES

BEYOND PB&Js, 66

BUTTERS, 75

FOCACCIA TOPPINGS, 69

Stonehenge Bread

2/3 cup warm water (110 degrees)

1 package dry yeast

Pinch of sugar

Pinch of ground ginger

6 tablespoons butter or margarine

1/3 cup honey or 1/2 cup firmly packed brown sugar

1 tablespoon salt

2 cups milk, scalded

3-1/2 cups stone-ground whole wheat flour

1/2 cup cracked wheat

1/2 cup bran

1/4 cup sesame seeds, unhulled

1/3 cup soy flour

2 tablespoons cornmeal

1/3 cup old-fashioned oats

1/3 cup sunflower seeds

2-1/2 to 3 cups unbleached flour

In a small bowl, mix water, yeast, sugar and ginger. Let stand until foamy, about 5 minutes. In a large bowl, mix butter, honey, salt, milk, wheat flour, cracked wheat, bran, sesame seeds, soy flour, cornmeal, oats and sunflower seeds. Beat well. Let stand for 10 minutes.

Add yeast mixture and beat into the batter. Add unbleached flour and knead for 10 minutes. Dough won't be smooth or satiny. Cover and let rise for 1 to 1-1/2 hours. Punch dough down, divide in half and place into 2 greased loaf pans. Let rise again for 1 to 1-1/2 hours. Bake in a 350-degree oven for 30 to 35 minutes.

Makes 2 loaves

A fabulous seven-grain bread that is worth the search for the varied ingredients. Check health food stores to find small quantities of the different grains and flours. For variety, form dough into rolls and bake for 18 to 25 minutes.

Sage Celery Seed Bread

1 package dry yeast

1/4 cup warm water (110 degrees)

3/4 cup milk

1-1/2 tablespoons sugar

2 tablespoons butter

1-1/2 tablespoons honey

2 teaspoons salt

1 egg, slightly beaten

1 tablespoon sage

1 tablespoon plus 1 teaspoon celery seeds

3 to 3-1/2 cups flour

Soften yeast in water. In a small pan over moderate heat, scald milk. Add sugar, butter, honey and salt. Cool, then add beaten egg, followed by yeast mixture. Transfer mixture to a large bowl.

Mix sage and celery seed with yeast mixture into liquid. Gradually mix in flour, 1 cup at a time, until dough can be worked with hands. Knead on a lightly floured surface until smooth. Place dough in a greased bowl, turning over once. Let rest for 10 minutes. Shape dough into a round ball and place in a 9-inch round cake tin. Cover and let rise again until double in size, about 1 hour.

Bake in a 400-degree oven for 20 minutes or until browned. Remove immediately from pan and let cool on a wire rack.

Makes 1 loaf

This wonderfully fragrant bread has a rather delicate taste that pairs well with many soups and stews. Dough also may be made into rolls.

Swedish Oatmeal Wheat Bread

2 cups old-fashioned oats, plus additional for garnish

2 cups boiling water

3/4 cup firmly packed brown sugar

3/4 cup warm water (110 degrees)

1 package dry yeast

2 teaspoons salt

2 tablespoons shortening

2-1/4 cups wheat flour

2-1/4 cups flour

1/2–3/4 cup sunflower seeds (optional)

1 egg white (optional)

1 tablespoon water (optional)

Pour boiling water over oats. Let stand for 1 hour.

Mix brown sugar, water and yeast until dissolved. Pour into oat mixture. Add salt and shortening. Gradually mix in flours and sunflower seeds and knead until smooth. Place in a greased bowl and cover with plastic wrap. Let rise for 90 minutes. Punch down and let rise again, about 90 minutes.

Divide dough and place in 2 greased loaf or baguette pans. Brush tops with mixture of beaten egg white and 1 tablespoon water and sprinkle with old-fashioned oats. Bake in a 350-degree oven for 1 hour.

Makes 1 loaf

A sweeter version of a classic. This makes a wonderful sandwich bread.

Roma Fennel Bread

1 tablespoon fennel seed, plus additional to garnish

4 tablespoons butter

1 large yellow onion, minced

2 cups warm water (110 degrees)

1 package dry yeast

1 tablespoon sugar

2 teaspoons salt

4 to 4-1/2 cups flour

Butter, melted

1 tablespoon cornmeal

Brown fennel seeds for 1 minute in a heavy dry skillet until golden. Add butter. After it has melted, add onion and sauté until golden, about 20 minutes. Set aside.

Combine water, yeast, sugar and salt and stir until yeast dissolves. Add reserved onion-fennel mixture and stir in flour (dough will be sticky). Place dough in a large greased bowl and cover with plastic wrap. Let rise in a warm place until doubled in bulk, about 45 minutes. Punch down and brush with melted butter to coat.

Grease a baguette pan and sprinkle with cornmeal. Butter hands and divide dough into 2 or 3 parts, depending on number of compartments in pan. Shape each into an oblong loaf. Do not knead. Brush tops of loaves with melted butter and sprinkle with a few fennel seeds. Let rise, covered with plastic wrap for another 45 minutes or until almost doubled.

Bake at 425 degrees for 10 minutes, then reduce oven temperature to 375 degrees and bake for 20 minutes more.

Makes 2–3 loaves

A delicious herb bread that complements any Italian meal, especially **Angel Hair Pasta with Spicy Sun-Dried Tomato Sauce.**

Deli Rye Bread

6 tablespoons yellow cornmeal, plus additional for baking sheet

3/4 cup cold water

1 cup boiling water

2 teaspoons salt

1 tablespoon butter or margarine

1 package dry yeast

2-1/2 cups rye flour

1-1/2 cups flour

1 cup mashed potatoes

1 tablespoon plus 1 teaspoon caraway seed

1/2 teaspoon cornstarch

Combine cornmeal and 1/2 cup cold water in a saucepan over medium-high heat. Add boiling water and cook for 2 minutes, stirring constantly. Stir in salt and butter. Allow to cool to lukewarm.

Combine yeast, flours, potatoes and 1 tablespoon caraway seed in mixing bowl and blend. Add cornmeal mixture and blend thoroughly. Turn dough out onto a lightly floured board and knead until stiff but slightly sticky. Place in a large, lightly greased bowl, turning to coat. Cover with plastic wrap and a hot, damp towel. Let rise in warm place until doubled, about 1 to 1-1/2 hours.

Grease a baking sheet and sprinkle lightly with cornmeal. Punch dough down, shape into a loaf or round and place on a baking sheet. Cover with plastic wrap and let rise again until double, about 90 minutes.

Remove wrap and bake at 375 degrees for 40 minutes. Meanwhile, combine 1/4 cup water and cornstarch and bring to a boil for 1 minute. When bread is finished baking, remove from oven and brush lightly with cornstarch glaze. Sprinkle with 1 teaspoon caraway seeds. Return to oven for 5 minutes or until top is glazed and loaf sounds hollow when tapped. Cool before serving.

Makes 1 loaf

This hearty bread is also lovely baked in a tube pan or baking mold. Serve with fresh cold cuts and crunchy kosher dills.

Fast Lane Bread Topping

1 (16-inch) baguette • 3 ounces Parmesan cheese, finely grated • 3 ounces extra sharp cheddar, finely grated • 1/4 cup olive oil • 1-1/2 teaspoons coarsely cracked pepper • 2 teaspoons chopped chives • 2 cloves garlic, minced • 1 teaspoon lemon juice (optional)

Combine cheeses and add to mixture of oil, pepper, chives, garlic and lemon juice until a paste forms.
(May be made up to 2 days in advance.)

Halve bread horizontally, leaving 1 long side attached at the seam.
Press cheese mixture evenly over cut surface of both halves,
leaving 1/2-inch border around outer edges. Place halves together,
wrap loaf tightly in foil and bake in a 350-degree oven
for 20 to 30 minutes.

Serves 8

Mustard Wheat Bread

1 package dry yeast

1/4 cup warm water (110 degrees)

1 tablespoon sugar

1/4 cup butter (1/2 stick) or margarine, melted

1/2 cup water

1 teaspoon salt

1/2 cup country Dijon or coarse-grained mustard

2 cups flour

1 cup whole wheat flour

1 egg white, beaten (optional)

1 tablespoon water (optional)

Dissolve yeast in warm water. Mix in sugar and let stand for 5 minutes. In a large bowl, combine butter, water, salt and mustard. Add yeast mixture. Mix in 1 cup flour, then follow with remaining flours and mix. On a floured board, knead for 10 minutes or until smooth, adding additional flour as needed. Place in a greased bowl. Cover and let rise until double in bulk, about 1 to 1-1/2 hours.

Punch dough down and shape into loaf or braid. Place in a greased loaf pan or on a cookie sheet for braid. Cover with plastic wrap and let rise until double in bulk, about 1 to 1-1/2 hours. Brush with a mixture of beaten egg white and 1 tablespoon water if desired.

Preheat oven to 375 degrees. Bake for 30 to 35 minutes or until golden brown.

Makes 1 loaf

The addition of mustard makes this a perfect complement to any hearty winter meal. Dough also may be made into rolls. To do so, roll into 8 individual logs. Tie each into a knot and tuck ends underneath. Let rise again and brush with egg white wash or butter. Bake until golden brown.

Red Bell Pepper Bread

1 cup minced red bell peppers (about 1 pepper)

2 tablespoons butter

1 tablespoon dry yeast

2-1/2 cups warm water (110 degrees)

1/2 cup warm tomato juice (110 degrees)

1/4 cup molasses

1-1/2 cups whole wheat flour

2 teaspoons tarragon

5 cups bread flour (no substitutions)

1-1/2 teaspoons salt

Sauté red peppers in butter until tender. Sprinkle yeast over 1/4 cup warm water and stir to dissolve. Combine peppers, remainder of water, tomato juice and molasses. Stir in yeast mixture, whole wheat flour and tarragon. Let mixture rise for about 20 minutes or until bubbly and active. Gradually add bread flour and salt. Knead for 10 minutes, cover and let rise until doubled, about 1 to 1-1/2 hours.

Punch dough down, divide in half and place in greased loaf or baguette pans. Let rise until

almost double, about 1 to 1-1/2 hours. Bake in a 375-degree oven 45 to 55 minutes or until golden.

Makes 2 loaves

*A nice accompaniment to **Chicken with Red Pepper Sauce**.*

Harlequin Loaves

1 package dry yeast
4 cups warm water (110 degrees)
8–9 cups flour
1-1/2 tablespoons salt
1/4 cup olive oil
1-1/4 cups chopped black olives

Dissolve yeast in warm water and let sit for 5 minutes. Stir in half of flour. Add salt and oil. Mix in 3 cups of remaining flour to form a sticky dough. Knead in olives and add remaining flour. Knead for 5 minutes more to form a smooth elastic dough. Place in a greased bowl and cover with plastic wrap. Let dough rise until double in bulk, about 1-1/2 hours.

Divide dough into 3 equal pieces and shape into loaves. Place each seam-side down on a lightly floured baking sheet and cover with plastic wrap. Let rise in a warm spot until double in bulk,

about 90 minutes. Slash top of each loaf with a serrated knife, 1/2-inch deep, and dust with flour. Bake in a 400-degree oven for 45 to 60 minutes. (If oven will not accommodate 3 loaves, place 1 in the refrigerator while the other 2 bake.)

Makes 3 loaves

Cut slices into festive shapes and top with **Black and White Spread** or **Olive Paste** to accompany soups or salads.

Beyond PB&Js

*H*ere are some sandwich combinations to tantalize the taste buds:

Raisin Spice Bread with chicken salad and chopped walnuts Toasted Italian bread brushed with vinaigrette and topped with mozzarella and oil-packed sun-dried tomatoes Herb bread with smoked turkey, cream cheese, and cranberry chutney Toasted Stonehenge Bread with avocado, tomato, cucumber and alfalfa sprouts, dabbed with mayonnaise Tuna melt with chopped cilantro, roasted red pepper and sliced Parmesan cheese on Mustard Wheat Bread Light rye bread with sliced roast pork and a dollop of apple butter A croissant stuffed with hard-cooked egg slices, smoked oysters, asparagus tips and lemon-flavored mayonnaise Grilled chicken breast with provolone cheese, grilled onions and flavored mustard on slices of Harlequin Loaf Melted cheddar and mozzarella cheese with tomato slices and artichoke hearts on Swedish Oatmeal Wheat Bread Baguette with slices of tenderloin, roasted shallots and Roasted Red Pepper Garlic Dip Sage Celery Seed Bread with cold Curried Turkey Breast and honey mustard Shrimp Salad Laced with Limes stuffed into pita pockets Cold meatloaf slices with Avocado Mayonnaise on sourdough bread

Anise Seed Bread

2 cups milk

1/2 cup (1 stick) butter

6 tablespoons sugar

1 teaspoon salt

1 package dry yeast

1/4 cup warm water (110 degrees)

7-1/2 to 8 cups flour

2 large eggs

2 tablespoons anise seed

Sesame seeds (optional)

In a large saucepan, scald 2 cups milk with butter. Stir in sugar and salt. Cool. In a separate bowl, dissolve yeast in water and let stand for 5 minutes. Blend 1 cup flour into milk mixture. Add yeast and 1 well-beaten egg, followed by anise seed. Gradually add remaining 6-1/2 to 7 cups flour. Knead dough mixture, then place in a greased bowl, turning to coat. Cover with plastic wrap. Let dough rise until doubled, about 1-1/2 hours.

Punch down and knead again. Divide dough in half and place in 2 greased loaf pans. Brush with beaten egg and sprinkle with sesame seeds. Let rise until almost double, about 1-1/2 hours. Bake in a 350-degree oven until golden brown, about 35 minutes.

Makes 2 loaves

This fragrant semisweet bread bakes quickly. As a variation, braid loaves or form small rolls and bake on a cookie sheet. For a softer crust, wrap hot baked loaves in a clean kitchen towel while cooling.

Rosemary Breadsticks

1 package dry yeast

1 teaspoon sugar

1/4 cup warm water (110 degrees)

1-1/2 cups flour

3/4 cup whole wheat flour

1-1/2 teaspoons rosemary

1 teaspoon salt, plus additional for glaze

2 tablespoons olive oil

3/4 cup cold water

Cornmeal

1 egg white, beaten

Pinch of salt

Dash of coarse salt, sesame seeds or poppy seeds

Mix yeast and sugar in warm water. Let sit until foamy, about 5 minutes. In a food processor fitted with a dough or metal blade, combine flours, rosemary and salt for 5 seconds. Add oil and cold water to yeast mixture and, with machine running, pour all through feed tube. Continue to process until dough forms a ball. Add more flour if necessary, 1 tablespoon at a time. Place dough in a greased bowl, cover with plastic wrap and let rise for 1-1/2 hours.

Divide dough in half. Roll each piece into a 12-inch log. Cut logs into 1-inch pieces. Roll each small piece into a 1/3-inch diameter log, fold logs in half and twist. Place on a greased baking sheet sprinkled with cornmeal.

Preheat oven to 300 degrees. Let sticks rise for about 15 minutes. Brush with glaze of beaten egg white and a pinch of salt. Sprinkle with coarse salt, sesame or poppy seeds. Bake for 30 minutes. Increase heat to 350 degrees and bake until brown, about 5 minutes.

Makes 24 small breadsticks

Substitute oregano, savory, marjoram, basil, sage or a combination of herbs for the rosemary, depending on the flavors of the meal you'd like these breadsticks to accompany. These freeze well.

1 package dry yeast

2 to 2-1/2 cups flour

3/4 cup milk

2 tablespoons butter or margarine

1 teaspoon salt

1 cup shredded cheddar, Swiss, Muenster or provolone cheese

2 eggs

Filling:

1 clove garlic, minced

1/4 cup (1/2 stick) butter or margarine

1 tablespoon snipped parsley

1/4 teaspoon tarragon, crushed (optional)

In a mixing bowl, combine yeast and 1 cup flour. In a saucepan, heat milk, butter and salt until warm and butter almost melts, about 110 degrees. Add to yeast mixture. Add 1/2 cup cheese and 1 egg. Beat with an electric mixer at low speed for 30 seconds, scraping bowl constantly, then beat for 3 minutes on high speed. Stir in 1 more cup of flour and mix at low speed.

Turn dough out onto a lightly floured surface. Knead in enough remaining flour to make a moderately stiff dough that is smooth and elastic, about 5 to 8 minutes. Place dough in a lightly greased bowl, then cover and let rise in a warm place until doubled, about 1 to 1-1/2 hours.

For filling: While dough is rising, prepare filling. In a small saucepan, sauté garlic in butter for about 1 minute. Stir in parsley and tarragon. Remove from heat. Cool slightly.

Punch down dough. Cover and let rise for 10 minutes. On a lightly floured surface, roll dough into a 20- by 9-inch rectangle. Spread dough with filling, then sprinkle with remaining 1/2 cup cheese. Roll up dough jelly-roll fashion, starting on the long side. Pinch edge to seal.

With a sharp knife, cut roll in half lengthwise, making two 20-inch portions. Place halves side by side, with cut edges up. Moisten 1 end of each portion and press together to seal. Twist

the 2 pieces together several times (intertwine), alternately lifting 1 portion of dough over the other. Moisten and seal remaining ends. Shape braid into a ring; seal ends together. Place ring on a greased baking sheet. Cover and let rise until nearly double, about 1 to 1-1/2 hours.

Preheat oven to 350 degrees. Bake for about 25 minutes. Beat remaining egg and brush on ring. Bake for 5 minutes more or until done. Let cool slightly on rack.

Makes 1 wreath-shaped loaf

This mouth-watering creation is deceptively easy and may be frozen after baking for up to 2 months. To reheat, thaw frozen ring and sprinkle lightly with water. Wrap in foil and place on a baking sheet. Bake at 325 degrees for 10 minutes or until heated through.

Focaccia

1 package dry yeast

3/4 cup warm water (110 degrees)

2 cups flour

1/2 teaspoon salt

4 tablespoons olive oil

Dissolve yeast in warm water and let stand for 5 minutes. In a food processor fitted with a dough or metal blade, combine flour and salt. Add yeast mixture and 3 tablespoons olive oil. Process until flour is absorbed. (May also be mixed by hand.) Turn dough out onto a floured surface. Knead until smooth and elastic, adding more flour as necessary to keep dough from sticking, about 2 minutes. Place dough in a greased bowl, turning to coat. Cover with plastic wrap and let rise in a warm place until double in bulk, about 1 hour.

Preheat oven to 425 degrees. Punch dough down and let rest for 5 minutes. Form dough into a 10-inch round or 9- by 13-inch rectangle on a greased pizza pan or baking sheet. Pull dough apart in several places to form small holes. Brush with 1 tablespoon olive oil and sprinkle with a focaccia topping. Cover and let rise for 15 minutes. Bake for 20 to 25 minutes or until golden brown. Cool completely in pan on a wire rack. Remove before serving.

Makes 1 loaf

Focaccia, an Italian flat bread, is an excellent accompaniment to any meal.

To make a delicious focaccia sandwich, cut baked loaf in half horizontally. Place bottom half on a baking sheet. Cover evenly with 1/2 cup freshly grated Parmesan cheese, 1/2 cup pesto and 1 thinly sliced tomato. Top with other bread half. Brush top with 1 tablespoon olive oil and sprinkle with an additional 1/2 cup Parmesan cheese. Bake in a 350-degree oven for 10 minutes or until cheese inside melts. Cut into 8 wedges and serve warm (may be made in advance and reheated).

Focaccia Toppings

Sliced or quartered green and black olives * **Fennel seeds** * **Fresh snipped herbs (especially rosemary)** * **Caraway seeds** * **Freshly ground pepper and kosher salt** * **Chives** * **Thinly sliced onions** * **Roasted pimiento** * **Chopped leeks and lemon zest** * **Peppercorns** * **Shaved prosciutto and sliced mushrooms** * **Thinly sliced pepperoni** * **Gruyère cheese and anchovies** * **Chopped and/or roasted garlic** * **Pine nuts (add just before serving)**

Savory Olive Nut Bread

5 cups flour

2-1/2 tablespoons baking powder

2/3 cup sugar

1 teaspoon salt

1/2 teaspoon ground savory

2 eggs, beaten

2 cups milk

2 cups sliced pimiento-stuffed green olives

2 cups walnut pieces

1/4 cup chopped pimiento

Sift together flour, baking powder, sugar, salt and savory.

In a separate bowl, beat together eggs and milk until well blended. Stir egg mixture into dry mixture until just blended. Add olives, walnuts and pimiento.

Preheat oven to 350 degrees. Divide batter into 2 greased loaf pans and bake for 55 to 60 minutes. Cool in pans for 5 minutes, then remove and cool completely.

Makes 2 loaves

Delicious topped with sweet butter or a mild cheese spread. For a quick appetizer, bake as mini loaves and top with a flavored cream cheese.

Sesame Zucchini Bread

1-2/3 cups flour

1-1/3 teaspoons baking soda

1/4 teaspoon baking powder

3/4 teaspoon salt

2 teaspoons cinnamon

1/3 cup wheat germ

2/3 cup oil

1/2 cup sugar

1/2 cup firmly packed brown sugar

2 eggs

1-1/2 teaspoons vanilla

1-1/2 cups shredded zucchini (1-1/2 to 2 medium zucchini)

1/4 cup sesame seeds

2/3 cup walnuts

2/3 cup raisins

In a food processor, sift flour, baking soda, baking powder, salt, cinnamon and wheat germ and pulse 3 times. Set aside.

Combine oil and sugars in food processor. Add eggs and vanilla and process until well mixed and creamy. Add zucchini, sesame seeds and nuts. Mix briefly until nuts are coarsely chopped, pulsing. Add sifted dry ingredients and raisins. Process and pulse only until flour is incorporated.

Pour into a greased and floured loaf pan. Bake at 350 degrees for 60 to 75 minutes or until a toothpick inserted in the center comes out clean.

Makes 1 loaf

When the zucchini harvest reaches its peak, stock up on this hearty summer bread, which freezes well.

Caraway Bread

2 cups flour
1 cup whole wheat flour
3 tablespoons sugar
1 tablespoon baking powder
2 teaspoons caraway seeds
1/2 teaspoon salt
1/2 teaspoon nutmeg
1/2 teaspoon thyme
1 cup skim milk
1/3 cup corn oil
1 egg, beaten

Combine flours, sugar, baking powder, caraway seeds, salt, nutmeg and thyme.

In a separate bowl, mix milk, oil and egg. Add to flour mixture and stir until moistened. Turn dough into a greased loaf pan. Bake at 350 degrees for 55 minutes or until a toothpick inserted in the middle comes out clean. Remove from pan and cool on a wire rack for at least 30 minutes.

Makes 1 loaf

The best of both worlds—this quick bread can be in the oven in 20 minutes, but its consistency is almost like a yeast bread.

Plaza Popovers

2 eggs
1 cup milk
1 cup flour
1 teaspoon salt
Dash of cayenne pepper
2 tablespoons butter or margarine

In a blender or medium bowl, mix eggs, milk, flour, salt and cayenne pepper until smooth. (At this point, batter may be refrigerated until ready to use, up to 2 days.)

Preheat oven to 425 degrees. Grease well twelve 2-1/2-inch muffin cups or popover pans. Place 1/2 teaspoon butter or margarine in each cup and heat in oven until butter sizzles. Pour batter into cups, 1/2 to 2/3 full. Bake for 25 to 30 minutes or until popovers are puffed and brown. Serve immediately with additional butter.

Makes 12 small or 6 large popovers

Remember not to open the oven door until at least 20 minutes have passed. For a drier popover, poke the tops with a fork during the last 5 to 8 minutes of baking time.

As a fun variation to traditional butter molds, experiment using antique chocolate molds instead. Their interesting shapes, such as small chickens and bears, add flair to the theme or setting. Spray the mold first with nonstick cooking spray, add butter and freeze until ready to unmold.

White Swan Rolls

1 package dry yeast

1/2 cup warm water (110 degrees)

2/3 cup shortening

1/2 cup sugar

1 teaspoon salt

1 cup mashed potatoes

2 eggs

1 cup lukewarm milk

4–5 cups flour

In a large bowl, dissolve yeast in warm water. Add shortening, sugar, salt, potatoes, eggs and milk. Mix until well blended. Add 2 cups flour and stir until smooth. Gradually add remaining flour to form a stiff dough, stirring after each addition. Knead for 3 to 5 minutes. Cover loosely with plastic wrap or cover in a bowl. Refrigerate for at least 12 to 14 hours.

Punch dough down and roll out on a lightly floured board. Cut into rounds, then fold each round almost in half and seal. Cover and let rise for 2 hours.

Preheat oven to 400 degrees. Bake for 10 to 13 minutes and serve.

Makes 3 dozen small rolls, clovers or knots

Dough must be made in advance.

A nice dinner roll that rises well in the refrigerator. Great for entertaining because the dough can easily be made a day ahead.

Onion and Corn Spoonbread

1/4 cup (1/2 stick) butter

1 large red onion, chopped fine

1-1/2 cups dry corn muffin mix

1 egg

1/3 cup milk

1 cup canned creamed corn

1/4 teaspoon hot pepper sauce

1 cup sour cream

1/4 teaspoon salt

1 cup grated sharp cheddar cheese

1/4 teaspoon dill (optional)

1 (4-ounce) can mild chopped green chilies (optional)

Preheat oven to 425 degrees. Grease a 9-inch square pan. Melt butter in a skillet. Add onion and sauté until soft.

In a large bowl, combine corn muffin mix, egg, milk, corn and pepper sauce. Pour into prepared pan. Stir sour cream, salt, 1/2 the grated cheese, dill and green chilies into sautéed onion. Spread mixture over batter in pan. Sprinkle with remaining cheese. Bake for 30 minutes and serve warm.

Serves 8–10

This smooth-textured bread is a marvelous accompaniment to chicken.

Parmesan Bread Pudding

2 cups milk

6 cloves garlic, chopped

2 whole eggs

2 egg yolks

3 tablespoons minced fresh parsley leaves

1/2 teaspoon salt

Freshly ground pepper, to taste

1/2 cup freshly grated Parmesan cheese

2-1/2 cups 1/2-inch Italian bread cubes

Scald milk in a saucepan and add garlic. Remove mixture from heat and cool for 15 minutes, then strain through a sieve, discarding garlic.

In a bowl, slowly whisk together whole eggs and yolks. Add milk in a slow stream, whisking continuously. (Milk will curdle if added too quickly). Continue whisking and stir in parsley, salt and pepper. Add 1/4 cup Parmesan cheese to mixture.

Divide bread cubes among 8 well-buttered muffin tins, custard dishes or ramekins. Ladle custard mixture over bread, dividing evenly among tins or dishes. Let mixture sit for 10 minutes. (At this point, pudding can be prepared 8 hours in advance and chilled.)

Preheat oven to 350 degrees. Before baking, sprinkle remaining Parmesan cheese evenly among tins or dishes. If using muffin tins, add water to any empty tins. Bake puddings for 45 minutes or until golden brown and puffed. Allow to rest and cool for 10 minutes (puddings will sink a little). If using muffin tins, run a knife around the side of each pudding and lift out carefully with fork. Serve warm.

Serves 8

Try this instead of potatoes alongside **Spinach and Steak Pinwheels.**

Raisin Spice Bread

2 cups flour

2 teaspoons baking powder

1 teaspoon salt

1 teaspoon cinnamon

1/4 teaspoon ground nutmeg

1/2 cup firmly packed brown sugar

1 cup raisins

3/4 cup old-fashioned oats

1/4 cup shortening

2 eggs, beaten

1 cup milk

Preheat oven to 350 degrees. Combine flour, baking powder, salt, cinnamon and nutmeg. Add brown sugar, raisins, oats, shortening, eggs and milk and stir until just blended.

Pour batter into a greased loaf pan and bake for 55 to 60 minutes. Remove from pan immediately and cool on a wire rack.

Makes 1 loaf

A flavorful bread loaded with spices. For ease in slicing, wrap cooled bread and store for 1 day before slicing.

Confetti Loaf

3 eggs, beaten

1/2 cup vegetable oil

1/2 cup milk

3-1/2 cups flour

1 cup sugar

1 teaspoon baking powder

1 teaspoon baking soda

1 teaspoon cinnamon

1/2 teaspoon salt

1-1/3 cups shredded coconut

1/2 cup maraschino cherries

1/2 cup raisins

1/2 cup chopped pecans

In a mixing bowl, combine eggs, oil and milk. In a separate bowl, combine flour, sugar, baking powder, baking soda, cinnamon and salt. Add to liquid mixture. Stir in coconut, cherries, raisins and pecans.

Preheat oven to 350 degrees. Pour batter into a greased loaf pan and bake for 50 minutes or until a toothpick inserted in the center comes out clean.

Makes 1 standard loaf or 3 small loaves

A colorful bread full of goodies that's a most appreciated gift.

Blarney Bread

1 (14-ounce) package quick date bread mix (dry)

2/3 cup water

1/3 cup Irish Cream

1 tablespoon oil

1 egg

Filling:

2 (3-ounce) packages cream cheese, softened to room temperature

1/4 cup sugar

1 egg

Glaze:

1/2 cup powdered sugar

1 teaspoon Irish Cream

2–3 teaspoons milk

For filling: Place cream cheese, sugar and egg in a small mixing bowl. Beat at medium speed until smooth, about 1 minute. Set aside.

In a large bowl, combine dry bread mix, water, liqueur, oil and egg. Stir by hand until mix is moistened, about 50 to 75 strokes. Pour 1 cup of batter into a greased loaf pan. Carefully spoon filling over batter. Pour remaining batter over filling. (For a marbled effect, pull knife through batter in wide curves from side to side. Turn pan 90 degrees and repeat.)

For glaze: In a small bowl, mix sugar, liqueur and milk. Use enough milk for desired consistency. Set aside.

Preheat oven to 350 degrees. Bake for 50 to 60 minutes or until toothpick inserted in center comes out clean. Cool in pan for at least 45 minutes. Remove from pan and cool completely, then glaze. (Allow plenty of cooling time before slicing or bread will be gooey.) Store in refrigerator.

Makes 1 loaf

Great for brunch or dessert. Blarney Bread is festive to serve or give during the holidays. Package in a gold doily, wrap with clear plastic wrap and tie with silver and gold ribbons.

After making homemade breads or muffins, why settle for plain old butter?

Cranberry Butter

1 cup (2 sticks) unsalted butter, cut into pieces, softened

3/4 cup cranberries

6 tablespoons powdered sugar

2 teaspoons grated lemon zest

Coarsely chop cranberries with sugar and lemon zest. Add butter and blend until mixture is combined but slightly chunky. Cover and chill. Bring to room temperature before serving.

Makes about 1 cup

Curry Butter

6 tablespoons (3/4 stick) unsalted butter, softened

2 teaspoons curry powder

Cream together butter and curry powder. Chill covered for 30 minutes or until firm but of spreading consistency.

Makes about 1/2 cup

Orange Grand Marnier Butter

1/4 cup (1/2 stick) unsalted butter, softened

1/4 cup cream cheese, softened to room temperature

2 tablespoons orange zest

2 tablespoons Grand Marnier

Blend all ingredients, place in a mold and chill. Unmold when cold and serve at room temperature.

Makes 1 cup

Apricot Butter

1/2 cup (1 stick) unsalted butter, softened

1/4 cup honey

1/4 cup finely chopped dried apricots

1/2 teaspoon grated lemon zest

Whip butter until fluffy. Add remaining ingredients and mix well. Chill, then serve at room temperature.

Makes about 1 cup

Radish Butter

1 cup (2 sticks) unsalted butter, softened

1/2 cup sliced red radishes

2 tablespoons freshly grated or minced horseradish, or bottled horseradish, drained

Coarse salt, to taste

Mince radishes and combine well with butter, horseradish and salt. Chill, then bring to room temperature before serving.

Makes about 1 cup

Red Onion Butter

2 tablespoons plus 1/2 cup (1 stick) butter, softened

1 medium red onion, finely chopped

2 tablespoons dry red wine

1/4 teaspoon salt

Sauté onion in 2 tablespoons butter until soft, about 5 minutes. Add wine and cook until all liquid is evaporated. Cool thoroughly, then combine with remaining butter and salt. Beat until fluffy. Chill, then bring to room temperature to serve.

Makes about 1 cup

Crescent Moon Sweet Rolls

1 cup (2 sticks) butter, room temperature

1 (12-ounce) carton cottage cheese

2 cups flour

Dash of salt

___

Frosting:

1 cup powdered sugar

1 tablespoon butter or margarine

1/2 teaspoon vanilla

1 tablespoon fresh orange juice or 1-1/2 to 2 tablespoons milk

1/2 teaspoon grated orange zest

Cream butter and cottage cheese together. Add flour and salt. Dough will be very sticky. Refrigerate for 4 hours or overnight.

Divide dough into 3 parts. On a floured board, roll each part into a circle 1/8-inch thick. Cut each circle into 12 wedges. Roll and form wedges into crescent shapes, starting at the wide end and rolling to the point.

Preheat over to 350 degrees. Place rolls on a greased baking sheet and bake for 25 to 30 minutes. Cool and frost.

For frosting: Combine all ingredients, adjusting liquid to make a frosting of spreading consistency.

Makes 36 rolls

When defrosting, place frozen rolls on a rack until thawed to remove moisture. These little rolls also fill well. Place a tablespoon of one of the following sweet fillings at the wide end of the dough before rolling: peach or strawberry preserves, miniature chocolate chips, Mascarpone or ricotta cheese mixed with either cinnamon sugar or almond paste. Offer several varieties for a morning coffee or brunch buffet, served on pretty dessert plates.

When using a baking stone or tile to bake breads, remember to preheat the oven and stone for at least 30 minutes.

Almost all breads should be baked in the center of a preheated oven. For a hard brown crust, put the bread pan on the bottom rack of the oven after 15 minutes of baking.

When preparing quick breads, combine wet and dry ingredients just until moistened. Too much mixing will cause the dough to be tough and the bread to contain many air pockets.

To enhance the raisin flavor in baked goods, plump the raisins first. Place them in a microwave-proof bowl and cover with liquid (water, liqueur, brandy, etc.). Microwave covered on high for 45 seconds or until raisins are soft. Let stand covered for 1 minute, then drain and use.

Citrus Bows

1-1/4 cups milk, scalded

1/3 cup sugar

1/2 cup shortening

1 teaspoon salt

1 package dry yeast

2 eggs, well beaten

1/4 cup fresh orange juice

2 tablespoons grated orange zest

5 cups flour

Frosting:

2 tablespoons fresh orange juice

1 tablespoon grated orange zest

1 cup powdered sugar

Combine milk, sugar, shortening and salt. Cool to lukewarm, no higher than 110 degrees. Soften yeast in mixture. Add eggs, orange juice and zest. Beat thoroughly. Add flour, 1 cup at a time, beating after each addition. Cover and let rest for 10 minutes.

Knead dough on a lightly floured board. Place in a greased bowl, cover and let rise until double in bulk, about 2 hours.

Punch dough down and roll out on a lightly floured board into a rectangle, 1/2 inch thick and approximately 12 by 10 inches wide. Cut strips of dough 1/2-inch wide by 10 inches long. Tie each strip into a knot. Arrange on baking sheets. Spray a piece of plastic wrap with nonstick cooking spray, cover dough and let double in size for 1 to 2 hours.

For frosting: Mix orange juice, orange zest and sugar. Set aside.

Preheat oven to 400 degrees. Bake rolls for 15 minutes. Frost and serve warm.

Makes 24–30 rolls

To keep these enchanting rolls warm, heat a ceramic quarry tile in the oven while baking the rolls. Place it on top of a linen napkin in the bread basket and add rolls. The tile also helps keep any grease from soiling the napkin.

Pecan Muffins

1/3 cup butter or margarine, melted

1 cup firmly packed dark brown sugar

2 eggs, beaten

1/2 cup flour

1 teaspoon vanilla

1 cup chopped pecans

Melt butter over low heat. Remove from heat and add brown sugar, eggs, flour, vanilla and pecans.

Preheat oven to 350 degrees. Lightly grease small muffin tins and fill with batter 3/4 full. Bake for 15 minutes.

Makes 24 small muffins

Perfect brunch fare—these are best served warm.

Citrus Berry Muffins

1 cup (2 sticks) butter, softened to room temperature

1 cup sugar

4 egg yolks, well beaten

2 cups flour

2 teaspoons baking powder

1 teaspoon salt

1/2 cup fresh lemon juice

4 egg whites, stiffly beaten

2 teaspoons grated lemon zest

1 cup fresh blueberries

In a mixing bowl, cream butter and sugar by hand. Add egg yolks and beat until mixture becomes light in color. Sift flour with baking powder and salt. Add portions of lemon juice to butter and sugar mixture alternately with portions of flour mixture. Do not overmix. Fold in stiffly beaten egg whites and lemon zest. Gently fold in blueberries.

Preheat oven to 375 degrees. Pour batter into greased muffin tins and bake for 15 to 20 minutes.

Makes 12 muffins

If using frozen blueberries, toss lightly in flour while still frozen to prevent berries from "bleeding" in batter.

For a pretty presentation, sprinkle muffins with powdered sugar after they have cooled. A batch of mini Citrus Berry Muffins in a decorative basket will add appealing color to the table at a luncheon buffet or bridal shower.

Morningside Peach Muffins

1 egg

1 cup milk

1/4 cup (1/2 stick) butter, melted

2/3 cup sugar

1/2 teaspoon salt

1/4 teaspoon cinnamon

1 teaspoon fresh lemon juice

1/4 teaspoon vanilla

2 cups flour

3 teaspoons baking powder

1 cup chopped unpeeled peaches

Beat egg in a large mixing bowl. Stir in by hand milk, butter, sugar, salt, cinnamon, lemon juice and vanilla. Sift together flour and baking powder and mix into wet ingredients until just blended. Do not overmix. Gently fold in peaches.

Preheat oven to 350 degrees. Fill greased muffin tins 3/4 full and bake for 20 minutes.

Makes 12 muffins

A delicately sweet and fragrant way to say "good morning." When selecting fresh peaches, look for a creamy or yellow background color, a firm texture, a well-defined crease, and a sweet fragrance as indicators of quality and ripeness.

Roanoke Farm Muffins

2 cups flour

1-1/4 cups brown sugar

2 teaspoons baking soda

2 tablespoons cinnamon

1/2 teaspoon salt

1-1/2 cups finely shredded carrot

1-1/2 cups peeled and shredded apple (1 large)

3/4 cup coconut

1/2 cup dates

1/2 cup chopped pecans

1 teaspoon grated orange zest

3 eggs, beaten

1 cup vegetable oil

3/4 teaspoon vanilla

In a large bowl, combine flour, brown sugar, baking soda, cinnamon and salt. In another bowl, combine carrot, apple, coconut, dates, pecans and orange zest. Stir in beaten eggs, oil and vanilla. Add to dry ingredients, stirring just until moistened.

Preheat oven to 375 degrees. Pour battter into greased muffin tins and bake for 10 to 18 minutes. Cool on a rack for 10 minutes before serving.

Makes 18–20 muffins

A meal in a muffin. With a cream cheese frosting, these muffins can become "mini carrot cake" desserts.

Nutty Muffins

1 egg

1/2 cup milk

4 tablespoons butter or margarine, melted

1/2 cup sugar

1/4 teaspoon nutmeg (optional)

2 tablespoons baking powder

1/4 cup sour cream

1/4 cup pine nuts, lightly toasted

4 tablespoons chopped pecans, lightly toasted

4 tablespoons sunflower seeds

1-1/2 cups flour

Beat egg until foamy with an electric mixer. Blend in milk and butter. Stir in sugar, nutmeg and baking powder. Add sour cream, pine nuts, chopped pecans, sunflower seeds and flour.

Preheat oven to 400 degrees. Spoon batter evenly into lightly greased muffin tins. Bake until golden brown and a toothpick inserted in the centers comes out clean, about 20 to 25 minutes. Serve immediately.

Makes 8 muffins

Not very sweet, these dense, crunchy muffins would go well with a variety of soups.

Rosy Rhubarb Muffins

1-1/2 cups firmly packed brown sugar
1/2 cup vegetable oil
1 egg
2 teaspoons vanilla
1 cup buttermilk
1-1/2 cups fresh or frozen rhubarb, diced
1/2 cup pecans, chopped
2-1/2 cups flour
1 teaspoon baking powder
1/2 teaspoon salt

Topping:

1 tablespoon butter
1/3 cup firmly packed brown sugar
1 teaspoon cinnamon

In a large bowl, mix sugar, oil, egg, vanilla and buttermilk by hand. Stir in rhubarb and nuts. In a separate bowl, mix flour, baking powder and salt. Fold into rhubarb mixture. (Muffins are better when mixed with a light touch.) Spoon into greased muffin tins.

For topping: In a small bowl, combine butter, sugar and cinnamon. Sprinkle topping over filled muffin cups and press lightly into batter.

Preheat oven to 400 degrees. Bake for 20 minutes, 15 minutes if preparing miniature muffins. Remove from pans immediately and cool on wire racks.

Makes 12–16 muffins

These delicate pink-red muffins offer a perfect introduction to rhubarb.

Butterscotch Pumpkin Muffins

1-3/4 cups flour, sifted
1/2 cup firmly packed light brown sugar
1/2 cup sugar
1/2 teaspoon ground ginger
1/2 teaspoon ground mace
1 teaspoon cinnamon
1/8 teaspoon ground cloves
1 teaspoon baking soda
1/4 teaspoon baking powder
1/4 teaspoon salt
2 large eggs
1 cup canned pumpkin
1/2 cup (1 stick) butter, melted
1 cup butterscotch chips
1/2 cup chopped pecans, toasted (optional)

In a large bowl, mix flour, sugars, ginger, mace, cinnamon, cloves, baking soda, baking powder and salt. Create a well in the middle of the mixture.

In another bowl, whisk together eggs, pumpkin and butter. Stir in butterscotch chips and pecans and pour into the well of dry ingredients. Fold together just until dry ingredients are moistened. Do not overmix.

Preheat oven to 350 degrees. Spoon batter evenly into greased muffin tins. Bake for 20 to 25 minutes or until a toothpick inserted into the centers comes out clean. Place on a rack to cool.

Makes 18 muffins

A Halloween party natural!

Jeweled Oat Muffins

1 cup old-fashioned oats

1 cup buttermilk

1 large egg, beaten

1/2 cup (1 stick) butter, melted

1 cup flour

1/2 teaspoon cinnamon

1/2 cup firmly packed brown sugar

2 teaspoons baking powder

1 teaspoon baking soda

1/2 teaspoon salt

6 teaspoons plum jam

6 teaspoons apricot jam

In a medium bowl, combine oats and buttermilk and let stand for 2 minutes. Stir in egg and melted butter. In a small bowl, combine flour, cinnamon, brown sugar, baking powder, baking soda and salt. Add to oat mixture and stir until just combined.

Preheat oven to 350 degrees. Pour batter into greased muffin tins and top each with 1 teaspoon jam (alternate between plum and apricot). Bake until a toothpick inserted into the centers comes out clean, about 18 minutes. Cool slightly and serve.

Makes 12 muffins

Any fruit jam works well on top of these muffins. Children especially love them baked as mini muffins, served with cold milk or hot cocoa.

Macadamia Nut Coffee Cake

1/2 cup (1 stick) unsalted butter, softened

1 cup firmly packed dark brown sugar

1 egg

2-1/4 cups sifted flour

2 teaspoons baking powder

1/2 teaspoon baking soda

1/2 teaspoon salt

1 cup buttermilk

1 tablespoon Grand Marnier (optional)

1-1/2 cups coarsely chopped macadamia nuts

1/4 cup heavy cream

1 egg yolk

2 tablespoons sugar

2 tablespoons grated orange zest

With an electric mixer, beat butter until fluffy, about 3 minutes. Add brown sugar and mix to incorporate. Add whole egg and continue beating, scraping down sides of the bowl, for about 5 minutes.

In a separate bowl, sift together flour, baking powder, baking soda and salt. With mixer at low speed, add 1/4 of flour mixture to butter and sugar mixture. Add 1/4 cup buttermilk. Continue alternating between flour and buttermilk additions, beating well after each. Mix in liqueur and then add 1/2 cup macadamia nuts. Pour into a greased and floured 9-inch baking pan.

In a small mixing bowl, beat cream and egg yolk together. Pour over batter. Combine remaining macadamia nuts, sugar and orange zest. Sprinkle over batter.

Preheat oven to 350 degrees. Bake for 40 to 50 minutes, until center springs back when touched lightly. Let cool for 20 to 30 minutes before cutting.

Makes 1 coffeecake

A little bit of island fantasy in a luscious coffee cake. Its buttery, nutty aroma will fill your breakfast room.

Honey-Almond Coffee Cake

1/2 cup ricotta cheese

4 tablespoons milk

4 tablespoons vegetable oil

1/4 cup sugar

Dash of salt

2 teaspoons baking powder

1-1/2 cups flour

Topping:

5 tablespoons butter

1/4 cup sugar

1/3 cup honey

1 cup sliced almonds

1 teaspoon vanilla

In a large bowl, combine cheese, milk, oil, sugar and salt. Sift baking powder with flour and add to cheese mixture. Stir well and then knead lightly for about 5 minutes to form a smooth ball. Set aside for 10 minutes.

For topping: Melt butter in a heavy saucepan. Add sugar and honey and stir constantly over medium heat until mixture is thick and coats a wooden spoon. Add almonds. Remove from heat and add vanilla.

Preheat oven to 350 degrees. Grease the bottom and sides of a 9-inch springform pan. Place dough in pan and spread topping evenly over all. Bake for 25 to 30 minutes, making sure topping does not get too brown. Cool for 5 minutes, then remove sides of pan. Serve warm.

Makes 1 coffee cake

Set a sweet agenda by taking this to a morning meeting.

Substitute quick-rising yeast to cut rising times in half.

Rolls and breads brushed with olive oil before baking will have tender crusts. Those brushed with milk or a combination of 1 beaten egg and 1 tablespoon milk produce crisp crusts.

A loaf of frozen bread should be taken out of plastic wrap before thawing so that it does not become soggy. Thaw for about 1 hour.

For a nutty taste and a little extra crunch, oats may be browned before using in baked goods. In a 325-degree oven with rack in the center position, spread old-fashioned oats on a baking sheet and toast for 15 minutes. Stir frequently until they turn pale gold and smell nutty. Let cool. Great for breads and cookies.

Put a whole sprig of rosemary in the oven to flavor baking bread.

Harvest Brunch Cake

2 apples, 2 pears or 2–3 cups fresh fruit

1 cup (2 sticks) butter, plus additional for sautéing

Juice of 1 lemon

3 cups flour

2 cups sugar

2 teaspoon baking powder

1 egg

1 cup plus 1 tablespoon milk

1 teaspoon grated lemon zest

1 cup apricot preserves

2 teaspoons cinnamon

1 teaspoon nutmeg

1 cup powdered sugar, sifted

Peel, core and slice apples and pears. Sauté in butter for about 2 minutes per side, allowing 1 tablespoon butter per piece of fruit. Squeeze lemon juice evenly over sautéed slices, transfer to container and hold. Continue process until all fruit is sautéed and sprinkled with lemon juice.

In a large bowl, sift 2 cups flour, 1 cup sugar and baking powder. With a pastry blender, blend in 1/2 cup butter to form a consistent mixture. Add egg and 1 cup milk. Blend to incorporate. Pour into a greased 9- by 13-inch baking dish. Layer fruit slices on top of batter.

Heat lemon zest and apricot preserves in saucepan over moderate heat; whisk until melted. Drizzle over fruit. Mix 1 cup flour, 1 cup sugar, cinnamon, nutmeg and 1/2 cup butter until crumbly. Sprinkle evenly on top of fruit and preserves.

Preheat oven to 400 degrees. Bake for 30 to 35 minutes. Cool slightly. Add powdered sugar to 1 tablespoon milk to make a glaze. Spread over warm coffee cake. Cut into squares and serve warm or cooled.

Serves 12

A luscious, fruit-filled breakfast.

Rum Raisin French Toast

3/4 cup rum raisin ice cream, melted

3 eggs, beaten

1/3 cup ground walnuts

1 tablespoon amber rum

1/4 teaspoon grated orange zest

1/4 teaspoon cinnamon

8 slices raisin bread

4 tablespoons butter

Maple syrup

Additional rum raisin ice cream (optional)

In a large shallow pan, combine melted ice cream with eggs, walnuts, rum, orange zest and cinnamon. Dip bread slices into ice cream mixture, letting bread soak for about 1 minute per side.

In a large, heavy skillet, melt 2 tablespoons butter over medium heat. Place 4 bread slices in skillet and cook until browned (approximately 2 minutes per side). Repeat with remaining bread and butter. Serve immediately with maple syrup and additional ice cream.

Serves 4–8

Start the day with this fragrant French toast or offer it as dessert after Sunday night supper.

Stuffed French Toast with Orange Sauce

1 (1-pound) rectangular loaf challah or egg bread, unsliced

8 tablespoons butter

3 large eggs

1/2 cup milk

2 tablespoons Grand Marnier

Powdered sugar, to garnish

Sauce:

1/2 cup (1 stick) butter

1/3 cup sugar

2 oranges, thinly sliced, peeled and pith removed

1/4 cup fresh orange juice

1/4 teaspoon cornstarch

Filling:

1 (3-ounce) package cream cheese, softened to room temperature

3 tablespoons toasted, chopped pecans

2 tablespoons apricot preserves

For sauce: In a large skillet, melt butter and then add sugar. Cook until mixture is bubbly. Add orange slices and cook, stirring occasionaly for 5 minutes. In a small bowl, combine orange juice and cornstarch. Add orange juice mixture to butter mixture. Cook, stirring constantly until sauce thickens slightly, about 4 minutes. Remove sauce from heat and pour into a serving bowl. Keep warm.

For filling: Combine cream cheese, pecans and apricot preserves. Set aside.

With a bread knife, trim short ends from loaf. Cut bread into four 1-1/2-inch thick slices. With a sharp knife, on 1 edge of each slice, make a horizontal cut to center of bread to create a pocket. Stuff each pocket with cream cheese filling, taking care not to poke a hole through top or bottom of slice.

In a large skillet, melt butter over medium heat. In a pie plate or wide shallow bowl, combine eggs, milk and Grand Marnier. Dip each side of stuffed bread slices into egg mixture for several minutes until bread is saturated. Reduce heat and fry bread slices, turning once to brown both sides, about 7 minutes per side.

Spoon sauce onto plates. Cut slices in half diagonally, top with powdered sugar and place on plates.

Serves 4

A wonderful contrast of textures— crispy outside, creamy inside.

🍂 *Try baking eggs in hollowed-out baked potatoes, then top with freshly snipped chives, basil, chervil or dill.*

🍂 *The fresher and colder the eggs, the better they hold their shape while poaching.*

🍂 *Flavored honeys provide an appealing accompaniment at the breakfast table. To make, heat honey until lukewarm, then add herb sprigs such as mint or thyme. Use on breads or muffins (mint honey is especially good on broiled grapefruit).*

Hyde Park Waffles

1 egg

1/4–1/2 cup vegetable oil

1-1/3 cups club soda or citrus-flavored sparkling water

2 cups prepared biscuit mix

1 (6-ounce) can frozen orange juice concentrate, undiluted

_____

Syrup:

1/2 cup (1 stick) butter

3/4 cup sugar

Remainder of orange juice concentrate

1 tablespoon Grand Marnier (optional)

For waffles: Heat a well-greased waffle iron. Combine egg, oil, club soda, biscuit mix and 1/4 of the orange juice concentrate. Beat mixture until smooth. Pour approximately 1/4 of the batter (about 1/2 cup) into the waffle iron. Bake until golden and crisp. Repeat until batter is used. Serve with heated orange syrup.

For syrup: Heat all ingredients except Grand Marnier to boiling, stirring occasionally. Heat until sugar is dissolved and mixture thickens. Remove from heat, add Grand Marnier and serve.

Serves 4

For a special garnish, serve waffles and syrup with a few slices of orange and a flaming sugar cube. (Soak sugar cube in lemon or orange extract and light).

Creamy Ham Brioches

6 tablespoons butter or margarine

1/2 pound mushrooms, sliced

1/4 teaspoon dry mustard

1/4 teaspoon thyme leaves

3 teaspoons flour

1-1/2 cups milk

2-1/2 cups shredded cheddar cheese

1/2 teaspoon freshly ground pepper

1 tablespoon dry sherry

1 (8-1/2-ounce) can artichoke hearts, drained and quartered

2-1/2 cups cubed, cooked ham

Salt and freshly ground pepper, to taste

8 brioches or popovers

In a large skillet, melt 2 tablespoons butter over medium heat. Add mushrooms and cook until liquid evaporates. Add remaining butter, mustard and thyme. When butter melts, stir in flour and cook until bubbly. Gradually stir in milk. Cook, stirring constantly, until sauce thickens. Add cheese, pepper and sherry. Stir until cheese melts, then remove from heat. Stir in artichokes and ham and season with salt and (additional) pepper to taste. (At this point, mixture may be cooled, covered, and refrigerated overnight.)

To serve, reheat mixture, stirring gently, over medium-low heat.

Gently hollow out each brioche with a spoon, leaving a 1/4-inch thick shell. Spoon filling into each and serve immediately.

Serves 8

For a shower or special birthday luncheon, pastry shells can stand in as a "dressier" alternative to brioches or popovers.

5 cups cubed French bread

3 tablespoons melted butter

2 cups grated Swiss cheese

1/2 cup freshly grated Parmesan cheese

8 eggs

Sauce:

1 clove garlic, minced

1/4 cup chopped onion

3 tablespoons butter

3 tablespoons flour

1-1/2 cups chicken broth

3/4 cup dry white wine

Pinch of nutmeg

Pinch of dry mustard

Salt and freshly ground pepper, to taste

1/2 cup sour cream

For sauce: In a medium pan, sauté garlic and onions in butter. Add flour and mix well. Cook briefly, then pour in broth and wine. Add nutmeg, dry mustard, salt and pepper. Bring to a boil, reduce heat and simmer for 15 minutes. Remove from heat and stir in sour cream. Taste and adjust seasonings as needed. Set aside.

Grease a 9- by 13-inch baking dish. Place bread cubes in dish and pour melted butter over bread. Sprinkle grated cheeses over all.

Place eggs and sauce in a food processor and mix well. Pour over bread and cheese. Cover with plastic wrap and refrigerate for 24 hours.

Remove from refrigerator 1 hour before baking. Preheat oven to 350 degrees. Bake for about 30 minutes, until set.

Serves 8–12

Must be made 24 hours in advance.

Experiment with alternatives to the Swiss cheese, such as Gruyère, Jarlsberg and Emmenthaler.

---

3 eggs

1-1/2 cups half-and-half

1/2 cup dry white wine

1/4 teaspoon salt

1/2 teaspoon dry mustard

4 slices thin white bread, buttered and crusts removed

2 cups shredded Swiss cheese or 1 cup Swiss and 1 cup cheddar

Chopped scallions (optional)

Diced ham (optional)

1/2 cup sautéed mushrooms (optional)

In a medium bowl, mix together eggs, half-and-half, wine, salt and mustard. Set aside.

Place slices of buttered bread in the bottom of a baking dish (use more than 1 if necessary), making sure bottom is completely covered. Spread shredded cheese over bread only. Pour egg mixture over bread and cheese. Cover and chill overnight.

Preheat oven to 350 degrees. Before baking, top with chopped scallions, diced ham, sautéed mushrooms or any combination. Bake for 45 minutes and serve.

Serves 6–8

Must be started 24 hours in advance.

Perfect for after-the-theatre suppers or casual brunches.

Crab and Cheese Tarts

2 uncooked pie crusts

1-1/2 cups coarsely chopped fresh crabmeat

1/2 cup shredded Parmesan cheese

1/2 cup shredded Jarlsberg or Swiss cheese

2 tablespoons butter or margarine

3 tablespoons chopped fresh chives

4 large eggs

2 cups half-and-half

1/2 teaspoon salt

1/8 teaspoon freshly ground pepper

Dash of cayenne pepper

Spray six 10-ounce custard cups with nonstick cooking spray. Place cups in a jelly roll pan for easier handling.

Roll dough of 1 pie crust to 1/8-inch thickness. As a guide, use a 7-inch plate to cut 3 circles of dough. Place a circle of dough in each of 3 custard cups, gently fluting top edges of dough (about 4 to 6 flutes). Repeat using second pie crust and remaining custard cups. Evenly distribute crabmeat and cheeses into pastry-lined cups.

In a 2-quart saucepan, melt butter over medium heat. Add chives and cook for 2 minutes. Set aside.

In a medium bowl, mix eggs, half-and-half, salt and pepper with a wire whisk until well blended. Stir in butter and chive mixture. Add cayenne pepper. Pour over crabmeat and cheeses in pastry-lined cups.

Preheat oven to 425 degrees. Bake for 25 minutes. Reduce heat to 325 degrees and bake for 15 minutes or until a knife inserted in the center comes out clean. Cool for about 5 to 8 minutes, then remove from cups and serve.

Serves 6

Simple, yet sophisticated. These larger sized custard cups make main-dish servings. Garnish with a sprig of herbs, pimientos or red bell pepper and serve with a light salad. Baked in muffin tins, these also make appealing appetizers.

Apple Jack Compote

1-1/2 pounds mixed dried fruit (apricots, apples, pears, raisins, dates, currants, etc.)

1 tablespoon cinnamon

1 teaspoon nutmeg

1 teaspoon ginger

4 tablespoons apple brandy

1 cup shredded coconut

Whipped cream, to garnish

In a heavy saucepan, cover dried fruit with water and simmer until fruit is plump. Stir in cinnamon, nutmeg, ginger, brandy and coconut. Serve warm with whipped cream.

Serves 6–8

Any leftovers make a great filling for sweet bread or coffee cake. May be refrigerated for 3 to 4 weeks.

Cheese Soufflé Roll

7 eggs

1/3 cup butter

6 tablespoons unsifted flour

Dash of cayenne pepper

3/4 teaspoon salt

1-1/4 cups milk

1/2 cup freshly grated Parmesan cheese

1/2 cup coarsely grated sharp cheddar cheese

1/4 teaspoon cream of tartar

Filling:

2 (10-ounce) packages frozen, chopped spinach

2 tablespoons butter

1/4 cup finely chopped onion

1/4 teaspoon salt

1/4 cup grated sharp cheddar cheese

1/2 cup sour cream

Freshly grated Parmesan cheese

1/4 pound cheddar cheese, sliced

Separate egg whites and yolks into separate bowls. Let egg whites warm to room temperature (approximately 1 hour).

Grease the bottom of a 10-1/2- by 15-inch jelly roll pan. Line the bottom with waxed paper, then grease with butter. Preheat oven to 350 degrees.

In a saucepan, melt butter. Remove from heat. With a wire whisk, stir in flour, cayenne pepper and 1/2 teaspoon salt until smooth. Gradually stir in milk. Bring to a boil, stirring constantly. Reduce heat and simmer, stirring until thick and mixture leaves bottom of pan. Beat in Parmesan and cheddar cheeses.

With a wire whisk, beat yolks and blend into cheese mixture. With mixer on high speed, beat whites with 1/4 teaspoon salt and cream of tartar until stiff peaks form. With an under-and-over motion, fold 1/3 of egg whites into cheese mixture. Carefully fold in remaining whites. Turn mixture into prepared pan. Bake for 15 minutes or until surface is puffed and firm when pressed with fingertip.

For filling: Cook spinach as package directs. Turn into a sieve and press to remove all water. In a medium skillet, melt butter and sauté onions until golden. Add spinach, salt, sharp cheddar cheese and sour cream. Mix well.

With a metal spatula, loosen edges of souffle. Invert onto waxed paper sprinkled lightly with Parmesan cheese. Peel off waxed paper and spread surface evenly with spinach filling. From the long side, roll souffle up jelly-roll style. Place on a greased baking sheet, seam-side down. Arrange cheese slices over top of roll. Broil, about 4 inches from heat, just until cheese melts. Using a large spatula, remove to serving dish or board, slice and serve.

Serves 8–10

Serve these sunny yellow pin-wheels with **Apple Jack Compote** during the winter months or with garden fresh tomatoes in the summer.

Puerto Vallarta Crêpes

1 (15-ounce) can tomato sauce

1 clove garlic, minced

1/4 teaspoon crushed oregano leaves

2 tablespoons chopped green chilies

1/3 cup sour cream

1-1/2 cups grated Monterey Jack cheese

8 thin slices ham

Crêpes:

1 cup cold water

1 cup cold milk

4 eggs

1/2 teaspoon salt

2 cups flour

4 tablespoons butter, melted

For crêpes: In a blender or food processor, combine water, milk, eggs and salt. Add flour and blend again. Add butter and blend for 1 minute or until lumps disappear. Scrape down sides, cover and refrigerate at least 2 hours. (Batter should be consistency of light cream.) Cook in a lightly oiled crêpe pan, using 1/4 cup batter at a time. Set aside.

In a blender or food processor, combine tomato sauce, garlic, oregano, green chilies and sour cream until smooth. Place grated cheese and 2 slices of ham on each crêpe, reserving some cheese to sprinkle on top. Roll and place filled crêpes, seam-side down, in a greased baking dish or on a baking sheet. Pour tomato sauce over crêpes and top with more cheese.

Preheat oven to 350 degrees. Bake uncovered for 10 to 15 minutes, until bubbly.

Serves 4

To shorten preparation time, use prepared crêpes. This recipe makes more crêpes than you'll need to serve 4 guests; additionals freeze well with waxed paper separating them.

Poached Eggs in Avocado

2 avocados, peeled, halved and pitted

4 poached eggs

1 tablespoon grated orange zest, to garnish

Hollandaise:

1-1/2 cups fresh orange juice

4 egg yolks

6 tablespoons unsalted butter

1 teaspoon grated orange zest

Cook avocado halves in simmering water until heated through. Remove from water and pat dry. Set aside.

For hollandaise: In a heavy saucepan, boil orange juice until reduced to 1 to 2 tablespoons. Let cool slightly. Place egg yolks in top of a double boiler. Pour in reduced orange juice and whisk until thickened slightly. Whisk in butter, 1 tablespoon at a time, then whisk in orange zest. Set aside.

Place an avocado half on each of 4 plates and top with a poached egg and orange hollandaise sauce. Garnish with orange zest and serve.

Serves 4

When entertaining, the eggs may be poached a day ahead and stored in a dish of cold water in the refrigerator. (Trim ragged edges if desired.) Just before serving, carefully transfer to a pan of hot water until heated through. Drain on paper towels and serve.

Wild Mushroom Quiches in Acorn Squash

4 small acorn squash

1/2 cup chopped wild mushrooms

5 eggs

1-3/4 cups heavy cream

1 teaspoon salt

1-1/2 teaspoons savory

1/4 cup grated Gruyère cheese

Slice tops off squash and hollow out seeds and half of flesh. Trim bottoms so that squash sit upright. Spray a baking dish with nonstick cooking spray and place squash in the dish. Bake in a 350-degree oven for 30 minutes or microwave until cooked through. Remove and leave oven on.

Whisk together chopped mushrooms, eggs, cream, salt and savory. Divide Gruyère between squash halves, followed by mushroom mixture. Return to oven and bake for 1 hour until set and slightly puffed in the squash.

Serves 4

Wild mushrooms lend an earthy taste to this unusual quiche.

Italian Strata

1-1/2 pounds mild Italian sausage

1 pound zucchini, sliced

1/2 pound fresh spinach, torn into bite-sized pieces

1 onion, thinly sliced

1 teaspoon dry mustard

1 teaspoon salt

1/2 teaspoon freshly ground pepper

2 cups grated cheddar cheese

2 cups grated Swiss cheese

1-1/2 cups milk

7 eggs

10 slices white bread, torn

Cook sausage and drain. Sauté zucchini, spinach and onion in sausage drippings. In a large bowl, combine sausage, zucchini mixture, mustard, salt, pepper, cheeses, milk, eggs and torn bread slices. Mix well. Cover and refrigerate overnight.

Preheat oven to 325 degrees. Mix ingredients again and place in a greased 9- by 13-inch baking dish. Bake for 1-1/2 hours. (Watch closely during the last 30 minutes; strata tends to brown quickly.) Full baking time may not be necessary—just make sure mixture is set before removing from oven.

Serves 8–12

Must be prepared ahead.

Many markets now sell Italian sausage made with turkey. Cooks substituting this lower fat alternative may need to add a bit of margarine to the drippings in order to sauté the zucchini, spinach and onion.

1 cup finely ground almonds

3-1/2 cups unsifted flour

Pinch of salt

1/2 cup powdered sugar

3/4 cup (1-1/2 sticks) butter, softened

1 large egg

1 egg yolk

Filling:

1/2 cup chopped onion

1 tablespoon butter

1/3 cup smoked ham, finely diced

6–8 slices cooked bacon, finely crumbled

3 cups cream

8 eggs, beaten

1/4 teaspoon salt

1/2 teaspoon freshly ground pepper

1/4 teaspoon nutmeg

3 tablespoons finely chopped fresh basil

1 tablespoon finely chopped fresh thyme

1 (3-ounce) package cream cheese, cubed

1/2 cup grated cheddar cheese

1/2 cup grated Monterey Jack cheese

1 bunch scallions, chopped

1/3 cup sliced almonds

In a mixing bowl, combine almonds, flour, salt and sugar. Cut butter into cubes. Sprinkle over surface of dried ingredients. Using a fork or pastry cutter, cut butter into dried ingredients until mixture resembles coarse cornmeal.

Beat egg and yolk together and stir into flour mixture. Shape into 2 round disks and refrigerate for 30 minutes. Crumble dough over the bottom of two 9-inch tart pans or one 9- by 13-inch baking dish. Using fingers and hands, press dough over the bottoms and sides of each pan to shape shells. Bake in a 350-degree oven until barely brown.

For filling: Sauté onion in butter until translucent. Divide ham, bacon and onion into 2 equal portions and sprinkle over the bottom of each tart shell. Whisk together cream and beaten eggs. Add salt, pepper, nutmeg, basil and thyme and stir well. Pour egg mixture over bacon mixture. Sprinkle cream cheese cubes and grated cheeses over the top of each filled tart. Sprinkle scallions over cheese, followed by sliced almonds.

Preheat oven to 350 degrees. Bake for 30 to 40 minutes. Let cool slightly, then cut and serve.

Serves 16

A rich, enticing tart for "special morning" occasions. If you wish to freeze, cool thoroughly and wrap well.

MEAT & POULTRY

Autumn River Salad, 97
Berried Pork Salad, 95
Brookside Salad, 96
Flint Hills Beef Salad, 94
Mediterranean Chicken Salad, 95
Southwest Turkey Salad, 98
Won Ton Chicken Salad, 96

SEAFOOD

Dilled Prawns and Melon, 99
Madagascar Crab Salad, 99
Salmon and Apple Salad, 101
Shrimp Salad with Apricot Mayonnaise, 102
Shrimp Salad Laced with Limes, 100
Sole Primavera Salad, 101

FRUITS & VEGETABLES

Blue Cheese Potato Salad, 107
Bruschetta Salad, 104
Carrot and Apple Salad, 111
Cold Roasted Peppers with Mustard Dressing, 104
Fruited Snow Pea Toss with Poppy Seed Dressing, 106
Goat Cheese Salad with Nectarines and Walnuts, 112
Indian Maize Salad, 105
Minted Spinach and Apple Medley, 112
South of the Border Potato Salad, 107
Tomato Avocado Mold with
Creamy Horseradish Dressing, 105

PASTA, GRAIN & LEGUMES

Black Bean Salad, 111
Cobb Pasta Salad, 109
Cold Herbed Garbanzo Beans, 109
Minted Barley Salad, 110
Sesame Pasta Salad, 110
Szechuan Noodle Salad, 108

GREENS & SLAWS

"Bleuberry" Spinach Salad, 115
Marinated Mushrooms and Romaine Salad, 115
Queen of Hearts Salad, 116
Ruby Cole Slaw, 118
Seville Salad, 113
Southern Belle Salad, 113
Summer Palette Salad, 116
Technicolor Toss, 117
Thai Cabbage Salad, 117

DRESSINGS

Garden Creamy Basil Dressing, 119
Hazelnut Cognac Dressing, 119
Sour Cream Sherry Dressing, 118

MINI RECIPES

Curled Melba Toast, 94

Salads

Pictured finishing touch:

CUTTING

BELL PEPPERS

WITH CANAPÉ CUTTERS, 98

SPECIAL TOPIC BOXES

FRESH FROM THE GARDEN, 103

GREAT GREENS, 114

GARNISHES, 106

Flint Hills Beef Salad

2 pounds boneless sirloin, cooked to medium-rare and cubed

1 head cauliflower, separated into small florets

1 head broccoli, separated into small florets

1/4 cup milk

1 red bell pepper, chopped

1 yellow bell pepper, chopped

1 medium red onion, sliced thin

1/2 cup crumbled bacon, cooked and drained

1 cup freshly grated Parmesan cheese

1 head lettuce, torn into bite-sized pieces

Dressing:

1/2 cup olive oil

3 tablespoons tarragon vinegar

1 tablespoon Dijon mustard

1 teaspoon tarragon

1 teaspoon salt

For dressing: In a sealable container, blend olive oil, vinegar, mustard, tarragon and salt and refrigerate, covered, for several hours. Shake again before tossing with salad.

In a large bowl, combine sirloin, cauliflower, broccoli, milk, red pepper, yellow pepper, onion and bacon. Chill for 1 to 2 hours.

To serve, toss meat and vegetables with dressing. Toss in Parmesan cheese just before serving. Line plates with a bed of lettuce and mound salad into the center of each.

Serves 6–8

This main-dish salad offers a fresh solution to planning a meat-and-vegetable dinner. Cut ingredients in half for a smaller crowd.

Curled Melba Toast

1 loaf day-old, unsliced white bread

Freeze bread for 2 hours, or until firm but not frozen. With a sharp knife, cut into paper-thin slices.

Preheat oven to 250 degrees. Arrange slices on baking sheets, making sure they do not touch.

Bake, turning occasionally, for 1-1/2 hours, or until toasts curl and are golden brown. Store in an airtight container.

Berried Pork Salad

1 to 1-1/2 pounds boneless pork tenderloin, sliced thinly into bite-sized pieces

Red leaf lettuce

1 cup chopped green cabbage

1-1/2 cups raspberries

1-1/2 cups blueberries

1 cup strawberries

Toasted almonds or macadamia nuts, to garnish

_____

Dressing:

1/3 cup orange juice

2 tablespoons red wine or raspberry vinegar

1 tablespoon berry-flavored jam

1/2 teaspoon Dijon mustard

1 tablespoon canola or safflower oil

1 teaspoon poppy seeds

1 teaspoon finely chopped onion

For dressing: Combine all ingredients in a jar or container with a lid and set aside.

Clean and prepare all fruit. Halve strawberries.

Cook pork slices in a pan coated with nonstick cooking spray. Stir-fry until slightly pink, approximately 3 minutes. (Pork may be served barely warm or refrigerated.)

To serve, arrange lettuce, fruit and pork on each plate and pass dressing. Top with toasted almonds or macadamia nuts.

Serves 4 as a main dish
6–8 as a side dish

Absolutely beautiful. All items should be prepared ahead and kept separately until pork is cooked. Dressing may be prepared the day before and refrigerated, but brought to room temperature before serving

For more information on flavored vinegars, see "Cooking with Herbs" in Fish & Seafood.

Mediterranean Chicken Salad

1 large cucumber

4 cups cubed poached chicken

1-1/4 cups feta cheese

2/3 cup sliced Greek or black olives

1/4 cup chopped parsley

1/2 cup mayonnaise

3 garlic cloves, minced

1/2 cup plain yogurt

1 tablespoon fresh oregano

Salt and freshly ground pepper, to taste

Peel, seed and chop cucumber. Combine all ingredients by tossing lightly with a fork. (Better if made the day ahead.) Serve chilled or at room temperature.

Serves 4–6

Served on a bed of sliced tomatoes with **Toasted Pita Triangles** or in a pita pocket with chopped tomatoes and alfalfa sprouts.

Won Ton Chicken Salad

8 boneless, skinless chicken breast halves, cooked and cubed

1 small package won ton skins, fried, drained and crumbled

4 scallions, chopped

2 tablespoons sesame seeds

2 tablespoons chopped almonds

1 head romaine lettuce, torn

Dressing:

1/2 cup sugar

1 tablespoon salt

3/4 teaspoon freshly ground pepper

3/4 cup vinegar

1/4 cup sesame or vegetable oil

Toss chicken, won ton skins, scallions, sesame seeds, almonds and greens together in a large bowl.

For dressing: Mix salad dressing ingredients together in a glass container and shake well. Pour onto salad and toss.

Serves 6

A wonderful mix of flavor and texture. Try toasting the sesame seeds for a richer taste. For a festive presentation, place egg roll skins over 10-ounce inverted custard cups and bake at 350 degrees for 10 to 12 minutes. Spoon salad into these baked "bowls" and serve.

Brookside Salad

8–10 ounces smoked duck or chicken breasts, thinly sliced

1 red bell pepper, julienned

1 yellow bell pepper, julienned

1 carrot, julienned

1/2 jícama, julienned

2 tablespoons pine nuts, toasted

1 tablespoon chopped fresh basil

1 tablespoon chopped scallions

3 egg yolks, beaten

2 tablespoons balsamic vinegar

Salt and freshly ground pepper, to taste

1/2 cup buttermilk

1/4 pound bacon, cooked, drained and crumbled

3 ounces herb pasta, or other pasta

Vegetable oil, as needed

Combine chicken, red and yellow peppers, carrot and jícama and arrange on a salad platter. Sprinkle pine nuts, basil and scallions over chicken and vegetables.

Combine egg yolks, balsamic vinegar, salt and pepper in the top of a double boiler and cook, whisking constantly, until thickened. Remove from heat and let cool to room temperature. Add buttermilk and bacon to mixture. Pour over salad and refrigerate until chilled.

Cook pasta according to package directions and drain. Deep fry in oil until crisp. Let cool, then crumble and sprinkle over salad.

Serves 6

A truly colorful salad. Fried pasta is also great sprinkled with salt and served as a snack.

3 large Red Delicious apples,
thinly sliced

1/3 cup crumbled blue cheese

4 tablespoons chopped walnuts

1 head romaine lettuce, trimmed and
cut lengthwise into thirds

1 bunch watercress, trimmed

2 cups thinly sliced smoked duck

Salt and freshly
ground pepper, to taste

Nutmeg, to taste

Vinaigrette:

1 tablespoon Dijon mustard

1/4 cup white wine vinegar

1/2 teaspoon dill

1/2 teaspoon freshly ground nutmeg

1 teaspoon sugar

1/8 teaspoon salt

1/8 teaspoon freshly ground pepper

1/2 cup extra-virgin olive oil

In a bowl, combine apple slices, blue cheese, walnuts and 3 tablespoons vinaigrette. Cover and refrigerate for up to 4 hours.

For vinaigrette: Combine mustard, vinegar, dill, nutmeg, sugar, salt and pepper. Add oil very slowly, whisking constantly. Stir vigorously before using. (Vinaigrette may be prepared up to 3 days in advance.)

To serve, arrange lettuce, watercress and chilled apple mixture on a platter. Add duck and top with vinaigrette. Season with salt, pepper and nutmeg.

Serves 8

Nutmeg adds a delicately warm, spicy-sweet taste to this beautiful salad. If smoked duck is unavailable, substitute smoked chicken. For a serving variation, substitute red oak leaf lettuce.

To toast sesame seeds, spread on a baking sheet and put in the oven until brown, or toast on top of the stove in a dry skillet, stirring often.

The most widely available walnut is the English walnut, which comes in many varieties and is found year-round. Shelled nutmeats should be refrigerated, tightly covered, for up to 6 months and can be frozen up to a year.

1 (16-ounce) package frozen corn

3 cups cubed smoked turkey

2 celery stalks, chopped

2/3 cup julienned red bell pepper,

2 avocados, sliced and drizzled
with lemon juice, to garnish

2 lemons, sliced in rings, to garnish

4 slices red bell pepper rings, to garnish

Lettuce leaves

Dressing:

1 cup olive oil

1 small clove garlic, crushed

2/3 cup fresh lemon juice

2 teaspoons ground cumin

2 tablespoons honey

3 tablespoons fresh oregano leaves or
1 tablespoon dried

1-1/2 teaspoons salt

1/2 teaspoon white pepper

1/8–1/4 teaspoon cayenne pepper

Prepare corn according to package directions, drain and cool.

For dressing: Combine ingredients in a blender until well mixed and oregano is chopped. Set aside.

Combine turkey, celery, red pepper and corn. Toss with dressing (reserving some) several hours or more before serving. Stir periodically to ensure blended flavor.

To serve, line 4 plates with lettuce. Peel and slice avocados thinly. Alternate slices of avocado and lemon on the edge of the lettuce. Spoon salad next to garnish of avocado and lemon. Drizzle reserved dressing on avocado slices. Top each salad with a red pepper ring.

Serves 4

Try smoking your own turkey rather than roasting. Leftovers transform into a colorful Southwestern salad. Serve with **Stonehenge Bread** for a quick and satisfying meal.

🍃 *When using fresh bell peppers in a salad, use small canapé cutters to cut pieces shaped like stars, hearts, diamonds and so on instead of simply chopping or cutting the peppers into strips.*

🍃 *To keep celery crisp, stand in a pitcher of cold water and refrigerate.*

🍃 *Citrus peels can be grated and then frozen for later use.*

Madagascar Crab Salad

1 head red leaf or Bibb lettuce

4 stalks celery, chopped

4 scallions, chopped

2 pounds king crab legs, cooked, cracked and chunked (reserve 1/4 cup)

Dressing:

3 tablespoons chutney

1 cup mayonnaise

2 tablespoons tarragon vinegar

2 tablespoons vegetable oil

3 teaspoons curry powder, or to taste

3–4 tablespoons half-and-half

Condiments:

Toasted coconut

Toasted slivered almonds

Chopped scallions

Golden raisins mixed with dark raisins

Chutney

Prepare condiments and set aside. (To toast nuts, place on a baking sheet and bake in a 350-degree oven for 5 to 8 minutes, stirring occasionally until lightly browned.)

Tear lettuce into bite-sized pieces and place in a large salad bowl. Add celery and scallions. Stir in crab.

For dressing: Pulse ingredients in a blender or food processor. Taste for seasoning. (Curry flavor should just bite or its flavor will be lost in the salad.) Dressing may be prepared a day ahead.

To serve, toss salad with dressing and garnish with 1/4 cup reserved crab. Serve condiments in separate bowls, either buffet style or passed around the table.

Serves 8

Serve this lovely salad in a large silver bowl or tureen or individually in hollowed-out coconut shells.

Dilled Prawns and Melon

3 cups melon cubes or balls (honeydew, cantaloupe, watermelon or a combination)

1-3/4 pounds cooked prawns, shelled and deveined

1-1/2 tablespoons lemon juice

Dill sprigs, to garnish

Sauce:

1/2 cup ricotta cheese

6–8 tablespoons buttermilk

Salt and freshly ground pepper, to taste

1 teaspoon dill vinegar or lemon juice

2 tablespoons chopped fresh dill

Drain melon and mix with prawns. Sprinkle mixture with lemon juice.

For sauce: In a food processor, puree cheese with 2 tablespoons of buttermilk at a time until mixture reaches consistency of medium-thick cream. (The quantity of buttermilk needed will depend on the consistency of the ricotta.) Add more buttermilk if mixture is too thick. Add salt and pepper, dill vinegar and chopped dill.

Mix dill sauce with prawns and melon and chill for 1 hour. Toss before serving and garnish with sprigs of dill.

Serves 8

Serve in tall margarita glasses for a brunch or luncheon. For a lighter variation, try plain yogurt in place of ricotta cheese.

Shrimp Salad Laced with Limes

1 cup dry white wine

1 cup clam juice

1/2 lemon, sliced

3 parsley sprigs

3 celery tops

1 large onion, studded with 3 cloves

1 bay leaf

3 pounds uncooked medium shrimp, shells on

1 clove garlic, peeled and flattened

1 large bunch celery

3 heads fresh fennel

4 shallots, finely minced

Juice of 1 lime

1 (15-ounce) can pitted black olives, drained

1/2 cup chopped fresh basil

Salt and fresh cracked pepper, to taste

Lime slices, to garnish

Chopped chives, to garnish

Vinaigrette:

1/3 cup white wine vinegar

1 tablespoon Dijon mustard

2 tablespoons lime juice

1 cup virgin olive oil

In a large saucepan, combine wine, clam juice, lemon, parsley sprigs, celery stalk tops, studded onion and bay leaf and bring to a boil. Place shrimp in the boil and simmer for 2 to 4 minutes, until shrimp turn opaque. Remove shrimp, shell and devein.

For vinaigrette: Combine vinegar, mustard and lime juice in a small bowl. Drizzle oil in slowly, whisking constantly. Set aside.

Rub a large bowl with garlic and discard. Mince celery and fennel together and add to bowl. Add shallot and lime juice. Toss well. Add shrimp, black olives and basil. Refrigerate in vinaigrette for 1 hour.

Season to taste with salt and cracked pepper. Toss and serve garnished with lime slices and chives.

Serves 8

A delightful mingling of fresh flavors. To shorten preparation time, use packaged frozen medium shrimp, precooked, shelled and deveined. Drop shrimp into clam juice boil until shrimp thaws, then continue with preparation as above.

Pull out all the stops for an alfresco "seaside" meal. Cover the table with a gauzy fabric to catch the breeze, sprinkle the tabletop with seashells and nestle candles in painted pails of white sand. Encircle the area with citronella torches and complete the ambience with a tape of ocean sounds.

Salmon and Apple Salad

1 pound salmon fillets

1 tablespoon lemon juice

1 cup cubed, tart apples (such as Granny Smith)

1/4 cup thinly sliced celery

1/4 cup chopped fresh parsley

2 scallions, thinly sliced

1/4 cup mayonnaise

1/4 cup plain yogurt

1 tablespoon balsamic vinegar

4 cups mixed salad greens

Lemon or apple slices, to garnish

Place salmon fillets in a 9-inch pie pan, with the thicker sections toward the outside, and sprinkle with lemon juice. Cover tightly with plastic wrap, turned back slightly to vent steam, and microwave on medium for 9 to 11 minutes, turning over once. Chill in refrigerator.

Remove skin from cooled salmon and drain. Place fish in a medium mixing bowl and flake with a fork. Mix in apples, celery, parsley and scallions.

In a small bowl, combine mayonnaise, yogurt, and vinegar. Toss with salmon mixture to moisten.

Serve on a bed of mixed greens, garnished with lemon or apple slices.

Serves 4–6

A crisp, intriguing salad, perfect for an outdoor luncheon. For a taste variation, use grilled salmon fillets.

Sole Primavera Salad

1 cup chopped broccoli florets

1 cup chopped peeled carrots

2 cups snow pea pods

1 cup chopped cauliflower florets

1 cup uncooked shell pasta

1 cup sliced celery

1/4–1/2 cup scallions

1-1/2 pounds sole fillet

1-1/2 cups water

2 lemon slices

2 peppercorns

Dressing:

2 tablespoons lemon juice

1/8 teaspoon pepper

1/4–1/2 cup mayonnaise

1/2 cup Italian dressing

Steam or blanch broccoli, carrots, snow peas and cauliflower for 1-1/2 minutes. Cook pasta to package directions.

In a large saucepan or fish poacher, bring 1-1/2 cups water, lemon slices and peppercorns to a boil. Poach sole for 5 to 7 minutes or until flaky. Remove from pan. Flake sole into large chunks with a fork.

Mix broccoli, carrots, snow peas, cauliflower, pasta, celery, scallions, and sole together in a large bowl.

For dressing: Combine all ingredients and blend well. Mix with sole and vegetable salad and serve.

Serves 8–10 as a first course
4–6 as an entree

A taste of the sea mingled with fresh garden flavors. Substitute scallops or other white fish for the sole, if desired.

Shrimp Salad with Apricot Mayonnaise

6 cups water

1 small onion, sliced

1 bay leaf

3 cloves

1 cup dry white wine

1 teaspoon salt

1-1/2 pounds medium to large shrimp, shelled and deveined

16 snow pea pods

16 large mushrooms, thinly sliced

3 tablespoons finely minced red onion

8 or more lettuce leaves plus additional chopped lettuce

8 fresh or canned apricots, sliced, to garnish

Apricot mayonnaise:

3/4 cup mayonnaise

1/2–1/3 cup apricot preserves

For apricot mayonnaise: Whisk mayonnaise and apricot preserves in a medium bowl to blend well. Cover and refrigerate. (May be prepared 2 to 3 days in advance.)

In a large pot, combine water, onion, bay leaf, cloves, white wine and salt. Bring to a boil. Add shrimp and cook until pink. Remove shrimp and refrigerate.

Blanch snow peas for 2 minutes in boiling, salted water. Drain well and pat dry. Cut each into 3 pieces. Slice shrimp diagonally into small pieces, reserving 8 largest shrimp (or 1 to 2 shrimp per person) for garnish. Combine sliced shrimp with snow peas, mushrooms and onion. Toss with apricot mayonnaise.

To serve, line each plate with a lettuce leaf and top with a small layer of chopped lettuce. Mound salad on top and garnish with whole shrimp and sliced apricots.

Serves 8

The pale pinks and oranges in this salad look beautiful garnished with nasturtiums, variegated sage or mint leaves.

Apricots are highly perishable and seasonal—90% of them are marketed in June and July. When purchasing apricots, look for fruit that's plump and rather firm. They should also be a uniform color, which can range from pale yellow to deep burnt orange. Store in a plastic bag in the refrigerator for 3 to 5 days.

A familiar element used in an unexpected way brings an extra dimension of pleasure to dining. Such is the case with flowers. No longer bound to an arranged centerpiece, edible flowers turn up as colorful garnishes to soups, salads, desserts and more. Beyond the beauty they impart to any meal, some edible flowers also lend a unique flavor to the dishes they accompany. When using flowers with food, remember to identify your choice as edible (some look-alikes may be poisonous) and check to see that they are pesticide-free.

Petal Perfect

🍃 ***Anise hyssop***—Purple and blue flowers are pretty as garnishes and delicious in baking, in sweet-and-sour marinades or in Chinese-style dishes. This is sometimes called the root beer plant. 🍃 ***Apple blossom***—A delicate floral flavoring makes these white and pink petals an excellent garnish. 🍃 ***Borage***—These dainty, vivid blue, star-shaped flowers add a cool cucumber flavor and a pretty highlight of color to any salad or fruit. They're also good frozen in ice cubes for cold drinks. 🍃 ***Calendula***—Yellow, orange or apricot petals add color to eggs and cheese and can be added for a saffron-like nuance in many rice dishes. 🍃 ***Chamomile***—These small, white, daisy-like flowers impart a lovely scent and mild taste. They make a soothing tea and offer an excellent garnish. 🍃 ***Chive blossoms***—An eye-catching garnish, these blossoms are also good in meat broths, salads, eggs, cream cheese or any dish where a mild, subtle-onion flavor is called for. 🍃 ***Dandelion flowers***—Yellow and slightly bitter, dandelions may be used in soups and salads. 🍃 ***Honeysuckle***—These pale yellow blossoms offer a floral-honeyed flavor. Use sparingly on ice cream. 🍃 ***Johnny jump-ups***—Use these small purple or blue flowers with cheese plates or to set off sliced fruit. Beautiful with freshly grilled salmon. 🍃 ***Lavender***—Accent soups and salads with this strongly flavored purple flower. A wonderful garnish, but use it sparingly. 🍃 ***Lemon blossom***—Sprinkle these cream-colored, citrus-flavored petals over salads and soups. 🍃 ***Marigolds***—These blooms produce yellow-orange petals with a mildly peppery taste. Try them in pasta dishes. 🍃 ***Mustard flowers***—The pleasant taste of these yellow or white flowers makes them an excellent addition to soups and salads as well as a wonderful garnish. 🍃 ***Nasturtiums***—Choose these beauties for strong visual appeal (wonderful colors and rounded leaves) and intriguing flavor (a taste of watercress with a hint of honey). Add to salads and cream cheese for a dip, or use as a substitute for capers. 🍃 ***Rose petals***—Choose from a myriad of colors. Rose petals may be used in, as well as on, salads, butters, jellies and vinegars. 🍃 ***Squash blossoms***—Orange and yellow blossoms add a mild zucchini-like flavor to soups and salads. These also can be stuffed, sautéed and fried. 🍃 ***Violets***—These bluish flowers are wonderful crystallized or used plain as a garnish.

Bruschetta Salad

1/2 small baguette

1 large clove garlic, crushed

1/2 cup olive oil plus additional for brushing on bread

6 medium-to-large tomatoes, cut into large chunks

1/2 medium onion, chopped

3 tablespoons coarsely chopped fresh basil

1/4 cup balsamic vinegar

Fresh basil sprigs, to garnish

Preheat oven to 300 degrees. Split baguette in half lengthwise. Rub 1 side with crushed garlic and brush liberally with olive oil. Cut bread in half again lengthwise and then cut into 3/4-inch pieces. Place pieces on a baking sheet, crust-side down. Bake until dark golden brown (approximately 45 to 60 minutes). Set aside.

Place tomatoes in a bowl. Add onion and basil. In a separate bowl, whisk together vinegar and 1/2 cup oil. Pour over salad and toss. Add reserved croutons just before serving. Serve at room temperature or well chilled, garnished with fresh basil sprigs.

Serves 6

Rich ripe tomatoes make this simple salad a sure winner. For a crouton variation, grill the oiled bread before cutting into 3/4-inch pieces instead of baking.

Cold Roasted Peppers with Mustard Dressing

3 green bell peppers

3 red bell peppers

1/3 cup olive oil

3 tablespoons red wine vinegar

Coarse salt, to taste

Freshly ground pepper, to taste

Pinch of dry mustard

1/4 cup finely chopped fresh chives, to garnish

Skewer whole peppers and blacken over a gas or electric burner on top of the stove, turning to char all sides. Place in a brown paper bag, fold closed and let steam for 5 to 10 minutes. Skins should peel easily.

Remove and discard fibrous portions and seeds. Cut peppers into strips and place in a serving dish.

Combine oil, vinegar, salt, pepper, and mustard in bowl and whisk into a sauce. Pour over peppers and refrigerate. Serve well chilled, sprinkled with finely chopped chives.

Serves 8

For a splash of color on a summer buffet, use a combination of red, green, orange, yellow and purple bell peppers. This dish should be prepared several hours in advance to allow time for the flavors to blend.

Tomato Avocado Mold with Creamy Horseradish Dressing

4 envelopes unflavored gelatin

3/4 cup cold water

7 cups tomato juice

3 tablespoons white wine vinegar

3–4 celery leaves

1 bay leaf

1 tablespoon salt

1 tablespoon sugar

3 tablespoons chopped scallions
(white parts only)

1 large avocado

Lemon juice

***

Dressing:

1 cup sour cream

1/4 cup mayonnaise

1/3 cup Dijon mustard

1 tablespoon prepared horseradish

1/2 teaspoon grated lemon zest

1 tablespoon lemon juice

1 clove garlic, pressed

1/2 teaspoon red pepper flakes

2 tablespoons milk

2 tablespoons dry white wine

Sprinkle gelatin over water to soften. Simmer tomato juice in a nonaluminum pan for 10 minutes with vinegar, celery leaves, bay leaf, salt, sugar and scallions. Strain. Add gelatin mixture to hot juice mix. Stir to dissolve. Chill until thick and syrupy.

Peel avocado and cut into thin slices. Sprinkle lemon juice over slices to prevent browning. Arrange slices into a pattern in the bottom of a mold. Top with a little of refrigerated gelatin mixture and chill to set. Pour in remaining gelatin mixture and chill for approximately 3 hours.

For dressing: Combine first 8 ingredients in a small container. Refrigerate for several hours to allow flavors to incorporate. Prior to serving, mix in milk and wine to desired consistency. Serve in dollops over molded salad.

Serves 12–14

A classic first-course starter. For a milder taste, try a clam and tomato juice mixture instead of plain tomato juice. The dressing also makes an excellent dip for crudités.

When preparing a molded salad, rinse the mold with cold water, wipe it dry and then coat it with vegetable oil for easy removal.

Indian Maize Salad

5 ears fresh corn, husked

1 to 1-1/2 cups diced
red and green bell peppers

1 red onion, chopped

2 tablespoons fresh lime juice

2 tablespoons white vinegar

4 tablespoons vegetable oil

Fresh chopped cilantro, to taste

Maple syrup, to taste

Salt, to taste

To roast corn, place clean ears (wrapped in aluminum foil) on a baking sheet in the middle of a 400-degree oven. Bake for 20 minutes, turning several times. Cut kernels off the cob.

Mix corn with red and green peppers, lime juice, vinegar, oil, cilantro, maple syrup and salt. Chill (cilantro flavor gets stronger with time).

Serves 8

Crisp and colorful, this salad is great for outdoor entertaining. Offer servings in small bunches of corn husks tied at the ends.

Fruited Snow Pea Toss with Poppy Seed Dressing

4 cups fresh snow pea pods, blanched

1 cup seedless red grapes

1 cup fresh orange sections
(about 2 oranges)

1 cup fresh grapefruit sections
(about 2 grapefruit)

1 green or red bell pepper, julienned

1/2 cup roasted sunflower seeds

1 small red onion, sliced thin (optional)

Dressing:

2 cups sugar

1-1/4 cups white vinegar

3-1/3 cups vegetable oil

2 tablespoons plus
2 teaspoons poppy seeds

1/4 cup chopped fresh chives

2 teaspoons dry mustard

3-1/2 teaspoons salt

Snip ends off snow peas, string and discard. Combine snow peas, grapes, orange sections, grapefruit sections, bell pepper, sunflower seeds and onion. Toss with poppy seed dressing and serve.

For dressing: Stir sugar into vinegar and then whisk until blended. Whisk in oil and add poppy seeds, chives, mustard and salt.

Serves 4–8

The combined shapes, textures and colors in this medley dress up any simple entree.

Garnishes

The look, taste and texture of salads can be enhanced by myriad garnishes.

Berries Broken tortilla chips Capers Carrot curls Chives Chopped or sliced hard-cooked egg Chopped or julienned prosciutto Chopped celery Chopped fennel tops Citrus curls Cornichons Croutons Crumbled blue cheese Currants Dried fruits Flavored cream cheese (to reflect the tastes in the dish; put into a candy mold, freeze for 20 minutes, warm in your hand and squeeze out of mold) Fresh snipped herbs Fried pasta and Chinese noodles Grated citrus rind Hazelnuts Homemade herbal bread crumbs Kumquats Light dusting of ground herbs/spices (careful—not too much!) Olives Parsley sprigs Pecans Pine nuts Pistachios Pomegranate seeds Poppy seeds Raisins, golden or dark Toast points Toasted seeds Toasted fresh coconut Tomato roses Walnuts Whole peppercorns

Blue Cheese Potato Salad

10 medium new potatoes

1 (4-ounce) package crumbled blue cheese

1 cup chopped celery

2 tablespoons chopped chives

Dressing:

3/4 cup sour cream

3/4 cup mayonnaise

3 tablespoons white wine vinegar

Wash potatoes (do not peel) and boil until tender. Drain, cool and cut into large pieces. Toss together with blue cheese, celery, and chives. Blend dressing ingredients and stir into potato mixture. Chill and serve.

Serves 6–8

A potato classic with a blue cheese surprise. Perfect for tailgating or potluck gatherings.

South of the Border Potato Salad

20 new potatoes

1 large tomato, peeled and chopped

1/4 cup chopped scallions (tops included)

1/4 cup chopped or minced cilantro leaves

1/4 cup chopped red onion

1/4 cup chopped green chilies

Chopped scallions, to garnish

Chopped tomatoes, to garnish

Dressing:

2 cups mayonnaise

2 tablespoons fresh lime juice

1 clove garlic, crushed

1/4 teaspoon cayenne pepper

2 tablespoons Dijon mustard

Wash potatoes (do not peel) and boil until tender. Drain, cool and cut into bite-sized pieces.

For dressing: Blend mayonnaise, lime juice, garlic, cayenne pepper and mustard. Cover and chill.

To assemble, mix potatoes with tomato, scallions, cilantro, onion and chilies. Toss with dressing mixture and chill well. Garnish with additional scallions and chopped tomato and serve.

Serves 6–8

Green chilies give this potato salad a real Southwestern zing. Serve it with hamburgers straight from the grill.

Szechuan Noodle Salad

1 (8-ounce) package thin whole wheat noodles, cooked

1-1/4 cups cooked, slivered chicken breast

1-1/4 cups slivered carrots

1 cup slivered scallions

2 cups fresh bean sprouts

Sauce:

2 tablespoons finely minced ginger

1 tablespoon finely minced garlic

1 tablespoon finely minced scallions

6 tablespoons smooth peanut butter

2 tablespoons soy sauce

4 tablespoons red wine vinegar

1 tablespoon chili paste

1 teaspoon sugar

1 tablespoon sesame oil

2 tablespoons vegetable oil

1 teaspoon dry mustard

1/2 teaspoon salt

1 tablespoon dry sherry

1/2 cup hot chicken broth

For sauce: Combine all ingredients and set aside. Do not refrigerate.

Combine noodles, chicken, carrots, scallions and bean sprouts. Add sauce and mix thoroughly. Note: Noodles and sauce must be at room temperature when tossed and served or dressing will lose its creamy consistency.

Serves 6

A main dish pasta salad with an intriguing Asian flavor. Chili paste can be found at most Asian specialty stores. If unavailable, try chili-flavored sesame seed oil.

To rid hands of onion odor, rub skin with salt or vinegar and rinse with cold water. Wash again with soap and water.

Try making croutons with various types of bread—whole wheat, pumpernickel and sourdough.

Cobb Pasta Salad

1 pound ruote (wagon-wheel pasta)

2 cups cooked chicken,
cut into bite-sized pieces

10 ounces bacon, fried and crumbled

2 cups fresh spinach, shredded

1 cup pitted black olives, halved

1 (4-ounce) package
crumbled blue cheese

2 ripe tomatoes, diced

_____

Dressing:

1 teaspoon Dijon mustard

1/4 cup red wine vinegar

1 cup olive oil

1/2 teaspoon freshly ground pepper

1 teaspoon sugar or honey

1 clove garlic, pressed

For dressing: Combine mustard, vinegar, oil, pepper, sugar and garlic. Shake well and set aside for 15 minutes to allow flavors to blend.

Cook pasta until al dente. Drain and rinse. In a large bowl, combine pasta, chicken, bacon, spinach, black olives, cheese and tomatoes, reserving some spinach, bacon and cheese for garnish. Add dressing and gently toss. Garnish with reserved spinach leaves, bacon and cheese.

Serves 6–8

A tip of the hat to the famous lettuce-based Cobb salad, this updated version is full of hearty flavor.

Cold Herbed Garbanzo Beans

2 cups canned garbanzo beans,
rinsed and drained

1/4 cups chopped parsley

1/2 cup chopped tomato

1/4 cup chopped black olives

1 teaspoon ground cumin

1 teaspoon minced garlic

1 teaspoon white wine vinegar

1 teaspoon dry mustard

2 tablespoons olive oil

In a large bowl, combine garbanzo beans, parsley, tomato and black olives. In a separate bowl, whisk together cumin, garlic, vinegar, mustard and olive oil. Add to bean mixture and toss well. Chill for several hours.

Serves 8

*Present in lettuce or cabbage cups, garnished with sliced olives and parsley. As a serving variation, puree all ingredients in a blender or food processor and offer as a hearty dip with **Toasted Pita Triangles**.*

Sesame Pasta Salad

1 (10-ounce) package long, thin pasta (such as spaghetti or soba noodles), uncooked

1 tablespoon vegetable oil

1 (10-ounce) package frozen sugar snap peas, thawed and sliced into 1/4-inch strips

6 scallions, sliced diagonally

2 red bell peppers, sliced into 1/4-inch strips

2 medium carrots, sliced into 1/4-inch strips

Sesame seeds, to garnish

Dressing:

1/4 cup red wine vinegar

1/4 cup soy sauce

3 tablespoons sesame oil

2 tablespoons sugar

1 tablespoon minced fresh ginger

3 garlic cloves, minced

1/4 teaspoon cayenne pepper

For dressing: Combine all ingredients. Cover and let stand at room temperature for 2 hours.

Cook spaghetti until al dente. Drain and toss with oil. Combine sugar snap peas, scallions, bell peppers and carrots with cooked spaghetti. Toss with dressing and serve either chilled or at room temperature.

Serves 6–8

Serve this flavorful salad in white porcelain lotus bowls, garnished with toasted sesame seeds, or pack it in a sealed container and tote to a neighborhood gathering.

Minted Barley Salad

4 cups cooked barley

1/3 cup extra-virgin olive oil

3 tablespoons fresh lemon juice

2 cloves garlic, minced

3/4 cup coarsely chopped mint leaves

1/2 cup chopped fresh dill

2 cups seeded and diced plum tomatoes

2 cups seeded and diced cucumbers

1/2 cup thinly sliced scallions

Salt and freshly ground pepper, to taste

Mint or dill, to garnish

In a large bowl, toss barley with olive oil, lemon juice and garlic. Add chopped mint and dill. Toss in tomatoes, cucumbers and scallions. Season with salt and pepper. Toss again gently but thoroughly. Let sit for at least 1 hour. Garnish with mint or dill.

Serves 6–8

This refreshing salad is wonderful as a side dish or as a nest for grilled chicken, lamb or fish. Best when prepared the day before.

Black Bean Salad

2 cups dried black beans, rinsed and picked over

5 cups chicken broth

1 cup chopped red onion

2 scallions, chopped

6 pear tomatoes, chopped

1 red bell pepper, chopped

1 yellow bell pepper, chopped

2 cups cooked corn

Juice of 1 lemon

1 celery stalk, chopped

Dressing:

2 small jalapeño peppers

2 cloves garlic

1/4 cup chopped parsley

1/4 cup chopped cilantro

1 cup mild olive or vegetable oil

1/2 cup red wine vinegar

1 teaspoon cumin, or less to taste

Salt and freshly ground pepper, to taste

In a stockpot, combine beans with 4 cups broth. Bring to a boil and cook for 2 minutes. Cover, remove from heat and let stand for 1 hour. Boil again. Add 1 cup chicken broth and simmer for 1-1/2 hours, stirring until tender. Drain and refresh under cold water. Drain again and place in a large bowl. Set aside.

For dressing: Place all ingredients into a food processor (jalapeños and garlic mince better if thrown in first with machine running, then add herbs, etc.)

Combine red onion, scallions, tomatoes, bell peppers and corn to beans. Pour dressing over all. Serve chilled or at room temperature.

Serves 8

When the menu says "potato salad," try this medley instead.

Carrot and Apple Salad

1/2 cup honey

1/2 cup apple cider vinegar

2 cups peeled and grated carrot

2 cups grated apples

Mixed greens

Melt honey in vinegar. Toss with carrots and apples and serve on a bed of mixed greens.

Serves 6–8

A quick and easy salad to toss together. Try including pineapple chunks for an added twist. Garnish with a baby carrot.

Goat Cheese Salad with Nectarines and Walnuts

1 head Bibb lettuce

1 head curly endive

3 ounces fresh goat cheese, quartered

1/4 cup chopped walnuts, toasted

4 nectarines

Coarsely ground pepper, to taste

Vinaigrette:

4 nectarines, pitted and coarsely chopped

1 tablespoon red wine vinegar

1 tablespoon water

1 small clove garlic

Thyme, to taste

1 tablespoon olive oil

For vinaigrette: In a food processor or blender, combine nectarines, vinegar, water, garlic and thyme. Blend until smooth. With motor running, drizzle in olive oil and blend for 15 seconds longer. Chill. (Dressing may be prepared ahead.)

Arrange greens by lining each plate with whole leaves of Bibb lettuce and curly endive. Top whole lettuce leaves with remaining torn pieces of lettuce and curly endive.

Preheat oven to 350 degrees. Shape goat cheese into 4 disks (2-1/4 inches by 1/2 inch). Roll each disk in walnuts and place on a baking sheet lined with foil. Bake for 5 minutes to heat through. Place 1 warm disk in the center of each plate of greens.

Slice remaining nectarines into wedges and fan around cheese. Drizzle vinaigrette onto each salad and sprinkle with freshly ground pepper.

Serves 4

Indulge your guests with this special salad. The dressing also is wonderful on other salads. As a variation, prepare goat cheese as directed and serve on toast squares as an appetizer.

Minted Spinach and Apple Medley

2 red apples

Juice of 1 lemon

2 tablespoons red wine vinegar

1 cup low-fat vanilla yogurt

1 medium cucumber, peeled, seeded and sliced

1 tablespoon chopped fresh mint

6 ounces fresh spinach leaves, cleaned and torn

8 strawberries, to garnish

Core apples and slice into a bowl. Toss with lemon juice to prevent browning. Remove apple slices and reserve, leaving lemon juice in the bowl. Add vinegar and yogurt to juice, stirring until well mixed. Add apples, cucumbers and mint and toss well.

To serve, place a bed of fresh spinach on each plate and spoon apple mixture on top. Garnish with strawberries and serve.

Serves 4

A wonderful pairing of cool mint and crisp apples.

Seville Salad

1/2 head red leaf lettuce

3 navel oranges

12 pitted black olives

4 slices red onion

Dressing:

2 small cloves garlic

4 teaspoons fresh lemon juice

1 tablespoon chopped fresh tarragon

4 tablespoons olive oil

Salt and freshly ground pepper, to taste

Line plates with leaf lettuce and top with additional torn pieces. Peel oranges and divide into sections. Arrange on lettuce mounds. Slice olives and place over oranges. Separate onion rings and place on each plate.

For dressing: In a food processor fitted with steel blade, process garlic. Add lemon juice and tarragon and pulse 3 to 4 times. With processor running, pour olive oil through chute. Season with salt and pepper. Drizzle over individual salads and serve.

Serves 4

A fragrant combination of oranges, olives and onion to honor Kansas City's Spanish sister city.

Southern Belle Salad

4 cups torn arugula leaves

4 cups torn Bibb lettuce

2–3 ripe peaches, sliced

1/2 cup toasted pecan pieces

Dressing:

3 tablespoons raspberry or white wine vinegar

1 teaspoon Dijon mustard

5 tablespoons olive oil

Pinch of sugar

Pinch of salt

For dressing: Combine ingredients and mix well. Set aside.

Combine greens and peach slices in a bowl. Pour dressing over all and toss. Arrange salad on individual plates and sprinkle with pecans before serving.

Serves 6

Peppery arugula combined with sweet peaches offers a pleasant mélange of flavors. For information on flavored vinegars, see "Cooking with Herbs" in Fish & Seafood.

When planning a floral centerpiece, slip in a few herbs appropriate

to the occasion, such as rosemary for

friendship, lavender for luck and marjoram for happiness.

*T*ime was when a nice head of iceberg lettuce was the standard base of any salad. Not so in today's supermarkets, where an expanded selection allows cooks to experiment with a marvelous array of taste, texture and color.

*G*reens, like fine wines, require a little tender loving care before serving. For best results, choose those that look and smell fresh, avoiding wilted leaves or slimy stems. Once home, give your greens a proper wash to eliminate sand and grit, and then dry thoroughly. Greens may be kept in the crisper up to a week if wrapped loosely in paper towels and stored in plastic refrigerator bags.

Super Salads

Arugula—A spicy, peppery taste provides the same punch as green onions without the aftertaste. *Belgian endive*—Curly, pale green or yellow leaves make a beautiful statement when combined with lettuce, adding body and texture. This slightly bitter member of the chicory family is also an excellent dipper for flavored mayonnaises, creamy dressings and dips. *Bibb lettuce*—Long preferred in Europe, Bibbs are prized for their buttery flavor and delicate texture. *Dandelion*—These greens offer an excellent source of vitamins and minerals. Small younger leaves tend to be less bitter. *Escarole*—This pleasantly bitter member of the chicory family is best when served alone with a hearty dressing. *Frisée*—Serve this pale, mildly bitter green in a light vinaigrette. *Garden cress*—Similar in taste to watercress, this makes an excellent garnish and a wonderful substitute for salt. *Iceberg lettuce*—Crisp and cool, iceberg is a salad classic. *Kale*—Curly blue-green leaves lend a cabbage-like flavor to salads. Try kale chopped and cooked with olive oil and garlic. *Leaf lettuce*—Soft red-tipped or green leaves impart a delicate flavor. A wonderful plate-liner. *Mâche (lamb's lettuce)*—Also known as corn salad, mache has a soft and buttery flavor. The French wait for this lettuce every spring. Wash it well before using. *Mustard greens*—Add zip to salads by tossing in a few of these spicy greens; younger leaves are best. Mustard greens may also be steamed, sautéed or simmered and served as a side dish. Wash them well. *Oak leaf lettuce*—Try this nut-flavored lettuce with a splash of fruity olive oil and a squeeze of fresh lemon. *Raddichio*—These beautiful red-white variegated leaves produce a tangy, peppery taste and are visually pleasing as plate-liners or mixed into salads. *Romaine*—Long crisp romaine leaves lend a nutty flavor to salads with hearty dressings. *Sorrel*—Similar in appearance to spinach, this has a sharp, lemony bite that's wonderful in salads or cooked into soups, sauces, breads, omelets and frittatas. *Spinach*—Dark green, iron-rich leaves add color and texture to salads. Equally good fresh or cooked, remember to wash well before using. *Watercress*—This pungent peppery flavor gives a lift to any mixture of greens. Use it as a flavor spike to tomatoes, cucumbers and potato salad.

"Bleuberry" Spinach Salad

1 pound fresh spinach or Bibb lettuce, torn into pieces

1 cup fresh blueberries

1 (4-ounce) package crumbled blue cheese

1/2 cup toasted pecans

Raspberries, to garnish (optional)

Dressing:

1/2 cup vegetable oil

3 tablespoons blueberry or white wine vinegar

1 teaspoon Dijon mustard

1 teaspoon sugar

Salt, to taste

For dressing: Combine all ingredients well and set aside.

Place torn greens, blueberries, blue cheese and pecans in a salad bowl. Just before serving, toss gently with dressing. Garnish with raspberries, if desired.

Serves 8

Crunchy, sweet and pungent! For information on flavored vinegars, see "Cooking with Herbs" in Fish & Seafood.

Marinated Mushrooms and Romaine Salad

1 head romaine or other greens

3 ounces fresh mushrooms, halved

3 tablespoons snipped chives, to garnish

Vinaigrette:

1/4 cup white wine vinegar

4 teaspoons sugar

3 teaspoons lemon juice

1/4 teaspoon dry mustard

3/4 cup vegetable oil

3 large scallions, sliced

3 cloves garlic, minced

Clean and tear greens into bite-sized pieces. Place mushrooms in a covered dish or plastic storage bag.

For vinaigrette: In a jar with a tight fitting lid, mix vinegar, sugar, lemon juice, mustard, oil, scallions and garlic. Shake vigorously. Pour over mushrooms, cover and chill for 4 hours or overnight, stirring occasionally.

Drain mushrooms, reserving vinaigrette. Spoon mushrooms over salad greens and drizzle remaining dressing over all. Garnish with snipped chives and serve.

Serves 8

For visual effect, try using a variety of mushrooms. For more information, see "Just Wild About Mushrooms" in Vegetables & Grains.

Summer Palette Salad

2 oranges, peeled

1-1/2 cups raspberries, rinsed

1 large red onion, thinly sliced

3–4 heads Bibb lettuce

Dressing:

2 tablespoons fresh orange juice

1 tablespoon raspberry vinegar

1/4 cup olive oil

2 teaspoons snipped fresh chives

Salt and freshly ground pepper, to taste

Cut oranges into slices 1/8- to 1/4-inch thick and then halve. Remove seeds. Mix with raspberries and onion slices. Prepare early in the day and refrigerate, allowing flavors to blend.

For dressing: Combine orange juice and vinegar. Slowly add oil, whisking constantly. Add chives and season with salt and pepper. (Dressing may be prepared ahead.)

Tear lettuce into bite-sized pieces and combine in a large salad bowl with fruit and onion mixture. Toss with dressing and serve.

Serves 8–10

Serve this pretty salad in clear or colored glass bowls as a prelude to game or turkey.

Queen of Hearts Salad

1 (14-ounce) can water-packed artichoke hearts, chopped

1 (14-ounce) can water-packed hearts of palm, diced

1 head romaine lettuce, torn into bite-sized pieces

1 head leaf lettuce, torn into bite-sized pieces

1/2 red onion, very thinly sliced

Dressing:

1/2 cup olive oil

1/3 cup balsamic vinegar

1/2 cup freshly grated Parmesan cheese

1 tablespoon sugar

For dressing: Combine ingredients in a glass or plastic container and shake well. Set aside. (Dressing may be prepared ahead.)

Layer lettuce, onion slices, artichoke hearts and hearts of palm on serving plates. Drizzle with dressing just before serving.

Serves 8–10

*The sweet-tart taste of balsamic vinegar gives this classic salad a rich flavor. For a milder variation, use tarragon vinegar instead of balsamic. Or substitute **Hazelnut Cognac Dressing** for the dressing and garnish salad with chopped hazelnuts.*

Thai Cabbage Salad

1 head green cabbage, chopped

1/3 cucumber, peeled and diced

1 carrot, peeled and shredded

1 cup dry roasted peanuts,
coarsely chopped

3 scallions, chopped

2 Serrano chilies, chopped

Dressing:

1/3 cup vegetable oil

1/3 cup white vinegar

3 tablespoons sugar

3 tablespoons soy sauce

1 cup chopped fresh cilantro
or 1/3 cup dried

1–2 tablespoons red salsa
or green chili paste

3 cloves garlic, chopped

1/2 Thai chili pepper, chopped

For dressing: Combine vegetable oil, vinegar, sugar, soy sauce, cilantro, salsa, garlic and Thai pepper and set aside.

In a large bowl, combine cabbage, cucumber, carrot, peanuts, scallions and Serrano chilies. Pour dressing over cabbage mixture and toss.

Serves 8–10

This is a side dish with fire! Tone down the heat by substituting jalapeños for the Serrano chilies and red bell pepper for the Thai chilies.

Technicolor Toss

2 cups shredded green cabbage

2 cups shredded red cabbage

1 cup peeled, shredded carrots

1/2 cup diced green bell pepper

1/2 cup diced red bell pepper

4 scallions, thinly sliced

Vinaigrette:

1/4 cup tarragon vinegar

1/4 cup sugar

1 tablespoon Dijon mustard

Salt and freshly ground pepper, to taste

3/4 cup olive oil

For dressing: In a medium bowl, mix tarragon vinegar, sugar, Dijon mustard, salt, pepper and olive oil, whisking in oil a little at a time. Set aside.

Combine green and red cabbage with carrots, peppers and scallions. Toss with dressing, to taste. Refrigerate until ready to serve.

Serves 8

A bright blend of red, green and orange, this salad is prettier when chopped by hand. Garnish with raisins, sliced baby carrots and fresh tarragon.

Ruby Cole Slaw

1 head red cabbage

1 large red onion

3/4 cup plus 1 teaspoon sugar

1 cup cider vinegar

1-1/2 tablespoons salt

2 teaspoons celery seed

1 teaspoon dry mustard

1 teaspoon sugar

1-1/2 cups vegetable oil

Cut cabbage into long fine strips. Slice onion in fine circles. In a large crock, alternate layers of cabbage and onion. Spread 3/4 cup sugar over all. Set aside.

In a small saucepan, combine vinegar, salt, celery seed, mustard and 1 teaspoon sugar. Bring mixture to a boil. Add oil and bring to a boil again. Pour over cabbage mixture while hot. Cover tightly and refrigerate. After 3 hours, toss gently and continue to refrigerate. Toss again in 1 hour; refrigerate. Repeat in 1 hour and refrigerate. Toss again before serving.

Serves 8–10

Red cabbage is the key to this slaw's appealing "look." Garnish with toasted nuts and serve alongside barbecued chicken, ribs or brisket. Better if prepared the day before.

Sour Cream Sherry Dressing

1 (3-ounce) package cream cheese, softened to room temperature

1 cup sour cream

1/4 cup sherry

1 teaspoon grated onion

3/4 teaspoon salt

1/2 teaspoon garlic salt

1/8 teaspoon freshly ground pepper

1 tablespoon white wine vinegar

2 tablespoons mayonnaise

Combine all ingredients and toss with mixed greens.

Makes approximately 1-1/2 cups

This luscious dressing would add interest to a simple menu of **Mesquite Grilled T-Bones** *and* **Grilled Potatoes.**

🍃 *To store lettuce that has already been torn, toss with a small amount of oil and refrigerate in a large plastic bag.*

Hazelnut Cognac Dressing

1 cup sour cream

1/2 cup mayonnaise

1/2 cup plain yogurt

1/2 cup crushed toasted hazelnuts

2 teaspoons finely minced onion

1 teaspoon freshly ground pepper

1 teaspoon seasoned salt

1 small clove garlic, crushed

Dash of Worcestershire sauce

Dash of hot pepper sauce

1-1/2 tablespoons cognac

2 tablespoons lemon juice

In a medium bowl, combine sour cream, mayonnaise, yogurt, hazelnuts, onions, pepper, seasoned salt, garlic, Worcestershire and hot pepper sauce. Mix together well. Stir in cognac and lemon juice. Cover and refrigerate until ready to serve. Pour over mixed salad greens and toss.

Makes approximately 2 cups

Hazelnuts may be more readily available in the fall. Remove skins after toasting.

Garden Creamy Basil Dressing

2/3 cup light to mild olive oil

6 tablespoons red wine vinegar

6 tablespoons finely chopped fresh basil

4 tablespoons heavy cream

2 tablespoons lemon juice

Salt and freshly ground pepper, to taste

Whisk all ingredients together until well mixed. Adjust seasonings as needed. Serve with mixed greens and toasted pine nuts.

Makes 1-3/4 cups

Basil darkens if left to stand. This dressing is better when prepared just before serving.

Thick, creamy mayonnaise serves as the start for countless other mixtures—salad dressings, sauces, rémoulades and more. The luscious homemade variety lasts only a few days; its commercial counterparts will store up to 6 months after opening.

(For a basic recipe plus flavored variations, see "Mayonnaise" in Meats.)

CHILLED

Amaretto Peach Soup, 141
Cool Blueberry Soup, 140
Creamed Zucchini Soup, 134
Dilled Tomato Soup, 137
Garden Green Gazpacho, 138
Indian Summer Soup, 140
Minted Kiwi Cream, 139
Tomato Soup with Basil Cantaloupe Balls, 138

HOT

Broccoli Blue Soup, 133
Cauliflower Stilton Velouté, 135
Classic Wild Rice Soup, 130
Corn, Shrimp and Penne Soup, 128
Mushroom Ravioli in Beef Consommé, 129
Rajah Chicken Soup, 130
Red Onion Soup with Apple Cider, 132
Red Pepper Soup, 133
Tuscan Tortellini Soup, 128
Vegetable Port Consommé, 136

HEARTY

Country Veal Stew, 125
Curried Butternut Squash Soup, 134
Fennel Soup with Oysters, 124
Garden Tomato Soup, 132
Green Chili Stew, 123
Harvest Stew in Maple Baked Acorn Squash, 122
Hearty Lentil Potage, 125
Herbed Black Bean Soup with Smoked Chicken, 123
Minestrone Parmesan, 129
Mushroom Feta Soup, 137
Old-Fashioned Vegetable Soup with Homemade Noodles, 131
Three Pepper Chili, 126

MINI RECIPES

Bagel Croutons, 126
Garlic Croutons, 126
Maple Baked Acorn Squash, 122
West Indian Cream, 136

Soups & Stews

Pictured finishing touch:

USING

SMALL POTS OF HERBS

AS PLACECARDS, 141

SPECIAL TOPIC BOXES

KNOW YOUR CHILIES, 127

PLACECARDS, 141

SOUP GARNISHES, 139

Harvest Stew in Maple Baked Acorn Squash

4 medium onions, unpeeled

6 pounds boneless pork shoulder, trimmed and cut into 1-1/2-inch cubes

1/2 cup fresh orange juice

1/2 cup soy sauce

1/4 cup dry sherry

3 tablespoons minced fresh ginger

2 tablespoons cornstarch

2 tablespoons water

1 cup pitted prunes

1 cup diced (large chunks) apple

Salt and freshly ground pepper, to taste

Dash of sugar

Dash of cinnamon

3/4 cup water

Preheat oven to 325 degrees. Set 2 onions in the center of each of 2 jelly roll pans. Add pork in a single layer. Bake for 1 hour, stirring pork occasionally. Cool onions slightly, then peel and quarter lengthwise.

Transfer onions to a large baking dish. Add pork. Gently mix in orange juice, soy sauce, sherry and ginger. Continue baking until pork is tender when pierced (approximately 1 hour).

Reduce juices in pan and pour into a large, heavy saucepan over medium heat. Dissolve cornstarch in 2 tablespoons water. Add cornstarch and stir until sauce boils and thickens (approximately 3 minutes). Stir in pork, onions, prunes, apples and seasonings. Heat through. Ladle into **Maple Baked Acorn Squash** halves.

Serves 12

A luscious blend of spices and fruit. For a more tender meat, substitute pork tenderloin for pork shoulder. **Maple Baked Acorn Squash** *makes excellent containers for serving vegetables and rice as well. Place on pewter chargers and surround with colorful fall leaves.*

Maple Baked Acorn Squash

6 large golden acorn or other squash • Salt, to taste

1/3 cup butter • 1/2 cup maple syrup

Preheat oven to 325 degrees. Cut squash in half lengthwise and seed. Sprinkle cut sides with salt and arrange, cut-sides down, in a baking dish. Bake until tender (easily pierced with a sharp knife), about 45 to 60 minutes. Run fork over cut sides of squash, then spread with butter and drizzle with maple syrup. Continue baking for 3 minutes more.

Makes 12 containers

Herbed Black Bean Soup with Smoked Chicken

1/4 cup (1/2 stick) unsalted butter

1 cup peeled, diced broccoli stems

1/2 cup chopped carrot

1/2 cup chopped onion

1/2 cup chopped celery

1 tablespoon thyme, crumbled

1 teaspoon Cajun seasoning

1 tablespoon oregano

1 tablespoon basil, crumbled

1/2 cup dry white wine

4 cups chicken broth

2 cups broccoli florets

1 (16-ounce) can black beans, rinsed and drained

8 ounces smoked chicken, shredded and chopped

1 tablespoon Worcestershire sauce

1/2 teaspoon hot pepper sauce

2 cups heavy cream

Salt and freshly ground pepper, to taste

In a soup pot, melt butter over medium heat. Add broccoli stems, carrots, onion and celery and sauté for 5 minutes. Add thyme, Cajun seasoning, oregano and basil and sauté for 5 minutes more. Pour in wine and bring mixture to a boil. Add broth and cook until liquid is reduced by half, stirring occasionally (approximately 12 minutes).

Stir broccoli florets, beans, chicken, Worcestershire sauce and hot pepper sauce into soup and simmer for 5 minutes, stirring occasionally. Add cream and simmer for 5 minutes more. Season with salt and pepper and serve.

Serves 6

*A smoky, spicy soup that's even better when prepared a day in advance. Garnish with cilantro, broccoli florets, pimiento, curled carrots or homemade croutons and serve with **Sage Celery Seed Bread**.*

Green Chili Stew

2 pounds top sirloin steak, cubed

1/2 cup chopped onion

2 tablespoons olive oil

3 tablespoons flour

4 cloves garlic, chopped

2 pounds tomatoes, chopped

3 cups fresh or canned chopped green chilies

1 cup water

1 tablespoon cumin

Salt and freshly ground pepper, to taste

Sauté steak and onion in olive oil until onions are transparent. Add flour and brown. Transfer to a Dutch oven or crockpot and add remaining ingredients. Simmer on low heat for at least 3 hours.

Serves 8–10

Serve this hearty, garlicky stew in deep, rustic bowls. Garnish with grated cheese, sour cream and scallions, and offer a basket of steamed tortillas on the side. As variations, add pinto beans, cubed potatoes, sliced carrots or sliced zucchini.

Fennel Soup
with Oysters

1 medium whole fennel head
(leafy top included)

1 shallot

3 tablespoons unsalted butter

2 cups chicken broth

1 cup heavy cream

1/2 cup milk

1/3 cup fish stock or clam juice

2 dozen freshly shucked oysters,
halved, liquor reserved

1-1/2 teaspoons ground coriander seed

1 teaspoon freshly ground pepper

Clean and peel fennel bulb under cold water. Slice sufficient portion of bulb into julienne strips to make 1 cup. Chop remaining bulb and blend in a food processor. Set aside. Mince leafy top and reserve for garnish.

In a large heavy pan, sauté shallots in 1 tablespoon butter. Whisk in chicken broth and reduce to medium-low heat. Whisk in processed fennel, cream, milk, fish stock and oyster liquor. Bring to a simmer.

In a heavy pan, sauté fennel strips in remaining butter for approximately 2 minutes until crunchy. Add fennel strips to stock mixture and bring to a simmer.

Just before serving, increase heat to boil. Add oysters and boil for 3 minutes, until oysters curl. Stir in coriander and pepper. Transfer to serving bowls and garnish with minced fennel top.

Serves 6–8

Fragrant fennel lends a delicate hint of sweetness to oyster soup. Choose clean, crisp bulbs with no sign of browning. Refrigerate, tightly wrapped in a plastic bag, for up to 5 days.

A leaf of cabbage dropped into a pot of soup

absorbs the fat from the top.

To thicken soups, puree cooked vegetables in a blender and stir into soup.

To save a soup that is too salty, simmer with a sliced potato for a

few minutes. Repeat with fresh potato slices until desired seasoning is achieved.

Chilling will mute the seasoning of any soup.

If water evaporates when making stock, add cold water,

not warm, to prevent lumping.

Garlic can be kept indefinitely in the freezer. Peel and chop before thawing.

2 tablespoons flour

1 teaspoon salt

1/2 teaspoon freshly ground pepper

2 pounds stew veal, cut into
1-inch pieces

2 tablespoons butter

1 large onion, coarsely chopped

1 large clove garlic, minced

2 cups chicken broth

2 (16-ounce) cans whole
tomatoes, chopped

3 carrots, peeled and julienned

1/2 pound mushrooms, thickly sliced

1/2 pound zucchini, thickly sliced

1 large red or yellow bell pepper,
cut into 1-inch squares

1/2 cup country Dijon mustard

Combine flour, salt and pepper in a plastic bag. Add veal and coat with flour mixture.

In a large skillet or Dutch oven, brown veal in butter. Add onion, garlic, chicken broth, tomatoes and carrots. Cover and simmer, stirring occasionally, for 1 hour, or until meat is tender. Add mushrooms, zucchini and bell pepper. Cover and simmer for 10 minutes or until vegetables are tender. Stir in mustard just before serving.

Serves 8

*Combine with crusty **Mustard Wheat Bread** and a tossed salad for an early spring meal, when nights are still nippy.*

1/4 cup vegetable oil

3 cups diced cooked ham

2 large yellow onions, chopped

1 clove garlic, minced

1/2 pound Polish sausage,
cut into 1/2-inch slices

2 cups chopped celery (leaves included)

1 (16-ounce) can tomatoes with liquid

1 pound uncooked lentils, washed well

1 teaspoon hot pepper sauce,
or to taste

1-1/2 teaspoons salt

1 (10-ounce) package frozen chopped
spinach, thawed and drained

Heat oil in a large pot and add ham, onion, garlic and sausage. Cook for 10 minutes over medium heat. Add celery, tomatoes, lentils, hot pepper sauce, salt and water to cover. Cover and cook over low heat for 2 hours. Add spinach to soup and simmer about 15 minutes more.

Serves 8

Make a double batch and take some to a friend. Place in a large glass jar (with plastic wrap under the lid), tied with a big plaid bow.

Three Pepper Chili

5 slices bacon

1/2 pound Italian sausage, casings removed

1-1/2 pounds ground chuck

1 cup chopped onion

1/2 cup chopped green or red bell pepper

1 clove garlic, crushed

2 dried red chili peppers, seeded and chopped

2 jalapeño peppers, seeded and chopped

1-1/2 tablespoons chili powder

1/2 teaspoon salt

1/4 teaspoon oregano

2-1/2 cups water or beef broth

1 (12-ounce) can tomato paste

1 (16-ounce) can pinto beans

Cook bacon until crisp. Remove from pan and crumble. Cook and crumble sausage in same pan. Remove from pan and drain, saving 2 tablespoons fat. Set bacon and sausage aside.

In reserved fat, sauté ground chuck, onion, green peppers and garlic. Add bacon, sausage, chili peppers, jalapeños, chili powder, salt and oregano. Stir in water and tomato paste and bring to a boil. Reduce heat and simmer for 1-1/2 hours. Stir in beans and continue cooking for 30 minutes more.

Serves 4–6

For those who like it hot! Serve buffet style with bowls of sour cream, lime wedges, grated cheeses, guacamole and soft tortillas.

Bagel Croutons

1 bagel • Melted butter • Freshly grated Parmesan cheese (optional)

Slice a bagel in half, then cut halves into sections and brush with butter. Place on a cookie sheet and bake for 1 hour at 250 degrees.

For vegetable soups, try adding freshly grated Parmesan cheese on top of the crouton.

Makes about 12 croutons

Garlic Croutons

Stale baguette, diced • Melted butter or olive oil, to taste • Fresh garlic, to taste

Toss bread cubes with butter and garlic. Place in a shallow baking dish and bake at 325 degrees for 30 to 45 minutes, stirring 2 to 3 times.

For an interesting flair, cut bread into favorite shapes instead of dicing.

*Some like it hot, while others seek milder pleasures.
Fortunately, chili peppers come in a wide assortment of shapes, sizes and
colors—and degrees of fire. Here are a few selection guidelines:*

*Generally, the longer and thinner the pepper, the more fiery the taste.
(Most of the fire comes from the seeds and the veins—to tone
down the "bite," remove these parts.)*

*Look for firm peppers with glossy skins. Use fresh chilies
whenever possible. Canned chilies will alter the
flavor and texture of a recipe.*

*Fresh chilies may be refrigerated for up to 2 to 3 weeks,
wrapped in paper towels and stored in a paper bag. Dried chilies should be
stored in a tightly covered container in a cool, dark spot.*

*When preparing fresh chilies, wear rubber gloves and avoid
touching your eyes or face. If you accidentally do so, flush with cold water.
If you do not wear gloves, remember to wash your hands thoroughly
with soap and water before continuing with the recipe.*

Picking Peppers

Anaheim or Californian—Long and thin, this popular medium-hot pepper comes in red or green. Great for stuffing. **Cayenne**—These small, red, green and yellow-green peppers are most often found in dried form (cayenne pepper). Whether fresh or dried, they add fire to any recipe. **Fresno**—This is similar to the jalapeño, but with a lighter green or bright yellow skin. **Habanero**—Careful! These tiny, neon-orange chilies pack a lot of punch for their size—a little goes a long way. Use care in handling. **Jalapeño**—Popular throughout the United States, these green, thick-skinned chilies can vary from hot to very hot. Tone down the heat by roasting. **Chipotle**—This is the ripened, dried version of the jalapeño. **Poblano**—The medium heat of this long, triangular-shaped chili is best sampled when the pepper has been charred and peeled. **Ancho**—This all-purpose mild chili is the dried version of the poblano. **Pasilla**—This long, narrow, black-hued dried chili is very pungent. Try combining with poblanos. **Serrano**—Go for the burn! This small, dark green pepper has a distinctive fire. **Thai**—Small and powerful, these can be used to flavor many dishes.

Tuscan Tortellini Soup

1/4 pound bacon, cut into small pieces

2 cloves garlic, pressed

4 cups chopped fresh spinach

4 cups chicken broth

1 (16-ounce) can small white beans with liquid

1 (28-ounce) can tomatoes with liquid

1 medium yellow bell pepper, cubed

1 (8-ounce) package tricolor tortellini (freezer fresh)

Sauté bacon and garlic for 5 to 8 minutes or until bacon is brown. Remove from pan. Cook spinach in pan drippings for 2 minutes or until wilted. Stir in broth, beans, tomatoes and bell pepper and bring to a boil. Stir in pasta and bacon and simmer until pasta is al dente.

Serves 6–8

*Friends will appreciate this colorful, warming soup. Substitute spinach tortellini if tricolor is unavailable. Serve with **Toasted Pita Triangles**.*

Corn, Shrimp and Penne Soup

1 tablespoon olive oil

1 teaspoon minced garlic

1 small shallot, minced

1/2 pound shrimp, peeled and deveined

1/4 cup corn (reserved from corn used in broth)

1/4 cup chopped Roma tomatoes

1/4 cup chopped arugula

7–8 ounces cooked penne

Salt and freshly ground pepper, to taste

1 tablespoon chopped cilantro, to garnish

Broth:

1 medium yellow onion, diced

1 carrot, diced

2 celery stalks, diced

4 tablespoons minced garlic

1 tomato, diced

1/4 cup olive oil

2 ears corn

1 gallon chicken broth

Salt and freshly ground pepper, to taste

For broth: In a large, heavy stockpot, sauté onion, carrot, celery, garlic and tomato in olive oil until transparent and browned. Grill corn until just brown, then cut kernels off cob. Reserve kernels and add cobs to vegetable mixture. Stir in chicken broth, salt and pepper. Reduce stock by half and strain vegetables off. Set broth aside.

Sauté garlic and shallot in olive oil for a few seconds. Add shrimp and partially cook. Add corn, tomatoes and arugula and sauté for about 5 minutes. Add broth, penne, salt and pepper to shrimp mixture. Top with chopped cilantro and serve.

Serves 6

The best soups still start with homemade stocks. Serve this one in sunny Italian ceramic bowls.

Minestrone Parmesan

1/4 cup olive oil

1 cup minced onion

2 cloves garlic, minced

1/4 cup minced fresh cilantro

3 cups finely diced smoked ham

4 quarts beef broth, boiling

1 cup diced fresh or canned tomatoes

1 cup diced carrots

1 cup diced celery

1/2 cup corn

1 cup diced raw white potatoes

1 cup cooked garbanzo beans

1 cup uncooked small pasta
(macaroni or smaller)

2 cups shredded fresh spinach

Freshly ground pepper, to taste

Freshly grated
Parmesan cheese, to taste

Heat oil in a large stockpot and sauté onions, garlic, cilantro and smoked ham until onions are soft. Add boiling beef broth and simmer on medium-low heat for 20 minutes. Add tomatoes, carrots, celery, corn, potatoes and garbanzo beans all at once. Cover and barely simmer until vegetables are tender. Add pasta and spinach and cook until pasta is al dente. Season with pepper. Stir in freshly grated Parmesan cheese and serve hot.

Serves 10–12

This hefty soup is best prepared a day ahead and reheated to serve. Make 2 batches and freeze the extra. Serve with buttered slices of **Cheese and Herb Twist.**

Mushroom Ravioli in Beef Consommé

1 pound fresh mushrooms, thinly sliced

1 pound shiitake mushrooms,
thinly sliced

2 cloves garlic, crushed

1 large shallot, minced

1/2 bunch celery (4–6 stalks),
thinly sliced crosswise

4 tablespoons unsalted butter

40 won ton skins (round or square)

2 egg whites

5 cups hot beef consommé

Sauté mushrooms, garlic, shallot and celery in butter. Cook until liquid is evaporated. Place 1 teaspoon of mushroom mixture on a won ton skin and cover with another skin. Brush edges with egg white and crimp with fork tines. Steam won tons lightly for 10 minutes, being careful not to let them stick together. Ladle consommé into bowls and place 1 to 2 won tons in each.

Serves 10

Shiitake mushrooms lend a rich, smoky flavor to beef consommé. When steaming ravioli, spray the steam basket with cooking oil to prevent sticking.

These ravioli also make an excellent appetizer. Try serving with this intriguing sauce: Combine 2–3 tablespoons country Dijon mustard, 1 tablespoon sugar or honey, 2 tablespoons soy sauce and 1–2 tablespoons tarragon or wine vinegar.

Rajah Chicken Soup

4 tablespoons butter

1 cup chopped onion

4 carrots, sliced

3/4 cup diced green bell pepper

1 cup cauliflower florets

1/4 cup uncooked long grain white rice

1 quart chicken broth

2 cups chopped, cooked chicken

1/4 cup minced parsley

3/4 pound cherry tomatoes, quartered

1 tablespoon tomato paste

1-1/2 teaspoons curry powder

1 clove garlic, pressed

In a large pot, sauté onion in butter until soft. Add carrots, green pepper, cauliflower, rice and broth. Simmer for 20 minutes. Add chicken, parsley, tomatoes, tomato paste, curry powder and garlic, and simmer for 20 minutes more.

Serves 4–6

A West Indian blend of garden goodness.

Classic Wild Rice Soup

1/2 cup uncooked wild rice

6 slices bacon, chopped into 1/2-inch pieces

3 cloves garlic, pressed

1 onion, finely chopped

3 celery stalks, finely chopped

1 carrot, finely chopped

2 cups chicken broth

2 cups half-and-half

1/2 teaspoon Worcestershire sauce

1/4 pound diced ham

Run cold water over rice for 1 minute in strainer. Set aside.

Cook bacon and garlic in a large saucepan until partially browned. Add onion, celery and carrot. Cook and stir for 8 minutes until tender. Drain fat. Add drained rice and chicken broth. Bring to a boil. Reduce heat and simmer for 40 minutes or until rice is tender. Add water to thin if necessary. Stir in cream and Worcestershire sauce and cook over medium heat, stirring occasionally until heated (approximately 5 to 10 minutes). Sprinkle with ham and serve.

Serves 8

This soup doubles easily for large groups, whether strictly casual or all dressed up.

Old-Fashioned Vegetable Soup with Homemade Noodles

1 tablespoon butter

1 large onion, chopped

2 cloves garlic, minced

4 carrots, cut into medium slices

4 celery stalks, cut into medium slices

1 tablespoon flour

4-1/2 cups chicken broth

2 large tomatoes, peeled and chopped

Salt and freshly ground pepper, to taste

4 small pieces lemon zest, finely chopped, to garnish

1 large clove garlic, finely chopped, to garnish

1/2 cup parsley, stems removed, finely chopped, to garnish

Noodles:

1 tablespoon melted butter

1/4 teaspoon salt

1 egg

2/3 cup flour

In a large pot, melt butter and sauté onions and garlic for 5 minutes or until limp. Add carrots and celery and sauté for 3 minutes. Sprinkle flour over all. Cook, stirring constantly with a wooden spoon, for 2 minutes. Slowly add broth, continuing to stir constantly. Simmer for 30 minutes.

For noodles: In a bowl, combine butter, salt and egg with a fork. Work in flour by hand to form dough. Roll into a ball and wrap in plastic until ready to use. Thirty minutes before serving, roll dough out on floured board as thinly as possible. Cut into 1/2-inch strips and lightly toss with flour. Set aside.

Add tomatoes, salt and pepper to soup mixture. Cover and simmer for 10 minutes. Drop noodles into soup and simmer for 4 minutes. Sprinkle with lemon zest, garlic and parsley and serve.

Serves 6–8

This soothing vegetable soup comforts the soul. Serve in a rustic country crock or earthenware bowls. To save time, substitute frozen egg noodles for the homemade ones.

Vegetable stocks are more delicate than those that are meat-based and tend to deteriorate in flavor if simmered longer than 30 minutes.

Store leftover stocks as ice cubes. After stock has cooled, refrigerate until fat congeals at the top. Skim off fat, pour stock into ice cube trays and freeze. Store stock cubes in plastic freezer bags and use as needed.

Add grated horseradish to crème fraîche to create a standout garnish for hearty soups.

Red Onion Soup with Apple Cider

2 tablespoons unsalted butter

1-1/4 pounds red onions, thinly sliced

2 teaspoons flour

1 teaspoon minced garlic

3 cups beef broth

3 cups chicken broth

1/2 cup dry white wine

1/2 cup apple cider

1 bay leaf

1-1/2 teaspoons dried thyme, crumbled

Salt and freshly ground pepper, to taste

1 baguette, sliced 1/2-inch thick

Freshly grated Swiss or white cheddar cheese

Melt butter in a large, heavy saucepan over medium heat. Add onions and cook until light golden brown, stirring frequently (approximately 20 minutes). Add flour, stir for 2 minutes, and then add garlic and stir for 1 minute. Add both broths, wine, cider and bay leaf. Bring to a boil, skimming the surface occasionally. Add thyme, then reduce heat and simmer for 40 minutes. Remove bay leaf and season with salt and pepper.

Preheat broiler. Place bread slices on a baking sheet. Top with cheese and broil until cheese melts. Ladle soup into preheated bowls and top with croutons.

Serves 4

An interesting blend of tart flavors —sure to chase away the winter blues. For a touch of color, add a red-skinned apple slice on top of each cheesy crouton.

Garden Tomato Soup

1/2 cup (1 stick) butter

1 clove garlic, chopped

1 cup grated celery

1 cup grated carrot

1 medium onion, grated

1 cup grated unpeeled zucchini

1/4 cup flour

1 pound fresh tomatoes, peeled and pureed

2 tablespoons brown sugar

1 tablespoon chopped fresh basil

1 teaspoon marjoram

1 bay leaf

4 cups chicken broth

1 teaspoon paprika

1/2 teaspoon curry powder

Salt and freshly ground pepper, to taste

1/2 cup half-and-half

Sauté garlic, celery, carrot, onion and zucchini in butter. Stir in flour, tomatoes, brown sugar, basil, marjoram, bay leaf, chicken broth, paprika, curry, salt and pepper and simmer for 30 minutes. Remove bay leaf, stir in half-and-half and serve.

Serves 16

Old-fashioned flavor fresh from the garden. Top with homemade croutons cut into interesting shapes and sprigs of parsley. Fresh herbs lose flavor when cooked long—add a sprinkling just before serving.

Broccoli Blue Soup

2 cups finely chopped broccoli

1 small onion, finely chopped

3 cups chicken or turkey broth

2 cups milk or half-and-half

3 cups finely chopped cooked potatoes
(1 cup potato water reserved)

Salt and freshly ground pepper, to taste

3 ounces crumbled blue cheese

Dash of paprika or 1 teaspoon
chopped parsley, to garnish

In a 3-quart pot, cook broccoli and onion in broth and reserved potato water. Add milk and potatoes and simmer. Do not let mixture boil. Season with salt and pepper. Add blue cheese just before serving, stirring until it melts. Garnish individual servings with a dash of paprika or a sprinkle of parsley.

Serves 6

A creamy, rich first course. For a smoother texture, whirl soup in a blender or food processor. Try serving in hollowed-out individual rounds of sourdough bread or a brioche. Brush the inside with olive oil and toast in a 350-degree oven for 10 minutes. Add soup and serve immediately.

Red Pepper Soup

2 large red bell peppers, roasted

2 cups chicken broth

1 cup peeled, seeded and
chopped tomatoes

1 tablespoon fresh lemon juice

1/2 cup diced raw potato

1 clove garlic, minced

1/4 cup heavy cream

Dash of hot pepper sauce

Salt and freshly ground pepper, to taste

Peel and chop peppers coarsely and place in a medium saucepan. Add broth, tomatoes, lemon juice, potato and garlic. Bring to a boil and reduce heat to a simmer. Cover and cook for 20 to 25 minutes or until potatoes are smooth.

Slightly cool mixture. Transfer half at a time to a blender or food processor and whirl until mixture is very smooth. Add heavy cream, hot pepper sauce, salt and pepper, and blend until smooth.

Return mixture to saucepan and stir in more broth if too thick. Heat through but do not boil.

Serves 6

Ladle into china bowls and garnish with fresh basil, Italian parsley or edible flowers.

4 tablespoons butter or margarine

2 cups chopped onion

4 teaspoons curry powder

2 Granny Smith apples,
peeled and chopped

4 cups chicken broth

3 pounds baked butternut squash,
peeled, seeded and diced

Salt and freshly ground pepper, to taste

Seasoned croutons, to garnish

Toasted squash seeds, to garnish

In a large saucepan, melt butter and add onion and curry powder. Sauté for 15 minutes or until onion is soft. Add apples and chicken broth. Cover and simmer for 25 minutes or until apples are tender. Add squash and puree mixture, about 2 cups at a time, in a blender. Return to saucepan and season with salt and pepper. Serve hot, topped with seasoned croutons and toasted squash seeds.

Serves 6–8

A spicy blend of squash and apples just meant for brisk fall evenings. Serve in hollowed-out squash halves decoratively carved on the sides.

4 medium zucchini, unpeeled,
quartered and sliced

3-1/2 cups chicken broth

1 bunch scallions, chopped

1 teaspoon salt

1 teaspoon freshly ground pepper

Fresh dill, to taste

2 (8-ounce) packages cream cheese,
softened to room temperature

1 cup sour cream with chives

Chopped chives or paprika, to garnish

In a saucepan, combine zucchini, chicken broth, scallions, salt, pepper and dill. Cook mixture until soft (approximately 20 to 30 minutes).

Combine cream cheese and sour cream in a blender until smooth. Stir in zucchini mixture, a portion at a time, until smooth. Chill overnight or until very cold. Garnish with chopped chives or paprika.

Serves 8

Serve in clear bowls or cups nestled in cracked ice. Garnish variations could include chopped fresh basil, chopped fresh dill or thin lemon slices.

To toast squash seeds, first remove seeds from squash with a spoon or fork tines. Remove and discard string and pulp. Spread on a baking sheet in a single layer and allow to dry for 1-1/2 to 2 hours. (At this point, coat seeds with vegetable oil and salt if desired.) Bake in a 350-degree oven for approximately 15 minutes until golden brown. Check seeds every 5 minutes and stir them around on the sheet to ensure even browning.

Cauliflower Stilton Velouté

1/2 pound cauliflower, cut into florets (approximately 2-1/2 cups)

1 onion, finely chopped

2 celery stalks, strings discarded, finely chopped

3 tablespoons unsalted butter

2 cups chicken broth

1 cup plus 2 tablespoons milk

Salt and white pepper, to taste

1 tablespoon cornstarch

4 ounces Stilton cheese, crumbled (about 1 cup)

1/2 cup light cream

In a saucepan, sauté cauliflower, onion, celery in butter over moderately low heat for 10 minutes, stirring occasionally. Add chicken broth and 1 cup milk, bringing liquid to a boil. Cover and simmer for 25 minutes or until cauliflower is very soft.

In a blender or food processor, puree mixture in batches until smooth. Return mixture to a clean pan and season with salt and pepper.

In a small bowl, dissolve cornstarch in remaining 2 tablespoons milk. Add mixture to cauliflower puree and bring to a boil. Simmer, whisking, for 2 minutes. Stir in cheese and cream and mix well. Simmer, whisking, for 1 minute or until Stilton is melted and soup is smooth.

Serves 2–4

An interesting and substantial soup with a sophisticated air. Top with homemade croutons and a sprinkling of celery leaves.

Put a top hat on your soup with the help of puff pastry.

Simply roll out puff pastry to 1/4-inch thickness. Cut pastry into circles slightly larger than the diameter of your serving bowls.

Refrigerate puff pastry circles for 30 minutes.

Heat soup slightly. Ladle soup into ovenproof serving bowls and cover with puff pastry circles. Use a fork to fold the puff pastry over the edge of the bowl. Refrigerate for 1 hour.

Beat an egg yolk with 2 teaspoons water and brush lightly over pastry.

Bake in oven according to package directions or in a preheated 425-degree oven for 12 to 15 minutes until puffed.

Nestle soups in folded napkins for a festive touch. This also helps avoid burns.

Vegetable Port Consommé

2 tomatoes
2 carrots, peeled
2 celery stalks
1 onion
8 cups water
1 sprig fresh thyme or 1 teaspoon dried
1 bay leaf
2 cloves garlic, unpeeled
1/2 teaspoon red pepper flakes
4 parsley sprigs
6 beef stock cubes
1/2 cup port
2 egg whites and crushed egg shells
Salt and freshly ground pepper, to taste
Parsley sprigs, to garnish

Matignon:

2 carrots, peeled
1 celery stalk
1/2 pound mushrooms
1/2 cup water
Pinch of salt

Coarsely chop tomatoes, carrots, celery and onion. Place in a large pot and add water, thyme, bay leaf, garlic, red pepper flakes, parsley and beef stock cubes. Cover and simmer over low heat for 2 hours.

Strain stock, discarding vegetables and return to pot. Heat to simmer and stir in egg whites and crushed shells. Simmer for 5 minutes. (Egg whites and shells clarify the stock.) Strain stock through cheesecloth. Consommé will be a beautiful clear golden color. Add port and check seasoning. Add salt and pepper to taste.

For matignon: Quarter carrots lengthwise. Remove cores. Finely dice carrots, celery and mushrooms. Cook carrots in salted water over medium heat for 3 minutes. Add celery and cook for 3 minutes more. (Add more water if necessary.) Add mushrooms and cook for 3 minutes longer. Drain vegetables and reserve.

To finish soup, divide matignon evenly between 6 ovenproof soup bowls or 8 ovenproof consommé cups. Ladle warm consommé over matignon, taking care not to overfill cups. Garnish with sprigs of parsley and serve.

Serves 6–8

*This beautiful soup is well worth the effort. As a serving variation, "float" dabs of **West Indian Cream** onto tops of consommé servings (this may cloud the soup slightly). Place cups or bowls under the broiler for 2 minutes or until nicely browned and puffed.*

West Indian Cream

2/3 cup mayonnaise • 1-1/2 teaspoons curry powder • 1/2 cup heavy cream

Mix mayonnaise with curry powder until thoroughly blended. Add cream a little at a time, stirring constantly.

Makes about 1 cup

Dilled Tomato Soup

2 medium onions, chopped

2 cloves garlic, crushed and peeled

1 tablespoon butter

2 pounds chopped fresh tomatoes or 1 (26-ounce) can crushed tomatoes with liquid

2 chicken or beef stock cubes

1-1/2 tablespoons chopped fresh dill or 1 teaspoon dried

2 tablespoons mayonnaise

2 cups buttermilk

Salt and freshly ground pepper, to taste

Chopped tomatoes, to garnish

1/4 cup chopped fresh parsley, to garnish

In a large saucepan, sauté onions and garlic in butter over medium heat until onions are translucent. Add tomatoes, stock cubes and dill. Cover and simmer mixture for 10 minutes. Remove from heat and cool. Puree in a blender until very smooth. Add mayonnaise. Blend until combined. Pour into a large bowl and stir in buttermilk. Season with salt and pepper. Chill for 2 hours or overnight.

To serve, ladle into chilled bowls and garnish with chopped tomatoes and parsley. Top with a grind of fresh pepper.

Serves 4

Creamy tomato flavor offers the perfect beginning for a light summer meal. Garnish variations could include a spoonful of lightly whipped, salted cream sprinkled with chopped chives.

Mushroom Feta Soup

1–2 cloves garlic, crushed

1 cup (2 sticks) unsalted butter or margarine

1 onion, diced

2 tablespoons chopped scallions

3/4 pound fresh mushrooms, sliced

1/2 cup flour

1 (12-ounce) can beer

2 cups chicken broth

1 cup milk

1 (12-ounce) can evaporated milk

1/2 pound feta cheese, crumbled

1/2 cup grated Parmesan cheese

1 teaspoon thyme

1 teaspoon basil, plus additional for garnish

1 tablespoon Worcestershire sauce

Salt and freshly ground pepper, to taste

Cayenne pepper, to taste

In a medium skillet, sauté garlic in 2 tablespoons butter. Add onion, scallions and mushrooms and cook until soft. Set aside.

In a large pot, melt remaining butter. Add flour and cook over low heat until golden brown, about 5 to 8 minutes. Whisk beer into mixture and cook until thick and smooth.

Combine chicken broth and milks and pour slowly into beer mixture. Cook until thick and smooth. Add vegetable mixture, 1/2 of feta cheese, Parmesan cheese, thyme, basil, Worcestershire, salt and peppers. Simmer for 10 to 15 minutes. Serve garnished with basil and remaining feta cheese.

Serves 8–10

Feta cheese, made from sheep's or goat's milk, is cured in brine. Rinse in cold water to "tone down" the salty taste.

Garden Green Gazpacho

3 large avocados, halved

1 tablespoon seeded and chopped
mild jalapeño pepper

1 tablespoon minced scallions

1 green bell pepper, seeded and
chopped

2 large cloves garlic, minced

1 celery stalk, chopped

1 cucumber, peeled and chopped

1 (28-ounce) can whole
tomatoes with liquid

1 cup chicken broth

5 tablespoons red wine vinegar

With a spoon, scoop out avocado flesh. Process in a blender with remaining ingredients for 1 minute. Chill for at least 3 hours before serving.

Serves 6

Serve this crisp-tasting summer soup with something hot off the grill. Pour into chilled glasses and garnish with chopped tomatoes, onions, olives or croutons.

Tomato Soup with Basil Cantaloupe Balls

6–8 medium tomatoes

1 large cucumber, peeled,
seeded and chopped

1/2 cup finely chopped onion

1 cup sour cream
or plain low-fat yogurt

1/2 teaspoon ground ginger

Salt and white pepper, to taste

4 teaspoons lemon juice

1 tablespoon grated lemon zest

1 large cantaloupe

2 tablespoons chopped fresh basil

Blanch tomatoes until skins start to crack. Remove and peel. Puree in a blender or food processor at high speed (should yield approximately 5 cups of puree). Puree cucumber and onion and add to tomato puree. Stir in sour cream and season with ginger, salt, pepper, lemon juice and lemon zest.

Halve cantaloupe, remove seeds and either use a melon baller or cut into chunks. Toss melon with chopped basil. Chill soup and melon separately for several hours.

To serve, either pour soup into chilled bowls and add a few pieces of melon to each, or place melon in the soup bowls first and ladle in soup at tableside.

Serves 6

For an eye-catching effect, dip the rims of each bowl in chopped fresh basil. These cantaloupe balls also make a pretty garnish for a dinner plate.

Minted Kiwi Cream

6–8 very ripe kiwis, peeled

12–15 small fresh mint leaves, to taste

1-1/2 cups plain yogurt

1-1/2 cups heavy cream

3 tablespoons fresh lemon juice

3/4 cup sugar

3/4 cup apricot nectar

Mint sprigs or mandarin orange segments, to garnish

Place kiwis and a few mint leaves in a blender. Puree, adding just a few more mint leaves at a time and tasting after each addition. Add yogurt, 1/2 cup cream, lemon juice, 1/2 cup sugar and apricot nectar. Blend until smooth. Pour into a large bowl.

In a small mixing bowl, whip remaining heavy cream to soft peaks, beating in remaining sugar. Fold into kiwi mixture and chill.

When ready to serve, pour into champagne glasses and garnish with mint sprigs or mandarin orange segments.

Serves 6–8

A beautiful pale green soup, sure to tame a summer's heat. Ripe kiwis will keep in the refrigerator up to 2 weeks.

Soup Garnishes

Garnishes can add both taste and visual appeal to the soups they enhance. Following are a few suggestions:

Apple slices or curls of peel ❧ *Avocado slices or puree* ❧ *Berries* ❧ *Capers* ❧ *Carrot strips or flowers* ❧ *Caviar* ❧ *Celery leaves or seeds* ❧ *Chopped fresh herbs* ❧ *Chopped scallions* ❧ *Chopped bell peppers* ❧ *Chopped radishes* ❧ *Croutons* ❧ *Crumbled or grated cheese* ❧ *Fennel seeds* ❧ *Kiwi slices* ❧ *Lemon or orange slices or peel* ❧ *Mushroom slices or tiny caps* ❧ *Pimiento strips* ❧ *Sliced or chopped hard-cooked egg* ❧ *Slivered or chopped nuts* ❧ *Sorbet* ❧ *Sour or whipped cream* ❧ *Tofu* ❧ *Whole or cracked peppercorns* ❧ *Yogurt*

Cool Blueberry Soup

1/2 cup frozen, unsweetened pineapple juice concentrate, undiluted

1/2 cup water

1 teaspoon fresh lemon juice

3 cups fresh or unsweetened frozen blueberries

Vanilla yogurt, to garnish

Mint leaf or orange zest, to garnish

Combine pineapple juice concentrate, water and lemon juice in a blender. Add 2 cups blueberries and pulse 4 to 5 times until coarsely chopped (pulsing rather than pureeing holds the beautiful colors of the berries). Add remaining blueberries and pulse. Chill.

When ready to serve, garnish with a dollop of vanilla yogurt and a mint leaf or orange zest.

Serves 4–6

A refreshingly smooth addition to any summer menu. Stir vanilla yogurt into soup for a creamy variation.

Indian Summer Soup

8 large Golden Delicious apples

2 cups apple juice

1/4 cup fresh lemon juice

1 tablespoon sugar (optional)

3 cinnamon sticks

2 teaspoons vanilla extract

1–2 teaspoons freshly grated nutmeg, plus additional to garnish

2 cups fresh orange juice

2 cups vanilla yogurt

1 cup half-and-half

3 tablespoons Triple Sec

Crème fraîche, to garnish

Grated tart red apple, unpeeled and tossed in lemon juice, to garnish

Quarter, core and peel apples. In a large saucepan, combine apples, apple juice, lemon juice, sugar, cinnamon sticks, vanilla and nutmeg. Cover and simmer over medium heat until apples are very tender (approximately 20 to 30 minutes). Let cool. Cover and refrigerate for 24 hours.

Remove cinnamon sticks. Puree apple mixture in a blender until smooth. Add orange juice, yogurt, half-and-half and Triple Sec. Garnish with crème fraîche, grated apple and ground nutmeg.

Serves 8

Must be started 24 hours in advance.

A luscious blend of fall flavors and perhaps a prelude to **Autumn River Salad**.

Strips of fruit peel become pliable enough to form after soaking in warm water. Shape into twists or curls, or tie into bows, for colorful natural accents.

Amaretto Peach Soup

1-1/2 pounds peaches, peeled, pitted and sliced

2 cups sour cream or plain low-fat yogurt

1 cup fresh orange juice

1 cup pineapple juice

1/2 cup Amaretto

2 tablespoons fresh lemon juice

Sugar, to taste (optional)

Mint leaf, to garnish

Raspberries, to garnish

Puree peaches in a food processor until smooth. Add sour cream, orange juice, pineapple juice, Amaretto and lemon juice and blend well. (May have to blend in batches.) Pass soup through a fine strainer or leave as is for a coarser texture. Add sugar and chill.

When ready to serve, garnish with mint leaves and raspberries.

Serves 8

A midsummer's dream, perfect for an elegant first course. Serve in chilled, flat glass bowls or ruby-red goblets, garnished with orange zest. Substitute dry sherry for the Amaretto, if you prefer.

Placecards

*U*sing *placecards and placecard holders needn't be limited to formal entertaining. Interesting options abound for lunches, brunches and dinner parties of any description:*

Painted chocolate molds   Kitschy salt and pepper shakers   Small pots of herbs or cacti   Little picture frames with Polaroids of guests   Small pumpkins or large mushrooms   Wooden Christmas ornaments   Lengths of wired ribbon   Tiny teacups and saucers   Miniature bottles of liqueur   Small bouquets of dried flowers or herbs   Personalized baked dough cutouts   Miniature watercolors reflecting the theme or menu   Tiny baskets filled with marbles   Little jars of assorted honeys and jams   Small brandy snifters floating miniature gardenias   Small calendars for New Year's parties   Colorful bicycle nameplates   Clusters of little pinecones   Assorted chessmen or game pieces   Old brooches and hat pins   Raffia packets of potpourri   Votive candles in colored glass   Jumbo pasta shells

PORK

Apricot-Honey Baked Ham, 150
Canadian Bacon with Ginger Pineapple Sauce, 149
Garlic Grilled Pork Tenderloin, 144
Honey-Roasted Sesame Pork, 145
Mustard-Ginger Pork Chops, 147
Pacific Rim Tenderloin, 146
Peppered Pork Chops with Madeira Glaze, 148
Pomander Pork, 147
Pork Tenderloin with Lime Cilantro Pesto, 144
Pork with Dijon Caper Sauce, 149
Spicy Apple Sausage Patties, 150

BEEF

Burgundy Shepherd's Pie, 157
Filet Marchand du Vin, 158
Herbed Meat Loaf with Cream Sauce, 153
Mesquite Grilled T-Bones, 152
Orange Fennel Brisket, 156
Pepper-Coated Stuffed Flank Steak, 151
Royal Beef Tenderloin, 154
Savory Steaks, 153
Smoky Brisket, 154
Spinach and Steak Pinwheels, 152
Teriyaki-Glazed Flank Steak, 151

VEAL

Arrowhead Veal Chops, 158
Veal Imperial, 159
Veal Roast with Cognac Sauce, 159

LAMB

Blue Lamb, 160
Butterflied Leg of Lamb, 162
Grilled Lamb Pita Pockets, 161
Lamb Brochettes, 163
Rack of Lamb Dijon, 163
Red Sun Lamb Shanks, 160
Stuffed Leg of Lamb, 162

MINI RECIPES

Flavored Mayonnaises, 155
Pear Chutney, 145
Wine-Soaked Apple Lemon Relish, 146

Meats

Pictured finishing touch:

ADDING

SPECIAL TOUCHES

TO THE TABLE, 161

SPECIAL TOPIC BOXES

CHUTNEY, 145

MAYONNAISE, 155

SETTING THE TABLE, 161

Pork Tenderloin with Lime Cilantro Pesto

1 (1-1/2-pound) pork tenderloin

1/2 cup grated jalapeño cheese

1/4 cup toasted pine nuts, to garnish

Marinade:

1/2 cup white wine

2 cloves garlic, minced

1 tablespoon olive oil

Pesto:

4 cloves garlic, minced

3 tablespoons minced fresh ginger

3/4 cup minced scallions (tops included)

3 tablespoons minced cilantro

1 tablespoon minced jalapeño pepper

6 tablespoons fresh lime juice

6 tablespoons olive oil

For marinade: Combine all marinade ingredients and set aside. Cut tenderloin lengthwise, almost in half, and lay out flat in a glass baking dish. Top with marinade, cover and refrigerate overnight.

For pesto: In a food processor or blender, combine garlic, ginger, scallions, cilantro, jalapeño, lime juice and olive oil and puree. Slowly add olive oil until mixture thickens.

Remove from marinade and spread half of pesto mixture over tenderloin. Sprinkle grated cheese over pesto. Reform tenderloin and tie with kitchen twine to secure. Spread remaining pesto over tenderloin and chill for several hours.

Preheat oven to 400 degrees. Place tenderloin on a rack and bake until firm (about 25 minutes). Remove from oven and cover to keep warm. Reserve all juices. Remove string and cut tenderloin into slices. Fan slices on a platter. Top with warm sauce and sprinkle with toasted pine nuts.

Serves 4–6

Must be marinated overnight.

A knockout dish with a glorious, garlicky aroma. The dark, rich colors get a pleasant spike from a bright "pepper flower" garnish. To make one, select a narrow pepper, snip off the tapered end and, using a knife or scissors, create "petals" by slitting the pepper several times from the cut end to within 1/2 inch of the stem.

Garlic Grilled Pork Tenderloin

2 (3/4-pound) pork tenderloins

Marinade:

2 tablespoons olive oil

1 tablespoon white wine vinegar

2 teaspoons chopped fresh rosemary

1/2 teaspoon salt

1/4 teaspoon freshly ground pepper

2 cloves garlic, minced

For marinade: Combine all marinade ingredients and stir well. Place tenderloins in a 9- by 13-inch dish and coat thoroughly with marinade. Cover and chill for 3 hours.

Grill tenderloins, covered, over hot coals for 30 to 45 minutes, turning once.

Serves 4–6

For a smoky flavor, place tenderloins on the side of the grill and smoke over hickory chips for 1 hour.

Honey-Roasted Sesame Pork

1 (3/4-pound) pork tenderloin

1/4 cup honey

1 cup sesame seeds, lightly toasted

Marinade:

1/4 cup soy sauce

2 cloves garlic, sliced

1 (2-inch) piece ginger, peeled and sliced thin

For marinade: Combine soy sauce, garlic and ginger in a dish just large enough to hold pork tenderloin. Add meat, cover and refrigerate for 1 hour, turning several times.

Drain tenderloin and pat dry. Spread honey on a plate and roll meat in it. Spread sesame seeds on another plate and roll honeyed tenderloin in them, coating all over.

Preheat oven to 400 degrees. In a roasting pan, bake pork tenderloin for 20 minutes or until no longer pink at the thickest part. Let meat stand for 5 minutes and slice on the diagonal to serve.

Serves 2–4

Sesame seeds add a delightful visual effect to this tenderloin. For a slightly stronger flavor, marinate longer than the recommended 1 hour.

Chutney

Chutney is a sweet-and-sour condiment made from fruit, vinegar, sugar and spices. A spicy, aromatic chutney can be a colorful finishing touch to a meat or poultry entree, a curry dish, plain or seasoned rice, chicken salad, potatoes or a cold meat tray. Sweeter versions make interesting bread spreads and are delicious served with cheese, such as Stilton, Gorgonzola or warm Brie. Try mixing small amounts of chutney into stuffings to spice them up and sharpen the flavor.

There are three basic types of chutney: **uncooked**, which make wonderful, relish-like dipping sauces or nice accompaniments; **freshly cooked,** made with fruits and vegetables; and **preserved.** All chutney should be stored in a cool, dark, dry place. Some varieties keep for many years and improve greatly in the aging process. Here's a sample to get you started:

Pear Chutney

1-1/2 cups fresh orange juice

1/2 cup cider vinegar

1/4 teaspoon cinnamon

1/4 teaspoon ground ginger

2 tablespoons slivered orange peel

4 pears, peeled, cored and chopped fine

1/3 cup dark raisins

1/3 cup golden raisins

2 teaspoons diced candied ginger

1/3 cup slivered almonds

1/4 cup sugar

1/3 cup finely packed light brown sugar

In a large saucepan, combine orange juice, vinegar, cinnamon, ground ginger, orange peel and pears and simmer for 10 minutes. Add remaining ingredients and simmer until mixture is tender and thick, about 45 minutes. Cool and serve.

Makes 3 cups

Pacific Rim Tenderloin

1 (2-pound) pork tenderloin

Marinade:

4 tablespoons soy sauce

2 tablespoons dry sherry

2 tablespoons firmly packed light brown sugar

2 tablespoons peanut oil

3 teaspoons honey

1 teaspoon garlic salt

1 teaspoon ground cinnamon

1 cup toasted peanuts, chopped

Sauce:

1/2 cup firmly packed light brown sugar

1/4 cup catsup

1/2 cup pineapple juice

1/3 cup cider vinegar

1/2 teaspoon garlic powder

2 tablespoons cornstarch

1/3 cup water

For marinade: Combine all ingredients and stir well. Pour into a large resealable plastic bag and add tenderloin. Seal and refrigerate for 8 hours, turning occasionally.

Remove tenderloin from marinade. Grill 6 inches from hot coals for 30 to 35 minutes, turning often. To serve, slice thinly and garnish with peanuts. Present with warm sauce.

For sauce: In a saucepan, combine all ingredients except cornstarch and water. Bring mixture to a boil. Mix cornstarch and water, then add to sauce and stir to thicken. Serve warm.

Serves 6

An attractive and easy entree. The sweet and sour sauce is easily doubled or tripled.

Wine-Soaked Apple Lemon Relish

3 thin-skinned lemons, washed well • 5 sweet, firm, red apples, washed, halved and cored • Light brown sugar • 1/2 cup dry white wine

Slice lemons very thin, discarding all seeds. Thinly slice apples to about twice the thickness of lemons.

In a straight-sided glass serving bowl, make a layer of lemon slices and sprinkle with brown sugar. Follow with a layer of apple slices and sprinkle with a little brown sugar. Continue layering in this manner until fruit is all used, ending with a layer of lemons. (Use brown sugar sparingly.) Pour wine over layered fruit. Cover with plastic wrap and chill for at least 4 hours. Add a little more wine just before serving with cold or warm roasted meat. Serves 10–12.

Pomander Pork

1 (5-pound) boneless pork loin

Marinade:

1/2 cup fresh lemon juice

1/2 cup soy sauce

1/2 cup red wine

1/2 teaspoon ground ginger

Sauce:

2/3 cup sugar

1 tablespoon cornstarch

1/2 teaspoon salt

20 whole cloves, tied in cheesecloth

1/2 teaspoon cinnamon

1 tablespoon grated orange zest

1 cup fresh orange juice

3 orange slices, halved (optional)

For marinade: Combine ingredients and pour over pork. Cover and refrigerate overnight, turning occasionally.

Remove pork from marinade. Bake in a 350-degree oven for 2-1/2 hours, basting often with marinade. Serve with orange sauce.

For sauce: In a saucepan, combine sugar, cornstarch, salt, cloves, cinnamon, orange zest and orange juice. Simmer over medium heat until thickened and clear. Remove cloves. Add orange slices, if desired. Cover and remove from heat.

Serves 6–8

Must be marinated overnight.

A tantalizing blend of spices and fruit to crown a festive holiday table. Substitute 8 pork chops, 1-inch thick or 2 (3/4-pound) pork tenderloins for pork loin.

Mustard-Ginger Pork Chops

4 thick pork chops

Marinade:

1/2 cup dry white wine

1/4 cup soy sauce

2 tablespoons vegetable oil

1/2 teaspoon ground ginger

1/2 teaspoon dry mustard

1 teaspoon sugar

For marinade: In a glass bowl or baking dish, combine all ingredients and pour mixture over pork chops. Cover and refrigerate for 2 hours or longer, turning several times.

Remove pork from marinade and reserve liquid. Grill pork chops for 15 minutes per side (or bake at 350 degrees for 8 to 10 minutes per side), basting often with reserved marinade. Bring remaining marinade to a boil and serve with the pork chops.

Serves 4–6

Great for people on the go or a quick weekend meal. Pair with Thai Zucchini.

Peppered Pork Chops with Madeira Glaze

6 pork chops, 1-inch thick

2 teaspoons peppercorns, coarsely ground

2 teaspoons thyme

1 teaspoon salt

2 teaspoons sugar

3 tablespoons olive oil

Glaze:

1 medium onion, finely chopped

2 medium carrots, thinly sliced

1 celery stalk, thinly sliced

2 cloves garlic, unpeeled

2 cups chicken broth

1 tablespoon tomato paste

1/8 cup dry Madeira

1 teaspoon cornstarch or arrowroot

1 tablespoon water

Combine pepper with thyme, salt and sugar. Rub mixture evenly into both sides of pork chops. Wrap in foil and refrigerate overnight.

In a large sauté pan, heat olive oil over high heat. Add chops and sauté until browned, about 2 minutes per side. As they are browned, place chops on baking sheets, cover tightly with plastic wrap and freeze for 25 minutes or refrigerate overnight.

For glaze: In the pan in which chops were browned, combine onions, carrots, celery and garlic and sauté over moderate heat until onions are softened but not browned, about 5 minutes. Add broth and tomato paste. Bring to a boil, reduce heat to medium-high and simmer, uncovered, for 30 minutes.

Strain broth through a fine-mesh sieve, pressing gently to extract all liquid; discard vegetables. Adjust broth by boiling off or adding water to equal 1 cup.

In a small saucepan, return broth to a boil and add Madeira. Combine cornstarch and water and whisk into broth, stirring constantly to prevent lumps, until sauce thickens (about 2 minutes). Remove from heat and cover tightly.

About 20 minutes before serving, preheat broiler. Place chops on baking sheets under broiler for about 8 minutes per side.

Heat reserved Madeira glaze until hot. Brush chops with glaze and serve. Pass any additional sauce.

Serves 6

Must be prepared in advance.

These juicy flavorful chops are the perfect choice for a special evening with friends. Serve with **Leek Timbales** *and* **Lemon Carrot Sheaves.**

🍂 *Wine vinegar is a natural tenderizer. An economical cut of meat can become quite tasty when marinated with it.*

🍂 *When stirring a sauce, stir in a constant, one-way motion. Changing directions will affect cooking and texture.*

🍂 *When a sauce curdles, remove pan from heat and plunge into a pan of cold water to stop the cooking process. Beat sauce vigorously or pour into a blender and process until smooth.*

Pork with Dijon Caper Sauce

6 center-cut or boneless pork chops

Sauce:

1 shallot, minced

2 teaspoons butter

2 cups heavy cream

3-1/2 tablespoons Dijon mustard

1/4 cup capers

For sauce: In a heavy saucepan, sauté shallot in butter until translucent. Pour in cream and bring mixture to a boil. Reduce heat to low and cook until cream thickens (about 10 minutes), stirring occasionally. Remove mixture from heat and whisk in mustard and capers.

On a broiling pan, bake pork chops or cutlets in a 500-degree oven for about 12 minutes. To serve, arrange pork chops on dinner plates and spoon warm sauce over meat.

Serves 6

Serve this tangy sauce with fish or veal as well.

Canadian Bacon with Ginger Pineapple Sauce

3 tablespoons butter

12 thick slices Canadian bacon

Pineapple slices, to garnish

Sauce:

2-1/2 cups chopped fresh pineapple

2 tablespoons chopped ginger

1/3 cup plus 1 tablespoon sugar

3 tablespoons fresh lemon juice

For sauce: Combine all ingredients in a food processor fitted with steel blade and process until combined. (Pineapple can be left chunky if desired.) Pour into a saucepan and boil over moderate heat until thickened (about 15 minutes). Let mixture cool, then refrigerate. (Sauce will keep up to 1 week.)

In a heavy skillet, melt butter. Heat Canadian bacon, cooking for 1 to 2 minutes per side. Remove from skillet and top each slice with 1 tablespoon ginger pineapple sauce (mixture will melt and form a glaze). Serve garnished with pineapple slices.

Serves 6

Ginger and pineapple lend this dish an unusual flavor. For a low-calorie version, cook Canadian bacon in just enough pineapple juice to cover the bottom of the skillet.

Apricot-Honey Baked Ham

1 (12-pound) smoked ham, partially boned

1/2 pound dried apricots

3 tablespoons Dijon mustard

2 tablespoons white wine vinegar

1/4 cup honey

1-1/2 cups water

2 (8-ounce) cans apricot nectar

1/4 cup melted apricot preserves

2 tablespoons melted butter

Preheat oven to 325 degrees. Place ham, fat-side up, on a rack in a roasting pan. With a sharp knife, cut semicircle pockets (1-inch deep) in rows. Continue until all fat is cut into pockets. Place apricots within, anchoring with toothpicks.

In a small bowl, combine mustard, vinegar and honey. Brush over ham and apricots. Pour 1-1/2 cups water into roasting pan and loosely cover with foil. Bake for 1 hour. Remove foil and continue baking, basting ham with apricot nectar and pan juices every 20 minutes until internal temperature reaches 140 degrees (about 2 hours).

Remove ham from oven and place on a carving board. Combine apricot preserves with melted butter and 2 tablespoon basting liquid. Brush ham with glaze, then let rest for 15 minutes before carving. Serve warm or at room temperature.

Serves 8–10

Celebrate spring's arrival with this spicy sweet ham. Serve with **Asparagus Flans** *and* **White Swan Rolls**.

Spicy Apple Sausage Patties

1/4 pound pork sausage

1/2 pound ground turkey

1 egg, lightly beaten

1/4 cup dried bread crumbs

1 clove garlic, minced

1/2 teaspoon ground ginger

1/4 teaspoon red pepper flakes

1/4 teaspoon savory

1/4 teaspoon thyme

1/3 cup shredded apple

1/2 teaspoon salt

3 tablespoons vegetable oil

In a large bowl, combine all ingredients except vegetable oil and mix thoroughly. Mixture can be held overnight.

Shape mixture into eight 2-1/2-inch patties. In a heavy skillet, heat oil. Brown patties on both sides and cook through (about 10 minutes). Drain and serve immediately.

Serves 8

Serve these versatile patties for a mid-week scrambled egg supper or for a weekend brunch buffet.

Teriyaki-Glazed Flank Steak

1-1/2 pounds flank steak

Glaze:

1/4 cup sesame seeds

2 cups soy sauce

3/4 cup sugar

1-1/2 tablespoons hot pepper sauce

3/4 teaspoon freshly ground pepper

1 tablespoon minced garlic

1 tablespoon minced ginger

1/4 cup sesame oil

1 tablespoon cornstarch

1/4 cup water

1 tablespoon firmly packed light brown sugar

1 tablespoon honey

For glaze: In a dry skillet, toast sesame seeds over medium heat until golden and nutty smelling. Transfer seeds to a saucepan and add soy sauce, sugar, pepper sauce, pepper, garlic and ginger. Stir in sesame oil and bring to a simmer. (Glaze may be prepared a day ahead.)

In a separate bowl, mix cornstarch, water and brown sugar until smooth. Stir into hot glaze and simmer until thickened. Stir in honey. Store covered in the refrigerator until ready to use.

Brush glaze over flank steak and grill, basting often.

Serves 6

Spicy grilled flank steak with an Asian twist. Marinate overnight for fuller flavor. If serving glaze on the side, be sure to bring to a boil first.

Pepper-Coated Stuffed Flank Steak

2 pounds flank steak

4 tablespoons olive oil

1/4 cup minced red onion

1 pound fresh mushrooms, chopped (combine 1–2 ounces shiitake or other fresh wild mushrooms and 14–15 ounces button mushrooms)

1 teaspoon salt

1 teaspoon chopped fresh rosemary

1 clove garlic, minced

1/4 cup dry bread crumbs

1 egg, beaten

1 teaspoon freshly ground pepper

Pierce both sides of steak with fork tines. Create pockets for stuffing by making crosswise slits in the center of the steak to within 1 inch of the sides.

In a large skillet, heat 2 tablespoons oil. Add onion and sauté until golden (about 1 minute). Add mushrooms, 1/2 teaspoon salt, rosemary and garlic. Sauté until all liquid is evaporated, about 8 minutes. Add bread crumbs and egg. Mix and cool.

Spoon mushroom mixture into steak pockets. Close openings with skewers or toothpicks. Brush both sides of steak with remaining 2 tablespoons oil. Sprinkle meat on both sides with pepper and remaining 1/2 teaspoon salt. Place steak over hot coals or in a broiler pan. Grill over coals or broil under a preheated broiler for about 4 minutes per side (for medium rare).

Serves 6

*Wild mushrooms, rosemary and garlic give this steak a luscious bouquet. Serve with **Polenta Pepper Soufflés**.*

Spinach and Steak Pinwheels

1-1/2 pounds flank steak or boneless top round steak

Salt and freshly ground pepper, to taste

2 tablespoons olive oil

1 medium onion, chopped

1 (10-ounce) package frozen chopped spinach, thawed and drained

1 teaspoon snipped fresh thyme

1 teaspoon paprika

3 cloves garlic, minced

1/4 cup grated Parmesan cheese

Score steak by making shallow diagonal cuts about 1/4-inch deep at 1-inch intervals across meat, forming a diamond pattern. Repeat on second side. With a meat mallet, working from the center to the edges, pound steak into a 12- by 8-inch rectangle. Sprinkle with salt and pepper.

In a skillet, heat oil and sauté onion until almost translucent. Add spinach, thyme, paprika and garlic. Toss and remove from heat.

Spread spinach mixture over meat and sprinkle with Parmesan cheese. Roll up, beginning with a short side. Secure meat loosely with kitchen string at 1-inch intervals, starting 1/2 inch from one end. Cut between string (about 2/3 way through) into eight 1-inch slices. Place meat on a broiler pan, cut-side down. Broil 3 inches from heat for 6 minutes. Turn and broil for 6 to 8 minutes more for medium doneness. Remove string and serve. (May also be prepared on the grill.)

Serves 8

A colorful, flavorful dish sure to please family and friends. For more tender meat, marinate flank steak overnight in 1/3 cup red wine, 2 to 3 tablespoons olive oil, salt and pepper to taste, 1 tablespoon fresh thyme and 2 cloves of garlic before preparing.

Mesquite Grilled T-Bones

8 T-bone steaks, 1-1/2-inches thick

2 to 2-1/2 teaspoons seasoned salt

1-1/2 cups beer

8 large cloves garlic, minced

Freshly ground pepper, to taste

Soak mesquite wood chips in water for 1 to 24 hours.

Trim fat around steaks to 1/4– 1/2-inch thick. Pierce steaks with a fork on each side. Sprinkle each side of meat evenly with salt, beer and garlic. Cover and let stand at room temperature for 1 hour.

Heat coals and place mesquite chips directly on hot coals. Grill steaks for 8 to 10 minutes per side or until desired degree of doneness. Continue basting with beer while cooking. Sprinkle with pepper and serve.

Serves 8

*A classic grilled steak with the slightly sweet flavor of mesquite. Serve with **South of the Border Potato Salad, Adobe Corn with Jalapeño Lime Butter** and mugs of frosty beer. What a way to spend a summer evening.*

2 eye of the round steaks,
3/4–1-inch thick

Marinade:

1/4 cup salsa

2 tablespoons chopped cilantro

2 tablespoons fresh lime juice

1 tablespoon oil

1 clove garlic, minced

1/4 teaspoon cumin

For marinade: In a shallow glass dish, combine all ingredients and pour over steaks. Cover and refrigerate for 6 to 24 hours.

Remove steaks from marinade and grill over medium-hot coals for about 12 minutes (for rare). If using a covered grill, reduce time by about 2 minutes.

Serves 2

Serve these sizzling steaks with Sesame Pasta Salad.

Herbed Meat Loaf with Cream Sauce

1 pound lean ground beef

1/2 pound ground veal

3/4 cup ground bread crumbs

1 egg

1/4 cup grated Parmesan cheese

1 tablespoon chopped capers

1 tablespoon chopped parsley

1/4 teaspoon freshly ground pepper

1 tablespoon olive oil

3 shallots or 1 small onion, minced

1/4 cup chopped fresh sage

1 teaspoon chopped sweet marjoram

1 teaspoon chopped fresh thyme

2 strips bacon

Sprigs of fresh sage, to garnish

Sauce:

1 tablespoon tomato paste

3/4 cup heavy cream

2 tablespoons chopped fresh sage

Preheat oven to 350 degrees. In a large bowl, combine beef, veal, bread crumbs, egg, Parmesan cheese, capers, parsley and pepper. Set aside.

In a heavy skillet, warm olive oil over medium heat. Add onion and sauté until translucent. Reduce heat and add sage, marjoram and thyme. Continue to cook for 2 to 3 minutes. Remove from heat and allow to cool.

Add cooled herb mixture to meat mixture and combine well. Form into a loaf and set on a rack or use a well-greased 9- by 5-inch loaf pan. Top loaf with bacon strips and bake for 45 minutes until browned and firm to the touch. Allow loaf to cool for 10 minutes before serving. Reserve pan drippings.

For sauce: In a small saucepan, warm 3 tablespoons reserved pan drippings over high heat. Whisk in tomato paste and allow mixture to boil. Whisk in cream and reduce heat to low. Allow mixture to simmer, stirring regularly until reduced and thickened, for about 10 minutes. Whisk in sage.

Remove bacon strips, slice meat loaf and place on serving plates. Spoon sauce over slices and garnish with sprigs of sage.

Serves 8

Capers and sage combine to give this meatloaf a pungent aroma. Served with a heavenly cream sauce, it offers a beautiful and flavorful dish.

Smoky Brisket

1 (5–6 pound) beef brisket

1 teaspoon celery salt

1 tablespoon onion salt

2 cloves garlic, minced

3 ounces liquid smoke

Salt and freshly ground pepper, to taste

2 teaspoons Worcestershire sauce

Sauce:

1/2 medium onion, finely chopped

1 cup tomato puree

3/4 cup water

3 tablespoons cider vinegar

2 tablespoons Worcestershire sauce

1 teaspoon salt

1 teaspoon paprika

1 teaspoon chili powder

1/2 teaspoon freshly ground pepper

1/4 teaspoon cinnamon

Dash of ground cloves

Sprinkle brisket generously with celery salt, onion salt and garlic. Pour liquid smoke over brisket, cover and refrigerate overnight.

Pour off all but 2 tablespoons of liquid. Sprinkle meat with salt, pepper and Worcestershire sauce. Cover and bake for 3-1/2 to 4 hours at 275 degrees.

For sauce: In a medium saucepan, combine all ingredients and bring to a boil. Reduce heat and simmer until mixture thickens. Set aside.

Remove brisket from oven and top with sauce. Bake for 1 hour more. Remove from sauce and let cool for 2 hours before slicing. Slip back into a warm oven after slicing, if desired, and serve topped with warm sauce.

Serves 8–10

Serve this tender smoky beef with *Ruby Cole Slaw*.

Royal Beef Tenderloin

1 to 1-1/2 pounds beef tenderloin

1/2 cup dry red wine

2 tablespoons cider vinegar

1 tablespoon minced garlic

2 shallots, peeled and minced

1 tablespoon Dijon mustard

1 teaspoon freshly ground pepper

1/4 teaspoon dried thyme leaves

1/4 cup chopped parsley

1 tablespoon Worcestershire sauce

1/4 cup soy sauce

1/2 cup olive oil

In a food processor, combine wine, vinegar, garlic, shallots, mustard, pepper, thyme and parsley. Process for 1 minute. Add Worcestershire sauce, soy sauce and olive oil and process for 1 minute more. Reserve 1/2 cup to baste beef while grilling and pour remainder into a shallow glass dish. Add tenderloin and coat completely. Cover with plastic wrap and let stand for at least 1 hour.

Grill tenderloin, basting and turning often, until internal temperature reaches 145 degrees (for rare), then serve.

Serves 6–8

Combine this hearty tenderloin with **Parmesan Bread Pudding** and **Chinese Fried Asparagus**.

Store-bought versions of mayonnaise abound, but the taste of homemade mayonnaise is far superior—and it's surprisingly easy to make.

For best results, begin with ingredients at room temperature. Use patience when adding oil— the slower, the better. (Egg yolks may only absorb 3/4 cup oil.)

Start with a basic recipe, then experiment with different flavorings, such as pestos, green chilies, pink peppercorns, citrus juice and zest, garlic, mustard, horseradish, dill, tomato puree, tarragon, chives, shallots, capers, watercress—let your imagination wander. Homemade mayonnaise may be refrigerated for up to 1 week in a covered jar.

Basic Mayonnaise

1 egg yolk

1 teaspoon dry mustard

1 teaspoon sugar

1/4 teaspoon salt

Dash of cayenne pepper

2 tablespoons fresh lemon juice

1 cup vegetable oil

In a small bowl, beat egg yolk, mustard, sugar, salt, cayenne pepper and 1 tablespoon of lemon juice at medium speed until blended. Continue beating, adding oil drop by drop. As mixture thickens, increase rate of addition. Slowly stir in remaining lemon juice. Beat thoroughly. Chill.

Makes about 1-1/2 cups

Dijon Mayonnaise

1 egg

1 teaspoon fresh lemon juice

1 teaspoon red wine vinegar

1 teaspoon Dijon mustard

1 teaspoon salt

Freshly ground pepper, to taste

1-1/2 cups oil (preferably safflower with 3 tablespoons olive oil)

In a food processor or blender, combine egg, lemon juice, vinegar, mustard, salt, pepper and 3 tablespoons oil and mix for 5 seconds. With machine running, begin adding remaining oil in a thin, steady stream until mayonnaise thickens. Taste and adjust seasonings.

Makes about 1-3/4 cups

Avocado Mayonnaise

1 small avocado

1/2 cup mayonnaise

Dash of cayenne pepper

Juice of 1/2 lemon

Remove skin and seed from avocado, then cut flesh into chunks. In a blender or food processor, combine all ingredients. Refrigerate before serving.

Makes about 1 cup

Green Chili Mayonnaise

2 egg yolks, room temperature

1 tablespoon fresh lime juice

1 tablespoon chopped scallions

1-1/2 cups vegetable oil

1/2 teaspoon salt

Pinch of freshly ground pepper

2 tablespoons chopped green chilies

In a food processor or blender, mix yolks and lime juice. Blend in scallions. With machine running, add oil in a slow, steady stream, processing until mayonnaise is smooth and thick. Mix in salt and pepper. Transfer to a bowl and stir in chilies. Cover and refrigerate.

Makes about 2 cups

Lemon Mayonnaise

1/4 cup fresh lemon juice

1-1/2 cups mayonnaise

Slowly add 1/4 cup lemon juice to mayonnaise. Excellent in chicken and seafood salads.

Makes 1-3/4 cups

Orange Fennel Brisket

4–6 pounds first-cut brisket
or rump roast

1 tablespoon safflower or corn oil

1/2 cup oil-packed sun-dried tomatoes,
drained, patted dry and cut into strips

3 tablespoons capers

6 tablespoons orange marmalade

2 tablespoons fennel seeds

3/4 cup dry red wine

3/4 cup beef broth

1 pound baby carrots

1-1/2 tablespoons grated orange zest

Cut slits 1/4 inch deep and 1 inch apart in top of brisket. In a small bowl, combine oil, tomatoes, 2 tablespoons capers, orange marmalade and 1 tablespoon fennel seeds. Spread mixture over brisket, pressing into slits. Add wine and broth. Cover and refrigerate overnight.

Preheat oven to 350 degrees. Place brisket in a roasting pan and bake for 1 hour, basting regularly. Add baby carrots to pan, arranging around brisket. Cover and roast, basting regularly, until done. (Total roasting time should be about 30 minutes per pound.) Add water to basting liquid if necessary.

Transfer meat to a carving board. Allow to rest at least 20 minutes before carving.

Pour pan juices into a small saucepan. Add additional broth to make 2 cups. Stir in orange zest and remaining capers and fennel seeds and simmer for 4 minutes. (If a thicker sauce is desired, mix 1 tablespoon cornstarch with 2 tablespoons cold water. Whisk into saucepan and bring mixture back to a simmer for 1 minute.)

Slice brisket crosswise on the diagonal into 1/2-inch slices. Top with sauce and tomatoes and serve with baby carrots.

Serves 8–10

Must be marinated overnight.

A cosmopolitan twist to a basic cut of meat.

Remember that cooking time on the grill is affected by many variables, including the temperature of the food (straight from the refrigerator or at room temperature), the temperature of the coals and the outside temperature. Timing will also be affected by the size and thickness of the meat, and whether (and what kind) a marinade was used. Additionally, the distance between the coals and the rack is a factor. Keeping these elements in mind, use cooking times given in recipes as guidelines only.

When cooking meat, add salt toward the end, as salt tends to take moisture out of meat.

2 pounds sirloin steak, trimmed and cut into 1-inch pieces

1/4 cup red wine vinegar

2-1/4 cups Burgundy

5 tablespoons unsalted butter

1 tablespoon vegetable oil

1/4 cup cognac

2 tablespoons flour

1 teaspoon thyme

1 teaspoon freshly ground pepper

2 cloves garlic, minced

1 bay leaf

3 large carrots, peeled and sliced

1 cup frozen pearl onions

1/2 pound small mushrooms

1 cup peas

1/2 tablespoon melted butter

1 teaspoon nutmeg

Topping:

2-1/2 pounds baking potatoes

1/2 teaspoon salt

4 tablespoons melted unsalted butter

2 egg yolks

1/3 cup milk

1 teaspoon nutmeg

Place steak in a shallow baking pan and top with vinegar and 1/4 cup Burgundy. Marinate for at least 2 hours at room temperature.

Remove steak from liquid and pat dry. In a heavy pan, melt 2 tablespoons butter in oil over high heat. Add meat and sauté, turning constantly, until browned on all sides (about 5 minutes). Transfer to a plate and set aside.

Add cognac to pan and deglaze by igniting. Add remaining butter and melt. Add flour and heat for 2 minutes, stirring constantly. Whisk in remaining Burgundy. Bring mixture to a boil and scrape pan. Add meat, thyme, pepper, garlic and bay leaf to pan and simmer over low heat for 30 minutes. Add carrots and onions and continue cooking for another 30 minutes.

In a sauté pan, melt remaining 2 tablespoons butter over medium heat. Sauté mushrooms until they release their liquid and are browned (about 5 to 7 minutes). Add peas to pan.

For topping: Clean, peel and cut potatoes into 1/2-inch slices. In a large pot, boil potatoes until tender, about 10 minutes. Mash potatoes. Beat in salt, melted butter, egg yolks and milk. Set aside.

Transfer beef mixture to a 1-1/2-quart baking dish and remove bay leaf. Spread potato topping over meat. Drizzle melted butter over the top and dust with nutmeg. Bake in a 350-degree oven for 15 to 20 minutes. If desired, brown potatoes by running under the broiler for 2 minutes.

Serves 8–10

*Take the chill off a winter's night with this robust, one-dish meal. Finish with **Apple Pie Cake with Rum Butter Sauce**.*

Filet Marchand du Vin

3 pounds beef tenderloin

1 ounce Scotch

1 ounce Drambuie

6–8 thick baguette slices

6–8 mushroom caps, sautéed

Sauce:

1/2 cup beef broth

1 cup red wine

2 shallots, chopped

2 cloves garlic, crushed

2 sprigs fresh thyme or
1/2 teaspoon dried

1/3 cup heavy cream

4–8 tablespoons unsalted butter,
cut into small pieces

Salt and freshly ground pepper, to taste

For sauce: In a medium saucepan, combine beef broth, wine, shallots, garlic and thyme. Over high heat, reduce mixture to 1/2 cup. Add cream and reduce heat to medium. Continue to cook until sauce reduces and thickens.

Strain sauce and return to low heat. Whisk in 4 tablespoons butter, 1 piece at a time. Add salt and pepper to taste. Whisk in additional butter, if desired.

Preheat oven to 550 degrees. Place tenderloin on a broiler pan, tucking tapered end under. Combine Scotch and Drambuie. Baste tenderloin with liquor mixture and bake for 15 minutes. Lower temperature to 325 degrees, baste again and cook for 10 minutes per pound, basting every 10 minutes. (At this rate, ends will be well done and middle will be rare.)

To serve, slice tenderloin and serve on baguette slices topped with marchand du vin sauce. Top meat with additional sauce and a mushroom cap.

Serves 8–10

Pull out all the stops and make this entree the centerpiece for an elegant evening. Use a hearty, full-bodied red wine to give the sauce a refined taste and color. Because the flavor of the sauce is largely dependent on the wine, select a good one.

Arrowhead Veal Chops

4 thick veal chops

3–5 tablespoons butter or olive oil

1 (10-1/2-ounce) can tomato puree

1 cup dry white wine

1 teaspoon salt

1/4 teaspoon freshly ground pepper

1/2 cup finely chopped parsley

2–3 cloves garlic, crushed

1 tablespoon grated lemon zest

Cooked brown rice

Pine nuts or slivered
almonds, to garnish

In a large skillet, brown meat in oil (add more oil if necessary). Combine tomato puree, wine, salt and pepper and pour over meat. Cover and simmer for 55 to 75 minutes, until tender.

Just before serving, combine parsley, garlic and lemon zest and spoon over chops. Cover and simmer for 10 minutes on low heat. Serve over brown rice, topped with pine nuts or slivered almonds.

Serves 4

A cinch to prepare. Preface with tossed greens in **Hazelnut Cognac Dressing**.

Veal Imperial

1/4 cup (1/2 stick) butter

2-1/2 pounds veal, cut into
1-1/2-inch cubes

3/4 cup finely chopped onion

2 tablespoons instant
beef bouillon granules

1-1/2 cups boiling water

1/2 cup dry white wine

1 tablespoon paprika

1 teaspoon fresh lemon juice

1/8 teaspoon thyme

1/2 cup sour cream

2 tablespoons sherry

In a large skillet, melt butter and brown veal. Add onion and cook until tender.

In a bowl, dissolve bouillon in boiling water. Stir in white wine, paprika, lemon juice and thyme. Pour into skillet over veal and onions. Cover and simmer over low heat for 1-1/2 hours or until meat is tender. Stir in sour cream and sherry just before serving.

Serves 4–5

Serve this creamy Old World dish over a bed of couscous or orzo. Garnish the platter with sprigs of fresh thyme.

Veal Roast
with Cognac Sauce

1 (3-1/2 pound) veal rump roast

1 cup dry white wine

6 cloves garlic

1 teaspoon salt

2 teaspoons freshly ground pepper

1/4 cup cognac

1/4 cup olive oil

4 tablespoons thyme

Sauce:

4 cups veal stock or 2 cups beef
or chicken broth

1 tablespoon tomato paste

2 tablespoons cornstarch

1/4 cup water

1/4 cup cognac

1 tablespoon thyme

4 tablespoons unsalted butter

Preheat oven to 350 degrees. In a food processor or blender, combine garlic cloves with cognac, olive oil, thyme, salt and pepper. Rub veal roast with cognac mixture and place in a roasting pan.

Bake roast, basting every 10 to 15 minutes by pouring a few tablespoons of wine over meat and brushing with pan juices. Roast until internal temperature reaches 150 degrees (about 1-1/2 hours). Remove from oven and allow to cool 20 minutes before slicing.

For sauce: In a medium saucepan, boil stock for 15 minutes to reduce to 2 cups. Whisk in tomato paste. Mix cornstarch in 1/4 cup water and whisk into paste. Reduce heat to medium and allow sauce to simmer for 5 minutes to thicken. Whisk in cognac and thyme. Remove saucepan from heat and whisk in butter, 1 tablespoon at a time.

Slice veal roast. Fan slices on serving plates and spoon on a small amount of sauce. Pass remaining sauce.

Serves 8

An easy entree that makes an elegant impression. The sophisticated sauce beautifully complements the full-flavored roast.

Red Sun Lamb Shanks

6 lamb shanks
(about 5-1/2 pounds total)

2 cups water

1/4 cup soy sauce

1/3 cup dry sherry

1/4 cup minced fresh ginger

3 tablespoons sugar

3 scallions, chopped

2 cloves garlic, minced

1 tablespoon cornstarch

2 tablespoons water

6 cups hot cooked noodles

Chopped parsley, to garnish

In a 9- by 13-inch baking dish, place lamb shanks in a single layer and bake uncovered at 400 degrees until browned (about 35 minutes). Turn shanks over and add water, soy sauce, sherry, ginger, sugar, scallions and garlic. Cover tightly with foil, reduce heat to 300 degrees and bake until meat is so tender it pulls apart easily (about 2 to 2-1/2 hours). Transfer shanks to a serving platter and keep warm.

Skim fat from cooking broth and pour broth into a measuring cup. If needed, add water to make 1-1/2 cups. Set baking pan with broth over high heat and bring to boiling. If there is more than 1-1/2 cups, boil to reduce.

In a small bowl, mix cornstarch with water. With a wire whisk, stir enough of cornstarch mixture into boiling broth to thicken broth to desired consistency. Pour into a sauce bowl.

To serve, arrange noodles in a ring around lamb shanks and sprinkle with parsley. Pour sauce over all and serve.

Serves 6

For an interesting buffet presentation, mound pasta in the center of a platter, surrounded by lamb shanks arranged in a spoke pattern. Present sauce in a hollowed-out head of cabbage.

Blue Lamb

2 loin lamb chops, 1-1/2-inches thick

1 ounce blue cheese

2 tablespoons Worcestershire sauce

Preheat broiler. Trim fat from lamb chops, then make a deep slit in the "fat" side of each to make a pocket. Divide blue cheese in half and stuff each pocket. Press to close pockets. Sprinkle one side of each chop with 1/2 teaspoon Worcestershire.

Place chops on a broiler pan and broil for 7 minutes. Turn and sprinkle with remaining Worcestershire and cook for 7 more minutes or until pink.

Serves 2

A romantic dinner can be a snap with these bold-flavored lamb chops.

Grilled Lamb Pita Pockets

2 pounds boneless leg of lamb, trimmed and cut into 1-inch cubes

2/3 cup fresh lemon juice

1/4 cup olive oil

2 tablespoons soy sauce

1 small onion, minced

1/2 teaspoon freshly ground pepper

2 tablespoons melted butter

1 tablespoon plain yogurt, room temperature

1/2 teaspoon cumin

Dash of salt

6 rounds pita bread, warmed

1/2 cup chopped scallions

1 cup chopped fresh tomatoes

2 tablespoons chopped fresh mint

In a bowl, whisk together lemon juice, olive oil and soy sauce until blended. Stir in onion and pepper. Add lamb and toss to coat. Cover and refrigerate for several hours or overnight, stirring occasionally.

Bring lamb to room temperature 1 hour before grilling. Thread cubes onto 6 metal skewers and set aside. In a small bowl, whisk together melted butter, yogurt, cumin and salt. Grill meat 4 to 6 inches away from the fire, turning occasionally and basting with yogurt mixture 2 to 3 times while cooking to desired doneness (best when rare).

Tuck lamb into warmed pitas and sprinkle in scallions, tomato and mint. Serve remaining yogurt sauce on the side.

Serves 4

Excellent for summer lunches or evening picnics. Serve these colorful sandwiches with **Creamed Zucchini Soup.**

Setting the Table

Setting the table means more than just counting out the plates and flatware—it's also setting the scene.

Tablecloths—Try using granny quilts, beach towels, gossamer netting, bold fabric remnants or pretty floral sheets. Kraft paper just tosses away after an enthusiastic lobster-eating crowd and will keep little ones busy with markers until dinner or dessert. **Napkins**—Try pretty old handkerchiefs, bright bandannas, painted cotton squares, or rolls of paper towels on stands for pizza or "peel your own" shrimp suppers. **Table tops**—Try a scattering of buttons, shiny pennies, dried legumes or fall leaves. Tendrils of wired ribbon or leafy ivy arc beautifully over each plate, or you can create circlets of herbs or grapevines.

Butterflied Leg of Lamb

1 (4–5 pound) leg of lamb

2 cloves garlic, minced

1/4 cup grated onion

1 teaspoon salt

1 teaspoon fine herbes

1/2 teaspoon freshly ground pepper

1/2 teaspoon thyme

1/2 cup vegetable oil

1/2 cup fresh lemon juice

Have butcher bone leg of lamb and slit lengthwise. Spread flat and trim off excess fat.

In a large dish, combine remaining ingredients. Cover and marinate meat in this mixture for at least 1 hour or overnight, turning occasionally. Remove meat and reserve marinade.

Insert 2 skewers at right angles through meat. Grill for 20 minutes per side, basting often with reserved marinade. Check for doneness in the thickest part of the meat. To serve, carve meat across the grain into thin slices.

Serves 6–8

This lamb also may be broiled instead of grilled. Place meat on a broiler pan 3 inches from heat for 8 minutes per side, brushing once or twice with reserved marinade. Reduce heat to 325 degrees and roast meat for 50 to 55 minutes or until desired doneness, basting occasionally.

Stuffed Leg of Lamb

1 (7–8-pound) leg of lamb

3 tablespoons plus 1/4 cup olive oil

1 green bell pepper, chopped

4 medium onions, chopped

2 bunches leeks, trimmed and sliced

1/2 cup pitted Greek olives, chopped

2 cups seasoned dry bread crumbs

Salt and freshly ground pepper, to taste

2 cloves garlic, crushed

Juice of 2 lemons

Have butcher bone leg of lamb and leave shank in place to give meat shape.

In a skillet, heat 3 tablespoons olive oil and sauté green pepper, onions and leeks until wilted. Stir in olives and bread crumbs. Remove from heat and set aside.

Sprinkle lamb inside and out with salt and pepper. Spoon 1/3 of green pepper mixture into lamb. Wrap closely in foil or plastic wrap and freeze. Spoon remaining stuffing into a 1-quart baking dish and cover with foil and freeze.

When ready to cook, unwrap lamb and place in a shallow foil-lined baking pan. Combine garlic, lemon juice and 1/4 cup olive oil to brush over lamb every 30 minutes while roasting. Roast in a 350-degree oven for 2-1/2 hours

or until meat thermometer registers 150 degrees. Heat covered stuffing baking dish in the oven with lamb during the last hour of cooking.

Serves 8

Create the ambience of relaxed elegance with this savory stuffed lamb. Serve with a full-bodied Merlot or Zinfandel wine and a bit of fruit and let the conversation flow.

Lamb and stuffing will hold together better when frozen before roasting. If prepared unfrozen, reduce roasting time to 1-1/2 hours.

Lamb Brochettes

2 pounds (leg or shoulder cut) lamb,
cut into 1-1/2-inch cubes

Marinade:

1 onion, minced

1/2 teaspoon Worcestershire

1/2 cup red wine

1/4 cup fresh lemon juice

1/4 cup olive oil

2 cloves garlic, minced

Freshly ground pepper, to taste

For marinade: In a glass bowl, combine all ingredients. Cover and refrigerate lamb for several hours or overnight, stirring occasionally.

Thread lamb onto skewers and brush with marinade. Grill 3 inches from heat for about 15 minutes, basting and turning several times. Center of lamb should be pink when done. Remove from skewers and serve.

Serves 6

*Offer the brochettes with **Cold Herbed Garbanzo Beans** and warm pitas. Add pretty peppers, lemon halves and small whole onions to skewers for additional color and flavor.*

Rack of Lamb Dijon

1 (8-rib) rack of lamb (about 2 pounds)

1/4 cup Dijon mustard

2 slices day-old white bread

1/2 teaspoon thyme, crumbled

1/4 teaspoon rosemary, crumbled

1/4 teaspoon freshly ground pepper

2 tablespoons minced fresh parsley

Trim fat layer on lamb to 1/4 inch. Place lamb, fat-side down, in a large skillet over high heat. As fat begins to render, reduce heat to medium. Brown lamb well on all sides, about 10 minutes. Meat should still be very rare. Remove from pan and cool slightly. Spread mustard evenly over fat side of lamb.

Tear bread into small pieces and rub through a course sieve. In a small bowl, combine bread crumbs, thyme, rosemary, pepper and parsley and toss. Pat crumb mixture firmly onto mustard-coated lamb.

Arrange lamb, bone-side down, in a roasting dish and place in the center of a 500-degree oven. Roast until a meat thermometer inserted into the thickest part of the meat registers 130 degrees for

rare (about 15 to 20 minutes) or 150 degrees for medium (about 25 to 30 minutes). Let meat cool for 5 minutes before serving.

Serves 4–6

The mustardy, herbed crust lends a rich taste to this lamb. For ease of carving, have the butcher trim all meat and fat from the top 1-1/2 inches of rib bones.

GRILLED CHICKEN

Brochettes of Chicken and Sage, 167
Charcoaled Lemon-Lime Chicken, 172
Chicken in Black Bean Pecan Sauce, 173
Chicken with Red Pepper Sauce, 171
Fruit-Glazed Chicken, 167
Grilled Hedaki Chicken Sandwich, 181
Lotus Chicken, 168
Pesto Chicken with Basil Cream, 166
Saffron Chicken and Vegetables, 174
Taos Tequila Chicken, 180

BAKED CHICKEN

Baja Lasagna, 175
Chicken and Onion Quesadillas, 176
Chicken in Madeira Cream Sauce, 179
Lemon Chicken Turnovers, 181
Pink Peppercorn Chicken, 175
Reggae Chicken, 170

CHILLED CHICKEN

Chilled Chicken Spiral with Watercress Puree, 169
Dynasty Chicken, 172

STIR-FRIED, SAUTÉED CHICKEN

Chicken Medley Stir-Fry, 168
Feta Chicken on Couscous, 170
Ginger-Lime Chicken, 177
Orange Chicken with Acorn Squash, 178
Peppered Chicken with Artichoke Hearts, 176
Poulet Dijon, 179

TURKEY

Curried Turkey Breast, 184
Grilled Turkey Breast with Herb Butter, 183

GAME

Duck with Dried Cherries and Peppercorns, 185
Garlic Herbed Hens, 183
Pheasant au Vin, 184
Stuffed Cranberry-Pepper Game Hens, 182

MINI RECIPES

Caramelized Onions, 180
Tomatillo and Red Pepper Sauce, 180

Poultry

Pictured finishing touch:

SERVING

FLAVORED BUTTERS

IN TORTILLA CONES, 174

SPECIAL TOPIC BOXES

CENTER OF ATTENTION, 185

MAKING SUN-DRIED TOMATOES, 171

8 boneless, skinless chicken breast halves

8 (1-ounce) slices prosciutto or ham

1/2 cup pesto

4 tablespoons lemon juice

1/4 cup olive oil

3 cloves garlic, minced

Freshly ground pepper, to taste

Pesto:

1 cup tightly packed fresh basil

2 cloves garlic

1/2 cup toasted pine nuts

1/4 teaspoon freshly ground pepper

1 cup freshly grated Parmesan or Romano cheese

1/4 cup olive oil

Basil cream:

1/4 cup chopped shallots

2 tablespoons butter

1/3 cup dry white wine

1-1/2 cups heavy cream

1/4 cup oil-packed sun-dried tomatoes, halved and patted dry

1/4 cup shredded fresh basil

2 tablespoons lemon juice

1/2–1 tablespoon cornstarch

1 tablespoon water

For pesto: Remove stems from basil and wash leaves thoroughly. In a food processor, blend basil, garlic, pine nuts, pepper and Parmesan cheese until smooth. With processor running, add oil through the food chute in a slow steady stream until combined. Set aside.

Place each piece of chicken between 2 sheets of waxed paper and pound to 1/4-inch thick. Place 1 slice prosciutto and 1 tablespoon pesto in the center of each breast and spread across the whole piece. Roll breast up from the small end and secure with a wooden pick. Drizzle with 3 tablespoons lemon juice. Place in a covered dish and refrigerate overnight.

For basil cream: Sauté shallots in butter until translucent. Add wine and bring to a boil. Cook for 2 minutes or until liquid is reduced to about 1/4 cup. Add cream and return to a boil. Cook for 8 to 10 minutes or until sauce is reduced to approximately 1 cup. Whisking constantly, add tomatoes and cook for 2 minutes. Whisk in basil and lemon juice and cook until heated. If a thicker sauce is desired, combine cornstarch with water and stir into the cream mixture while boiling.

Let chicken stand at room temperature for 30 minutes before grilling. Combine olive oil, garlic, 1 tablespoon lemon juice and pepper. Grill chicken over medium coals for 15 to 20 minutes or until

done, turning and brushing occasionally with olive oil mixture. Serve with basil cream, garnished with fresh basil if desired.

Serves 8

Must be marinated overnight.

This chicken also may be baked in a 350-degree oven for 20 to 30 minutes. Coat first with olive oil, garlic and pepper and cover with foil before baking. For an eye-catching effect, slice breast halves into 5 or 6 pieces and fan onto a bed of pasta.

Fruit-Glazed Chicken

2 (3-1/2-pound) frying chickens, skinned and quartered or cut into pieces

1/2 teaspoon salt, or to taste

2 tablespoons savory, to garnish

Glaze:

1/3 cup apricot preserves

2/3 cup orange marmalade

1 cup Dijon mustard

1/4 cup honey

1 tablespoon curry powder, or to taste

2 tablespoons fresh lemon juice

For glaze: In a small heavy saucepan, simmer apricot preserves, orange marmalade, Dijon mustard, honey, curry powder and lemon juice over low heat for 5 minutes. Stir constantly. Cool.

Place chicken in a baking dish and brush completely with 1/2 the glaze. Let stand at room temperature for 1 hour. Sprinkle with salt.

Place dark meat on the grill over medium heat and close grill lid. Cook for 7 minutes, then turn and arrange at the edge of the grill rack. Place white meat pieces on grill, meat-side down, then cover and cook for 7 minutes. Brush all pieces with glaze. (If glaze starts to burn, move chicken to outside edge of grill.) Continue cooking until brown and cooked through, turning pieces occasionally (approximately every 10 to 12 minutes).

To serve, arrange chicken on a platter, brush with remaining glaze (reserving some to serve as a sauce) and garnish with dried savory.

Serves 6–8

An aromatic blend of jams and curry give this grilled chicken a special rich flavor.

Brochettes of Chicken and Sage

1 pound sweet Italian sausage, cut into 2-inch pieces

4 boneless, skinless chicken breast halves

16 whole sage leaves

Marinade:

1 cup olive oil

1/4 cup fresh lemon juice

1/2 cup dry white wine

2 cloves garlic, crushed

Freshly ground pepper, to taste

Minced fresh chives, to taste

Precook sausage by simmering in water for 5 minutes or by heating in a microwave for 3 minutes. Cut chicken breasts in half lengthwise, then halve each piece crosswise (16 pieces total). Alternate pieces of sausage and chicken on 4 skewers, placing folded sage leaves between each piece.

For marinade: Combine olive oil, lemon juice, wine, garlic, pepper and chives and pour mixture over brochettes in a flat, nonmetal pan. Cover and refrigerate overnight.

Turn brochettes in the morning, cover and refrigerate until 30 minutes before grilling. When coals are ready, remove brochettes from marinade and grill, covered, until golden brown (approximately 8 to 10 minutes per side).

Serves 4

Must be marinated overnight.

Add color to this combination with charcoal-grilled peppers or squash, sliced into strips or rounds. Line kabobs on a platter and ring with sprigs of sage.

Lotus Chicken

8 (6-ounce) boneless, skinless chicken thighs or breast halves

Marinade:

4 tablespoons grated orange zest

4 cloves garlic, halved

4 tablespoons orange marmalade

2 tablespoons rice vinegar

1/2 cup vegetable oil

4 teaspoons minced fresh ginger

8 scallions, thinly sliced (tops included)

4 dried Szechuan peppers, crushed into fine powder

4 tablespoons soy sauce

For marinade: In a food processor, combine orange zest with garlic. Add marmalade, vinegar, oil, ginger, scallions, Szechuan powder and soy sauce. Process to mix. Let sit for 15 minutes to combine flavors. Pour sauce into a large, resealable plastic bag. Add chicken and seal. Turn plastic bag several times to coat chicken. Marinate overnight in the refrigerator.

Approximately 30 minutes before cooking, remove chicken from refrigerator and start charcoal grill. When coals are ready, remove chicken from bag and drain, saving marinade for basting.

Grill for approximately 20 minutes, or until juices run clear when chicken is pierced with a fork. Turn meat once during cooking and brush often with marinade.

In a small saucepan, bring remaining marinade to a boil and serve with chicken.

Serves 4–6

Must be marinated overnight.

Try serving this spicy chicken sliced into thin strips and arranged on shredded spinach leaves. Garnish with green onion brushes.

Chicken Medley Stir-Fry

1 pound boneless, skinless chicken breasts, cut into 1/2-inch chunks

1–3 tablespoons oil

1 teaspoon red pepper flakes

1 bunch broccoli, cut up and blanched

1/2 cup carrots, thinly sliced and blanched

1/2 cup cashews or peanuts

Glaze:

1 tablespoon yellow rice wine

3–4 tablespoons soy sauce

2 teaspoons vinegar (cider or chinkiany)

2 teaspoons sugar

For glaze: In a medium jar, combine all ingredients and set aside.

Heat a wok or skillet over high heat. Add oil and red pepper flakes. Add chicken and stir-fry for 1 to 2 minutes. Add broccoli and carrots and continue stir-frying for 1 to 2 minutes more. Add cashews and glaze mixture and heat for 30 seconds, or until sauce has thickened slightly and taken on a glaze-like quality. Serve hot.

Serves 4

Prepare a bed of Chinese noodles or freshly steamed rice, top with stir-fry and garnish with carrot flowers or fried won ton noodles.

1 cup tightly packed fresh basil leaves, stems removed

1 cup tightly packed fresh spinach, stems removed

6 boneless, skinless chicken breast halves

1/3 cup mild goat cheese

1/3 cup ricotta cheese

1/2 cup pine nuts, toasted, plus additional to garnish

1/4 cup oil-packed sun-dried tomatoes, chopped

3 tablespoons freshly grated Parmesan cheese

3 cloves garlic, minced

Toasted pine nuts, to garnish

Puree:

2 large bunches watercress, stems removed

2 tablespoons unsalted butter

2 tablespoons minced shallot

Wash basil and spinach, drain and pat dry. Flatten chicken breasts to 1/4-inch thick.

In a medium saucepan filled with water, cover and cook spinach and basil over medium-high heat for 1 minute or until wilted. Drain and rinse under cold water. Drain again. Place chicken breasts, skinned-side down, on a work surface. Cover each with an even layer of spinach and basil mixture.

For puree: Rinse watercress and shake lightly to remove excess water. In a large, heavy skillet, heat butter over medium-high heat. Add shallot and stir until translucent (approximately 3 minutes). Add watercress, reduce heat to low, then cover and cook until watercress is tender, stirring occasionally (approximately 6 minutes). Let cool. Squeeze mixture dry. Transfer to a food processor or blender and puree. Set aside.

In a small bowl, mix goat cheese, ricotta cheese, pine nuts, tomatoes, Parmesan cheese and garlic until well blended. Spread mixture evenly over spinach and basil to within 1/2-inch of the edges of chicken breasts. Roll each breast up jelly-roll style, starting from small side.

Preheat oven to 375 degrees. Lightly grease a shallow baking pan. Place rolls, seam-side down, in prepared pan. Cover with foil and bake for 20 to 25 minutes or until chicken is opaque and juices run clear when meat is pierced. Refrigerate. To serve, slice chicken breast rolls and garnish with puree or serve alongside.

Serves 6

An elegant brunch or luncheon entree. Fan slices on the dark side of several spinach leaves and top with toasted pine nuts.

To toast nuts in the microwave, spread 1 cup of nuts

evenly on a paper plate or paper towel.

Microwave on high for 2-1/2 to 4 minutes or until lightly roasted and

heated through, stirring every 2 minutes.

Feta Chicken on Couscous

2–3 cups cooked, chopped chicken breasts

3 scallions, sliced (including white and part of green)

3 large cloves garlic, crushed

2 tablespoons vegetable oil

1 (28-ounce) can tomatoes with liquid

2 tablespoons red wine vinegar or 1 tablespoon balsamic vinegar

2 tablespoons tomato paste

2 tablespoons chopped fresh dill or 1 tablespoon dried

8 ounces feta cheese, crumbled

2 cups water

1-1/2 cups uncooked couscous

In a large saucepan, sauté scallions and garlic in oil until translucent. Add tomatoes and liquid, vinegar and tomato paste, breaking up tomatoes with a spoon. Bring mixture to a boil. Reduce heat and simmer until thickened (approximately 10 minutes). Add chicken, dill and 1/2 of feta cheese. Cover and reduce heat to low.

In a medium saucepan, bring water to a boil. Stir in couscous and cover. Turn off heat and let rest for 5 minutes. (Note: Couscous also may be steamed instead of boiled.)

To serve, spoon chicken mixture onto a bed of couscous and top with remaining feta cheese.

Serves 4–6

Take your guests on a culinary trip to the Middle East. Garnish with lemon leaves.

Reggae Chicken

6 boneless, skinless chicken breast halves

Salt and freshly ground pepper, to taste

3 ripe bananas

1–3 tablespoons vegetable oil, plus additional for frying

4 tablespoons butter

1/2 cup shredded, sweetened coconut

Preheat oven to 325 degrees. Season chicken with salt and pepper and bake for approximately 45 minutes. Remove and arrange on a serving plate.

Halve bananas lengthwise. Fry for approximately 4 to 5 minutes in about a 1/2-inch of oil until soft and lightly brown. Place bananas, cut-side up, on top of chicken. Keep plate warm, but do not dry out meat.

Melt butter in a saucepan. Add coconut and sauté until coconut turns golden brown. Spoon mixture over bananas and chicken.

To serve, carefully lift each portion with a spatula, keeping fruit on top of chicken pieces.

Serves 4–6

For an island touch, line your serving platter with palm fronds and orange slices.

Chicken with Red Pepper Sauce

4 boneless, skinless
chicken breast halves

2 tablespoons Dijon mustard

1/4 cup lemon juice

4 tablespoons chopped fresh basil

2 cloves garlic, minced

2 tablespoons olive oil

Sauce:

1 (7-ounce) jar roasted
red peppers, drained

1 small jalapeño pepper,
cored and seeded

1/2 cup chicken broth

1/4 cup dry white wine

Salt, to taste

2 tablespoons butter

4 (6-inch) flour or corn tortillas

2 scallions, julienned (tops included) or
6 tablespoons chopped cilantro

Combine mustard, 2 tablespoons lemon juice and 1/2 of basil. Spread mixture on both sides of chicken breasts. Cover and refrigerate for 2 hours or overnight.

In a separate bowl, mix garlic, olive oil and 2 tablespoons lemon juice. Broil chicken until tender, turning occasionally, 4 to 6 inches from heat (5 minutes per side). Baste with olive oil mixture while cooking.

For sauce: In a blender or a food processor, blend red peppers, jalapeño, chicken broth, wine, remaining basil and salt until smooth. Transfer mixture to a medium saucepan and heat to boiling, stirring until reduced to 3/4 cup. Whisk in butter and reduce heat.

To serve, place heated tortillas on each plate. Top with chicken breasts and pepper sauce and finish with scallions or chopped cilantro.

Serves 4

A beautiful dish with a distinctively Southwest flavor. To heat tortillas, wrap in damp paper towels and microwave on full power for about 30 seconds or wrap in foil and place in a 200-degree oven for 5 minutes. Do not overcook or tortillas will become tough.

Making Sun-Dried Tomatoes

To fans of chewy, intensely flavored, sun-dried tomatoes, the opportunities to use them seem endless—pastas, pizzas, sauces, salads, sandwiches, hors d'oeuvre. You can dry tomatoes from your own garden at home in the oven. Roma tomatoes work best.

Using firm tomatoes, cut a 1/4-inch slice from the stem end of each. Then cut each tomato nearly in half lengthwise, leaving it attached at the opposite end, and open out flat so that the cut sides are exposed. Place tomatoes on cake racks, cut-side up and not quite touching each other, and place racks on baking sheets. Sprinkle cut surfaces with salt. Bake in a 200-degree oven for 6 hours, then turn off the oven and let tomatoes rest overnight. In the morning, turn oven to 200 degrees and continue baking for 1 to 3 hours more. Tomatoes are ready when they shrivel and feel dry. They should be flexible, not brittle. Pack them in clean, sterile jars and cover completely with olive oil. Store in a dark place for 4 weeks before using.

Charcoaled Lemon-Lime Chicken

6 small or 3 large boneless, skinless chicken breast halves

Chopped herbs, to garnish

Lemon slices, to garnish

___

Marinade:

3 medium cloves garlic, crushed

1-1/2 teaspoons salt, or to taste

1/2 cup firmly packed brown sugar

3 tablespoons coarse-grained mustard

1/4 cup cider vinegar

Juice of 1 lime

Juice of 1/2 large lemon

6 tablespoons vegetable oil

Freshly ground pepper, to taste

For marinade: In a bowl, combine garlic, salt, sugar, mustard, vinegar, lime and lemon juices. Blend well. Whisk in oil and pepper. Place chicken in a resealable plastic bag and add marinade. Refrigerate overnight, turning occasionally.

Bring chicken to room temperature 1 hour before serving. Grill breasts for 4 minutes per side. (Overcooking will toughen chicken.) Garnish with herbs and lemon slices.

Serves 6

Must be marinated overnight.

As a prelude to this crisp, flavorful chicken, serve guests chilled bowls of **Dilled Tomato Soup.**

Dynasty Chicken

6 boneless, skinless chicken breast halves

3 cups chicken broth or water

2–3 large cucumbers

___

Sauce:

1/4 cup peanut oil

1/4 cup peanut butter (smooth or crunchy)

3 tablespoons soy sauce

3 tablespoons vinegar

2 tablespoons sugar

3 tablespoons hot water

1 tablespoon sesame oil

2 cloves garlic, crushed

1 tablespoon hot chili oil

4 scallions, sliced (tops included)

1/8 teaspoon cayenne pepper, or to taste

Chopped peanuts or cashews (optional)

Poach chicken, partially covered, in simmering broth or water for 20 minutes or until just cooked through. Be careful not to overcook or chicken will be dry. Drain. When cool enough to handle, tear meat into shreds.

For sauce: Whisk ingredients together 1 at a time in the order given. Pour over chicken and chill in refrigerator for several hours.

To serve, peel cucumbers and split lengthwise, scooping out seeds. Cut into thin diagonal slices. Mound cucumbers onto each plate, top with chicken and sauce and sprinkle with scallions and chopped nuts.

Serves 6–8

Perfect for an evening outdoors. Hang Chinese paper lanterns and offer your guests chopsticks. For an added bit of color, place a red cabbage leaf underneath the sliced cucumbers on each plate.

Chicken in Black Bean Pecan Sauce

4 boneless, skinless chicken
breast halves

1-1/2 cups dry white wine

1/2 cup olive oil

2 tablespoons soy sauce

1 tablespoon coriander seed or
2 teaspoons ground coriander

2 Serrano chilies or jalapeño peppers,
seeded and chopped

6 cloves garlic (3 coarsely chopped)

1/3 cup chicken broth

4 flour tortillas

4 tablespoons chopped
fresh cilantro, to garnish

Sauce:

1/2 cup pecan halves

1/2 cup dry white wine

3 tablespoons butter

1/2 teaspoon grated lime zest

3 teaspoons fresh lime juice

1 jalapeño pepper, seeded and diced

2/3 cup canned or cooked black beans,
rinsed and drained

Salt and freshly ground pepper, to taste

Place chicken breasts in a shallow glass dish. Add white wine, oil, soy sauce, coriander seed, chilies and chopped garlic. Marinate for 4 hours or overnight.

For sauce: Preheat oven to 200 degrees. On a baking sheet, toast pecans until brown (approximately 10 minutes). Allow to cool, then coarsely chop or break (pieces should be the approximate size of black beans). In a medium saucepan, combine chicken broth and white wine. Bring mixture to a boil over medium heat and boil until reduced by half. Reduce heat to low and whisk in butter. Stir in lime zest and juice, jalapeño and pecan pieces. Cook for 2 minutes. Stir in black beans. Season with salt and pepper. Set aside.

Preheat grill or broiler. Grill or broil chicken until cooked through (approximately 7 minutes). Place a warmed tortilla on each plate, top with chicken breast and sauce and garnish with chopped cilantro.

Serves 2–4

A Southwestern marriage of springy chicken, crunchy pecans and creamy beans. Serve with **Festive Pepper Strips**. For instructions on warming tortillas, see **Chicken with Red Pepper Sauce**.

When grilling chicken, put the bone side next to the heat.

Bones act as an insulator and keep chicken from cooking too quickly.

Boning chicken will shorten any cooking time

but will also slightly diminish the flavor.

When a recipe calls for precooked chicken, bake in a 350-degree oven

for 20 minutes or simmer in seasoned water for 40 minutes.

Saffron Chicken and Vegetables

8 boneless, skinless whole chicken breast halves

Olive oil to coat vegetables, plus 2 tablespoons

2 cups julienned red and green bell peppers

18 Greek olives, pitted

1/4 cup sun-dried tomatoes, julienned

2 potatoes, cut into 1/2-inch pieces

2 carrots, cut into 1/2-inch pieces

Oregano, basil, thyme and salt to taste

Sauce:

4 cups chicken broth

2 cups dry white wine

1 teaspoon minced garlic

1 small shallot, minced

2 teaspoons tarragon

2 teaspoons saffron

4 cups heavy cream

Juice of 1/2 lemon

2 teaspoons butter

Kosher salt, to taste

For sauce: In a large saucepan, boil broth, wine, garlic and shallot until reduced by 1/2. Add tarragon, saffron and cream. Again, reduce mixture by 1/2. Add lemon juice and butter. Season with salt. Set aside.

Sauté peppers, olives and tomatoes in 2 tablespoons olive oil for 1 minute. Add prepared sauce and combine gently. Set aside.

Brush potatoes and carrots with olive oil and sprinkle with dry herbs. Bake at 350 degrees for 20 to 30 minutes.

Grill chicken for 4 minutes per side. Heat reserved vegetable sauce. Arrange breasts on top of potato-carrot mixture and cover with sauce.

Serves 6–8

*A golden-hued sauce accentuates the other colors within this pretty dish. Serve with **Caraway Bread** to complete the meal.*

🍂 *Saffron is available both in powdered form and in threads (stigmas). The powdered variety loses its flavor more readily. Although it is expensive, a little goes a long way in flavoring foods. Store saffron in a cool, dark place for up to 6 months.*

🍂 *To serve flavored butter for a cookout buffet, create small tortilla cones, secure them with raffia ties and spoon in softened butter, garnished if desired.*

Baja Lasagna

16–24 small corn tortillas

2 tablespoons safflower oil

2 cloves garlic, minced

1 pound boneless, skinless chicken breasts, diced

5 (8-ounce) cans tomato sauce

1 teaspoon salt

1/2 teaspoon freshly ground pepper

2 cups cottage cheese

1 (8-ounce) package cream cheese, softened to room temperature

1 cup sour cream

1/2 cup chopped Italian parsley

1 cup thinly sliced scallions (tops included)

2 (4-ounce) cans chopped green chilies, drained

1 cup grated sharp cheddar cheese

Grease two 9- by 13-inch baking dishes. Brush both sides of tortillas with safflower oil. Brown minced garlic in 1 tablespoon safflower oil for about 1 minute over medium-high heat. Add chicken and brown for 5 to 7 minutes.

In a large saucepan, combine tomato sauce, salt and pepper. Add chicken and simmer for about 30 minutes. Skim off any fat.

In a separate bowl, combine cottage cheese, cream cheese, sour cream, parsley, scallions and green chilies. Mix until smooth and creamy.

In each baking dish, place a layer of 4 to 6 tortillas, 1/4 of chicken sauce, 1/2 of cheese mixture, another layer of tortillas, and 1/4 of chicken sauce. Top each with 1/2 cup cheddar cheese. Cover with foil, tucking around the edges. Bake in a 350-degree oven for 25 minutes. Remove foil and bake uncovered for 25 minutes more. Let stand for 15 minutes before serving.

Serves 12 (each pan serves 6)

A south-of-the-border cousin to traditional Italian lasagna.

Pink Peppercorn Chicken

4 boneless, skinless chicken breasts

2 cups dry white wine

5 medium leeks, rinsed and julienned in 1-inch strips

2 tablespoons fresh rosemary

2 tablespoons pink peppercorns

2 tablespoons unsalted butter

Trim chicken breasts of any excess fat, place between 2 sheets of waxed paper and pound to an even thickness. Place flattened breasts into a shallow pan and cover with white wine. Marinate for 1 hour.

Fold 4 sheets of parchment in half and cut each into a half heart. Open out heart shape and butter 1 side of each sheet. Place 1/4 of leeks to the right of the crease on each heart shape. Top with a chicken breast. Sprinkle each with 1/2 tablespoon of rosemary and 1/2 tablespoon peppercorns. Fold parchment over and seal by folding with a twisting motion.

Place parchment packets on baking sheets and bake in a 375-degree oven for 30 minutes. To serve, place packets on individual plates and carefully snip open tableside.

Serves 4

Cutting the parchment packets open in front of your guests releases the woodsy fragrance of fresh rosemary.

Chicken and Onion Quesadillas

2 large yellow onions, thinly sliced

3 tablespoons olive oil

1 teaspoon basil

1/2 teaspoon cumin

2 tablespoons honey

1 cup chicken broth

1 to 1-1/2 cups coarsely chopped cooked chicken

Salt, to taste

6 (10-inch) flour tortillas

1 cup grated Monterey Jack cheese

1 cup salsa

Sour cream, to garnish

Chopped scallions, to garnish

Sliced black olives, to garnish

In a large skillet over medium heat, sauté onions in oil until they begin to soften. Sprinkle in basil and cumin and continue stirring over medium or medium-low heat for approximately 15 minutes. (The goal is to soften the onions, not brown them.) Stir in honey and continue cooking for 5 minutes more. Add chicken broth and barely simmer. Continue cooking and stirring until stock has almost totally evaporated. Add chopped chicken and continue sautéeing until chicken is heated through. Season with salt. Remove from heat and set aside.

Preheat oven to 350 degrees. Sprinkle cheese onto tortillas, then spoon on chicken and onion mixture. Fold each tortilla in half, creating a half-moon shape. Bake just long enough for cheese to melt (approximately 8 to 10 minutes). Do not dry out tortillas. Remove from oven and drizzle with salsa. Serve with sour cream, chopped scallions and sliced black olives.

Serves 6

Place quesadillas within a bed of fresh cilantro and drizzle with **Tomatillo and Red Pepper Sauce.**

Peppered Chicken with Artichoke Hearts

4 boneless, skinless chicken breast halves

1/2 teaspoon peppercorns

Salt, to taste

10 tablespoons butter or margarine (keep 6 tablespoons cold)

1 (14-ounce) can artichoke hearts, rinsed, drained and halved

3–4 tablespoons fresh lemon juice

1 tablespoon chopped fresh parsley

3 tablespoons dry white wine

1/2 teaspoon lemon zest

Pound peppercorns between waxed paper sheets to crush them. Place each breast between 2 sheets of waxed paper and pound to 1/4-inch thick. Rub crushed peppercorns into both sides of each chicken breast and sprinkle with salt.

In a large frying pan, heat 2 tablespoons butter over medium heat. Add breasts and sauté, turning once, for 3 to 5 minutes per side. Remove chicken from pan and keep warm in a 250-degree oven.

Add 2 tablespoons butter to pan drippings. Add artichoke hearts and sauté over medium heat for 2 to 3 minutes. Remove artichokes from pan drippings and keep warm in oven.

Add lemon juice, parsley, white wine and lemon zest to drippings and bring to a quick boil. Remove pan from heat and cool for 30 to 60 seconds. Whisk cold butter into pan drippings. If butter melts completely or sauce separates, place pan in cold water and whisk until thickened.

Arrange chicken on a serving platter. Top with artichoke hearts, pour sauce over all and serve.

Serves 4

A bed of lemon twists provides a fragrant preview to this delectable entree.

Ginger-Lime Chicken

6 boneless, skinless chicken breast halves

2 cups chicken broth

1 cup dry white wine

4 tablespoons grated fresh ginger

2–3 tablespoons peanut oil

3 tablespoons unsalted butter

Zest of 1 lime plus additional for garnish

1/4 cup fresh lime juice

12 thin lime slices

Marinade:

2 (12-inch) lemongrass stalks

1 small bunch fresh cilantro (approximately 3/4 cup)

4 cloves garlic

2 scallions, sliced

1 cup coconut milk

1/3 cup peanut oil

Juice of 1 lime

For marinade: Remove outer leaves from lemongrass and cut remainder into 1/2-inch pieces. In a food processor, chop lemongrass, cilantro, garlic and scallions. Transfer to a large bowl and combine with coconut milk, peanut oil and lime juice. Add chicken and stir to coat. Refrigerate for 4 hours.

Remove chicken from marinade and set aside on a plate. Place marinade, chicken broth, wine and ginger in a medium saucepan. Simmer over moderate heat until reduced to 1 cup (approximately 1 hour).

In a heavy saucepan, heat peanut oil. Sauté chicken over medium heat until opaque on each side (approximately 3 minutes per side). Place in an oven-safe dish and keep warm in a 250-degree oven until ready to serve. If serving immediately, sauté chicken about 4 minutes longer.

Just before serving, whisk butter, lime zest and lime juice into sauce. Place 1 chicken breast on each plate and top with sauce. Garnish with additional lime zest and lime slices, twisted for visual appeal. Serve hot.

Serves 4–6

Lemongrass adds a flowery, citrusy scent to this chicken. Look for it in Asian markets and in supermarkets with large, varied produce selections. Just before using, pound the upper stems and outer leaves lightly with a meat mallet (releasing the aromatic oils). Grind or mince lemongrass or leave it whole and remove before serving.

When the menu is Southwestern, cactus can take more than a decorative role. Available now in many supermarkets, the pads of edible varieties (with spines removed) can be used as paddles for dips or salsa, or as "trays" for crudités.

Orange Chicken with Acorn Squash

6 boneless, skinless chicken breast halves

2 acorn squash

2 tablespoons butter

1 (6-ounce) can frozen orange juice concentrate, thawed

2 tablespoons brown sugar

1-1/2 teaspoons ground ginger

1/2 teaspoon ground allspice

3 whole peppercorns

1/4 teaspoon hot pepper sauce

2 tablespoons fresh sweet savory or 1 tablespoon dried

2 medium oranges

Cornstarch (optional)

Cut squash in half and remove strings and seeds. Bake in a 300-degree oven for 30 minutes (or microwave for 13 minutes, turning after 9 minutes). Remove and let cool. Cut into 3/4-inch rings and then cut each ring in half.

In a large skillet, sauté chicken in butter. Combine orange juice concentrate, brown sugar, ginger, allspice, peppercorns and hot pepper sauce. Pour over chicken. Add squash and simmer with savory, covered, for 30 to 45 minutes or until done. Baste occasionally.

Cut oranges into 1/4-inch slices and then halve each slice. Place over chicken during the last 5 minutes of cooking. Remove chicken and squash to a serving platter and correct thickness of sauce by adding cornstarch, if desired.

To serve, pour sauce over chicken and squash. (If more sauce is desired, double sauce ingredients.)

Serves 4–6

Garnish with orange peel tied in a bow and serve with a simple green salad tossed with Sour Cream Sherry Dressing.

Squash divides generally into two categories—summer and winter. Summer squash produce thin, edible skins, soft seeds and flesh with a high water content. They are highly perishable and require refrigeration. The hard, thick skins of winter varieties such as acorn squash permit longer storage, and refrigeration is not necessary. They also require longer cooking than their summer counterparts.

Poulet Dijon

4 boneless, skinless chicken breast halves

1/4 cup (1/2 stick) butter

2 tablespoons Dijon mustard

1 clove garlic, minced, plus 1 whole clove, peeled

1 medium onion, finely diced

2-1/2 cups chicken broth

1 tablespoon flour

3/4 cup dry white wine

1/2 pound mushrooms, sliced

4 baguette slices, 1/8- to 1/4-inch thick

2 tablespoons finely chopped fresh parsley, to garnish

In a large skillet, heat butter and sauté chicken on all sides until browned. Remove from heat and set aside.

In a medium bowl, mix mustard, minced garlic, onion, broth, flour, wine and mushrooms until well blended. Pour mixture into a sauté pan and simmer, stirring until sauce has thickened slightly. Add chicken and reheat.

Toast baguette slices and rub with peeled garlic clove. Spoon 1 teaspoon sauce over each baguette slice. Serve chicken breasts over baguettes with remaining sauce spooned over the top. Garnish with chopped parsley.

Serves 4

Presenting the chicken breasts on baguette slices adds a touch of Provence to your table.

Chicken in Madeira Cream Sauce

6 chicken breast halves

1/4 cup (1/2 stick) butter

Sauce:

1/4 cup sliced mushrooms

2 teaspoons butter

1/4 cup beef broth

1/4 cup Madeira

1 cup heavy cream

Salt and freshly ground pepper, to taste

1/2 teaspoon fresh lemon juice

2 tablespoons finely chopped parsley, to garnish

In a large skillet, heat butter until slightly browned. Add chicken and brown lightly, 30 seconds on each side. Place chicken and drippings in a casserole and cover. Bake in a 400-degree oven for 6 to 8 minutes until chicken feels springy when touched. Do not overcook. Remove chicken to a hot serving dish, cover and keep warm while making sauce.

For sauce: Sauté mushrooms in butter. Add broth and Madeira to pan juices from chicken. Simmer until reduced by half. Add cream and simmer until slightly thickened. Add salt, pepper, lemon juice and mushrooms. Heat thoroughly.

To serve, spoon enough sauce over chicken to cover completely and sprinkle with parsley.

Serves 6

*A warming dish for cool winter nights. Serve with **Roma Fennel Bread**.*

Taos Tequila Chicken

6 chicken breast halves or
1 whole chicken, cut up

Marinade:

1 cup tequila

3/4 cup Rose's lime juice

1/2 cup olive oil

2 shallots, finely chopped

6 cloves garlic, minced

1/2 cup chopped cilantro

1/2 teaspoon oregano

1/2 teaspoon ground cumin

1/2 cup taco sauce, preferably green

For marinade: Combine all ingredients in a glass baking dish. Add chicken pieces and refrigerate overnight. (Chicken may be kept in marinade for up to 1 to 2 days.)

Prepare grill. When coals are red hot, grill chicken 4 to 5 inches from the heat. Turn frequently until done. Serve over **Caramelized Onions,** topped with **Tomatillo and Red Pepper Sauce.**

Serves 4–6

Must be marinated overnight.

A tasty delight for fans of Mexican cuisine. Add a pitcher of frozen margaritas and enjoy.

Caramelized Onions

6 tablespoons olive oil • 4–5 large yellow onions, very thinly sliced • 1 teaspoon cumin
1–2 teaspoons basil • 4 tablespoons honey • 2 cups chicken broth • Salt, to taste

In a large skillet over medium heat, sauté onions in oil until they begin to soften. Sprinkle in cumin and basil. Continue stirring over medium heat for 15 minutes. (The goal is to soften the onions, not brown them.) Stir in honey and continue cooking for 5 minutes. Add chicken broth and reduce heat to simmer slowly. Continue cooking and stirring until liquid is almost totally evaporated. (May take 30 minutes.) Serves 4–6.

Tomatillo and Red Pepper Sauce

6 fresh tomatillos • 3 red bell peppers, roasted and seeded • 1 jalapeño pepper, seeded and chopped • 3 tablespoons fresh lime juice • 1/4 cup chopped cilantro

Husk tomatillos, rinse in warm water and chop coarsely. Chop roasted peppers coarsely. In a food processor, combine 4 tomatillos, jalapeños and lime juice and process. Add remaining tomatillos and cilantro. Pulse 3 times. Transfer to a small bowl and keep covered until ready to serve. Makes about 4 cups.

Lemon Chicken Turnovers

4 boneless, skinless chicken breast halves

2 cups chicken broth

3 tablespoons grated lemon zest

1 cup chopped arugula

1/2 cup chopped pecans

1/2 cup golden raisins

3 tablespoons fresh lemon juice

1/4 teaspoon salt

Freshly ground pepper, to taste

1/4 cup sour cream

1/4 cup mayonnaise

1 (10-ounce) package frozen pastry shells, thawed or puff pastry sheets cut into 4- by 4-inch squares

1 cup hollandaise sauce

Place chicken in a shallow baking dish. Combine chicken broth and 2 tablespoons lemon zest and pour over breasts. Bake at 350 degrees for 30 minutes. Let chicken cool in liquid, then remove and cut into 1/2-inch chunks. Mix chicken with arugula, pecans, raisins, lemon juice, 1 tablespoon lemon zest, salt, pepper, sour cream and mayonnaise.

Roll out pastry shells to approximately 1/8-inch thick. Place 2 to 3 tablespoons chicken mixture in the center of each shell and fold over turnover-style, sealing edges with a fork. Place turnovers on a baking sheet. Bake in a 450-degree oven for 15 minutes or until golden brown. Serve with hollandaise sauce.

Serves 6–8

*A welcome change from everyday chicken salad, these turnovers burst with flavor. For a tasty hollandaise sauce, see **Pastry-Wrapped Salmon and Sole**.*

Grilled Hedaki Chicken Sandwich

6 boneless, skinless chicken breast halves

3 pita bread rounds, halved

6 slices baby Swiss cheese

Lettuce

Marinade:

1 clove garlic, finely minced

3/4-inch fresh ginger, minced

1/4 cup soy sauce

1/4 cup vegetable oil

1 teaspoon sesame oil

Sauce:

2 tablespoons reserved marinade

1/2 cup mayonnaise

2 tablespoons honey

For marinade: With a wire whisk, mix garlic, ginger, soy sauce and oils. Reserve 2 tablespoons marinade for sauce. Marinate chicken for about 30 minutes while charcoal grill is heating.

For sauce: Heat reserved marinade and add to mayonnaise and honey. Mix well with wire whisk and set aside.

Grill chicken breasts. Serve in a pita pocket with lettuce, cheese and sauce. Pass remainder of sauce.

Serves 6

Sweet and tangy hedaki sauce lends a wonderful spirit to these sandwiches. For an outdoor affair, line small, shallow baskets with brightly colored napkins. Arrange sandwiches in the baskets along with sliced fruit in hollowed-out oranges and tabouli in lettuce cups.

Stuffed Cranberry-Pepper Game Hens

4 Cornish hens, rinsed and dried

1 large shallot

2 celery stalks, cut into 1-inch pieces

1 medium Granny Smith apple, cored and quartered

1-1/2 cups cranberries

2 tablespoons unsalted butter

1 cup cooked wild rice

1/3 cup pine nuts

2 teaspoons plus 1 tablespoon jalapeño pepper jelly

1 teaspoon salt

1/2 teaspoon sage

Freshly ground pepper, to taste

Nutmeg, to taste

1 tablespoon vegetable oil

3/4 cup water

In a food processor, drop shallot through feed tube and mince finely. Add celery and chop finely. Set aside. Finely chop apple and transfer to a large bowl. Slice cranberries, using medium slicing blade. Reserve 3/4 cup and add remainder to apples.

In a skillet, melt butter and sauté celery-shallot mixture until soft (approximately 8 minutes). Add to apple mixture. Stir in rice, pine nuts, 2 teaspoons jelly, 1/2 teaspoon salt and sage. Season with pepper and nutmeg.

Stuff hens loosely with rice and fruit mixture. Tie legs together and place wings under body. Place in a roasting pan and brush with vegetable oil. Bake hens at 450 degrees for 30 minutes. Reduce temperature to 350 degrees and bake for 15 minutes more.

Meanwhile, cook reserved cranberries and water in a 1-1/2 quart nonaluminum saucepan until very soft. Add 1 tablespoon jelly and stir until dissolved. Remove from heat and strain glaze. Reserve cranberries.

Pour off fat in roasting pan. Brush hens with glaze. Bake for 10 minutes, brushing frequently with glaze.

Preheat broiler. Broil hens until brown (approximately 2 to 3 minutes), then let stand for 5 minutes.

Mix strained cranberries with pan drippings. To serve, spoon sauce over hens or pass separately.

Serves 4

Hot jalapeños and tart fruit orchestrate a complex, surprising flavor for these game hens.

Garlic Herbed Hens

4 Cornish hens, halved, rinsed and dried

1 teaspoon salt

1/2 teaspoon white pepper

1/4 cup chopped fresh parsley

1/4 cup chopped fresh sage

1/4 cup chopped fresh oregano

1/4 cup pine nuts, finely chopped

2 tablespoons minced garlic

1/2 cup (1 stick) butter, softened

1/2 cup fresh lemon juice

1/2 cup fresh lime juice

1 cup dry white wine

In a large bowl, mix salt, pepper, parsley, sage, oregano, pine nuts and garlic. Blend with butter to moisten. Place 1 to 2 tablespoons of mixture under the skin of each breast. Place hens in a 9- by 13-inch glass baking dish. Pour lemon and lime juices and wine over hens, cover and refrigerate overnight, turning occasionally to coat.

Grill hens on an oiled grill for 10 to 15 minutes per side. Serve warm.

Serves 4

Must be marinated overnight.

The flavor of these hens is delightfully enhanced by a trio of pungent fresh herbs.

Grilled Turkey Breast with Herb Butter

1/2 fresh turkey breast (about 3 pounds)

Marinade:

1/4 cup vegetable oil

1/4 cup soy sauce

2 tablespoons catsup

1 tablespoon vinegar

Freshly ground pepper, to taste

1 clove garlic, minced

1/4 teaspoon ground ginger

Herb butter:

1/4 cup melted butter

3/4 teaspoon thyme, crushed

1/2 teaspoon rosemary

1/8 teaspoon paprika

2 cloves garlic, minced

Combine marinade ingredients. Marinate turkey breast in the refrigerator for at least 8 hours, turning occasionally.

Grill over hot coals and hickory chips until a meat thermometer reaches 170 degrees (or approximately 20 minutes per pound at 350 degrees). Baste turkey while grilling. Remove lid for the last 10 to 20 minutes so that meat will brown.

For herb butter: Combine all ingredients and set aside.

Slice turkey, brush with herb butter if desired and pass with additional herb butter.

Serves 4

Try this and you'll be cooking turkey more often than just at Thanksgiving. The marinade is equally good on seafood and beef steaks.

Curried Turkey Breast

1 fresh turkey breast (4–6 pounds)
or whole turkey

1 tablespoon curry powder

1 teaspoon basil

1 teaspoon thyme

1 teaspoon oregano

1 teaspoon marjoram

2 tablespoons garlic salt

1/2 teaspoon paprika

2 onions, cut into eighths

3 carrots, peeled and sliced

2 celery stalks, cut into large pieces

1 orange, peeled and quartered

1 cup vodka

1-1/4 cups water

Zest of 1 orange

2–3 tablespoons cornstarch

Wash and dry turkey breast. If using whole turkey, wash, dry and stuff as desired. Combine curry powder, herbs, garlic salt and paprika and rub mixture onto turkey. (May need to increase dried ingredients to cover an entire bird.) Place turkey in a roasting pan with vegetables and orange quarters. Pour in vodka and 1 cup water.

Roast uncovered at 350 degrees until meat thermometer reaches 170 degrees (approximately 20 minutes per pound). Baste turkey regularly with the juices.

Allow turkey to cool for 30 minutes before slicing. Meanwhile, puree vegetables and drippings in a food processor or blender. Transfer to a saucepan and add orange zest. Simmer for 5 minutes. Mix cornstarch with 1/4 cup water and whisk into sauce. Simmer over moderate heat until thick. Pass sauce with turkey.

Serves 4–6

You'll pique the interest of dinner guests when they smell the wonderful aroma of this turkey. Add additional curry powder (2 teaspoons) to the sauce if desired.

Pheasant au Vin

1 or 2 pheasants (bone in, skin removed)

1 medium onion, sliced

Butter

Wild rice, cooked

___

Sauce:

2 cups beef broth or consommé

1 cup red wine (such as Zinfandel)

1 teaspoon Worcestershire sauce

2 tablespoons catsup

1 tablespoon flour

Salt and freshly ground pepper, to taste

Combine consommé, wine, Worcestershire sauce and catsup. Stir in flour, salt and pepper. Place pheasant in a 9- by 13-inch baking dish and pour sauce mixture over bird. Refrigerate overnight.

Place onion slices on top of pheasant. Spread butter on any parts that extend from dish. Bake in a 325-degree oven for 1-1/2 to 2 hours. Allow pheasant to sit for 15 minutes before carving.

Transfer sauce to a shallow pan and refrigerate for 15 minutes. Skim fat from top of sauce. Reheat and adjust seasonings. Serve sauce and pheasant over a bed of wild rice.

Serves 4

Must be marinated overnight.

*The perfect choice for a special occasion, served with **Wild Mushroom Ragoût**.*

Duck with Dried Cherries and Peppercorns

1 duck breast

2-1/2 cups red wine (such as Zinfandel)

5 tablespoons butter

1 cup cherry preserves

1/2 cup chicken broth

1 shallot, minced

1/3 cup dried cherries

1–2 tablespoons brine-packed green peppercorns, drained

Marinate duck refrigerated in 1 cup wine overnight, turning regularly. Reserve marinade.

In a large sauté pan, melt 2 tablespoons butter. Sauté duck on each side for 2 minutes. Transfer to a roasting pan and add marinade. In another pan, melt cherry preserves. Spoon 1/2 of preserves over duck breast. Roast duck in a 350-degree oven for 30 to 40 minutes. (Meat should be pink.)

Deglaze sauté pan with 1-1/2 cups wine. Add broth and shallot, heat and reduce to 1/3 cup. Sauce should be somewhat syrupy. Whisk in 3 tablespoons butter, 1 at a time. Add dried cherries and green peppercorns.

Allow duck breast to sit for 30 minutes to retain juices before carving. Carve by slicing lengthwise. Arrange slices on a plate, nap with sauce and top with additional dried cherries and peppercorns, if desired.

Serves 2

Must be marinated overnight.

Serve for a romantic dinner for two or as a first-course for a holiday dinner.

Center of Attention

A simple centerpiece may be all that's needed for most entertaining, but don't be limited by just a vase with a few stems:

🍂 *Glue a layer of asparagus stalks (tips up) to a hatbox or a milk carton cut in half. Tie with calico ribbon or raffia and fill with fruit and summer blossoms.* 🍂 *Mingle a variety of small framed pictures or collectibles—antique toys, vases and bottles, carved birds or animals, interesting trinket boxes—and unify by weaving fabric or ribbon through the collection.* 🍂 *Lay a grapevine wreath flat and line with grapes, small apples and unshelled nuts. Surround with ivy or grape leaves.* 🍂 *Toss dried apple, orange and lime slices with whole nutmegs, cloves and cinnamon sticks in a large footed bowl. In the fall and winter, add bits of juniper, bittersweet and pinecones.* 🍂 *Line a basket with lettuce—radicchio, arugula, endive, etc.—and create a leafy "garden" of colors and textures. Tuck in handpainted eggs or use produce such as eggplant, carrots, artichokes and rhubarb.*

SHELLFISH

Crab Tacos with Salsa, 192
Crusty Crab Burgers, 193
Scallops Florentine, 191
Shellfish Gratin, 191

SHRIMP

Corn Crêpes with Shrimp and Green Chilies, 188
Grilled Shrimp with Lemon Butter Sauce, 189
Shrimp Kabobs and Red Pepper Sauce, 189
Sticky Shrimp, 190

CATFISH & TROUT

Camden County Catfish, 203
Poached Trout Sauterne, 202

HALIBUT, SWORDFISH & TUNA

Broiled Tuna with Provençal Sauce, 193
Ginger-Lime-Cilantro Swordfish, 195
Grilled Halibut with Japanese Eggplant, 201
Grilled Swordfish with Melon Salsa, 195
Italian Grilled Tuna, 194

SALMON

Lime Dilled Salmon, 198
Rosemary Poached Salmon, 196
Tarragon Mustard Salmon Steaks, 196

WHITEFISH & REDFISH

Mediterranean Baked Whitefish, 200
Moroccan Ragoût, 200
New Year's Redfish, 202
Orange Roughy with Pecan Sauce, 199
Pastry-Wrapped Sole with Salmon, 198
Roughy Pepper Packets, 199

MARINADES & SAUCES

Basil Wine Marinade, 204
Creamy Mustard Sauce, 203
Herbed Mustard, 204
Lime-Red Pepper Hollandaise Sauce, 203
Orange Soy Marinade, 204

MINI RECIPES

Flavored Butters, 197

Fish & Seafood

Pictured finishing touch:

CREATING

A SPLASH WITH

CARVED LEMONS AND LIMES, 190

SPECIAL TOPIC BOXES

BUTTERS, 197

COOKING WITH HERBS, 205

FIRE UP THE GRILL, 201

1-1/2 pounds medium-sized shrimp, peeled and deveined

2-1/2 cups grated sharp cheddar cheese

2 tablespoons minced scallions, for garnish

Sauce:

2 tablespoons butter

2 (4-ounce) cans chopped green chilies, drained

1/2 cup minced scallions

1/4 teaspoon minced garlic

2 tablespoons flour

1 cup chicken broth

1 cup heavy cream

1 cup sour cream, room temperature

1/4 teaspoons salt

1/4 teaspoon freshly ground pepper

Crêpes:

1-1/4 cups milk

3/4 cup yellow cornmeal

2 eggs

1/3 cup flour

1 teaspoon sugar

1/4 teaspoon salt

4 tablespoons butter, melted

For crêpes: In a blender or food processor, combine milk, cornmeal, eggs, flour, sugar, salt and 2 tablespoons butter until smooth. Let stand for 20 minutes.

Heat a 6-inch crêpe pan or heavy skillet over high heat. Brush with remaining butter. Stir batter again to blend well. Remove pan from heat and ladle 3 tablespoons batter into corner of pan, then tilt pan so batter covers bottom. Return excess to bowl. Cook until bottom is golden brown. Turn and cook second side about 10 seconds. Repeat with remaining batter.

For sauce: Melt butter in a large heavy saucepan over medium low heat. Add chilies, scallions and garlic. Cook until onion is soft, about 5 minutes. Add flour and stir for 3 minutes. Mix in broth. Increase heat and bring to a boil, stirring constantly. Reduce heat and simmer until sauce is smooth, stirring often, about 3 to 5 minutes. Add cream and simmer until thick, about 2 minutes. Stir in sour cream, salt and pepper. Remove from heat and set aside.

Reserve 6 shrimp for garnish, and coarsely dice remainder. In a medium bowl, combine shrimp, 1 cup sauce and 1 cup cheese. Butter 9-inch by 13-inch baking dish. Spoon 2 tablespoons shrimp mixture into each crêpe. Roll up, tucking ends under and place, seam-side down, in dish. Pour remaining sauce and cheese over tops. Bake in a 350-degree oven for 15 minutes. Put reserved whole shrimp in sauce and bake for 5 minutes more, or until shrimp are opaque. Garnish with scallions and reserved whole shrimp.

Serves 6

A fancy first course for a gala evening or a memorable main event. Cooks who are unaccustomed to preparing crêpes may want to double the ingredients in order to practice. If crêpes are too thin, they will not roll properly.

Shrimp Kabobs and Red Pepper Sauce

1 pound large shrimp, peeled and deveined

1/4 cup vegetable oil

1/4 cup red wine vinegar

1/2 teaspoon salt

1 clove garlic, minced

1/8 teaspoon ground ginger

1/8 teaspoon ground nutmeg

1/2 teaspoon freshly ground pepper

8 large scallions, cut into 1-1/2-inch pieces

Spinach leaves, washed and patted dry, to garnish

Sauce:

1 teaspoon paprika

1 clove garlic, minced

1/4 teaspoon salt

1/4 teaspoon cayenne pepper

2 tablespoons vegetable oil

Place shrimp in a deep glass baking dish. In a small bowl, combine oil, vinegar, salt, garlic, ginger, nutmeg and pepper. Pour marinade over shrimp. Cover and refrigerate for 2 hours.

For sauce: Combine all ingredients and set aside.

Prepare grill. Drain shrimp, reserving marinade. Thread shrimp and scallions on skewers, using 3 shrimp to a skewer. Grill over very hot coals, brushing with reserved marinade until shrimp turn pink. (Do not overcook or shrimp will become tough.) Arrange on a spinach-lined platter, drizzle generously with sauce and serve immediately.

Serves 2–4

The natural springy texture of shrimp is enhanced by this lively marinade and peppery sauce.

Grilled Shrimp with Lemon Butter Sauce

2 pounds large shrimp, shelled and deveined

1 cup olive or vegetable oil

1 cup dry sherry

1 cup soy sauce

1 clove garlic, crushed

Sauce:

1 cup (2 sticks) butter

Juice of 1 lemon

1/4 teaspoon salt

1 teaspoon Worcestershire sauce

1 tablespoon soy sauce

3–4 dashes hot pepper sauce

In a glass baking dish, combine oil, sherry, soy sauce and garlic. Add shrimp and refrigerate for 1 hour.

For sauce: Melt butter in a small saucepan, then add lemon juice, salt, Worcestershire sauce, soy sauce and hot pepper sauce. Keep warm until serving.

Remove shrimp from marinade and cook over a hot charcoal fire for 2 to 3 minutes per side or until just opaque (or pink). Serve with sauce.

Serves 4

To create kabobs, skewer button mushrooms and chunks of different colored bell peppers between the shrimp.

1/4 cup (1/2 stick) butter

1 cup finely chopped onion

3/4 cup chopped celery

1 clove garlic

1/4 cup flour

1 teaspoon salt

1 tablespoon sugar

Dash of hot pepper sauce

1 teaspoon paprika

1 small bay leaf

1 (15-ounce) can tomatoes with liquid

3/4 cup chopped green bell pepper

4 cups raw shrimp, shelled and deveined

Rice:

3 cups water

1 tablespoon butter

1 teaspoon salt

1-1/2 cups uncooked rice

2 cups shredded cheddar or Swiss cheese

1 teaspoon Dijon mustard

Melt butter in a large skillet, add onion, celery and garlic, and cook until onion is soft, but not transparent. Blend in flour, salt, sugar, hot pepper sauce, paprika and bay leaf. Add tomatoes and green pepper, and simmer for 5 minutes. Add shrimp and stir until shrimp are pink, about 5 minutes. Remove bay leaf.

For rice: In a medium saucepan, bring water to a boil. Add butter, salt, and rice. When mixture boils again, reduce heat to low and cook covered until liquid is absorbed. Add cheese and mustard. Combine with shrimp mixture after cheese melts.

Serves 12

The shrimp mixture will at first appear watery and the rice will appear too sticky. They combine, however, to form a marvelous texture and flavor.

For casual outdoor entertaining, mound a child's plastic swimming pool with ice and fill it with bottled and canned beverages. Toss in a rubber ducky or two for whimsy.

Add a bit of splash to the lemons and limes you serve to accompany fresh seafood. Using a zester or vegetable peeler, carve simple designs into the peels and pile all into a basket, Easter egg style.

Scallops Florentine

1 pound fresh scallops

1/4 cup dry white wine

1/4 cup (1/2 stick) butter or margarine

1/4 cup flour

1/2 teaspoon salt

1/4 teaspoon freshly ground pepper

2 cups heavy cream

1 (10-ounce) package frozen chopped spinach, cooked and drained

3/4 cup sliced mushrooms, sautéed

1 tablespoon prepared mustard

6 frozen puff pastry shells, baked

Simmer scallops gently in wine until they release liquid and turn opaque (about 4 minutes).

In a separate skillet, melt butter over low heat. Stir in flour, salt and pepper. Slowly add cream, stirring until thickened. Drain scallops and stir into mixture, followed by spinach, mushrooms and mustard. Heat through and serve in pastry shells.

Serves 6

*Delightful as a luncheon entree preceded by **Amaretto Peach Soup**. For an elegant appetizer, serve in mini pastry shells.*

Shellfish Gratin

1/2 cup shrimp

1/2 cup sea scallops

1/2 cup diced lobster, cooked and chunked

1/2 cup lump crabmeat, cooked and chunked

2 bay leaves

2 teaspoons peppercorns

1/4 cup (1/2 stick) butter

1 tablespoon pressed garlic

3 tablespoons sherry

1/2 cup chopped mushrooms

1/2 cup chopped scallions

3/4 cup grated Swiss cheese

Sauce:

2 tablespoons butter

2 tablespoons flour

1-1/2 cups milk

Salt and freshly ground pepper, to taste

Boil shrimp in water spiced with bay leaves and peppercorns until pink, about 3 to 4 minutes. Cool and peel. Prepare scallops by sautéing lightly in 2 tablespoons butter with garlic and sherry. Sauté until scallops begin to shrink in size, about 3 minutes per side. Turn off heat and allow scallops to rest while preparing sauce.

Sauté mushrooms and scallions in remaining butter. Set aside.

For sauce: Melt butter in a large pan. Add flour and mix. Gradually stir in milk. Bring to a boil and cook, stirring, for 2 to 3 minutes. Season with salt and pepper.

When sauce is ready, add mushroom and onion mixture. Add shrimp, scallops, lobster and crabmeat and heat gently for 3 to 4 minutes. Pour into buttered ramekins and top with grated cheese. Bake in a 350-degree oven for 15 to 20 minutes or until cheese is melted.

Serves 4–6

As an alternative to ramekins, present this rich seafood quartet in shell-shaped serving dishes.

Crab Tacos with Salsa

8 (6–7-inch) flour tortillas

2 tablespoons vegetable oil

2 cups chunked or flaked crabmeat

2 cups fresh spinach, rinsed, dried and shredded

2 ripe avocados, peeled and sliced lengthwise

1 cup shredded Monterey Jack cheese

2 small limes, quartered

_____ Salsa: _____

2 cups ripe tomatoes, peeled, seeded and chopped, including juice

2 tablespoons finely minced jalapeño peppers

1/4 cup finely chopped green chilies

2 shallots, minced

2 cloves garlic, minced

1/4 cup chopped cilantro leaves

1 teaspoon salt

2 tablespoons fresh lime juice

2 tablespoons red wine vinegar

1 tablespoon maple syrup

For salsa: Mix tomatoes with peppers, chilies, shallots, garlic and cilantro. Toss with salt, lime juice, vinegar and syrup. Cover and refrigerate at least overnight.

Warm a stack of tortillas in the oven or microwave. In a skillet, heat oil, add crabmeat and toss until heated through.

To assemble, arrange 2 tortillas side by side on each plate. In the center of each, place 1/4 cup each of spinach, crab and avocado. Sprinkle with cheese. Fold or roll, then top with salsa and limes.

Serves 4

Salsa must be made in advance.

Mix up a pitcher of white wine sangria to serve with these "tacos with a twist."

Prepare fresh fish as soon as possible, preferably the day of the catch or purchase. If you cannot cook it immediately, wrap loosely in clear plastic wrap and refrigerate for a day. For longer storage, freeze.

To freeze fresh fish, use whole, cleaned fish with the head intact; the skin protects the flesh. Unskinned fillets will freeze better than skinned for the same reason. Wrap tightly to seal against contact with air. Oily fish may be frozen for up to 2 months; lean fish for up to 3 months.

Crusty Crab Burgers

1 pound cooked crabmeat, shell and cartilage removed, shredded

2 large scallions, finely chopped

2 teaspoons coarse-grained mustard

1/4 cup light or regular mayonnaise

1/4 teaspoon hot pepper sauce

1/4 teaspoon cayenne pepper

Salt and freshly ground pepper, to taste

1-1/2 cups fine, fresh bread crumbs

1 egg

1 tablespoon olive oil

4 tablespoons unsalted butter

4 soft onion or hamburger buns, or bagels

In a medium bowl, mix crabmeat, scallions, mustard, mayonnaise, hot pepper sauce, cayenne pepper, salt and pepper. Fold in 1/2 cup bread crumbs. Mold mixture into 4 patties and chill for at least 10 minutes.

Beat egg lightly in a wide shallow bowl. Slowly beat in oil. Spread remaining bread crumbs over a large plate. Dip each patty in egg mixture to coat both sides and press into bread crumbs until evenly coated.

Melt butter in a large skillet over medium high heat. When foam subsides, add crab patties and cook until bottoms are deep brown. Reduce heat to medium. Turn patties and cook until browned. Drain on paper towels. Serve on toasted buns.

Serves 4

A seafood alternative to hamburgers. For a heartier sandwich, add lettuce, fresh tomato slice and a dollop of mustard. These burgers may also be served open-faced with Creamy Mustard Sauce or Lime-Red Pepper Hollandaise Sauce.

Broiled Tuna with Provençal Sauce

4 tuna steaks, 1-inch thick

Salt and freshly ground pepper, to taste

1 tablespoon grated fresh ginger

1 tablespoon fresh lemon juice

1 tablespoon olive oil

Sauce:

1 large ripe tomato

2 tablespoons red wine vinegar

1/4 cup olive oil

1/4 cup finely chopped scallions

1 teaspoon finely minced garlic

1/4 cup finely chopped fresh basil or 1 tablespoon dried

1/2 teaspoon grated lemon zest

Salt and freshly ground pepper, to taste

For sauce: Drop tomato in boiling water for 1 minute, remove and skin. Halve tomato, discard seeds and core. Cut into 1/4-inch cubes (there should be about 1/2 cup). Pour vinegar into a small mixing bowl and add oil, scallions, garlic, basil and tomato. Follow with lemon zest, salt and pepper, and blend well with whisk. (Sauce may be prepared early in day and refrigerated until serving time.)

Preheat broiler or charcoal grill. Sprinkle both sides of tuna with salt and pepper. Rub ginger on both sides and sprinkle evenly with lemon juice and oil. Broil for 5 minutes, 6 inches from heat. Turn steaks and continue broiling for 5 minutes more. If grilling, put steaks on a hot grill, cover and cook for 5 minutes. Turn, cover and cook for 5 minutes more. Serve with sauce.

Serves 4

This succulent tuna should be moist—be careful not to overcook. The delicate accompanying sauce is best when made several hours before serving. Tuna also can marinate in Basil Wine Marinade or your favorite marinade early in the day.

6 (8-ounce) tuna steaks, 3/4-inch thick

3/4 cup extra virgin olive oil

1/2 cup minced parsley

1/2 (7-ounce) jar roasted red peppers, drained and diced

1/2 cup thinly sliced scallions

1/4 cup fresh lemon juice

2 tablespoons capers, drained

2 tablespoons minced fresh oregano or 2 teaspoons dried

1/4 teaspoon salt

1/8 teaspoon freshly ground pepper

In a medium saucepan, combine 1/2 cup olive oil with parsley, red peppers, scallions, 1 tablespoon lemon juice, capers, oregano, and salt. Simmer over low heat for 5 minutes, stirring occasionally to blend flavors. Remove from heat and set aside.

Arrange a single layer of tuna in a glass baking dish. Drizzle remaining 1/4 cup olive oil and 2 tablespoons lemon juice over fish. Season with pepper. Turn to coat both sides. Cover and marinate at room temperature for 30 minutes.

Prepare grill. Place fish on an oiled rack set 4 to 6 inches from coals. Reheat sauce. Grill tuna, turning once, until opaque throughout but still moist (about 8 to 10 minutes). Spoon sauce over each steak and serve.

Serves 6

*Make a splash with this boldly colored fish. Serve with a good-quality chianti and finish the meal with **Mascarpone** and tiny Amaretto cookies.*

🍃 Tips for selecting fresh tuna:

Mild-flavored albacore tuna has the lightest flesh and is the only tuna

that can be called white. Yellowfin tuna is pale pink and has

a flavor slightly stronger than albacore. Bluefins are among the largest

tunas. Young bluefins have a lighter flesh and a milder flavor.

As they grow, bluefins acquire a dark red flesh and their

flavor becomes more pronounced. Bonitos are the smallest of the tuna

family but also the most strongly flavored.

🍃 The texture of grilled fish is right when it just begins to flake.

"Flaking" is indicated when pressure applied with a fork at the thickest part

of the fish causes the flesh to split easily along its natural separations.

Ginger-Lime-Cilantro Swordfish

4 swordfish steaks

Olive oil

Salt and freshly ground pepper, to taste

Sauce:

1 teaspoon chopped shallots

1 cup dry white wine

1 tablespoon grated fresh ginger

1/2 cup heavy cream

3/4 (1-1/2 sticks) unsalted butter

Juice of 2 limes

1 tablespoon chopped cilantro

Salt and freshly ground pepper, to taste

For sauce: Combine shallots, wine and ginger in a medium saucepan. Simmer until reduced to 1/4 cup. Add cream, butter, lime juice, cilantro, salt and pepper. Whisk and simmer for 3 to 4 minutes to thicken. Hold over very low heat until ready to serve.

Grill swordfish rubbed with olive oil for 4 minutes on each side. Sprinkle with salt and pepper and serve hot surrounded by cream sauce.

Serves 4

Fresh ingredients lend a verdant flair to this light cream sauce. Garnish steaks with strips of lime zest and additional cilantro.

Grilled Swordfish with Melon Salsa

8 (1/2-pound) swordfish steaks, 1-inch thick

2/3 cup vegetable oil

2/3 cup soy sauce

1/2 cup fresh lime or lemon juice

2 teaspoons grated lime zest

2 tablespoons grated fresh ginger

8 cloves garlic, minced

Salsa:

1 cup finely diced cantaloupe or casaba melon

3/4 cup finely diced honeydew melon

1 cup finely diced Crenshaw melon

2 tablespoons olive oil

3 tablespoons fresh lime juice

2 tablespoons chopped fresh cilantro

3 scallions, sliced (tops included)

1 tablespoon grated fresh ginger

For salsa: Combine all ingredients in a medium bowl. Cover and refrigerate for up to 2 days.

Arrange swordfish steaks in a single layer in a large glass baking dish. Combine oil, soy sauce, lime juice, lime zest, ginger and garlic, and pour over fish. Cover and marinate in refrigerator for 1 to 2 hours, turning occasionally.

Prepare and oil grill. Add steaks when coals are hot. Grill for 5 to 6 minutes per side, turning once and moving as necessary to ensure even cooking (fish should be opaque in the center when done). Brush occasionally with marinade. Serve with melon salsa.

Serves 8

*A wonderful marriage of hearty fish and light fruit flavors. Serve extra salsa as a side dish with **Crusty Crab Burgers.***

Tarragon Mustard Salmon Steaks

4 salmon steaks

Fresh lemon juice

2–3 tablespoons olive oil

Sauce:

1 tablespoon Dijon mustard

1 teaspoon sugar

1 tablespoon white wine vinegar

2 tablespoons finely chopped fresh parsley

1 tablespoon chopped fresh tarragon or 1 teaspoon dried

1/4 cup olive oil

For sauce: In a small bowl, combine mustard, sugar, vinegar, parsley and tarragon. Blend well. Slowly add olive oil, blending well. Set aside.

Brush salmon with lemon juice and olive oil. Place under a preheated broiler for about 5 minutes. Turn and broil for 5 minutes more or until translucent. Spoon sauce over steaks and serve immediately.

Serves 4

This piquant sauce is also wonderful served with tuna. It may be made ahead of time and refrigerated before using.

Rosemary Poached Salmon

4 (6–8-ounce) salmon fillets, 1-inch thick

1 cup dry white wine

1/4 cup dry vermouth

4 tablespoons snipped fresh rosemary

1 cup heavy cream

4 tablespoons cup unsalted butter

2 tablespoons Dijon mustard

Salt and freshly ground pepper, to taste

4 sprigs rosemary, for garnish

Combine wines and 2 tablespoons rosemary in a large skillet. Boil until reduced by half. Add cream and bring to a boil. Reduce heat to low and add fish. Poach in liquid for about 10 minutes, 5 minutes per side. Transfer fish to a covered dish and hold in a warm oven (about 300 degrees).

Increase heat under poaching liquid to high. Boil until reduced by half, stirring occasionally. Reduce heat to low and gradually whisk in butter, 1 tablespoon at a time. Whisk in mustard and remaining rosemary. Season with salt and pepper as needed. Place each salmon fillet on a dinner plate and top with 3 to 4 tablespoons of sauce. Garnish with rosemary sprigs.

Serves 4

*Accompany this fragrant fish with **Salmon Biscuits** (see **Smoked Salmon with Salmon Biscuits**) and fresh steamed asparagus, preceded by **Goat Cheese Salad with Nectarines and Walnuts**.*

Easy to prepare, flavored butters can add tasty interest as well as visual variety to simple grilled or broiled fish and seafood.

Green Peppercorn Butter

1/2 cup (1 stick)
unsalted butter, softened

1/4 cup chopped
fresh parsley leaves

1 tablespoon water-packed green
peppercorns, drained

1 teaspoon fresh lemon juice

1/2 teaspoon Dijon mustard,
or to taste

Worcestershire sauce, to taste

Blend all ingredients until well combined. Cover and refrigerate for at least 1 hour before serving.

Makes about 1 cup

Wasabi Butter

6 tablespoons
unsalted butter, softened

1/4 cup wasabi (Japanese
powdered horseradish)

Combine butter and wasabi into a thick paste. Cover and refrigerate to set before serving.

Makes about 1/2 cup

Fiery Pepper Butter

1/2 cup (2 sticks)
unsalted butter, softened

1 (7-ounce) jar roasted
red pepper, drained

1 tablespoon tomato paste

1-1/2 teaspoons
firmly packed brown sugar

1/4 teaspoon (generous)
cayenne pepper

1/4 teaspoon hot pepper sauce

Salt, to taste

Puree peppers and combine well with butter, tomato paste, brown sugar, cayenne pepper and hot pepper sauce. Season to taste with salt. Cover and chill. Let stand at room temperature for 1 hour before serving.

Makes about 2 cups

Chili-Cumin Butter

1/2 cup (1 stick)
unsalted butter, softened

2 teaspoons ground
ancho chili (roasted and peeled),
or 2 finely chopped
jalapeño peppers

1/2 teaspoon ground cumin

Combine all ingredients well. Cover and refrigerate before serving.

Makes about 1/2 cup

Creamy Dill Butter

1/2 cup (1 stick)
unsalted butter, softened

2 hard-cooked egg yolks

4-1/2 teaspoons fresh dill

1/2 teaspoon salt

1/8 teaspoon freshly ground
white or black pepper

Press egg yolks through a wire strainer. Combine with remaining ingredients and beat until fluffy. Cover and refrigerate until serving.

Makes about 3/4 cup

Lemon Dijon Butter

1/2 cup (1 stick)
unsalted butter, softened

2 teaspoons fresh lemon juice

2 teaspoons minced parsley

1/4 teaspoon salt

1/8 teaspoon
freshly ground pepper

2 tablespoons Dijon mustard

Combine butter, lemon juice, parsley, salt and pepper, and beat until fluffy. Add Dijon mustard and mix well. Cover and refrigerate until serving.

Makes about 3/4 cup

Lime Dilled Salmon

4 (6–8-ounce) salmon fillets

Chopped scallion tops, to garnish

Lime wedges, to garnish

Sauce:

1/4 cup chopped fresh dill

3 tablespoons chopped scallions

3 tablespoons fresh lime juice

1 tablespoon hot honey mustard

1/2 teaspoon salt

1/4 teaspoon freshly ground pepper

2–4 tablespoons olive oil

Rinse fillets and pat dry. Place in a single layer in a greased baking dish.

For sauce: In a blender or food processor, combine dill, scallions, lime juice, mustard, salt, pepper and oil. (For a chunkier sauce, process liquid ingredients first, then add chopped scallions and dill).

Cover fish with sauce and bake uncovered at 375 degrees for 15 to 25 minutes or until just opaque. Garnish with scallion tops, lime wedges or both.

Serves 4

An unexpected collage of simple ingredients!

Pastry-Wrapped Sole with Salmon

1 sheet frozen puff pastry (half of a 17-ounce package), thawed

8 (3-ounce) sole fillets

Freshly ground pepper, to taste

1 (4-ounce) salmon fillet, skinned and cut in small pieces

2 tablespoons butter, softened

1/2 teaspoon fresh lemon juice

1 egg yolk, slightly beaten

Blender hollandaise sauce:

5 large egg yolks

5 tablespoons lemon juice

3/4 cup chicken broth

2 tablespoons melted butter

1/2 teaspoon salt

Dash of cayenne pepper

Dash of freshly ground pepper

Cut pastry sheet into 4 squares. On a lightly floured surface, roll each into an 8-inch square. In center of each square, place a sole fillet. Sprinkle with pepper and set aside.

In a blender, combine salmon, butter and lemon juice. Spread mixture down the center of each fillet on pastry and top with remaining fillets. Bring pastry up around fish to cover completely. Trim off excess and pinch seams to seal. Place seam-side down on a foil-lined baking sheet and chill overnight.

Brush pastry with beaten egg yolk. Bake in bottom third of a preheated 400-degree oven for 20 to 25 minutes until golden brown. Serve with hollandaise sauce.

For sauce: In a heavy 1-quart saucepan, boil 4 tablespoons lemon juice and broth until reduced to 2/3 cup. Cool slightly. Place egg yolks and 1 tablespoon lemon juice in a blender and process for 45 seconds. With blender on high, dribble in broth and lemon juice. Pour sauce back into saucepan and whisk over low heat until mixture thickens, about 2 to 3 minutes. Whisk in melted butter. Season with salt, cayenne and pepper. The sauce will continue to thicken when standing.

Serves 4

Must be started a day in advance.

Make designs and shapes from leftover puff pastry and arrange like appliqués on the tops of individual pastry pockets before baking.

Orange Roughy with Pecan Sauce

3 pounds orange roughy fillets, cut into 8 serving pieces

Marinade:

1 cup olive oil

6–7 tablespoons fresh lemon juice

1/4 teaspoon salt

1/8 teaspoon freshly ground pepper

2 bay leaves

1/2 onion, minced

4 cloves garlic, minced

Sauce:

1-1/4 cups (10 tablespoons) butter or margarine

1/2 cup chopped fresh parsley

1/3 cup ground pecans

1 tablespoon fresh lemon juice

2 tablespoons finely chopped scallion tops

1/4 teaspoon freshly grated nutmeg

1/2 teaspoon hot pepper sauce

1-1/4 cups pecan halves

For marinade: Combine all ingredients in a large, resealable plastic bag or glass baking dish. Add fish and seal bag or cover dish. Turn several times for marinade to coat fish completely. Let sit at room temperature for 1 hour, turning occasionally.

For sauce: Melt butter in a medium saucepan. Add parsley, ground pecans, lemon juice, scallion, nutmeg and hot pepper sauce. Simmer on low for 1 minute. Add pecan halves, tossing well with mixture. Turn off heat until ready to reheat and serve.

Grill fillets for 4 to 6 minutes or broil until fish is opaque. Serve each piece topped with pecan sauce.

Serves 8

The flaky fish and crunchy pecans produce a delightful contrast of textures. Garnish with pansies and parsley fresh from the garden for a beautiful presentation.

Roughy Pepper Packets

4 orange roughy fillets (about 1-1/2 pounds)

1 green bell pepper, sliced

1 red bell pepper, sliced

2 onions, sliced

1/2 cup melted butter

4 tablespoons fresh lemon juice

2 teaspoons salt

2 teaspoons paprika

Freshly ground pepper, to taste

Lightly grease 4 pieces of heavy-duty foil and place 1 fillet, skin-side down, on each. Top with peppers and onions. Combine remaining ingredients and pour mixture over fillets. Bring foil up over food and seal thoroughly.

Place foil packets on a grill about 5 inches from moderately hot coals. Cook for 30 minutes or until fillets flake easily. Cooking time will vary depending on temperature of coals and thickness of fish.

Serves 4

Fun, fast and easy! Guests will enjoy peeling back individual packages to reveal the colorful entree within. Fish may be prepared and refrigerated an hour before grilling.

Mediterranean Baked Whitefish

1-1/2 to 2 pounds firm whitefish (orange roughy or sole)

4 cloves garlic, minced

4 tablespoons olive oil

2 (2-ounce) tins anchovies (16 fillets)

2 (28-ounce) cans Italian plum tomatoes, drained and chopped

16 pitted black olives, sliced

1-1/2 tablespoons capers

1 teaspoon red pepper flakes

1 teaspoon fennel seed, crushed

Freshly ground pepper, to taste

Rinse fish, pat dry and arrange in a single layer in a greased baking dish.

Sauté garlic in oil. Add anchovies and stir until pasty. Add tomatoes and simmer for 10 minutes, then stir in olives, capers, red pepper, fennel seed and pepper. Simmer uncovered for 20 minutes or until thickened. Pour over fish. Bake uncovered in a 375-degree oven for 20 minutes or until fish is opaque.

Serves 6–8

Focaccia and delicate **Polenta Pepper Soufflés** *nicely balance the robust flavors of this fish.*

Moroccan Ragoût

2 large bell peppers, red, yellow, orange or green

1 medium yellow onion

4 tablespoons olive oil

4 cloves garlic, minced

1-3/4 cups dry white wine

1/2 cup chicken broth

1/2 teaspoon salt

1/2 teaspoon freshly ground pepper

1/4 teaspoon cayenne pepper

1/4 teaspoon paprika

1 teaspoon cumin

6 (3-ounce) sole or orange roughy fillets

6 whole long chives or strips of leek leaves

2/3 cup garbanzo beans

2 teaspoons grated orange zest

1/2 cup finely shredded sweet basil (or combined sweet basil and opal basil)

Slice peppers into 1/4- to 1/2-inch strips. Slice onion and then cut rounds in half. In a large covered baking dish, heat olive oil. Add bell peppers, onion and garlic. Sauté until limp (about 5 minutes), then add wine, broth, salt, pepper, cayenne pepper, paprika and cumin. Cover and simmer for 10 minutes on low heat. (May be prepared in advance up to this point.)

Roll each piece of fish and tie with a whole chive or strip of leek leaf (or use kitchen twine). About 10 minutes before serving, stir garbanzo beans and orange zest into vegetable mixture. Place fish bundles on top and cover the baking dish. Simmer for about 5 minutes or until fish is opaque and begins to separate when touched. Mix in basil and cover again for 1 minute.

To serve, spoon equal portions of vegetables and broth into shallow soup plates and top each with a fish bundle.

Serves 4 (main course) or 6 (first course)

The pale fish rolls stand out atop the vibrant pool of vegetables and broth.

Grilled Halibut with Japanese Eggplant

1 pound halibut steaks, cut into generous 1-inch cubes

3/4 cup olive oil

1 jalapeño pepper, minced

3/4 cup chopped cilantro

2 cloves garlic, crushed

8 miniature Japanese eggplants

1 small onion, quartered

8 new potatoes, approximately 1-inch in diameter

2 red and 2 green or yellow bell peppers, cut into 1-inch pieces

12 cherry tomatoes

In a medium bowl, combine 1/2 cup olive oil, jalapeño pepper, cilantro and garlic. Add fish and marinate in refrigerator for 2 hours. Reserve marinade for basting.

Place eggplants in a baking dish and cover with remaining 1/4 cup oil. Marinate for 1 hour. Precook potatoes in boiling water until tender but still crisp (about 5 minutes). Set aside.

Prepare coals and oil grill rack. Alternate onions, peppers, tomatoes and fish on 4 long metal skewers, ending with a pepper. Place whole eggplants and potatoes in center of grill and turn while cooking (about 10 minutes). Brush brochettes with reserved marinade, place around eggplants and potatoes on grill and cook, turning occasionally, for 8 to 10 minutes.

Serves 4

This recipe is also great with shark or swordfish and zucchini. If Japanese eggplant is not available, substitute regular eggplant that has been seeded, salted, drained and chopped into 2-inch cubes.

Fire up the Grill

Whether it's the sights and smells that tease our appetites or the pleasure of good company gathered around the coals, food just seems to taste better when it's cooked outside.

Aromatics delightfully boost grilled flavors. Fruitwoods (apple, peach, cherry) impart a smoky, sweet flavor to light entrees, as do grapevines, blueberry twigs or raspberry canes. The stronger, more pungent flavors of hardwoods (hickory, oak, mesquite) are well suited to robust foods. A pan of fruit juice, beer or wine on the coals adds flavorful moisture to grilled items. Lay stalks of soaked and drained fresh herbs or juniper twigs over hot coals just before putting meat on the grill. Tea leaves, strips of citrus zest, apple peels and onion skins also serve as flavor and fragrance enhancers. For additional interest when grilling fish, ask your fishmonger for seaweed. Lay it over the hot coals and place fish directly on it; seaweed preserves moisture in the fish as well as imparting flavor.

New Year's Redfish

4 redfish fillets
(about 3 pounds)

Juice of 1 lemon plus 1/4 cup

Lemon pepper, to taste

1 tablespoon minced fresh thyme

1/4 cup (1/2 stick) butter

2/3 cup flour

1/2 large Vidalia or sweet onion,
sliced into rings

1/4 cup dry vermouth

Wash fillets and pat dry. Place in a glass baking dish and drizzle with juice of 1 lemon. Season with lemon pepper and thyme and let marinate at room temperature for 30 minutes.

Melt butter in a large skillet, lightly dredge fillets in flour and quickly sauté over medium heat until lightly browned on both sides.

Transfer fillets to a warm serving platter. Place onion slices in the same skillet, and sauté for 5 minutes until translucent. Add vermouth and 1/2 cup lemon juice to deglaze pan and simmer until liquid is reduced by half. Pour over fillets and serve immediately.

Serves 4

Redfish season traditionally opens in Southern coastal waters on New Year's Day. If redfish is not available, substitute snapper, sea bass, grouper or sole.

Poached Trout Sauterne

1 fresh rainbow trout (3–4 pounds)

Salt and freshly ground
white pepper, to taste

Chopped fresh parsley, to taste

1/2 pound white seedless grapes,
plus additional to garnish

1/2 cup sauterne

4 tablespoons butter

2 tablespoons fresh lemon juice

Pimiento strips, to garnish

Lemon slivers, to garnish

Parsley sprigs, to garnish

Preheat oven to 350 degrees. Wash fish well, inside and out, and place in a long, shallow baking dish. Salt and pepper lightly and sprinkle with chopped parsley. Cover with grapes and sauterne. Dot fish with butter and sprinkle with lemon juice.

Bake for about 25 minutes or until fish flakes easily. Serve on a platter, garnished with pimiento strips, lemon slivers, parsley and grapes.

Serves 6–8

Serving this whole fish fully garnished makes a stunning buffet presentation. Choose salmon trout for a change of color and flavor.

Camden County Catfish

3 pounds catfish fillets

Buttermilk, chilled

1 tablespoon crushed oregano

1 tablespoon crushed basil

1 tablespoon lemon pepper

Salt and freshly ground pepper, to taste

Curry powder, to taste

Paprika, to taste

2 tablespoons freshly grated Parmesan cheese

1 cup yellow cornmeal

Peanut oil

Place fillets in a glass baking dish and cover completely with very cold buttermilk. Soak for at least 2 hours in the refrigerator.

Combine seasonings, Parmesan cheese and cornmeal in a large resealable plastic bag. Set aside.

In a deep skillet, heat peanut oil to 375 degrees. Drain fillets and place, 1 at a time, in plastic bag containing seasonings, gently coating thoroughly. Fry until golden brown and crunchy out-side, about 2 minutes.

Serves 4–6

The secret to this crunchy-textured catfish is to have the oil hot and the fish very cold.

Lime-Red Pepper Hollandaise Sauce

1/2 cup (1 stick) unsalted butter

1 tablespoon water

2 tablespoons fresh lime juice

3 egg yolks, beaten

1 teaspoon grated lime zest

1/4 teaspoon cayenne pepper

In a small bowl, microwave butter on high for 2 minutes or until completely melted. Add water, lime juice, and egg yolks and beat until smooth. Microwave on medium power for 1 minute, then whisk well. (Sauce will appear curdled, but after beating will become smooth.) If sauce is still not thick enough, microwave on medium for another 30 seconds (or more, depending on oven).

Beat in lime zest and cayenne pep-per. Serve with grilled or smoked fish, chicken or vegetables.

Makes 1 cup

The more finely grated the zest here, the stronger the lime flavor.

Creamy Mustard Sauce

1 cup sour cream

1 tablespoon Dijon mustard

1 teaspoon prepared mustard

6 dashes hot pepper sauce

Combine all ingredients and beat lightly. Serve with **Crusty Crab Burgers**, cooked shrimp or baked or poached fish.

Makes 1 cup

The bite of this sauce adds interest to many grilled dishes.

Herbed Mustard

1 cup dry mustard

1 cup white wine tarragon vinegar, or other herbed vinegar

3/4 cup sugar

3 egg yolks

Lemon juice, to taste (optional)

Mix dry mustard and vinegar and allow to stand for 2 hours or overnight. Place in the top of a double boiler, add sugar and egg yolks and whisk over hot water until thickened. Add lemon juice to taste. Chill and serve.

Makes about 3 cups

Drizzle over fish or serve with game, beef or pork. Serve individual portions in mushroom caps or baby eggplants.

Orange Soy Marinade

1/2 cup vegetable oil

3 tablespoons soy sauce

1 teaspoon grated orange zest

1/4 cup fresh orange juice

1 teaspoon ground ginger

Lemon pepper, to taste

Combine all ingredients. Use as an overnight marinade with halibut, shark, swordfish, tuna, orange roughy or mahi mahi.

Makes 1 cup

A flavorful accent to chicken and pork as well as fish. After marinating, heat remaining liquid to a boil and then simmer, reducing to half. Drizzle sauce on prepared seafood, chicken or meat.

Basil Wine Marinade

1/2 cup olive oil

1/4 cup dry white wine

1 clove garlic, minced

3 tablespoons chopped fresh basil or 1-1/2 teaspoons dried

1 tablespoon fresh lemon juice

1/4–1/2 teaspoon freshly ground pepper

Combine all ingredients. Use as an overnight marinade with halibut, shark, swordfish, tuna, salmon, orange roughy or chicken.

Makes 1 cup

Experiment with other fresh herbs and citrus juices in this simple, versatile combination.

*The difference between a recipe that suffices
and one that sings often points to the presence of herbs.*

Fresh vs. Dried

Be discerning when substituting fresh herbs for dried and vice versa. Dried herbs are usually stronger than their fresh counterparts, and certain varieties actually taste different. ❧ When substituting fresh for dried herbs, the standard formula is 2 to 3 times as much fresh as dried.

Storing

To keep most herbs fresh, wrap unwashed sprigs in a damp, wrung-out towel and refrigerate in a resealable plastic bag. Parsley and dill, however, keep longest when their stems are immersed in water. Wash fresh herbs just before using. ❧ To freeze fresh herbs, first wash and pat dry, then discard the stems. Put the leaves in a plastic bag, press out the air and tightly seal. They will freeze for up to 4 months. ❧ Fresh herbs also may be frozen in cube form. Puree them with a small amount of water and freeze in ice cube trays. Store the cubes in plastic bags and use to season soups, sauces and beverages.

Flavored Vinegars

Loosely pack fresh herbs in a jar and pour good-quality wine vinegar over all (red or white is typical, but rice wine vinegar offers a very mellow flavor). Cover and let stand for at least 2 weeks. (To speed the process, heat the vinegar slightly before adding to the herbs.) Strain vinegar if desired and pour into pretty storage bottles. Add herb sprigs or flowers or both.

Don't be reluctant to experiment with different combinations of herbs and vinegars—striking marriages abound: tarragon in cider vinegar, red and green basil in red wine vinegar, nasturtiums and salad burnet in rice wine vinegar and chive blossoms in white wine vinegar. ❧ Enjoy flavored vinegars as you would use any vinegar in marinades for meat, poultry and fish or in salad dressings. Try a mint vinegar in fruit salad, a tarragon vinegar in chicken salad or a lovage vinegar with caraway seeds in potato salad. ❧ Add herbed vinegar to cooking water when steaming vegetables. This addition not only boosts flavor; it also helps keep vegetables such as beets and artichokes from discoloring.

PASTA WITH CHICKEN

Chinese Garden Pasta, 210
Lemon Fettuccine with Hickory-Smoked Chicken, 208
Pepper Poulet Pasta, 209
Spinach Fettuccine with Chicken and Pesto, 208
Tagliatelle Verde, 211

PASTA WITH MEATS

Artichoke-Prosciutto Pasta, 215
Buttons and Bows, 214
Green Chili Lasagna, 213
Lasagna Bolognese, 212
Pork and Penne in Fennel Seed Sauce, 213
River Country Pasta, 215

PASTA WITH SEAFOOD

Basil Scallop and Shrimp Linguine, 218
Martini Scallops with Angel Hair Pasta, 218

PASTA WITHOUT MEAT

Angel Hair Pasta with Spicy Sun-Dried Tomato Sauce, 217
Baked Fettuccine, 220
Cheese Quartet Rigatoni, 219
Fettuccine with Tomato Basil Cream, 220
Heartland Pasta, 217
Pasta with Herbed Tomatoes and Cheese, 219
Pasta Sauté with Rice and Pine Nuts, 221
Potato Gnocchi with Fresh Tomato Basil Butter Sauce, 221
Spaghettini with Mushroom and Parsley Sauce, 216
Summer Bounty Pasta, 216

SAUCES

Tomato Basil Sauce, 222
Tomato Sauce Roma, 222

PIZZA

Calzone Napoli, 228
Grilled Pizza with Gorgonzola and Prosciutto, 225
Summer Phyllo Pizza, 223
Pizza Polenta, 224
Tortilla Stacked Pizza, 226
Upside-Down Pizza Pie, 226

MINI RECIPES

Calzone Fillings, 229
Parsley Pesto, 211

Pasta & Pizza

Pictured finishing touch:

MAKING

PASTA PARTY

NAPKIN RINGS, 220

SPECIAL TOPIC BOXES

OLIVE OILS: BEYOND THE BASICS, 227

PESTO: BEYOND BASIL, 211

Lemon Fettuccine with Hickory-Smoked Chicken

1 pound fettuccine

3 cups heavy cream

3 tablespoons chopped fresh basil

Zest and juice of 1 lemon

1 pound hickory-smoked chicken breast, julienned

3/4 cup toasted walnuts

3/4 cup peeled, diced tomato (about 1 medium)

Salt and freshly ground pepper, to taste

1/2 cup freshly grated Parmesan cheese

Cook fettuccine until al dente. Put cream in a skillet or Dutch oven and add basil, lemon zest and juice. Bring to a boil. Lower heat and simmer until cream has a sauce-like consistency and coats a spoon (at least 5 to 7 minutes).

Add chicken, walnuts and tomato. Remove from heat and stir. Let stand for 2 to 3 minutes. Add cooked pasta and stir to coat. Reheat and add salt, pepper and Parmesan cheese.

Serves 6

A complex blend of textures with a smooth, lemony flavor.

Spinach Fettuccine with Chicken and Pesto

3/4 pound spinach fettuccine, cooked

1 cup heavy cream

1 cup (2 sticks) unsalted butter, cut into pieces

3/4 cup freshly grated Parmesan cheese

2–3 tablespoons cooking oil

4 boneless, skinless chicken breast halves, cut into bite-sized pieces

4 tablespoons pesto

Salt and freshly ground pepper, to taste

Heat cream in a small heavy saucepan over medium heat. Add butter and stir until melted. Gradually add 3/4 cup Parmesan cheese and stir until melted. Reduce heat to low and keep sauce warm.

Heat oil over medium heat. Add chicken and stir until opaque (approximately 3 minutes). Transfer to a bowl, using a slotted spoon. Mix in 1 table-spoon pesto.

Toss cooked fettuccine with remaining pesto and cheese sauce. Arrange pasta on a platter. Spoon chicken over and season with salt and pepper. Serve immediately. Pass additional grated Parmesan cheese.

Serves 6

Take the chill off a winter evening with this full-bodied blend. Garnish with toasted pine nuts or fresh basil and serve with an oaky Chardonnay and crusty bread.

Pepper Poulet Pasta

8 ounces linguine, cooked

3 tablespoons flour

1/2 teaspoon salt

1/4–1/2 teaspoon cayenne pepper

1/8–1/4 teaspoon
freshly ground pepper

4 boneless, skinless chicken breast
halves, cut into 1-inch pieces

2 tablespoons vegetable oil

1 medium onion, chopped

1 red bell pepper, chopped

1 tablespoon chopped jalapeño pepper

2 cloves garlic, minced

3/4 cup chicken broth

1/2 cup milk

1 teaspoon Worcestershire sauce

1/4 teaspoon crushed red pepper flakes

1 cup grated Monterey Jack or
cheddar cheese

1 cup sour cream

Combine 1 tablespoon flour, salt, cayenne and pepper, then toss with chicken to coat. Sauté chicken in oil for 4 to 5 minutes over medium-high heat. Remove chicken and add onions, red bell pepper, jalapeño pepper and garlic. Cook until tender. Stir in remaining flour. Add broth, milk, Worcestershire sauce and red pepper flakes. Cook until bubbly. Add cheese and stir until melted. Stir 1 cup hot mixture into sour cream. Return sour cream mixture to pan in which chicken was cooked. Add chicken and heat through.

To serve, place linguine on the bottom of a serving platter. Top with sauce and decoratively arrange chicken strips. Present, then toss.

Serves 4

A hearty dish with a lively flavor that draws from a blend of peppers.

When serving pasta in large quantities, cook in small

amounts. Remove from heat and rinse immediately in cold water.

Keep large amounts of precooked pasta in cold water in refrigerator

until ready to serve. To heat, drop pasta into boiling water for

1 minute and drain before serving.

Once water reaches a hard rolling boil, a teaspoon of salt or

the juice of 1 lemon may be added for flavor. Add the pasta

gradually and allow water to return to a boil.

8 ounces linguine

1 pound boneless, skinless chicken breasts, cut into strips

3 tablespoons soy sauce

1/2 tablespoon brown sugar

6–7 tablespoons sesame oil

2 tablespoons sesame oil

1 tablespoon ginger

2 carrots, peeled and sliced thinly lengthwise

1/2 head fresh broccoli, cut into small florets

1/2 head cauliflower, cut into small florets

1 green bell pepper, seeded and sliced into strips

1 red bell pepper, seeded and sliced into strips

1 yellow bell pepper, seeded and sliced into strips

1 pound fresh button mushrooms, sliced

1 (8-ounce) can sliced water chestnuts, drained

1 bunch scallions, julienned

1/2 teaspoon fresh cracked pepper

1 tablespoon white wine vinegar

In a shallow dish, coat and marinate chicken strips in 1 tablespoon soy sauce, brown sugar and 1 tablespoon sesame oil for at least 2 hours.

Cook pasta al dente and drain.

In a wok, heat 2 tablespoons sesame oil over medium-high heat. Add garlic and ginger and sauté for 1 minute. Drain chicken and add to oil. Sauté for 5 minutes, stirring constantly. Add carrots, broccoli, cauliflower, peppers and mushrooms. Sauté for 4 to 5 minutes. Add more oil, 1 tablespoon at a time, if necessary. Add water chestnuts and scallions. Sauté for 1 to 2 minutes. Transfer all ingredients to a large serving bowl.

In wok, combine cracked pepper, vinegar, 2 tablespoons soy sauce and 1 tablespoon sesame oil. Simmer for 1 minute, scraping brown bits. Toss sauce with pasta and serve with stir-fried vegetables.

Serves 6

An intriguing marriage of Mediterranean and Orient. For an elegant presentation, serve stir-fried vegetables over nests of pasta.

Pasta should always be cooked al dente, tender-firm. A core of uncooked starch should be in the pasta when it is removed from the water to ensure that it won't be mushy when served.

Tagliatelle Verde

1/4 pound spinach tagliatelle

1 small onion, thinly sliced

1 clove garlic, pressed

1/2 cup sliced fresh mushrooms

1/4 cup extra-virgin olive oil

1/4 cup (1/2 stick) plus
2 tablespoons butter

4 ounces prosciutto, julienned

1/3 cup peeled, seeded and
chopped tomato

1 cup cooked chicken breast, julienned

1/4 cup heavy cream

1/4 teaspoon nutmeg

Salt, to taste

1/2 teaspoon freshly ground pepper

1 cup freshly grated Parmesan cheese

Sauté onion and garlic in olive oil until golden. Add mushrooms and sauté mixture for 2 minutes. Add 1/4 cup butter, prosciutto and tomatoes. Simmer mixture for 5 minutes. Stir in chicken, cream, nutmeg, salt and pepper. Bring liquid to a boil and simmer over heat, stirring frequently. Remove sauce from heat. Set aside and keep warm.

Cook tagliatelle until al dente. Drain. In a serving dish, toss pasta with 2 tablespoons butter. Cover with sauce and serve with freshly grated Parmesan cheese.

Serves 2

Although green pasta is usually made with spinach, don't overlook lovely variations such as parsley or asparagus.

Pesto: Beyond Basil

Versatile pesto is a familiar partner for pasta or soup. Imaginative cooks, though, are discovering its glory as a topping for grilled fish or meats; as a substitute for tomato sauce on pizza; as a dip with fried calamari; mixed with yogurt, mayonnaise or sour cream; blended with dressings for salad; combined with softened cream cheese or goat cheese and enjoyed as a cracker or sandwich spread.

Traditionally pesto combines olive oil, garlic, pine nuts, Parmesan or Pecorino cheese and fresh basil, but these ingredients represent options rather than boundaries. Instead of basil, try marjoram, mint, parsley, spinach, tarragon, cilantro or thyme; for the pine nuts, substitute walnuts, hazelnuts or peanuts.

Here's a fragrant variation to get you started:

Parsley Pesto

2 cups lightly packed chopped Italian parsley

Zest of 1 large lemon (large strips)

2 cloves garlic

3/4 cup freshly grated Parmesan cheese

3 tablespoons extra-virgin olive oil

Freshly ground pepper, to taste

In a food processor, finely mince parsley, lemon zest, garlic and Parmesan cheese, scraping down the sides of the bowl as needed. Toss pesto mixture with warm pasta, olive oil and pepper.

1 pound mozzarella cheese, grated

1/2 pound ricotta cheese

1 pound fresh lasagna noodles, preferably green

1/2 cup freshly grated Parmesan cheese

Meat sauce:

2 tablespoons butter

1 cup chopped onion

2 cloves minced garlic

1/2 cup chopped celery

2 tablespoons olive oil

1 pound sweet Italian sausage

1 pound ground round

1/2 cup dry white wine

2 cups peeled, seeded and chopped fresh tomatoes

4 tablespoons tomato paste

2 cups beef broth

1 bay leaf

1/2 teaspoon sugar

1/2 teaspoon oregano

1/8 teaspoon allspice

1/2 teaspoon basil

Salt and freshly ground pepper, to taste

Besciamello (Italian béchamel sauce):

3 tablespoons butter

6 tablespoons flour

2 cups milk

1 cup heavy cream

1 teaspoon salt

1/8 teaspoon fresh nutmeg

For meat sauce: In a heavy skillet, melt butter and sauté onion, garlic and celery over low heat until golden. Transfer to a heavy 3- to 4-quart saucepan. To the same skillet, add olive oil and sauté sausage and beef until lightly browned, stirring to break up any lumps. Drain excess fat. Add wine to meat and bring to a boil, stirring constantly, until wine is almost evaporated. Add meat to the saucepan containing onion mixture, then add tomatoes, tomato paste, beef stock, bay leaf, sugar, oregano, allspice, basil, salt and pepper. Simmer partially covered for 30 minutes, stirring occasionally. Remove and discard bay leaf. (Meat sauce may be frozen.)

For besciamello: In a heavy 2- to 3-quart saucepan, melt butter over low heat. Whisk in flour and cook slowly for 2 to 3 minutes or until flour is lightly browned, stirring constantly. Gradually add milk and cream, stirring with a whisk to prevent lumping. Heat to boiling, stirring constantly, until sauce thickens. Remove from heat and add salt and nutmeg. Set aside.

Mix 3/4 of the mozzarella cheese with the ricotta cheese and set aside. Grease a 9- by 13-inch baking dish. Cook lasagna noodles until al dente. When done, drain and cover with cold water. Then lift out strips and drain on paper towels.

To assemble, spread 1/4 inch of meat sauce evenly in prepared dish. Layer with 1/3 of the noodles, then 1/3 of the besciamello and 1/3 of the cheese mixture. Repeat twice. Top with reserved mozzarella and sprinkle with grated Parmesan cheese. Bake in a 350-degree oven until bubbly (approximately 30 minutes).

Serves 10–12

A hearty lasagna with a northern Italian flavor. Spinach noodles and creamy white béchamel sauce combine to make a very appealing presentation. Serve with a full-bodied red wine, crusty bread and a green salad.

Green Chili Lasagna

1 pound lasagna noodles

1 teaspoon butter

3 pounds lean ground beef

5 (8-ounce) cans tomato sauce

1 tablespoon sugar

2 teaspoons salt

1/2 teaspoon freshly ground pepper

1 teaspoon minced garlic

2 cups ricotta cheese

1 (8-ounce) package cream cheese, softened to room temperature

1 cup sour cream

1 cup thinly sliced scallions, including tops

2 (4-ounce) cans chopped green chilies, drained

1/2 cup freshly grated Parmesan cheese

Grease two 9- by 13-inch baking dishes. Cook noodles according to package directions. Drain and toss with butter. Brown ground beef. In a large saucepan, combine tomato sauce, sugar, salt and pepper. Add meat and garlic and simmer about 30 minutes. Skim off any fat.

In a separate bowl, combine ricotta cheese, cream cheese, sour cream, scallions and green chilies. Mix until smooth and creamy.

In each baking dish, place a layer of noodles, 1/4 of meat sauce, 1/2 of cheese mixture, another noodle layer, 1/4 meat sauce and Parmesan cheese. Cover with foil and chill thoroughly. Remove foil before baking. Bake in a 350-degree oven for 45 minutes.

Serves 12 (each pan serves 6)

Best when prepared the day before serving and also freezes well. Thaw overnight in refrigerator, then bring to room temperature and reheat. Try substituting shredded beef or chicken for the ground beef. Garnish with cilantro or slices of peppers, such as fresh jalapeños or Anaheims.

Pork and Penne in Fennel Seed Sauce

1 pound penne

1 medium onion, chopped

2 tablespoons vegetable or olive oil

1 pound ground pork

1–2 teaspoons fennel seeds, to taste

1/2 teaspoon salt

1/4 teaspoon freshly ground pepper

1 (28-ounce) can tomatoes with liquid

1 (6-ounce) can tomato paste

1 clove garlic, minced

1 tablespoon fresh oregano or 1 teaspoon dried

1 tablespoon fresh basil or 1 teaspoon dried

Sauté onion in oil until tender. Add ground pork, fennel seeds, salt and pepper. Cook until meat is browned. Drain fat. Add tomatoes and tomato paste, stirring, then add seasonings and garlic. Increase heat and bring mixture to a boil. Reduce heat to low. Cover and simmer 10 minutes to blend flavors.

Prepare penne according to package instructions. Drain. Add meat sauce and heat until warmed through, tossing gently to mix.

Serves 8

A robust flavor that even children love.

12–16 ounces farfalle (bow-tie pasta)

Tomato sauce:

1/2 medium onion, finely chopped

3 large cloves garlic, pressed

1-1/2 tablespoons olive oil

5 tablespoons finely chopped fresh basil

1-1/2 teaspoons oregano

1/4 cup chopped fresh parsley

1/4 teaspoon red pepper flakes

10 medium tomatoes, peeled, seeded and diced, or 2 (14-ounce) cans peeled Italian tomatoes

1-1/2 cups tomato puree

1-1/2 cups chicken broth

Meat filling:

1-1/2 pounds mild Italian sausage

2–3 tablespoons olive oil

3/4 pound fresh button mushrooms, sliced

1 clove garlic, pressed

Ricotta filling:

2 cups ricotta cheese

2 beaten eggs

3/4 cup chopped fresh parsley

Cheese layer:

1/4 cup freshly grated Parmesan cheese

3–4 cups mozzarella cheese

1/4 cup chopped fresh parsley

For tomato sauce: Sauté onion and garlic in olive oil until translucent. Stir in basil, oregano, parsley, red pepper flakes, tomatoes and tomato puree. Add broth. Bring to a boil, then reduce heat and simmer until reduced by half, about 50 to 60 minutes. (Sauce may be made ahead and refrigerated or frozen.)

For meat filling: Remove casings from sausage. Brown in 1 to 2 tablespoons olive oil. Crumble sausage as it cooks. Drain and remove from heat.

Sauté mushrooms and garlic in 1 to 2 tablespoons olive oil. Remove from heat, and drain and discard liquid. Add mushrooms to tomato sauce, then set aside 1-1/2 cups of this mixture. Add meat to remainder of sauce. Simmer for 5 to 10 minutes, then remove from heat and set aside.

For ricotta filling: Mix ricotta cheese, eggs and parsley by hand or with a mixer until well blended. Divide in half.

For cheese layer: Combine Parmesan cheese, mozzarella and parsley. Mix well.

Cook pasta according to package directions. Drain. Divide pasta in half.

To assemble, spread 1/2 of meat-filled sauce over the bottom of a 9- by 13- inch pan. Mix 1/2 of ricotta mixture with 1/2 of pasta to coat. Spread pasta over sauce.

Sprinkle 1/2 of cheese mixture over pasta and ricotta mixture. Repeat layers. Bake uncovered in a 375-degree oven for 25 to 30 minutes until bubbly. Let stand for 10 minutes before cutting. Serve with reserved sauce.

Serves 8

The long simmering of this sauce produces a heady bouquet of garlic, basil and oregano.

River Country Pasta

12 ounces fettuccine, cooked al dente and drained

2-1/2 pounds fresh wild mushrooms or 1-1/2 ounces dried

1/2 cup shredded or slivered ham

1/4 cup butter

1 bunch scallions, sliced thin (including tops and stems)

1/2 cup chopped pecans

1 tablespoon snipped fresh parsley

3-1/2 cups heavy cream

1/4 cup dry sherry

If using dried mushrooms, soak in enough hot water to cover for 30 minutes, then rinse and squeeze dry. Slice mushrooms, discarding tough stems. Lightly sauté ham and mushrooms in butter for 5 minutes or until mushrooms are tender.

Combine scallions with pecans and parsley.

In a large skillet, simmer cream and sherry until reduced by half, about 15 minutes. Stir in ham and mushrooms. Add pecans, parsley and scallions. Toss with pasta. Serve immediately.

Serves 8

The ribbons of fettuccine weave beautifully through the textures of mushrooms, scallions and pecans. If prepared in advance, add the pecans, parsley and scallions at the last minute. Serve with **Mustard Wheat Bread***.*

Artichoke-Prosciutto Pasta

1 pound spinach fettuccine, cooked

1/4 cup (1/2 stick) butter

1/4 cup olive oil

4 tablespoons flour

1-1/2 cups chicken broth

1 clove garlic, minced

1 tablespoon fresh lemon juice

Salt and freshly ground pepper, to taste

2 (7-ounce) packages frozen artichoke hearts or 2 (14-ounce) cans artichoke hearts, quartered

1/4–1/2 pound sliced prosciutto, cut into 1/2-inch strips

2–3 ounces Romano or Parmesan cheese, grated

In a heavy sauté pan, melt butter with olive oil. Whisk in flour and cook for 2 minutes. Add chicken broth, garlic, lemon juice, salt and pepper. Mixture will be similar to a white sauce. Add artichoke hearts and prosciutto to sauce, then mix all with fettuccine. Arrange in a serving bowl and top with grated cheese.

Serves 4

An appealingly colored presentation. For a pasta buffet, offer bowls of warm tomato, spinach and egg fettuccine.

Frozen artichoke hearts have a firmer texture and more pronounced flavor than canned. Defrost before using.

Summer Bounty Pasta

12 ounces fettuccine, cooked

2 tablespoons olive oil

3 cloves garlic, minced

1 medium onion, chopped

2 small zucchini, cubed

1/2 green or red bell pepper, chopped

1 (10-ounce) can chopped tomatoes and green chilies, with liquid

1/2 cup chopped fresh basil or 2 tablespoons dried

1/2 cup chopped fresh parsley

1/2 cup freshly grated Parmesan cheese

Heat olive oil in a large skillet. Add garlic and onion and cook until translucent. Add zucchini and peppers and stir over medium-high heat until tender-crisp, about 2 minutes. Add tomatoes and green chilies, basil and parsley. Stir frequently until hot.

In a heated serving bowl, toss fettuccine with vegetables. Sprinkle with Parmesan cheese and serve immediately.

Serves 4–6

For a spicier version, pass crushed red pepper flakes to sprinkle over each serving.

Spaghettini with Mushroom and Parsley Sauce

8 ounces spaghettini

1/2 cup (1 stick) butter

1 tablespoon olive oil

1/2 pound fresh mushrooms, sliced

1 small onion, minced

2/3 cup fresh chopped parsley

1/2 teaspoon nutmeg

1/4 teaspoon salt

1/4 teaspoon fresh cracked pepper

1/4 cup freshly grated Parmesan cheese

Melt butter. Add olive oil and sauté mushrooms and onion until soft. Add parsley, nutmeg, salt and pepper. Keep warm.

Cook pasta until al dente. Drain well and add mushroom mixture. Serve immediately in a warm bowl.

Serves 4

Long threads of spaghettini tangle beautifully on a platter.

When a recipe calls for flaked parsley, use fresh!

Freeze fresh parsley, then rub the leaf heads vigorously between

your palms. They will crush into fairly fine flakes.

Angel Hair Pasta with Spicy Sun-Dried Tomato Sauce

1 pound capellini (angel hair pasta)

3 medium cloves garlic, minced

3 tablespoons virgin olive oil

6 medium ripe tomatoes

3 tablespoons minced fresh basil

1 tablespoon minced fresh cilantro

1/4 teaspoon red pepper flakes

1/4 teaspoon fresh cracked pepper

1 teaspoon salt

1 cup oil-packed sun-dried tomatoes, drained and cut into small strips

1 cup freshly grated Parmesan cheese

Sauté minced garlic in olive oil until soft, but not browned. Drop tomatoes in boiling water for 1 minute; remove, slip skins off, remove stems and seeds, quarter and puree in food processor.

In a large pan, combine sautéed garlic and oil and pureed tomatoes. Add basil and cilantro. Add red pepper flakes, black pepper and salt. Simmer for 30 minutes until sauce thickens. Add sun-dried tomatoes and simmer for 10 minutes more.

Cook pasta until al dente. Drain. Pour sauce over pasta and toss. Sprinkle with 2 tablespoons Parmesan cheese. Pass additional cheese when serving.

Serves 6

This sauce is thinner than most red sauces, and heavier pasta will dilute its flavor. For a change of pace, spoon the sauce onto a plate, top with cooked ravioli and drizzle additional sauce over all.

For more information, see "Making Sun-Dried Tomatoes" in Poultry.

Heartland Pasta

1 to 1-1/2 pounds fettuccine, cooked

3 tablespoons olive oil

6 tablespoons cooked diced bacon

1 tablespoon chopped garlic

1 large onion, chopped

1 tablespoon fresh rosemary

1 pound fresh spinach, torn

1/4 cup white wine

Salt and freshly ground pepper, to taste

Red pepper flakes, to taste

Pecorino cheese, to taste

In a large sauté pan, add olive oil followed by bacon, garlic, onion and rosemary. Sauté until tender. Add spinach and continue to sauté. Remove mixture and deglaze pan with white wine. Return mixture to pan and add salt, pepper and red pepper flakes. Toss with fettuccine and serve with freshly grated Pecorino cheese.

Serves 6

Earthy bacon, onion and rosemary meld to create cosmopolitan flair.

Martini Scallops with Angel Hair Pasta

1 pound capellini (angel hair pasta), cooked al dente

3 large cloves garlic, minced

2 tablespoons olive oil

1-1/2 pounds sea or bay scallops

Juice of 1 lemon

1-1/2 teaspoons capers, drained

2/3 cup dry vermouth

Bread crumb mixture:

1/2 cup bread crumbs

1/2 cup freshly grated Parmesan cheese

1/4 teaspoon salt

1/4 teaspoon freshly ground pepper

Paprika, to taste

In a skillet, sauté garlic in olive oil. Add scallops and cook until opaque, about 2 to 3 minutes. Do not overcook.

For bread crumb mixture: Combine bread crumbs, Parmesan cheese, salt, pepper and paprika together in a small bowl. Set aside.

In a small bowl, mix lemon juice, capers and vermouth. Add to scallops. Heat through, about 1 minute. Drain scallops, reserving liquid. Toss half of reserved liquid with pasta on a large ovenproof serving platter. Ladle scallops over pasta. Top with bread crumb mixture. Broil and serve immediately.

Serves 6

*Present this delicate coastal medley in shell-shaped dishes and serve with **Roma Fennel Bread**. Pass remaining reserved liquid as a sauce and garnish with lemon slices.*

Basil Scallop and Shrimp Linguine

8 ounces linguine

1 tablespoon olive oil

3–4 shallots, minced

2 cloves garlic, crushed

2 tablespoons chopped fresh parsley or 2 teaspoons dried

2 tablespoons minced fresh basil or 2 teaspoons dried

1/4 teaspoon red pepper flakes

1/2 cup dry white wine

2 tablespoons tomato paste

1 (16-ounce) can tomatoes with liquid

3/4 pound combined sea scallops and large shrimp

1 (14-ounce) can artichoke hearts, drained and halved

3–6 tablespoons toasted pine nuts

1–2 cups freshly grated Parmesan cheese

In a large skillet, heat olive oil over medium heat. Add shallots and garlic and sauté for 3 minutes. Add parsley, basil, pepper flakes, wine, tomato paste and tomatoes. Break up tomatoes and bring to a boil. Reduce heat, cover and simmer for 20 minutes. Slice scallops in half. Add with shrimp and artichoke hearts to tomato mixture and cook for about 5 minutes.

Prepare linguine according to package directions and drain. Arrange on heated platter and top with seafood mixture. Sprinkle pine nuts and generous amounts of Parmesan cheese over dish. Serve with additional Parmesan cheese.

Serves 4

Just for fun, make this a real "feast from the sea" by using one of the shell-shaped pastas, such as maruzze, instead of linguine.

Cheese Quartet Rigatoni

1 pound rigatoni, cooked

8 ounces Gruyère cheese, shredded

8 ounces mozzarella cheese, shredded

8 ounces Gorgonzola cheese, grated

8 ounces Parmesan cheese, grated

1-2/3 cups heavy cream

1/4 cup (1/2 stick) unsalted butter

Fresh cracked pepper, to taste

Place cheeses in a saucepan and warm over low heat. Slowly stir in cream and butter as cheeses begin to melt. Stir constantly to blend. When cheeses are melted, add pasta and toss. Season with pepper and serve.

Serves 4

If a milder flavor is preferred, use Swiss cheese instead of Gruyère.

Pasta with Herbed Tomatoes and Cheese

1 pound small pasta shells or rotini

8 medium tomatoes, peeled, seeded and coarsely chopped

4 cloves garlic, minced

1 cup chopped fresh basil

2 tablespoons chopped fresh mint

2 teaspoons salt

1 teaspoon freshly ground pepper

3/4 teaspoon red pepper flakes

1/2 cup olive oil

1/2 cup freshly grated Parmesan cheese

1/2 pound Fontina cheese, finely diced (about 2 cups)

Fresh cracked pepper, to taste

In a medium bowl, toss together tomatoes, garlic, basil, mint, salt, black pepper, red pepper flakes and olive oil. Let stand at room temperature for 2 to 3 hours, tossing occasionally.

Cook pasta until al dente. Drain and transfer to a large serving bowl. Spoon off 1/4 cup of liquid from tomato mixture and toss with pasta to coat. While pasta is still warm, add Parmesan and Fontina and mix until cheeses begin to melt. Add tomatoes with liquid and blend until mixed. Serve warm or at room temperature.

Serves 6–8

Serve with bread and fruit for a warm weather meal, garnished with a sprig of fresh summer basil. For a heartier meal, add 1 pound of cooked, peeled and deveined shrimp just before serving.

🌿 Fresh mint is easy to grow in a windowsill pot or in the garden. Several dozen varieties are available, but spearmint is the most common type used in cooking.

Fettuccine with Tomato Basil Cream

8 ounces fettuccine,

1/2 cup heavy cream

1/2 cup chicken broth

1/4 cup olive oil

1/2 pound tomatoes, seeded and chopped

1/3 cup shredded fresh basil leaves

4 tablespoons freshly grated Parmesan cheese

In a large skillet, combine cream, broth and oil. Bring liquid to a boil, reduce heat and simmer vigorously for 5 minutes. Add tomatoes and basil and continue to simmer for 1 minute more.

While sauce is simmering, cook fettuccine until al dente. Drain well and toss in skillet with Parmesan cheese and sauce to coat well.

Serves 6 (as a side dish)

A light, colorful accompaniment to **Italian Grilled Tuna** or salmon steaks.

Baked Fettuccine

1 pound fettuccine

1/4 pound provolone cheese, grated

1/4 pound Gruyère or ricotta cheese, grated

1/4 pound Parmesan or Fontina cheese, grated

1/4 pound mozzarella cheese, grated

2 tablespoons bread crumbs

2 tablespoons unsalted butter, melted

1 cup heavy cream (can substitute up to 1/2 cup low-fat milk)

Bring a large pot half filled with water to a boil and cook fettuccine until al dente. Drain well. In a 2- or 3-quart casserole, mix the 4 cheeses (reserving 2 tablespoons Parmesan) and set aside.

Toss pasta with melted butter and add gradually to cheese mixture. Smooth top of casserole and pour cream evenly over all. Sprinkle with bread crumbs and reserved Parmesan cheese. Bake in a 400-degree oven for 20 to 30 minutes. If top begins to brown, cover with foil during the last 10 minutes of baking.

Serves 6

Comfort food for contemporary tastes. Although best served immediately, this dish may be prepared 24 to 48 hours in advance and baked before serving. Serve it as a main entree with salad and bread or as a side with fish or poultry.

🌿 Rule of thumb: The thinner the pasta, the thinner the sauce.

🍂 Pasta party napkin rings: Tie napkins with bows made of strands of fresh, flavored pasta or with colored cording threaded through or tied to different shapes of dried pasta.

Potato Gnocchi with Fresh Tomato Basil Butter Sauce

3-1/2 pounds baking potatoes

1-1/2 cups flour

Salt and freshly ground pepper, to taste

Sauce:

6 Roma tomatoes, seeded and diced

1 clove garlic, chopped

1/2 cup fresh basil, julienned

3/4 cup (1-1/2 sticks) unsalted butter

Salt and freshly ground pepper, to taste

Pecorino cheese, to garnish

Bake potatoes until tender. Scoop potato out of the skins and run through a potato ricer or mash well. Add salt and pepper.

On a clean surface, work flour into potato until a smooth dough forms. On a lightly floured surface, divide dough into 6 balls and roll out into 1-inch thick tubes. Cut into 1-inch pieces and lightly press with the tip of a fork. Arrange dumplings on a baking sheet, dust with flour, and refrigerate until firm, about 30 minutes.

For sauce: In a large sauté pan, melt butter. Add garlic and tomatoes, basil, salt and pepper. Sauté lightly until sauce is distributed evenly.

In a large pot, bring salted water to a boil. Add gnocchi. When dumplings float to the top, remove with a slotted spoon and add to tomato basil butter sauce. Serve immediately, garnished with freshly grated Pecorino cheese.

Serves 6

These traditional Italian dumplings are a labor of love!

Pasta Sauté with Rice and Pine Nuts

2 cups cooked egg noodles

1/3 cup butter or margarine

1-1/2 cups uncooked long grain rice

3-1/2 cups chicken broth

1/3 cup pine nuts, toasted

1/3 cup snipped fresh cilantro

Salt and freshly ground pepper, to taste

In a large skillet, sauté cooked noodles in butter, stirring often until noodles just turn brown, about 5 to 8 minutes. (Be careful when sautéing the noodles, as they tend splatter.) Add uncooked rice and stir. Add chicken broth and simmer, stirring occasionally until liquid is absorbed and rice is tender, about 18 to 20 minutes. Cover and let sit a few minutes before serving. Toss with pine nuts and cilantro. Season with salt and pepper and serve.

Serves 8

A delicious alternative to two standard side dishes—rice and noodles. Even though the noodles are fried here, they end up softened. Serve with swordfish marinated in **Basil Wine Marinade**.

Tomato Sauce Roma

3 tablespoons olive oil

2 tablespoons butter

1 cup chopped onion

1 tablespoon finely chopped garlic

4 cups fresh or canned tomatoes with liquid, peeled, seeded and chopped

1 tablespoon chopped fresh basil or 1 teaspoon dried

1 teaspoon salt

1 or 2 green chilies, chopped

1 bay leaf

1 cup tomato paste

3 tablespoons fresh oregano or 1 tablespoon dried

1 tablespoon rosemary

Heat oil and butter. Add onion and cook over medium heat for 7 minutes, stirring occasionally. Add garlic and cook for 1 to 2 minutes. Add tomatoes and remaining ingredients. Bring to a boil, then lower heat. Simmer for 1 hour, stirring occasionally. Sauce will be somewhat thick. Remove bay leaf before serving. Adjust seasoning to taste.

Makes 4–5 cups

Not just another tomato sauce—this one is absolutely fabulous.

Tomato Basil Sauce

1/2 cup dry white wine

1 medium onion, finely chopped

Pinch of red pepper flakes

1 pound fresh tomatoes (about 3), peeled, seeded and chopped

3 tablespoons butter

1 teaspoon sugar

1/2 teaspoon salt

1 teaspoon tomato paste

3/4 cup chopped fresh basil

In a medium saucepan, sauté onion in wine until liquid is reduced to a few tablespoons. Add all other ingredients except basil and simmer until fairly thick, about 15 minutes. Add basil, then remove from heat.

Makes about 3 cups

Basil is added at the last minute to prevent it from turning black. This delicious sauce may be frozen up to 6 months and refrigerated up to 2 weeks. It's especially good served over a calzone.

5 tablespoons unsalted butter, melted

7 (17- by 12-inch) sheets phyllo dough

7 tablespoons freshly grated Parmesan cheese

1 cup coarsely grated mozzarella or Gorgonzola cheese

1 cup very thinly sliced red onion

2 pounds tomatoes (about 5), peeled, seeded and sliced 1/4-inch thick

1/2 teaspoon oregano, crumbled

1 teaspoon fresh thyme or 1/4 teaspoon dried

Preheat oven to 375 degrees. Place phyllo between 2 sheets of waxed paper and cover with a damp towel to prevent drying out. Brush a baking sheet with butter. Lay 1 sheet of phyllo on top of butter. Lightly brush top of phyllo with butter. Sprinkle 1 tablespoon Parmesan cheese on top of butter. Lay on another sheet of phyllo and press so that it adheres to the first layer. Butter, sprinkle and layer remaining phyllo sheets in the same way, ending with a sheet of phyllo and reserving the last tablespoon of Parmesan cheese.

Sprinkle top sheet of phyllo with mozzarella. Scatter onion evenly over cheese. Arrange tomatoes in 1 layer over onions. Sprinkle with remaining cheese, oregano and thyme. Bake for 20 to 30 minutes, watching that phyllo only browns and does not burn. Use a sharp knife to cut into squares. Garnish with fresh thyme or basil.

Serves 6–8 as a main course
12–16 appetizer portions

A kaleidoscope of summer vegetables atop a light, crunchy phyllo crust. Try puff pastry in place of the phyllo dough. Experiment with other cheeses and vegetables, too, such as zucchini sliced paper thin.

Mozzarella is one of Italy's famous "stretched curd" cheeses. Called pasta filata, *the technique involves giving the curd a hot-whey bath, then kneading and stretching it to a pliable consistency. Provolone is another member of this special-process family.*

1-1/2 cups yellow cornmeal

1 cup cold water

1 cup boiling water

1/3 cup freshly grated Parmesan cheese

2 tablespoons oil

1-1/4 cups chopped onion

1/2–1 green bell pepper, sliced

1/2 cup sliced mushrooms

1 teaspoon oregano, or to taste

1 teaspoon basil, or to taste

Freshly ground pepper, to taste

1 clove garlic, minced

1 (8-ounce) can tomato sauce

1 cup grated mozzarella or Monterey Jack cheese

In a medium bowl, combine cornmeal and cold water. Stir into a pan of boiling water and cook over low heat until thick, stirring continuously. Stir in Parmesan cheese and pour into a greased 10-inch pie pan. Press to form an edge. Bake in a 350-degree oven for 25 to 30 minutes.

While crust is baking, heat oil in a skillet and sauté onion, green pepper and mushrooms until tender. Stir in oregano, basil, pepper and garlic.

Pour tomato sauce over hot crust and cover with seasoned vegetables. Sprinkle grated cheese over all and bake for 20 minutes or until cheese is melted.

Serves 4–6

This vegetarian pizza with a textured crust can be prepared an hour before serving and baked up until the last 10 minutes of cooking time (or until the cheese is melted), then returned to the oven before serving. Meat lovers may enjoy adding some crumbled Italian sausage.

Fresh pasta cooks from a few seconds after the water returns to a boil for thin noodles to 90 seconds for very wide ones. The noodles should not taste like raw dough, but should have a bit of a bite. Do not expect them to be al dente.

Storing pasta: Dried pasta will last almost indefinitely if stored airtight in a cool, dry place. Fresh pasta can be frozen for up to 1 month. Fresh pasta made with egg may be stored in the refrigerator for up to 4 days.

6 ounces pizza dough

1–2 tablespoons olive oil plus additional for brushing on crust

1/2 teaspoon minced garlic

1/2 cup shredded Fontina cheese

2 tablespoons crumbled Gorgonzola cheese

1/8–1/4 pound shredded prosciutto, to taste

4–5 tablespoons chopped canned tomatoes in heavy puree

8–10 spinach leaves, cleaned and torn

Prepare hot charcoal fire, setting a clean grill rack 3 to 4 inches above coals. On a large, oiled, inverted baking sheet, spread and flatten pizza dough with hands into a 10- to 12-inch free-form circle, 1/8-inch thick. Do not make a raised edge. When possible to hold hand over coals for 3 to 4 seconds at distance of 5 inches, lift dough gently with fingertips and drape onto grill. Catch loose edge on grill first and guide remaining dough into place over coals.

Within 1 minute dough will puff slightly, underside will stiffen and grill marks will appear. Using tongs, flip crust over onto coolest part of grill (this is done most easily by 2 people). Quickly brush grilled surface with olive oil. Sprinkle with garlic, Fontina and Gorgonzola cheeses. Top with prosciutto and tomatoes. Drizzle 1 to 2 tablespoons olive oil over top. Slide pizza back toward hot coals but not directly over top.

Using tongs, rotate pizza frequently so different sections receive higher heat. Check underside often for burning. Pizza is cooked when top is bubbly and cheeses are melted, about 6 to 8 minutes. Top with spinach leaves. Remove with two spatulas.

Serves 4 as a main course
8 appetizer portions

*Guests at an outdoor party will have fun watching pizza "happen" on the grill. Prepare toppings prior to starting the coals. Cut into squares for an appetizer or serve as a main dish with **Marinated Mushrooms and Romaine Salad**.*

Tortilla Stacked Pizza

12 (6-inch) flour tortillas

Vegetable oil

1 (16-ounce) can refried beans

1/2 cup minced onions

1 (4-ounce) can chopped green chilies

1-1/2 cups grated Monterey Jack cheese

1 cup chopped red bell pepper

1-1/2 cups grated cheddar cheese

2 cups picante sauce

4 tablespoons sour cream (optional)

Black olive slices (optional)

Fry tortillas in oil until lightly crisp. Pat dry with paper towels.

Preheat oven to 375 degrees. Spread refried beans on 4 tortillas. Place tortillas on 2 ungreased baking sheets (or 1 oversized sheet). Place a second tortilla on top of each of the tortillas with beans. Evenly divide onions, chilies, Monterey Jack cheese and peppers and sprinkle on second tortilla layers.

Cover with third tortillas. Sprinkle this layer with cheddar cheese. (Can be prepared ahead to this point.) Pour picante sauce over top of each stack and bake for 15 to 20 minutes until heated through and cheese is melted.

Use a spatula to carefully transfer each stack to individual plates. Just before serving, top with a tablespoon of sour cream and sliced olives, if desired.

Serves 4

One stack is a hearty meal; use a pizza cutter to cut into wedges for smaller appetites. For a more mellow flavor, sauté the onions and red bell peppers.

Upside-Down Pizza Pie

1 pound mild Italian sausage, casings removed

1 large onion, chopped

1 cup spaghetti sauce

4 ounces black olives, sliced

1/2 pound mushrooms, sliced

10 ounces sliced mozzarella cheese

2 large eggs

1 cup milk

1 tablespoon vegetable oil

1 cup flour

1/4 teaspoon salt

1/4 cup freshly grated Parmesan cheese

Crumble sausage in a large skillet over medium heat. Add onion and cook, stirring frequently, until onion is translucent and sausage is cooked through. Drain off fat. Stir in spaghetti sauce, olives and mushrooms. Heat until bubbly. Pour into an ungreased 9- by 13-inch baking dish. Arrange mozzarella cheese evenly over top.

In a food processor, blend eggs, milk, oil, flour and salt until smooth. Evenly pour over mozzarella, then sprinkle with Parmesan cheese. Bake uncovered in a 400-degree oven until crust is puffed and golden brown, about 25 minutes. Cut into squares and serve immediately.

Serves 6

*An easy dish for family or casual entertaining. Garnish the golden brown crust with a few quartered black olives and a sprig of parsley. Add or substitute other ingredients as suits your taste, such as pepperoni, ground beef and green or red bell peppers. For a variation on the spaghetti sauce, use **Tomato Sauce Roma**.*

Well-known as a cholesterol-friendly food, olive oil has become an important part of our cuisine—in salad dressings, sauces and marinades. Although incorporating olive oil into your way of life is easy, choosing the oil can present quite a confusing task. Taste and color often vary, depending on where and how the oil is produced.

Olive oils range in color from light amber to deep green, and in flavor from mildly "buttery" to semi-fruity to a full-bodied fruity taste. Nationalities of oils are also distinctive:

🌿 *Italian*—Known for intense olive taste, peppery flavor and deep green color. 🌿 *French*—More delicate and lightly flavored than Italian oils. 🌿 *Spanish*—Heavy and thick, with a strong flavor. 🌿 *Greek*—Thick in consistency and tending toward a lighter taste than Spanish olive oils. 🌿 *Californian*—May range from a delicate French-style taste to a heavy, rich Italian-style oil.

Olive oils are graded according to the process used in extracting the oil from the olive. Topping the list is extra-virgin olive oil, followed by superfine, fine and virgin oils. These are made from hand-picked olives that are cold pressed (without the use of heat), a process that allows the oil to retain its delicate flavor. Pure olive oil is often a blend of refined oil (extracted by further pressings using heat or chemicals) and virgin oil.

Flavored Oils

To flavor oils, loosely pack herbs in a jar or crock (stems and flowers alone or with the leaves) and fill with virgin olive oil. Cover and leave in a dark place for 2 weeks. Strain the oil through a sieve or cheesecloth and then pour through a funnel into clean, dry bottles. (To prepare bottles, arrange them on a baking sheet and place in the oven at 150–200 degrees for several hours.) Drop in a sprig of the herb used for flavoring and then cap. 🌿 Experiment with different oils and flavor combinations. Try orange peels, slivers of peppercorns and herb seeds, or basil and 1/4 pound of sun-dried tomatoes. For spicier oil, add 1 or 2 hot peppers. 🌿 Herb-infused oils offer a quicker variation of flavored oils. In a saucepan, combine 1 cup of fresh herbs (rosemary, sage, oregano, bay leaves or thyme) with 2 cups of extra-virgin olive oil. Heat over medium-high until herbs start to sizzle and oil begins to bubble. Remove pan from heat and let oil cool. Discard herbs and pour into decorative bottles. Insert beautiful sprigs of herbs (take care to submerge them completely), then cork or seal the bottles. Oil is ready to use immediately. 🌿 Try adding peppercorns or red pepper flakes once oil has been bottled. 🌿 Drizzle flavored oils on breads, in salad greens, or when sautéing vegetables and cooking meat. 🌿 Once oil has been opened, store it in a cool, dark place.

Crust:

1 package active dry yeast

1 cup warm water (110 degrees)

1 teaspoon salt

1/4 cup olive oil

2-1/2–3 cups flour

Meat filling:

1/2 cup tomato sauce

1 teaspoon basil

1 teaspoon oregano

6 ounces mozzarella cheese, shredded

1/2 cup freshly grated Parmesan cheese

1/2 pound Italian sausage, cooked, or pepperoni, sliced or diced

Glaze:

1 egg white, beaten

1 teaspoon fennel seed (optional)

For crust: In a large bowl, dissolve yeast in warm water. Let sit for 5 minutes. Add salt and olive oil. Add flour gradually until a stiff dough forms. Turn out onto lightly floured board and knead until dough is smooth and satiny, about 5 minutes. Add flour as needed to prevent sticking. Place in a lightly greased bowl. Cover and let rise in a warm place until dough has doubled, about 1 hour. Cover baking sheet with parchment paper or lightly grease and sprinkle with cornmeal. Roll out dough to make an oval about 14 by 10 inches. Transfer dough to prepared baking sheet.

Spread a 5-inch strip of tomato sauce down the center of the dough. Sprinkle with basil and oregano. Divide cheeses and sausage or desired filling over sauce and spread evenly. Lift up dough from both sides along the length of the covered oval and cover the filling, making a seam across the top center of the calzone.

Pinch edges together to seal completely. Let rise for 30 minutes, until dough looks puffy. Heat oven to 400 degrees. Pierce top of calzone in several places with a fork or skewer to make vent holes. Brush with beaten egg white and sprinkle with fennel seeds. Bake for 25 minutes or until golden.

Serves 4–6 as a main course
8–10 appetizer portions

*Serve with your favorite red sauce or **Tomato Basil Sauce**. We've included four different fillings here; pick your favorite and enjoy! Baked calzones are best when fresh, but may be frozen.*

Prosciutto and Cheese Filling

1/2 cup finely chopped onion • 1 teaspoon safflower oil • 1/2 cup finely chopped mixed red and green bell peppers • 3 ounces provolone cheese, shredded • 4 ounces mozzarella cheese, shredded • 2/3 cup freshly grated Parmesan cheese • 1/2 cup thinly sliced prosciutto • 2 eggs, beaten • 2 tablespoons chopped Italian parsley • 1 teaspoon coarsely ground pepper

Sauté onion in safflower oil over medium-high heat for 2 minutes.
Add peppers and sauté for another 2 minutes. In a large bowl,
with a fork or hands gently combine cheeses, prosciutto,
eggs, Italian parsley and pepper.

Spinach Filling

3 cloves garlic, minced • 2 tablespoons olive oil • 1 pound fresh spinach, cleaned • 1/2 teaspoon red pepper flakes • 8 ounces mozzarella cheese, sliced thick

In a skillet, sauté garlic in olive oil over medium-high heat for 1 minute.
Add spinach and cook until wilted, no longer than 2 minutes. Season
with red pepper flakes. Layer with 1/3 of the cheese, 1/2 the spinach,
another layer of cheese, then spinach and remaining cheese.

Cheese Filling

*1/3 pound Gruyère cheese • 1/3 pound mozzarella cheese
1/2 pound provolone cheese • 3 tablespoons cream cheese • 1/2 cup
coarsely chopped Italian parsley*

In a food processor fitted with steel blade, combine Gruyère,
mozzarella and provolone cheeses. Process until coarse.
Add cream cheese and Italian parsley.

ASPARAGUS, ARTICHOKES & MUSHROOMS

Chinese Fried Asparagus, 241
Classic Creamed Mushrooms and Artichokes, 232
Fresh Asparagus Flans, 241
Wild Mushroom Ragoût, 232

BEANS, BROCCOLI & BRUSSELS SPROUTS

Broccoli Amandine, 245
Broccoli with Onions and Pine Nuts, 245
Chili String Beans, 236
Honeyed Brussels Sprouts, 246
Liberty Green Beans, 236

CORN, CARROTS & CAULIFLOWER

Adobe Corn with Jalapeño-Lime Butter, 237
Grilled Herb Corn on the Cob, 238
Lemon Carrot Sheaves, 233
Spiced Grapes and Carrots, 233
Sunburst Florets, 246
Zesty Carrot Gratin, 234

EGGPLANT, FENNEL & LEEKS

Braised Fennel with Sage Sauce, 234
Eggplant Prosciutto, 242
Leek Timbales, 240
Leeks in Lemon Cream, 240
Ratatouille, 243

PEPPERS, PEAS & SQUASH

Festive Pepper Strips, 246
Minted Peas, 233
Orange Blossom Zucchini, 245
Polenta Pepper Soufflés, 247
Spaghetti Squash with Sun-Dried Tomatoes, 242
Thai Zucchini, 244
Thyme Veggie Bundles, 244

TOMATOES & POTATOES

Basil Tomatoes with Gorgonzola, 243
Grilled Potatoes, 238
New Potatoes with Caviar Cream, 239
Rosemary Potato Tart, 238
Sherried Sweet Potatoes, 239
White Cheddar Parsnips and Potatoes, 235

GRAINS & LEGUMES

Calypso Black Beans, 247
Crunchy Baked Barley, 249
Emerald Asparagus Pinwheel, 250
Kaleidoscope Fried Rice, 251
Lemon and Chive Risotto, 249
Ozark Caviar, 248
West Indian Apricot Rice, 251
Wild Rice with Plantains, 250

MINI RECIPES

Flavored Butters, 237

Vegetables & Grains

Pictured finishing touch:

SERVING

PORTIONS OF RICE IN

CORN HUSKS, 250

SPECIAL TOPIC BOXES

HERE WE GLOW, 235

JUST WILD ABOUT MUSHROOMS, 248

Wild Mushroom Ragoût

4 tablespoons unsalted butter

4 tablespoons olive oil

1 large onion, cut into 8 pieces

1 teaspoon sugar

3 cloves garlic, coarsely chopped

8 large shallots, halved

4 ounces chanterelle mushrooms, cut into 2-inch pieces

4 ounces shiitake mushrooms, halved or quartered into 1-inch pieces

8 ounces cremini (brown Italian) mushrooms, halved

Salt and freshly ground pepper, to taste

1 teaspoon crushed rosemary

3 ounces cognac

2 heaping tablespoons flour

1/2 cup beef broth

Heat butter and oil in skillet. Add onion and sugar and sauté on high heat until well browned and caramelized, about 20 to 25 minutes, stirring constantly. Add garlic and shallots and sauté on medium heat until soft, about 10 minutes. Add mushrooms and sauté over medium heat for 5 to 8 minutes, stirring several times. Add salt, pepper and crushed rosemary.

Turn heat to high, then add cognac and ignite. When flame subsides, reduce heat to medium. Add flour and stir well. Add broth, bit by bit, stirring constantly until consistency is slightly liquid. Turn off heat and serve. (May be kept covered for 30 minutes and warmed before serving.)

Serves 4–6

Other varieties of wild mushrooms may be substituted. The earthy flavor blends well with game, beef or fowl dishes. As a first course, serve in puff pastry shells with a rosemary sprig garnish.

Classic Creamed Mushrooms and Artichokes

1 (9-ounce) package frozen artichoke hearts

1 pound fresh mushrooms, halved

2 tablespoons plus 2/3 cup water

1/4 cup sliced scallions

2 tablespoons butter

2 tablespoons flour

1 teaspoon instant chicken bouillon granules

1/4 teaspoon crushed thyme

Dash of ground nutmeg

1/2 cup shredded Swiss cheese

1/3 cup sour cream

1/2 cup chopped pecans, toasted

Place frozen artichoke hearts in a colander and run under cool water until separated. Drain and halve each lengthwise. Combine with mushrooms and 2 tablespoons water in a baking dish. Microwave, covered, for 8 to 10 minutes, stirring twice. Drain. Return to baking dish.

In a 4-cup microwave-safe dish, combine scallions and butter. Cook covered for 2 minutes. Stir in flour, bouillon, thyme and nutmeg, followed by 2/3 cup water. Microwave uncovered for 2 to 3 minutes until thick, stirring every minute. Stir in cheese until melted, then add sour cream. Fold into artichoke-mushroom mixture. Return to microwave and cook uncovered for 2 minutes more, stirring once. Top with pecans and serve.

Serves 6–8

A rich partner for a simple roasted meat.

Minted Peas

2 cups fresh or frozen peas

2 tablespoons unsalted butter

2 tablespoons chopped fresh mint leaves

4 mint sprigs, to garnish

Steam or boil peas for 5 minutes. Drain and toss with butter and mint in a colander so excess butter drains off. Garnish with fresh mint sprigs.

Serves 4

Arrive early at the farmer's market to select the freshest mint and succulent green peas.

Lemon Carrot Sheaves

1-1/2 pounds carrots, peeled

6 leek strips, for tying bundles

1/3 cup fresh lemon juice

2 tablespoons sugar

3 tablespoons butter

1/4 teaspoon salt

Julienne carrots into 3-inch sticks. Steam in 1/2 inch of water in a covered saucepan for 8 to 10 minutes. Rinse with cold water.

Separate carrots into 6 bundles. Drop each leek strip into boiling water for 1 minute. Remove and rinse with cold water, then drain. Carefully tie a leek strip around each carrot bundle.

Combine lemon juice, sugar, butter and salt in a heavy sauté pan. Bring to a boil. Reduce heat and simmer for 1 minute, stirring until sugar dissolves. Add carrot bundles and cook over medium heat for 3 minutes. Spoon mixture over carrots to serve.

Serves 6–8

These vibrant little bundles enliven any pork or lamb entree.

Spiced Grapes and Carrots

8–10 carrots, French cut and steamed

3 tablespoons firmly packed light brown sugar

3 tablespoons Grand Marnier

Dash of cinnamon

Dash of nutmeg

Dash of allspice

1-1/2 teaspoons cornstarch

2 teaspoons water

1-1/2 cups seedless green grapes

Place cooked carrots in a saucepan. Stir in brown sugar, Grand Marnier, cinnamon, nutmeg and allspice. In a small bowl, mix cornstarch and water until smooth. Stir into carrots. Bring to a boil, stirring constantly. (May be kept covered at room temperature for several hours.)

Just before serving, add grapes and warm until heated through.

Serves 8

This attractive combo jazzes up simple beef or chicken dishes.

Zesty Carrot Gratin

1-1/2 pounds carrots, peeled

3/4 cup water

1 teaspoon paprika

2 tablespoons grated onion

1 tablespoon prepared
horseradish, drained

1/2 cup mayonnaise

1/4 cup grated cheddar cheese

1/2 teaspoon salt

1/4 teaspoon freshly ground pepper

1 cup fresh bread crumbs

1/4 cup butter, melted

Slice carrots into 1/4-inch thick rounds. Boil in water for 5 minutes. Drain, reserving 1/4 cup of water.

Combine reserved water, paprika, onion, horseradish, mayonnaise, cheese, salt and pepper. Add carrots and spoon into a buttered 2-quart baking dish. Combine bread crumbs and melted butter and sprinkle over carrot mixture. Bake in a 350-degree oven for 20 minutes.

Serves 8

For special gatherings, prepare in individual ramekins. In season, use Vidalia onions for a sweeter flavor.

Braised Fennel with Sage Sauce

2 heads fennel

5 tablespoons butter

3/4 cup chicken broth

1/4 cup fresh lemon juice

1 tablespoon flour

Grated zest of 1 lemon

4 fresh sage leaves, shredded or
2 teaspoons dried

Trim fennel, cut in half and wash well. Place heads broadside down in a large baking dish. Dot with 4 tablespoons butter. Pour chicken broth and 1/8 cup lemon juice over fennel. Bake in a 300-degree oven for 1 to 1-1/2 hours, turning and basting regularly. When fennel is soft, remove with a slotted spoon to a serving dish. Reserve liquid.

Mix flour, 1 tablespoon butter and remaining lemon juice to form a smooth paste. Drop by bits into simmering reserved liquid. Simmer, whisking constantly in the same direction until thickened. Whisk in lemon zest and sage. Pour over fennel and serve.

Serves 4

Sage is a key ingredient in this interesting side dish.

When buying fresh fennel, look for firm stalks and white bulbs. Fennel may be stored in a plastic bag in the refrigerator for up to 5 days.

White Cheddar Parsnips and Potatoes

2 pounds parsnips

2 pounds potatoes

1/3 cup heavy cream (more as needed)

3–4 tablespoons butter, or to taste, plus additional for topping

Salt and freshly ground pepper, to taste

2 tablespoons freshly grated nutmeg, or to taste

1 pound white cheddar cheese, grated

Peel parsnips and potatoes and cut into small pieces. Combine in a deep saucepan, cover with water and cook until tender. Drain. Whip potatoes and parsnips with cream and butter to the consistency of mashed potatoes. Season with salt, pepper and nutmeg.

Butter a 9- by 13-inch baking dish. Layer the bottom with half the potato-parsnip mixture and top with half the grated cheese. Repeat, finishing with remaining cheese on top. Dot with butter. Bake in a 350-degree oven for 15 to 20 minutes, or until hot.

Serves 8–10

As an alternative presentation, transfer puree to a pastry bag with a large star tip and pipe individual portions onto a baking sheet. Sprinkle with cheddar cheese and bake until cheese melts.

Here We Glow

Nothing creates a special mood like soft, flattering candlelight. Alternatives to the expected can add an extra spark of flair.

Fresh bay leaves, dill, coriander, lavender or Sweet Annie tied to votive holders will emit a soft fragrance from the warmth of the candle. Set crystal candlesticks en masse on a mirror for a dazzling chorus of flickers. Use hurricane lanterns instead of candles. Tint the oil or add sprigs of herbs or flowers to it. Intersperse floating candles and greenery in a clear glass bowl filled with water. Place votive candles in a napkin "nest" in the center of each dinner plate and light just before guests enter. Stabilize candles in unusual holders with sand, dried legumes, aquarium gravel, rock salt, sunflower seeds, potting soil or rice.

Liberty Green Beans

1 cup sugar

1/2 cup vegetable oil

1 cup white vinegar

1/2 teaspoon salt

1/2 teaspoon freshly ground pepper

4 pounds fresh green beans, trimmed and steamed, or 4 (16-ounce) cans

1 (8-ounce) can sliced water chestnuts, drained

1 red onion, thinly sliced

4 ounces crumbled blue cheese

Bring first 5 ingredients to a boil. Put beans, water chestnuts and red onion into a large bowl. Pour vinegar mixture over all. Add crumbled blue cheese and mix well.

Serve chilled or at room temperature.

Serves 12

Great for picnics and buffet meals, this combination is best prepared a day before serving.

Chili String Beans

16 raw almonds, coarsely chopped

4 teaspoons chili oil (see below)

3/4 pound fresh string beans, trimmed and blanched

1 red bell pepper, julienned

1/4 teaspoon salt

Freshly grated Parmesan cheese, for garnish

Chili oil:

3 cloves garlic, peeled

1/2 cup light olive oil

1 to 1-1/2 teaspoons red pepper flakes

1/2 lemon

For oil: Crush garlic cloves with the flat edge of a knife. Preheat a heavy sauté pan over low heat, then add garlic, olive oil, red pepper flakes and lemon half, cut-side down. Simmer for 20 minutes (do not boil). Remove from heat and cool to room temperature. Pour mixture through a fine strainer and discard garlic, pepper flakes and lemon. Keep oil refrigerated in a covered jar.

Preheat a heavy sauté pan or wok over medium heat. Add almonds and stir until lightly toasted, about 2 minutes. Remove from pan and set aside.

Heat chili oil in the same pan. Add beans and stir-fry for 3 minutes. Add red pepper strips and stir-fry for 3 minutes more. Season with salt and add almonds, then stir. Sprinkle with Parmesan cheese and serve.

Serves 4

Spicy infused oil gives these crisp green beans a tasty kick.

For more information on flavored oils, see "Olive Oils: Beyond the Basics" in Pasta.

Adobe Corn with Jalapeño-Lime Butter

8 ears sweet corn

1/2 jalapeño pepper, seeded, veins removed, and finely minced

8 tablespoons unsalted butter

1 tablespoon fresh lime juice

1/2 teaspoon grated lime zest

1/2 teaspoon salt

For butter: In a medium bowl, combine jalapeño, butter, lime juice, lime zest and salt. Cream together until well blended. Place dollops on waxed paper and shape into an 8-inch log. Wrap in waxed paper or plastic wrap and refrigerate. Slice into 8 pieces just before serving.

Boil corn for 5 to 6 minutes and serve each ear with 1 tablespoon jalapeño-lime butter. To grill, wrap corn and 1 tablespoon of jalapeño-lime butter in foil wrap. Place on grill and cook until tender, 20 to 30 minutes, turning occasionally. To bake, follow grilling directions for assembly and bake in a 400-degree oven for 20 minutes.

Butters

Basil-Parmesan Butter

1 cup (2 sticks) unsalted butter, softened

1/2 cup chopped fresh basil

4 cloves garlic, minced

2 tablespoons toasted pine nuts, or more to taste

2 tablespoons freshly grated Parmesan cheese

1 tablespoon dry vermouth

Salt, to taste

Combine all ingredients in a food processor (or by hand for a chunkier texture) and chill before serving. Great with freshly roasted corn or any fresh vegetables.

Makes about 2 cups

Ancho Oregano Butter

1/2 cup (1 stick) unsalted butter, softened

1 ancho chile, toasted and finely ground (about 1 tablespoon)

2 tablespoons chopped fresh oregano

3 tablespoons chopped pecans

3 cloves garlic, minced

1 tablespoon tequila

Combine all ingredients and chill before serving. Add to corn, sauces and soups, or melt over grilled chicken or steaks.

Makes about 1 cup

Royal Rosemary Butter

1/2 cup (1 stick) unsalted butter, softened

3 teaspoons fresh rosemary leaves, removed from stem

2–3 cloves garlic, minced

1/2 teaspoon grated lemon zest

1 tablespoon fresh lemon juice

1/4 teaspoon red pepper flakes

Salt, to taste

Combine all ingredients and chill before serving. Great dabbed on potatoes as well as steak, chicken or fish.

Makes about 1 cup

Grilled Herb Corn on the Cob

6 ears sweet corn

6 sprigs rosemary

6 sprigs mint

6 pats butter

Salt and freshly ground pepper, to taste

Place each ear of corn on a foil square. Place a pat of butter, a rosemary sprig and a mint sprig on each. Sprinkle with salt and pepper. Seal foil tightly and grill for 15 minutes, turning every 5 minutes so that packages do not burn on one side.

Serves 6

*Rosemary and mint make a delicious pairing. Serve with **Mesquite Grilled T-Bones** and French bread with **Fast Lane Bread Topping**, wrapped in foil and heated on the grill.*

Rosemary Potato Tart

2 to 2-1/2 pounds baking potatoes, peeled if desired

1 tablespoon olive oil

1-1/2 teaspoons fresh rosemary, minced

1-1/2 teaspoons salt

1/2 teaspoon freshly ground pepper

6 tablespoons butter, melted

1 teaspoon minced garlic

Slice potatoes very thin and place in a large bowl of ice water. Set aside.

Coat the inside of a cast-iron skillet or springform pan with olive oil. Arrange 1/4 of the potato slices, overlapping, to fill bottom of pan. Sprinkle with 1/2 teaspoon rosemary, 1/4 teaspoon salt, 1/8 teaspoon pepper and 2 tablespoons butter. Repeat layers with remaining ingredients, topping the last layer with minced garlic.

Bake in a 450-degree oven for 45 minutes. Loosen sides of tart with a knife and invert onto a platter. Cut into wedges for serving.

Serves 4–6

For a cheesy variation, substitute Parmesan cheese for the rosemary and garlic.

Grilled Potatoes

3–4 large baking potatoes or 10 new potatoes

2 cloves garlic, minced

2 tablespoons chopped onion

1/4 cup chopped fresh chives

Salt and freshly ground pepper, to taste

2 tablespoons butter, quartered

2 tablespoons vegetable oil

Scrub potatoes and cut into wedges. Place on a large piece of foil and sprinkle with garlic, onion, chives, salt and pepper. Top with butter and oil. Wrap foil, sealing end twice, and place on a hot grill for 45 minutes. (Hotter grills may require less time.) Keep away from direct flame.

Serves 3–4

These also may be prepared in individual packets. Substitute other fresh herbs for the chives as your tastebuds dictate. Delicious with barbecued pork chops.

New Potatoes with Caviar Cream

1/2 cup heavy cream

4 ounces salmon caviar

2 tablespoons chopped fresh chives

1 hard-cooked egg, chopped

30 small new potatoes

Fresh dill, to garnish

With an electric mixer, whip cream until soft peaks form. In a bowl, combine whipped cream, caviar, chives and egg and mix well. Refrigerate.

Boil new potatoes until tender. Allow to cool. Halve each potato and hollow out the centers with a melon baller. Leave a 1/4-inch shell. Slice off a small portion of the bottoms so potatoes can stand upright. Spoon cream mixture into hollowed potatoes. Serve well chilled, garnished with fresh dill.

Serves 8–10

These stuffed potatoes are equally delicious as a side dish or as an appetizer.

Sherried Sweet Potatoes

1-1/2 tablespoons cornstarch

2 teaspoons orange juice

1-1/4 cups firmly packed brown sugar

2 cups canned apricot halves, drained (reserve syrup)

1/8 teaspoon cinnamon

2 tablespoons butter

5 tablespoons sherry

2 (20-ounce) cans sweet potatoes, sliced

1/2 cup golden raisins

1 teaspoon salt

Dissolve cornstarch in orange juice. In a saucepan, combine brown sugar, cornstarch mixture, reserved apricot syrup, cinnamon and butter. Cook, stirring until mixture comes to a boil. Add sherry and remove from heat.

Arrange sweet potatoes, apricots and raisins in a 9- by 13-inch pan. Sprinkle with salt and pour sauce mixture over all. Bake in a 350-degree oven for 30 minutes or until bubbly.

Serves 6–8

Try this with fresh sweet potatoes. Boil 2-1/2 pounds sweet potatoes for 5 minutes, then slice and prepare as directed.

Adding a few drops of lemon juice to the cooking water will keep vegetables such as potatoes and parsnips whiter.

Add slices of raw sweet potatoes to a tray of crudités. They taste like chestnuts.

Leek Timbales

2 medium leeks (bulb and part of stem)

2 tablespoons unsalted butter

3 eggs

1-1/2 to 2 cups heavy cream, as needed

1/2 teaspoon nutmeg, plus additional to garnish

Salt and freshly ground white and black pepper, to taste

Preheat oven to 350 degrees. Grease four 4-ounce soufflé dishes or ramekins. Slice leeks in half lengthwise under running water, rinsing between layers to remove sand, then slice again into thin strips. Melt butter in a saucepan and cook leeks until wilted. Puree half the leeks in a food processor and then stir into remaining wilted leeks. Transfer to a 4-cup measure.

Whisk eggs and stir into leeks. Add enough cream to mixture to make 4 cups. Mix well and add nutmeg, salt and peppers. Spoon into prepared molds and place molds in a baking dish. Pour enough water into dish to cover halfway up sides of molds. Butter a piece of foil and lay over baking dish, butter-side down. Bake for 25 to 30 minutes or until a knife inserted into the center of the molds comes out clean. Unmold onto individual plates, sprinkle with a pinch of nutmeg and serve.

Serves 4

These rich vegetable custards are wonderful served with Apricot-Honey Baked Ham. They also make a lovely first course.

Leeks in Lemon Cream

4 small leeks

4 tablespoons unsalted butter

1/2 teaspoon salt

1/2 teaspoon freshly ground pepper

2 tablespoons heavy cream

1 teaspoon grated lemon zest

Juice of 1/2 lemon

Trim bottom and dark green portions of leeks. Julienne into 1-inch strips. Discard hard, bitter center portions. Transfer to colander and rinse very well under cold running water.

Heat a heavy sauté pan and add butter and leeks. Sauté for about 10 to 15 minutes until tender. Mix in salt, pepper, cream, lemon zest and lemon juice. Serve immediately.

Serves 6

This delicately flavored side dish pairs well with fish or seafood.

Chinese Fried Asparagus

1 tablespoon cornstarch

1 tablespoon water

3/4 cup chicken broth

1 tablespoon soy sauce

1 large clove garlic, minced

1-1/2 pounds fresh asparagus

1 tablespoon vegetable oil

Dissolve cornstarch in water. In a saucepan, combine chicken broth, soy sauce, cornstarch mixture and garlic. Bring to a slow boil and cook until thickened. Set aside and keep warm.

Cut asparagus into 1/2-inch pieces, using only the tender portions. Sauté in oil for approximately 5 minutes until barely tender. Do not overcook. Cover with warm sauce and serve immediately.

Serves 6

For more tender, attractive asparagus, prepare it French style by peeling the stems, beginning 1/2 inch below the tip.

Fresh Asparagus Flans

20–24 medium-sized fresh asparagus spears

3 eggs

1 cup crème fraîche

Salt and freshly ground pepper, to taste

Pinch of nutmeg

3 slices toasted bread, halved diagonally and crusts removed

Sauce:

3/4 cup fresh or frozen baby peas

3 tablespoons chopped onion

4 tablespoons unsalted butter

Pinch of curry powder

1/3 cup crème fraîche

Salt and freshly ground pepper, to taste

Trim asparagus spears to the same length and tie into a bunch. In a deep saucepan, bring 2 quarts salted water to a boil. Stand spears in pan with tips extending just above water line. Simmer until just tender. Drain well, trim and reserve tips.

In a food processor, blend asparagus stems with eggs and crème fraîche until smooth. Strain and season with salt, pepper and nutmeg. Turn mixture into 6 small greased molds or 4-ounce ramekins. Place molds in a baking pan with enough water to cover halfway up sides of molds. Bake in a 325-degree oven for 30 minutes or until a knife inserted into centers of molds comes out clean.

For sauce: In a small saucepan, bring salted water to a boil. Add peas and simmer for 3 minutes. Drain and set aside. In a skillet, sauté onions with 2 tablespoons butter until softened. Add curry powder and crème fraîche. Season with salt and pepper and simmer for 3 minutes. In a food processor, combine cream mixture, peas and remaining butter until smooth.

To serve, divide sauce among 6 plates. Unmold flans and place in center of sauce. Garnish each with reserved asparagus tips (reheat if necessary) and a toast triangle.

Serves 6

A real showstopper! Cut toasts with cookie cutters for a festive presentation.

Eggplant Prosciutto

2 pounds eggplant

1/4 cup melted butter

Freshly ground pepper, to taste

4 ounces prosciutto, thinly sliced

1-1/4 pounds Fontina cheese, thinly sliced

6 black olives, halved, to garnish

Peel eggplant and cut crosswise into twelve 3/4-inch slices. Preheat oven to 375 degrees. Arrange eggplant slices on a baking sheet and brush with butter. Sprinkle lightly with pepper. Completely cover each slice with single layer of prosciutto. Top with cheese, pressing lightly.

Bake until eggplant is tender and cheese is melted and browned, about 10 to 15 minutes. Arrange on a serving platter and garnish with olive halves.

Serves 12

Try this as an appetizer with miniature Japanese eggplants or serve as a nice first course preceding **Italian Grilled Tuna**. *Cholesterol-conscious cooks may prefer to substitute olive oil for the butter.*

Spaghetti Squash with Sun-Dried Tomatoes

1 spaghetti squash

1 (7-ounce) jar oil-packed sun-dried tomatoes (reserve liquid)

1 tablespoon cider vinegar

1/4 cup fresh orange juice

1 tablespoon olive oil

1 tablespoon oil from sun-dried tomatoes

1/2 teaspoon cumin

1/2 teaspoon ground coriander

1/2 teaspoon red pepper flakes

Grated zest of 1 orange

3 cloves garlic, minced

12 basil leaves, shredded, to garnish

Halve squash and discard seeds. Place halves cut-side down in a heavy pan. Add 2 inches of water. Bring to a boil and cover. Reduce heat to medium and simmer squash for 20 minutes or until tender. Drain and cool.

With a fork, remove spaghetti-like fibers from squash and set aside. Halve tomatoes and combine with spaghetti squash in a bowl. Toss well. Place all remaining ingredients, except basil, into a jar, then cover and shake well. Add to squash mixture and toss several times. Bake in a 375-degree oven for 30 to 45 minutes.

To serve, mound squash and tomato mixture onto plates and garnish with shredded basil.

Serves 4–8

Serve warm or at room temperature as an accompaniment to **Garlic Herbed Hens**. *For a buffet presentation, mound into reserved squash shells.*

Basil Tomatoes with Gorgonzola

1/4 pound Gorgonzola cheese

6 large tomatoes

1/4 cup shredded basil

3 tablespoons sliced shallot

2 teaspoons fresh lemon juice

2 teaspoons Dijon mustard

1/3–1/2 cup olive oil

Salt and freshly ground pepper, to taste

Freeze cheese for 30 minutes or until firm enough to grate. Slice tomatoes thinly and arrange on a platter. Grate Gorgonzola, then combine with basil and shallot and sprinkle over tomatoes.

In a small bowl, whisk together lemon juice, Dijon mustard and olive oil. Season with salt and pepper and pour over tomatoes. Serve at room temperature.

Serves 6–8

Gorgonzola cheese adds a rich and pungent flavor to sliced fresh tomatoes. Garnish with squash blossoms and serve as an accompaniment to any baked, broiled or grilled meat.

Ratatouille

1 pound eggplant, peeled and diced

Salt

1-3/4 pounds tomatoes, peeled and chopped

Bouquet garni of thyme and bay leaf

2 cloves garlic

3 tablespoons olive oil

1 pound onions, sliced

1/2 pound carrots, peeled and cut into thin sticks

1-3/4 pounds zucchini, diced

Salt and freshly ground pepper, to taste

Place eggplant in a bowl or on a wire rack and sprinkle generously with salt. Let rest for 30 minutes, then rinse and squeeze dry.

Place tomatoes in a saucepan with bouquet garni and garlic. Simmer uncovered for 30 minutes to make a thick sauce. Remove bouquet garni and garlic.

Heat oil in a large pot, add onions and carrots, and sauté lightly. Add zucchini, then cover and simmer for 15 minutes, stirring occasionally. Add eggplant and tomato sauce. Season with salt and pepper, then cover again and simmer for 1 hour, stirring occasionally.

Serves 8–10

This becomes a meal in itself when served over brown rice, couscous or bulgur and topped with farmer's cheese.

A bouquet garni is easily made by placing herbs in a tied cheesecloth bag. The herbal flavor permeates the dish, and the bagged leaves are easily discarded.

Thyme Veggie Bundles

2 carrots, peeled

1 yellow squash

1 medium zucchini

4 tablespoons butter

1 tablespoon fresh thyme

6–8 whole chives or scallion tops

Julienne vegetables into 2-1/2-inch lengths. Discard the center, seedy pieces of squash and zucchini. Steam vegetables, tossing occasionally, until bright in color but still crisp, about 2 minutes. Rinse in cold water.

In a heavy pan, melt butter over low heat. Add vegetables and thyme. Toss until all pieces are coated with butter. Remove from heat.

Remove vegetables from pan, evenly divide into bundles and tie together with a chive or scallion top. Leave butter and thyme in pan. Just before serving, reheat bundles in butter mixture over low heat for 2 to 3 minutes or in microwave for 1 minute.

Serves 4

Easy and fun! Experiment with different types of ties for the bundles. For example, cut a zucchini or yellow squash into 1/2-inch slices and then hollow. Insert vegetables into squash rings and cook bundles over low heat for 2 to 3 minutes.

Thai Zucchini

1 pound (about 5 medium) zucchini

2 teaspoons olive oil

1 clove garlic, finely chopped

1 teaspoon finely chopped fresh ginger

Pinch of red pepper flakes

2 tablespoons soy sauce

3 tablespoons rice vinegar

3 tablespoons chicken broth

1/3 cup finely chopped peanuts

Pinch of sugar

Julienne unpeeled zucchini into 2- to 3-inch sticks and set aside.

In a large skillet, heat oil, garlic, ginger and red pepper flakes. Sauté until softened, no more than 1 minute. Add soy sauce, rice vinegar, chicken broth, peanuts, and sugar. Next add zucchini sticks and sauté just until tender crisp, about 3 to 5 minutes. Serve hot immediately.

Serves 4–6

Do not substitute for the rice vinegar; other vinegars are too tart. For a festive presentation, spoon zucchini into cups made from red cabbage leaves.

Orange Blossom Zucchini

2 large or 3 small zucchini

2 tablespoons butter

1/4 cup Cointreau

1 tablespoon orange marmalade

Freshly ground pepper, to taste

Julienne zucchini into 2-inch sticks. Sauté in butter until tender crisp, about 3 minutes. Add Cointreau and marmalade and heat through. Sprinkle lightly with pepper and serve warm.

Serves 6

Pale green and soft orange intermingle beautifully here. Use a good-quality marmalade so as not to miss the added texture of tender orange zest.

Broccoli Amandine

2 pounds fresh broccoli, cut into florets

1 cup sour cream

1/2 teaspoon grated lemon zest

1 tablespoon lemon juice

1/4 teaspoon salt

Dash of freshly ground pepper

1/4 cup toasted slivered almonds

Steam broccoli and place in a shallow baking dish. Combine sour cream, lemon zest, lemon juice, salt and pepper. Spoon mixture over broccoli and sprinkle with almonds.

Place under the broiler 5 inches from heat and broil for 3 minutes.

Serves 6–8

Tangy touches of lemon juice and sour cream dress up basic broccoli.

Broccoli with Onions and Pine Nuts

4 cups chopped broccoli

2 medium onions, chopped

2 tablespoons butter or margarine

2 tablespoons olive oil

1/4 cup pine nuts, toasted

2 tablespoons dry white wine

2 tablespoons fresh lemon juice, or to taste

Salt and freshly ground pepper, to taste

Steam broccoli and set aside.

Sauté onions in butter and oil. Add broccoli, then pine nuts and wine. Add lemon juice a bit at a time. Season with salt and pepper. Cover and simmer until liquid is absorbed.

Serves 8

Tender crisp broccoli and crunchy pine nuts make an interesting counterpoint to soft, flaky fish.

Honeyed Brussels Sprouts

2 quarts (8 cups) fresh brussels sprouts

Salt and freshly ground pepper, to taste

6 tablespoons butter

6 teaspoons honey

1/2–1 clove garlic, crushed

2 cups seedless red grapes, halved

Cook sprouts in boiling water until just tender but still firm, about 5 to 8 minutes. Drain well, then season with salt and pepper.

Melt butter and honey in a saucepan. Add garlic, sprouts and grapes, and heat through. Serve warm.

Serves 8

Even children love these sprouts! Cut an "X" in the bottom of each sprout before cooking and it will hold its shape.

Sunburst Florets

1 medium head cauliflower, cut into florets

2 tablespoons water

1/2 cup mayonnaise

1 teaspoon finely chopped onion

1 teaspoon prepared mustard

1 teaspoon lemon pepper

1/2 cup shredded cheddar cheese

Place cauliflower in a 1-1/2-quart glass baking dish, add water and cover. Microwave on high for 8 to 9 minutes until tender crisp. (Cauliflower also may be steamed for 10 to 15 minutes.)

Combine mayonnaise, onion, mustard and lemon pepper and spoon onto cauliflower. Sprinkle with cheese. Microwave or broil for 1-1/2 to 2 minutes to heat topping and melt cheese. Let stand for 2 minutes before serving.

Serves 6–8

For an impressive presentation, leave cauliflower whole when cooking. Microwave whole cauliflower for 8 minutes, then turn dish and microwave for 5 minutes more or until done.

Festive Pepper Strips

4 large bell peppers

4 tablespoons butter

1/4 cup shredded fresh basil

1 teaspoon lemon zest

2 teaspoons fresh lemon juice

Salt and freshly ground pepper, to taste

Seed and cut peppers into 1/4- to 1/2-inch strips.

Melt butter over medium heat in a large saucepan or skillet. Sauté peppers with basil and lemon zest, tossing gently, until just heated through, about 3 to 5 minutes. Season with salt and pepper, toss with lemon juice and serve.

Serves 6–8

*Brilliant red peppers provide a simple, snappy accent to **Pepper-Coated Stuffed Flank Steak**.*

Polenta Pepper Soufflés

4 large bell peppers, preferably red, orange or purple

3 tablespoons butter

2 Anaheim chilies, seeded and minced

1 leek, top plus 1-inch green, sliced

1 teaspoon oregano

1 teaspoon basil

1/4 cup polenta (coarsely ground cornmeal)

3/4 cup heavy cream

1/2 cup shredded Monterey Jack cheese

3 egg yolks

4 egg whites

Slice off tops of peppers. Finely chop tops, then hollow out peppers (core and seed).

In a heavy skillet over medium heat, melt butter and sauté chopped pepper tops, Anaheim chilies and leek until tender. Add oregano, basil, and polenta and cook for 1 minute. Add cream and stir. Bring mixture to a boil and simmer for 5 minutes. Remove from heat. Add cheese and egg yolks and stir until incorporated. Beat egg whites with electric mixer until stiff. Stir 1/4 of egg whites into vegetable mixture, then stir resulting mixture into remaining egg whites.

Place hollowed-out peppers into an 8-inch square baking pan and spoon filling evenly into each. Bake in a 375-degree oven for 35 minutes until browned and puffed.

Serves 4 (whole) or 8 (halves)

An easy, fabulous soufflé for "first timers." Choose flat-bottomed peppers that can stand upright.

Calypso Black Beans

12 ounces uncooked black beans, soaked overnight

1/4 cup olive oil

2 teaspoons cumin

2 teaspoons chili powder

1 teaspoon celery salt

1 teaspoon Creole seasoning

1 teaspoon freshly cracked peppercorns

2 cloves garlic, minced

1 large onion, chopped

Sour cream

6 strips bacon, fried and crumbled

Rice vinegar, to taste

In a large pot, combine beans, oil, cumin, chili powder, celery salt, Creole seasoning, pepper and garlic. Add enough water to cover and simmer for about 4 hours. Add additional water as needed to prevent beans from drying out.

Serve with chopped onion and a dollop of sour cream. Sprinkle with bacon and vinegar.

Serves 4–6

Ladle over a bed of rice, or pour individual servings over polenta cakes.

Ozark Caviar

2 (15-ounce) cans black-eyed peas
1/2 red bell pepper, chopped fine
1/2 cup vegetable oil
1/4 cup raspberry vinegar
2 cloves garlic, lightly crushed
1/4 cup finely chopped onion
1/2 teaspoon salt
Cracked or freshly ground pepper, to taste

Rinse and drain black-eyed peas and place in a ceramic or glass bowl. Add remaining ingredients and stir well. Cover tightly and refrigerate for at least 24 hours. Remove garlic after 24 hours.

Serves 8–10

Must be prepared 24 hours in advance.

The flavored vinegar adds a touch of summer freshness to year-round pantry staples. This combination keeps well for up to 2 weeks.

Just Wild About Mushrooms

*B*utton, button, who's got the button? When it comes to mushrooms, just about every market does. These days, however, the selection goes much further. Many wild mushrooms now have been cultivated and, while not always as richly flavored as those found in the wild, are more easily obtained.

A Wild Hunt

Look for tight, firm mushrooms with solid color; avoid those with open caps or a slimy feel. Cover your mushrooms with a slightly damp paper towel and refrigerate in a paper bag. Just before serving, wipe with a damp cloth. Listed below are a number of mushroom options:

Angel trumpet—White and delicate, these have a subtle flavor. **Button**—Mildly flavored and extremely versatile, button mushrooms are among the most familiar. **Chanterelle**—Serve these mild-flavored wild mushrooms as a complement to chicken, veal and eggs. **Clamshell**—These offer a distinct nutty taste. **Cremini**—Similar to the button, these present a more intense flavor. **Elephant ear**—A staple in many Asian dishes, these are usually sold in dried form. **Enoki**—A crisp, fruity taste makes these an excellent addition to salads and sandwiches. **Hen-of-the-woods**—Use these rich, garlicky-tasting mushrooms in long-cooking soups and stews. **Morel**—A growing season of 3 weeks makes these peppery, full-flavored mushrooms difficult to find and a wonderful indulgence when you can. **Oyster**—These versatile, silky-textured mushrooms have an almost seafood-like flavor when cooked. **Pom pom blanc**—Baked at high heat, these take on a subtle seafood flavor. **Porcini**—Also known as *cèpes*, these offer a rich, smoky, buttery flavor. **Portobello**—A cuplike cap and meaty texture make these mushrooms an excellent candidate for stuffing. **Shiitake**—These add a wonderful smoky, earthy flavor wherever they're added.

Lemon and Chive Risotto

1 small onion, minced

2 tablespoons butter

1-1/2 cups Arborio rice, well rinsed

1/3 cup dry white wine

3–4 cups hot chicken broth

2–3 tablespoons fresh lemon juice

2 egg yolks

1/2 cup heavy cream

Salt and freshly ground pepper, to taste

2–3 tablespoons chopped fresh chives

Grated zest of 1 lemon

In a large, heavy saucepan, sauté onion in butter for 3 to 4 minutes or until soft, but not browned. Add rice and stir well. Add wine and cook over medium-high heat until wine evaporates. Begin adding broth 1/2 cup at a time, stirring constantly. Keep heat medium-high so rice absorbs liquid but does not dry out too quickly. Continue to add 1/2 cup broth at a time. If still chewy, partially cover and cook more slowly, stirring every minute or so.

In a bowl, combine lemon juice, egg yolks and cream. Whisk until well blended. Five minutes before rice is done, whisk in lemon cream. Add salt, pepper, chives and lemon zest. Adjust seasonings to taste and serve.

Serves 4

This Italian rice dish takes some attention but is well worth the effort. Do not substitute for the Arborio rice; if it's not available in your regular grocery, check gourmet or ethnic food stores.

Crunchy Baked Barley

2 tablespoons butter or margarine

1 cup uncooked barley, rinsed and drained

1 celery stalk, chopped

1-1/2 teaspoons minced parsley

1-1/2 teaspoons salt

1/4 teaspoon freshly ground pepper

2 cups chicken broth

1 (8-ounce) can sliced water chestnuts, drained

1/4 cup sliced scallions

1/4 cup toasted sliced almonds

In a skillet, melt butter, add barley and briefly sauté. Do not brown. Add remaining ingredients, except almonds. Heat to boiling and pour into an 8- by 8-inch covered baking dish.

Bake in a 350-degree oven for 50 minutes, stirring occasionally. Top with almonds and bake for 10 minutes more.

Serves 4–6

Barley offers a wholesome alternative to rice or potatoes.

Emerald Asparagus Pinwheel

1/2 cup (1 stick) butter

1 cup uncooked long grain white rice

Grated zest of 1 lemon

1-1/2 cups chicken broth

Juice of 1 lemon

1/8 teaspoon saffron (optional)

1/2 cup heavy cream

4 tablespoons freshly grated Parmesan cheese

10 or more asparagus spears, blanched

Melt butter in a saucepan over low heat. Add rice and lemon zest. Cook over medium heat, stirring, until rice is opaque, about 5 minutes. Add broth and bring to a boil. Reduce heat, cover and simmer for 20 minutes. Stir in lemon juice and saffron. Slowly stir in cream, followed by Parmesan cheese. Turn off heat and cover. Let mixture sit for 5 minutes to absorb remaining liquid.

Arrange asparagus spears in a pinwheel design on a serving platter and top the center with hot rice.

Serves 4

Creamy lemon rice is a delicious foil to the tender crunch of fresh asparagus.

Wild Rice with Plantains

1 cup uncooked wild rice

2-1/2 cups water

1 tablespoon butter

4 tablespoons soy sauce

2 tablespoons orange zest

2 ripe plantains, sliced and chunked

1/4 cup pecans, chopped and toasted

Simmer rice in water and butter for 25 minutes. Add soy sauce, orange zest and plantains. Cook until plantains and rice are tender, about 20 more minutes. Top with pecans before serving.

Serves 6–8

This striking blend of pale, peach-toned plantains and dark, nutty rice offers a delicious contrast of textures.

Despite its impressive name and glorious tang, crème fraîche is quite simple to create. Combine 2 tablespoons of buttermilk with 1 cup of whipping cream in a glass jar. Cover and let the mixture stand at room temperature for 8 to 24 hours (or until very thick). Stir well, then cover and refrigerate. The mixture will keep up to 10 days.

Trimmed corn husks, rolled cornucopia style and tied at one end, make pretty serving packets for individual portions of rice.

Kaleidoscope Fried Rice

2-1/2 tablespoons peanut oil

1 large clove garlic, minced

1 cup sliced Napa cabbage

6 ounces fresh
snow pea pods, julienned

1 red bell pepper, finely julienned

2 carrots, julienned

2 scallions, chopped diagonally

1/2 small onion, sliced

1 egg, beaten

2 cups cooked white rice, cold

2 tablespoons soy sauce

Heat 1 tablespoon oil in a wok and add garlic. Stir in cabbage, snow peas, bell pepper, carrots, scallions and onion. Stir-fry for 2 minutes, then remove. (Do not overcook vegetables; they are better a little crisp.)

Pour 1/2 tablespoon oil into wok and heat. Add egg and quickly form an omelet. Cut into strips and remove.

Pour 1 tablespoon oil into wok and add rice. Cook, stirring until heated. Add reserved vegetables and omelet strips. Season with soy sauce and mix well.

Serves 4

A whirl of color and texture that can become a meal in itself.

West Indian Apricot Rice

3 tablespoons butter

1 small onion, chopped

1/2 cup chopped celery

1 (1/2-inch) piece fresh ginger,
peeled and minced

1 cup uncooked long grain rice

2 cups chicken broth

1/4 cup diced dried apricots

1/4 cup light-colored chutney
(large pieces cut up)

Salt and freshly ground pepper, to taste

1/2 cup slivered almonds

3 tablespoons minced fresh parsley,
to garnish

In a saucepan, melt butter and add onions, celery and ginger. Sauté over medium heat until soft, about 5 minutes (do not brown). Add rice and continue to sauté until grains are coated and turn white. Add broth, apricots and chutney. Bring to a boil, then reduce heat, cover and simmer slowly for 25 minutes or until rice is tender. Season with salt and pepper.

Transfer mixture to serving bowl, top with almonds and mix slightly. Sprinkle with minced parsley and serve hot.

Serves 6–8

A fragrant rice with a nutty, fruity flavor. In place of chutney, try this substitute: 2 tablespoons peach or apricot preserves, 1/4-inch cube of fresh ginger, minced, and 2 teaspoons cider vinegar.

To preserve ginger, peel and place in a clean jar. Top with sherry to cover.

Treated this way, it will keep in the refrigerator for 3 months.

CAKES & CHEESECAKES
Apple Pie Cake with Rum Butter Sauce, 267
Chocolate Raspberry Cream Cake, 267
Gingerbread with Hot Caramel Sauce, 266
Graham Cracker Cake with Praline Glaze, 265
Lime Cheesecake, 269
Pecan Rye Cake, 264
White Chocolate Buttercream Frosting, 257
White Chocolate Cheesecake, 269

TORTES & TARTS
Alpine Torte, 256
Apricot Marzipan Tart, 261
Chocolate Mousse Torte, 258
Frozen Truffle Loaf, 255
Gypsy Torte with Lemon Sauce, 259
Hazelnut Tart, 263
Pear Tart, 264
Pecan Ganache Tart, 262
Phyllo Tortes with Honey Cream, 260

CREAMS, CUSTARDS & SOUFFLÉS
Almond Russe, 270
Apricot Mousse, 274
Chocolate Soufflés with Apricot Nectar, 273
Chocolate Chip Crème Brûlée, 256
Chocolate Coconut Mousse with Caramel Sauce, 270
Chocolate Pâté with
Crème Anglaise and Raspberry Coulis, 254
Coconut Flans, 271
Cold White Chocolate Soufflé, 272
Mascarpone, 257
Orange Custard, 274
Trifle St. Croix, 255
Zuccotto Frangelico, 268

SHERBETS & SORBETS
Champagne Strawberry Sherbet, 279
Creamy Lemon Sherbet with Marinated Strawberries, 278
Fresh Ginger Sorbet, 279
Pink Grapefruit Sorbet, 279

FRUIT
Blackberry Pinwheels, 276
Citrus Blossoms, 278
Cloaked Apples, 275
Crème de Menthe Grapes, 277
Fresh Fruit Torte, 277
Gewurztraminer Pears, 276
Peach Kuchen, 275

COOKIES & BARS
Bittersweet Ravioli, 283
Chocolate-Filled Pastry Puffs, 284
Chocolate Sherry Cream Brownies, 284
Coconut Truffles, 285
Irish Lace Sandwich Cookies, 282
Lily Cookies, 282
Lime Almond Squares, 281
Princess Cookies, 283
Raspberry Bars, 281
Terrific Truffles, 285

MINI RECIPES
Flavored Coffees, 280

Desserts

Pictured finishing touch:

MAKING

MELON "NESTS"

FOR SCOOPS OF SORBET, 265

SPECIAL TOPIC BOXES

FLAVORED COFFEES, 280

PRESENTING . . . , 266

Chocolate Pâté with Crème Anglaise and Raspberry Coulis

1 pound bittersweet chocolate

1 cup heavy cream

4 tablespoons unsalted butter, cut into slices

4 egg yolks

1 cup powdered sugar, sifted

1/4 cup eau-de-vie (Kirsch or Framboise)

1/4 cup sliced almonds

1/2 pint raspberries, to garnish

Crème anglaise:

3 egg yolks

1/4 cup sugar

1/8 teaspoon salt

1 cup heavy cream

1 vanilla bean

2 tablespoons Amaretto

1/2 teaspoon vanilla extract

Coulis:

1-1/2 cup raspberries

1/4 cup powdered sugar

1/4 cup Framboise

In a double boiler over low heat, partially melt chocolate. Add cream and butter. Heat, whisking frequently, until chocolate is fully melted and mixture is smooth. Whisk in egg yolks 1 at a time. Gradually mix in sugar and liqueur. Line a loaf pan with waxed paper, using enough to extend up and over the sides. Pour mixture into pan and let cool.

Toast almond slices in a low oven until golden. Sprinkle almonds on top of chocolate mixture, pressing down slightly so that portions stick in the chocolate. Cover and refrigerate overnight or a minimum of 6 hours. Invert pâté onto a platter and peel off waxed paper. Keep refrigerated until serving time.

For crème anglaise: Whisk egg yolks, sugar and salt together in a bowl until light and thick. In a heavy saucepan, combine cream and vanilla bean and bring to a boil. Allow mixture to cool slightly, about 5 minutes. Add cream mixture to egg mixture, whisking constantly. Pour combined cream and egg mixtures into saucepan and cook over low heat until thickened (coats the back of a spoon). Do not allow mixture to boil or it will curdle. Remove pan from heat and stir in Amaretto and vanilla extract. Remove vanilla bean. Pour mixture through sieve if necessary. (May be refrigerated up to 3 days.)

For coulis: Blend or process ingredients and strain. Keep refrigerated until serving time.

To serve, cut pâté into 1/2-inch slices with a knife dipped in cold water. Pool 2 tablespoons of crème anglaise on the left side of plate and 2 tablespoons of raspberry sauce on the right. Place a few raspberries along the outer edges of the sauces and place pâté in the center.

Serves 12–16

Must be prepared in advance.

The two sauces and fresh raspberries make a gorgeous presentation. This pâté is ideal to serve when inviting guests for "just dessert."

Trifle St. Croix

5 egg yolks, beaten

4 cups milk

1 tablespoon vanilla extract

1 cup sugar

Pinch of salt

2 heaping tablespoons cornstarch

1-1/2 teaspoons freshly grated nutmeg

4 tablespoons dark rum

1 angel food cake

1 (13-ounce) package macaroon cookies, crushed

Whipped cream, to garnish

Toasted coconut, to garnish

In a double boiler, combine egg yolks, milk, vanilla, sugar, salt and cornstarch. Cook until thickened. Remove from heat. Add nutmeg and rum. Set aside.

Lightly oil a springform pan with nonstick vegetable spray. Cover bottom of pan with slices of angel food cake. Add 1/2 cup crushed macaroons, followed by 1/2 the custard mixture. Repeat cookie layer and custard. Cover and refrigerate overnight.

Remove sides of springform pan and serve with whipped cream and toasted coconut.

Serves 8–10

Must be prepared in advance.

A symphony of harmonious textures set to a calypso beat.

Frozen Truffle Loaf

12 ounces semisweet chocolate chips

1/2 cup (1 stick) butter or margarine

4 large egg yolks

3/4 cup milk

3 tablespoons Kahlúa

1 tablespoon instant espresso powder

1-1/2 cups heavy cream

1/2 cup shaved or grated chocolate, plus additional to garnish

Raspberry puree, to garnish

Fresh raspberries, to garnish

Mint leaves, to garnish

In a heavy saucepan over low heat, melt chocolate and butter until smooth, stirring frequently. Remove from heat. In a 3-quart saucepan, whisk egg yolks. Add milk and simmer over low heat, stirring until mixture thickens and coats a spoon well (about 8 minutes). Do not let mixture curdle. Stir in melted chocolate, liqueur and espresso powder. Cover mixture with plastic wrap. Refrigerate until chilled, about 1 hour.

Spray a loaf pan with nonstick vegetable spray and line with plastic wrap. Whip cream. When chocolate mixture is cool, fold in 1/3 cup whipped cream to lighten it. Fold in remaining whipped cream and grated chocolate until

blended. Pour mixture into prepared loaf pan. Cover with plastic wrap and freeze overnight or until firm.

To serve, make a pool of pureed raspberry sauce to cover a small dessert plate. Place a slice of chocolate truffle on top. Garnish with shaved or grated chocolate, raspberries and mint.

Serves 16

Must be prepared in advance.

When dessert needs to star, serve this heavenly creation.

Alpine Torte

2 cups blanched almonds

1/4 cup flour

8 ounces good-quality white chocolate

3/4 cup (1-1/2 sticks) unsalted butter, softened

3/4 cup sugar

5 eggs, separated

Pinch of salt

In a food processor, finely grind almonds. Sift in flour. Melt chocolate in a double boiler or microwave. Stir until smooth. Cool.

In a large mixing bowl, cream butter and sugar, then beat for 2 minutes. Add egg yolks, 1 at a time, beating well after each addition. Add chocolate to mixture and stir well to blend ingredients. Fold in almond-flour mixture.

In a separate bowl, beat egg whites with a pinch of salt until stiff. Fold beaten egg whites into batter with a spatula. Grease the bottom of a 9-inch round cake pan. Line with parchment paper and grease paper. Pour batter into pan, spreading to gently smooth top. Place on a baking sheet. Bake at 350 degrees for 45 minutes. Torte will be firm to the touch when done.

Cool pan for 10 to 15 minutes. Run knife around edges and invert torte onto a flat plate. Cool completely before frosting. Serve chilled. (Unfrosted, torte freezes well.)

Serves 10–12

Drizzle melted white chocolate over torte or frost with **White Chocolate Buttercream Frosting**. *Garnish with fresh raspberries.*

Chocolate Chip Crème Brûlée

1/2 cup miniature semisweet chocolate chips, plus additional to garnish

3 cups heavy cream

1 vanilla bean

2 eggs

4 egg yolks

1/4 cup sugar

1 teaspoon vanilla extract

1/4 cup firmly packed light brown sugar

8 mint leaves, to garnish

Divide chocolate chips between six 4-ounce ramekins or oven-proof dessert plates or cups. Heat cream and vanilla bean, stirring or whisking several times. Do not boil.

In a medium bowl, whisk together eggs and sugar until frothy. While whisking, pour heated cream into sugar mixture. Remove vanilla bean. Strain mixture back into the saucepan. Cook over low heat, stirring constantly, until thick enough to coat the back of a spoon. Stir in vanilla extract.

Divide egg mixture into ramekins. Set ramekins in a baking dish and fill dish with hot water that reaches halfway up the sides of the ramekins. Bake in a 350-degree oven for 30 minutes until custard is set. Let ramekins cool, then cover and chill for 3 hours.

Just before serving, sift sugar over ramekins. Broil just until sugar caramelizes. Garnish with mint leaves and chocolate chips.

Serves 6

Spoon into this rich custard to find luscious chocolate morsels.

White Chocolate Buttercream Frosting

3 tablespoons water

1/2 cup plus 2 tablespoons sugar

1/3 cup egg whites (about 3 large eggs)

1-1/2 cups (3 sticks) unsalted butter, softened

4 ounces good-quality white chocolate, melted

In a heavy saucepan, combine water and 1/2 cup sugar. Stir to blend well. Cook over low heat to dissolve sugar. When sugar has dissolved, increase heat to medium. Wash down sides of the pan using a pastry brush dipped in water to remove crystals. Bring syrup to a boil. When mixture reaches 245 degrees (soft ball stage), remove from heat.

In a large mixing bowl, beat egg whites until frothy. Begin adding remaining sugar, 1 teaspoon at a time, until soft peaks form. Continue beating egg whites until stiff and glossy, but not dry.

Pour hot syrup into egg whites. Stir to incorporate, using beater. Egg whites will expand, almost tripling in volume. Whip for 2 to 3 minutes. Begin adding butter, 1 tablespoon at a time, and continue until all is incorporated. (If at any time mixture appears to curdle, whip on high speed until smooth again, then add remaining butter.) While still whipping buttercream, add melted chocolate.

Make 3 cups

*A sublime complement to the **Alpine Torte**. This recipe makes more than enough to frost a regular-sized cake. Use leftovers on a simple cookie or cupcake. It may also be refrigerated for 1 week or frozen up to 1 month. To use after refrigeration or freezing, bring to room temperature and mix until smooth.*

Mascarpone

2 (8-ounce) packages cream cheese, softened to room temperature

1/2 cup ricotta cheese

2 tablespoons sour cream

2 tablespoons heavy cream

1 tablespoon sugar

1 tablespoon fresh lemon juice

Grated lemon zest, to garnish

Blend all ingredients in a food processor until thoroughly mixed and very smooth, stopping machine once or twice to scrape down sides. Place in a covered container and refrigerate. (Cheese will keep for 6 to 7 days.) Sprinkle with lemon zest before serving.

Makes about 2-3/4 cups

Serve as a dip for tiny Amaretto cookies or pipe onto slices of apple.

3 cups finely crushed chocolate wafer cookies

1/2 cup (1 stick) unsalted melted butter, softened

1 pound semisweet chocolate

6 eggs

2 cups heavy cream

6 tablespoons powdered sugar

Chocolate leaves:

8 ounces semisweet chocolate

1 tablespoon vegetable shortening

Camellia or rose leaves, or other waxy leaves

Topping:

2 cups whipping cream

2 teaspoons powdered sugar, or more to taste

Combine crumbs and butter. Press onto bottom and sides of a 10-inch springform pan. Refrigerate for 30 minutes or chill in freezer.

Melt chocolate in top of a double boiler over simmering water. Cool to lukewarm. Add 2 whole eggs and mix well. Add 4 yolks and mix well. Whip cream with powdered sugar until soft peaks form. Beat egg whites until stiff but not dry. Stir a little of the cream and egg whites into the chocolate to lighten, then fold in remaining cream and whites. Turn into crust and chill for at least 6 hours, preferably overnight.

For chocolate leaves: Line a baking sheet with waxed paper. Melt chocolate and shortening in a double boiler. Arrange leaves, tops down, on waxed paper. Using a spoon, spatula or pastry brush, generously coat undersides with chocolate mixture. Chill or freeze until firm. Gently remove leaves by peeling, starting with the stem. It's best to hold leaf in one hand and work with the other. Be careful not to allow chocolate to run off of leaf or onto underside.

To serve, prepare topping by whipping cream with sugar until stiff. Loosen crust of chilled torte with a sharp knife. Remove sides of springform pan. Spread all but 1/2 cup cream over top. Use remaining cream to make rosettes, and top with chocolate leaves. (The mousse torte must be kept cold before serving or the filling will become runny.)

Serves 16–20

A chocolate lover's delight! The chocolate leaves are an attractive extra (ask the florist for unsprayed leaves). Try pairing them with candied violets for a garnish that is a visual feast.

Gypsy Torte with Lemon Sauce

1-1/2 cups heavy cream

3 tablespoons powdered sugar

32–35 large gingersnaps (2-1/2 inches in diameter)

1/4 cup medium-dry sherry

Strawberry slices, to garnish

Mint leaves, to garnish

Sauce:

2 eggs

1 cup sugar

Juice of 2–3 lemons (equal to 4 tablespoons)

Zest of 1 lemon, finely grated

4 tablespoons butter or margarine

1 tablespoon cornstarch

1 cup cold water

Whip cream until thickened. Add powdered sugar and continue beating cream until stiff. Dip gingersnaps one at a time in sherry, shaking off excess. To form torte, sandwich together 4 or 5 cookies at a time with whipped cream (about 1/4-inch thickness between each cookie). Stand sandwiched cookies on edge, forming a horizontal log as you go. When all cookies form 1 log, frost the sides. Place in the refrigerator and chill for 4 to 6 hours.

For sauce: Beat eggs in the top of a double boiler. Gradually add sugar. Add lemon juice, zest and butter. Dissolve cornstarch in cold water. Add to lemon mixture and cook in top of double boiler over simmering water until mixture has consistency of a thin sauce, about 5 minutes. Cool to room temperature, then chill. Serve cold.

To serve, slice each portion diagonally. Using the back of a spoon, spread about 2 tablespoons of sauce on a dessert plate and top with a slice of torte. Garnish with fanned strawberry slices and mint leaves.

Serves 6–8

The striking, graphic appearance of this confection is easy to make using store-bought gingersnaps. The lemon sauce is served cold with this torte, but is wonderful warm with other desserts.

When juicing lemons, remember that room-temperature lemons will yield more juice than chilled ones. If they are cold, place lemons in the microwave for 30 seconds on high before juicing.

After microwaving, roll the lemon on a countertop, pressing with the heel of your hand to help break open the juice sacs.

When grating a lemon, remove the thin yellow layer (the zest) only. It has all of the oils and flavor. The white part is bitter.

Leftover fresh lemon juice may be refrigerated up to 3 days and freezes well. Freeze the juice in ice cube trays. Once frozen, store in an airtight plastic bag for up to 4 months. Keep on hand for recipes and to put in beverages.

6 (17- by 12-inch) sheets
frozen phyllo dough, thawed

1/4 cup melted butter

1 cup ground pecans

2 tablespoons sugar

5 teaspoons boiling water

Honey cream:

1-1/4 cups half-and-half

3 tablespoons honey

1 tablespoon cornstarch

3 beaten egg yolks

1–2 tablespoons Grand Marnier
(optional)

1/2 cup heavy cream

Glaze:

1 ounce semisweet chocolate, chopped

1 tablespoon butter

3/4 cup sifted powdered sugar

1/2 teaspoon vanilla extract

3–4 teaspoons very hot water

Unfold phyllo. Lightly brush 1 sheet with some melted butter. Top with another phyllo sheet, brush with butter and repeat, using all phyllo and all butter. Cut phyllo into 6 strips. Cut each strip into fourths, making 24 pieces total.

Using a spatula, transfer phyllo to baking sheets. Combine ground pecans and 2 tablespoons sugar. Sprinkle over pastries. Bake at 425 degrees for 4 to 5 minutes. Cool on baking sheets on wire racks. (May store pastries at this point in container at room temperature for 2 to 3 days.)

For honey cream: In a small saucepan, combine half-and-half, honey and cornstarch. Cook and stir over medium heat until thickened. Cook and stir 2 more minutes. Remove from heat. Gradually whisk about half of hot mixture into beaten egg yolks. Return mixture to saucepan. Cook over medium heat until thickened, stirring occasionally. Add Grand Marnier. Transfer to a medium bowl, cover with plastic wrap and chill for about 4 hours. Before serving, beat whipping cream until soft peaks form. Fold into honey cream. Set aside.

For glaze: In a double boiler, melt chocolate and butter over low heat, stirring constantly. Remove from heat. Stir in sugar and vanilla until a coarse meal forms. Stir in 2 teaspoons hot water. Add in 1 to 2 teaspoons additional hot water, 1 teaspoon at a time until glaze is of drizzling consistency.

To assemble, place 1 phyllo square on each plate. Spread each with about 2 tablespoons honey cream. Top with another phyllo square and more honey cream. Top with a third phyllo square and a dollop of honey cream, then drizzle chocolate glaze over top.

Serves 8

These light do-ahead pastries are very elegant, especially when garnished with fresh fruit and mint leaves.

Apricot Marzipan Tart

1-1/4 cups flour

1 tablespoon sugar

1/2 cup (1 stick) butter, softened

1 egg yolk

1 cup canned apricots, drained well and patted dry

4 tablespoons brandy

3/4 cup preserves (half apricot and half pineapple)

Sliced almonds, toasted, to garnish

Filling:

1/2 cup (1 stick) butter, softened

1/2 cup sugar

1 (1-ounce) can almond paste

2 large eggs

2 teaspoons flour

Mix flour and sugar. Using a pastry blender or the metal blade of a food processor, combine butter and egg yolk. Add flour and sugar combination and blend until mixture resembles a coarse meal. Spread into a 10-1/2-inch flan dish or a 10-inch springform pan. Bake at 350 degrees for 15 minutes on lowest rack of oven. Do not brown.

For filling: Cream butter and sugar until light. Work in bits of almond paste until smooth. Add eggs, 1 at a time, then add flour. Pour mixture into prepared crust and bake in a 350-degree oven for 20 minutes or until brown. (Watch closely.) Place dish on a cake rack and add apricots at once. Apricot halves may be sectioned for a more attractive design.

In a saucepan, over low heat, melt brandy and preserves. Pour over tart, topped with a sprinkling of toasted almonds. Refrigerate for several hours or overnight before serving.

Serves 8

Marzipan, a paste of ground almonds, sugar and egg white, adds a sweet bonus to this fruited dessert.

Delicate phyllo dough is easier to handle when kept moist. Start by unrolling the paper-thin sheets of dough and topping with waxed paper and then a damp kitchen towel (if damp towel touches dough directly, it will become gooey). Keep towel in place as you work, pull aside to peel off layers of dough.

Phyllo tears very easily, so work carefully. Keep any scraps or trimmings to use later when patching. Brush very lightly with melted butter; do not saturate the paper-thin dough or it will come out greasy.

6 ounces unsalted pecans
(about 1-1/2 cups)

1/2 cup plus 1/3 cup sugar

3 tablespoons butter, softened

10 ounces bittersweet chocolate

1 cup heavy cream

1/3 cup sour cream

1 egg yolk

2 ounces semisweet chocolate

2 tablespoons Kahlúa

Powdered sugar or cocoa, to garnish

12 toasted whole pecans, to garnish

Sauce:

1 cup heavy cream

1 tablespoon Kahlúa

1 teaspoon instant coffee

1 vanilla bean

2 egg yolks

1/4 cup sugar

In a food processor, finely chop nuts. Add 1/2 cup sugar and process to combine. Add softened butter and pulse to combine until mixture sticks together. Press dough into a 9-inch tart pan. Bake at in a 350-degree oven for 15 to 18 minutes. Cool on rack.

In a double boiler or heavy saucepan, melt bittersweet chocolate. In another heavy saucepan, combine heavy cream, sour cream and egg yolk. Whisk over medium heat until the mixture is hot. Do not allow mixture to bubble or the egg will curdle. Add semisweet chocolate and Kahlúa and remove immediately from heat.

Stir melted bittersweet chocolate and 1/3 cup sugar into cream mixture until fully incorporated. Pour into cooled crust. Refrigerate until set, about 4 hours.

Thirty minutes before serving, remove tart from refrigerator. Set a paper doily on top of tart and sprinkle on powdered sugar or cocoa for garnish. Remove doily.

For sauce: Bring cream, Kahlúa, instant coffee and vanilla bean to a boil. Remove from heat and steep for 15 minutes. Remove vanilla bean. Whisk yolks and sugar together, then whisk cream mixture into eggs and sugar. Return to heat and cook for 5 minutes.

To serve, spoon 3 tablespoons or more of sauce onto serving plates and swirl to create a thin layer. Top with a slice of tart, sprinkle with pecans and serve.

Serves 10–12

Cut this nutty mocha tart into very thin slices and serve with a dessert coffee.

Hazelnut Tart

10-inch prebaked tart crust

1-1/2 cups heavy cream

2 tablespoons powdered sugar

1/2 tablespoon vanilla extract

1-1/2 cups hazelnuts

1-1/4 cups sugar

3 tablespoons water

Pinch of cream of tartar

2 large eggs

In a chilled bowl, whip 1/2 the cream to form stiff peaks. Add powdered sugar and vanilla. Beat until stiff peaks form again. Place mixture into a strainer lined with cheesecloth and set over a bowl. A concentrated whipped cream will form in strainer. Reserve for garnish (discard liquid).

Remove skin from hazelnuts by placing on a baking sheet and roasting 20 to 30 minutes in a 350-degree oven or until skins pop off. Remove from oven and rub several nuts in a coarse dish towel to loosen skins. (Don't worry if all of the skins come off.) Keep 1/2 cup of skinned nuts warm.

In a heavy saucepan, bring 1/2 cup sugar and 3 tablespoons water to a boil. Add cream of tartar and continue cooking and stirring constantly until color is a light brown, about 5 minutes. Lightly oil a baking sheet. When the nougatine mixture turns into a light brown syrup, pour into warm nuts and stir with a wooden spoon until nuts are coated. Immediately pour out onto oiled sheet. Let cool and harden for 10 minutes. Chop coarsely with a knife into bite-sized pieces.

In a food processor, grind remaining nuts with 3/4 cup sugar until smooth, about 6 to 10 minutes. Scrape down sides of bowl occasionally. The oils must emerge from the nuts to get the consistency of peanut butter.

In a separate bowl, mix remaining cream and eggs. Add to nut butter and pour into tart shell. Sprinkle hazelnut candy pieces over the top. Bake in a 375-degree oven for 25 to 35 minutes until brown and set.

Serve tart at room temperature with dollops of concentrated cream or pipe cream through a pastry bag.

Serves 10

The rich, nutty aroma of this traditional French tart is reminiscent of an Old World pâtisserie.

Pear Tart

1 cup flour

2 teaspoons sugar

1/4 teaspoon salt

6 tablespoons unsalted butter

2 tablespoons cold water

3–4 medium, ripe pears

Filling:

1/4 cup (1/2 stick) butter, softened

3/4 cup sugar

1 tablespoon flour

2 egg yolks

1/4 cup heavy cream

3/4 teaspoon vanilla

Combine flour, sugar and salt in a food processor. Add butter and process until mixture becomes coarse crumbs. Add water and process until a ball forms. Cover ball with plastic wrap and chill for about an 1 hour. Roll out onto a lightly floured surface, until round is large enough to fit in a 10-inch tart pan (one with a removable bottom is best). Refrigerate while preparing filling and fruit.

For filling: Cream butter and sugar. Add flour and mix well. Stir in egg yolks. Mix in cream and vanilla. Mixture will be thick. Spread on bottom of pastry shell.

Peel and halve pears. Core with a melon baller. Place fruit cut-side down on cutting board. Slice at a right angle 1/8-inch thick. Spread slices over filling around edge of tart pan. Save smaller end pieces for center.

Bake in a 400-degree oven for 10 minutes. Lower oven temperature to 325 degrees and bake until custard is set in center, about 30 minutes.

Serves 8

The perfect ending to **Poulet Dijon** _and_ **Thyme Veggie Bundles**_. For an autumn variation, substitute 3 tart cooking apples for the pears._

Pecan Rye Cake

6 eggs separated, yolks beaten

1-1/2 cups sugar

3/4 cup ground, dried rye bread crumbs (without seeds)

1 cup ground pecans

2 tablespoons whiskey

1/2 teaspoon vanilla

Frosting:

2 eggs

3/4 cup sugar

2 ounces unsweetened chocolate

1 teaspoon vanilla

4 tablespoons butter

Blend beaten egg yolks and sugar. Fold crumbs, pecans, whiskey and vanilla into mixture. Beat egg whites until soft peaks form. Fold into mixture.

Grease bottoms of two 8- or 9-inch round cake pans, line with parchment and grease. Add batter and bake in a 350-degree oven for 15 to 20 minutes.

For frosting: In a double boiler, add eggs, sugar, chocolate and vanilla. Stir until sugar is dissolved and chocolate is melted. Remove from double boiler and add butter a tablespoon at a time and whisk. Cool well. Ice cake when cooled.

Serves 8–10

The rye bread lends color and texture to this dark, dense, delicious cake. Serve with a dollop of fresh whipped cream garnished with nasturtiums or pansies.

Graham Cracker Cake with Praline Glaze

2 cups finely ground graham cracker crumbs

2 teaspoons baking powder

1/4 teaspoon salt

1/2 cup (1 stick) unsalted butter, softened

1 cup firmly packed light brown sugar

3 large eggs

1 cup milk

1 teaspoon vanilla extract

Pinch of cream of tartar

Glaze:

3 cups firmly packed light brown sugar

1 cup light cream

1/2 teaspoon salt

1/3 cup butter

1 teaspoon vanilla extract

Cream:

1-1/2 cups heavy cream

6 tablespoons powdered sugar

Grease the bottoms of two 9-inch round cake pans, then line with waxed paper. In a bowl, stir together graham cracker crumbs, baking powder and salt.

In a food processor or in a large bowl using an electric mixer, cream together butter and brown sugar until mixture is light and fluffy. Beat in egg yolks, 1 at a time, beating well after each addition. Stir in crumb mixture in batches, alternating with milk. Stir in vanilla.

In a separate bowl, beat egg whites with cream of tartar until mixture just hold stiff peaks. Stir 1/4 of mixture into batter, then fold in remaining whites gently but thoroughly. Divide batter between prepared pans and bake in the middle of a 350-degree oven for 20 minutes. Let cool before assembling cakes.

For glaze: Cook brown sugar, cream and salt until mixture reaches the soft ball stage. Remove from heat and add butter and vanilla. Cool for about 15 minutes without stirring, then beat by hand until smooth.

In a separate bowl, beat cream and powdered sugar to make whipped cream.

After cake and glaze have cooled, place cake on a stand. With the back of a spoon, spread glaze so that it drizzles over edges of cake. Then add whipped cream layer. Add next cake and glaze it. Put remaining whipped cream in a pastry bag and make a free-form design on top.

Serves 8–10

"Down home" flavor dressed up with an elegant praline glaze.

Serve scoops of sorbet in nests of melon ribbons for a cool, colorful presentation. Quarter a cantaloupe or other firm melon, then, using a vegetable peeler, cut thin strips of flesh and use them to line serving bowls or long-stemmed glasses.

Gingerbread with Hot Caramel Sauce

1 cup dark molasses
2 teaspoons baking soda
1 teaspoon cinnamon
1 teaspoon ginger
1/4 teaspoon nutmeg
1/2 cup sugar
1/2 cup (1 stick) butter, melted
2 cups flour
1 cup boiling water
2 eggs
Powdered sugar, to garnish
Whipped cream, to garnish

Sauce:

1 cup firmly packed light brown sugar
1/3 cup sugar
1/3 cup melted butter (no margarine)
2 heaping tablespoons flour
1 teaspoon vanilla extract
Dash of salt
1/4 teaspoon nutmeg
1 cup boiling water

In a large bowl, mix molasses, baking soda, cinnamon, ginger and nutmeg. Add sugar, butter, flour and boiling water. Stir in beaten egg yolks. Beat egg whites until stiff and fold into batter. Pour into a greased ring mold or Bundt pan. Bake in a 350-degree oven for 40 minutes or until done. Cool.

Turn gingerbread out onto a cake stand and sift powdered sugar over the top. Serve with hot caramel sauce and whipped cream.

For sauce: In a medium saucepan, combine sugars to melted butter and stir until sugars are dissolved. Add flour, stirring constantly over medium heat. Add vanilla, salt and nutmeg. Add boiling water. Cook for 10 to 15 minutes, stirring sauce until thickened. Serve over gingerbread or pool beneath.

Serves 12

Delicious with coffee or served at brunch instead of sweet rolls. The caramel sauce is also good over pound cake or ice cream.

Presenting . . .

*M*ake your edible gifts feasts for the eyes as well as the palate.

Wrap breads or cookies in patterned cotton napkins or bandannas, and tie with complementary cords or ribbons. ❧ *Nestle treats in pretty doilies inside flea market finds—old teacups, trinket boxes, pressed glass bowls, mismatched plates.* ❧ *Use floral wallpaper scraps to cover a "hat box" container for cakes.* ❧ *Glue ribbons and buttons onto wooden or cardboard containers.* ❧ *Sponge color onto inexpensive baskets, line with crumpled tissue paper and fill with tiny muffins or truffles.* ❧ *Make a "bouquet" of cookies by pressing thin wooden dowel "stems" into them while still warm and then arrange in small clay pots or a florist's box.*

Apple Pie Cake with Rum Butter Sauce

1/4 cup (1/2 stick) butter or margarine, softened

1 cup sugar

1 egg

1 cup flour

1/2 teaspoon salt

1 teaspoon cinnamon

1/2 teaspoon grated nutmeg

2 tablespoons hot water

1 teaspoon vanilla extract

3 cups peeled, diced cooking apples (such as Granny Smith or Jonathan)

1/2 cup chopped pecans (optional)

Whipped cream, to garnish

_____

Sauce:

1/2 cup firmly packed dark brown sugar

1/2 cup sugar

5 tablespoons butter or margarine, softened

1/2 cup heavy cream

1 tablespoon rum

Cream butter, then gradually add sugar, beating well at medium speed with an electric mixer. Add egg and beat until blended. Combine flour, salt, cinnamon and nutmeg and mix well. Add to creamed mixture. Beat on low speed until smooth. Stir in water and vanilla. Fold in apples and pecans and spoon into greased and floured 9-inch pie pan.

Bake at 350 degrees for 45 minutes or until a toothpick inserted in the center comes out clean.

For sauce: Combine brown sugar, sugar, butter and cream in a small saucepan and mix well. Bring to a boil and cook for 1 minute. Stir in rum. Serve warm or at room temperature with cake and whipped cream.

Serves 6–8

Cake-like texture, shaped and served like a pie.

Chocolate Raspberry Cream Cake

1 (3-layer) German chocolate cake, unfrosted

6 tablespoons Chambord

1-1/2 cups raspberry spreadable fruit

_____

Cream:

4 cups heavy cream

2 cups sifted powdered sugar

2/3 cup sifted cocoa

Dash of salt

For cream: In a mixing bowl, combine cream, sugar, cocoa and salt. Refrigerate, covered, for 30 minutes. Beat until stiff. (Do not overbeat.)

Place 1 layer of cake on a serving plate. Sprinkle with 2 tablespoons Chambord and spread with half of fruit. Frost with 1 cup cream mixture. Repeat process with second layer. For top layer, sprinkle cake with liqueur and frost with remaining cream mixture. Cake may be decorated using cream mixture in a pastry bag.

Serves 10–12

Grab a few items from the market and in less than an hour a show-piece is ready for your guests!

1 cup blanched hazelnuts

5 ounces semisweet chocolate chips

1 (10–12-ounce) pound cake

6 tablespoons Frangelico

2 cups heavy cream, cold

3/4 cup powdered sugar

Whipped cream, to garnish

Toast hazelnuts in a 400-degree oven for about 5 minutes. (If blanched hazelnuts are not available, toast with skins on, then rub with a dry dish towel to remove; some skins may remain.) Cool and chop. Chop 3 ounces of chocolate chips and combine with nuts. Set mixture aside.

Line a 1-1/2 to 2-quart round-bottomed bowl with a damp layer of cheesecloth or with plastic wrap (spray plastic wrap with nonstick cooking spray after lining bowl). Cut several 3/8-inch thick slices from pound cake, then halve each slice diagonally to form 2 triangles. Moisten each triangle on 1 side with Frangelico and lightly press, dry-side down, against lining of bowl (narrow end of triangle should point down). Cover interior of bowl with cake, filling in "holes" with smaller pieces. Reserve uncut portion of cake.

Melt remaining 2 ounces chocolate chips. In a well-chilled bowl, whip cream and sugar until stiff. Stir in reserved chocolate chip–nut mixture. Divide whipped cream mixture and spread 1/2 evenly over entire cake surface in bowl. Fold melted chocolate into remaining 1/2 and spoon mixture into bowl (completely fill cavity). Level off surface of bowl contents, trimming away any protruding cake. Slice additional pieces from remaining pound cake, moisten with Frangelico, and use, liqueur-side down, to seal off top of bowl. Trim edges to make them round.

Cover bowl with plastic wrap and refrigerate overnight or up to 2 days.

When ready to serve, uncover, place a flat serving dish over the top and turn upside down. Lift off bowl and carefully remove cheesecloth. Serve chilled, garnished with additional whipped cream if desired.

Serves 6–8

Must be prepared in advance.

Insert tiny sparklers into this dome-shaped sweet and celebrate!

White Chocolate Cheesecake

5 (8-ounce) packages cream cheese, softened to room temperature

1-3/4 cups sugar

5 eggs

2/3 cup heavy cream

2/3 cup flour

4 ounces good-quality white chocolate, melted

2-1/2 cups crushed graham crackers

2/3 cup sugar

1/2 cup (1 stick) butter, melted

1/2 cup sour cream

2 cups white chocolate shavings, to garnish

Whip cream cheese and sugar until soft. Add eggs, cream, flour and melted white chocolate. In a separate bowl, mix graham crackers, sugar and butter. Press cracker mixture firmly onto bottom and sides of a 10-inch springform pan. Pour cream cheese mixture into pan.

Bake in a 400-degree oven for 20 minutes. Reduce temperature to 300 degrees and bake for 40 minutes more. Cool.

Before serving, spread sour cream over the top of cooled cake and sprinkle with white chocolate shavings.

Serves 12

Mounds of white chocolate shavings form a pristine bed for a sprinkling of dark, chocolate-covered coffee beans. Good-quality chocolate makes all the difference!

Lime Cheesecake

1-1/2 to 2 cups butter cookies

5 tablespoons butter, melted

3 (8-ounce) packages cream cheese, softened to room temperature

1 1/4 cups sugar

2 tablespoons flour

4 eggs

1/3 cup fresh lime juice

1 heaping teaspoon grated lime zest

2 drops green food coloring (optional)

2 cups sour cream

3 tablespoons sugar

Break cookies into bowl of food processor and process into fine crumbs. Add butter and process briefly to combine. Press mixture into bottom and sides of a 10-inch springform pan.

Beat cream cheese until light and fluffy. Gradually add sugar and flour and mix until combined well. Add eggs 1 at a time, beating well after each addition. Blend in lime juice, zest, and food coloring. Pour into prepared pan and bake in a 325-degree oven for 55 minutes or until just set.

Remove from oven and let rest for 10 minutes. Mix sour cream and sugar until well blended.

Spread over cheesecake and bake for 10 minutes more. Cool completely and refrigerate until chilled thoroughly.

Serves 8–10

Limes add a refreshing twist to this creamy cheesecake. Key limes are not readily available outside of Florida, but are wonderful when you can get them.

Almond Russe

2 envelopes unflavored gelatin

3/4 cup sugar

1/4 teaspoon salt

4 eggs, separated

2 cups milk

1 cup sour cream

1 teaspoon almond extract

1 teaspoon vanilla extract

18 lady fingers, split

1 cup heavy cream, whipped, plus additional to garnish

Toasted almonds, to garnish

In a small saucepan, combine dry gelatin, sugar and salt. In a separate bowl, blend egg yolks and milk. Add to mixture in saucepan. Cook over low heat until mixture thickens to coat a spoon. Remove from heat and add sour cream, almond and vanilla extracts. Chill until mixture mounds slightly.

Line bottom and sides of a 9-inch springform pan with ladyfingers. Make sure ladyfingers are close together; cut to fit if necessary. Beat egg whites until stiff and fold into chilled mixture. Fold in whipped cream. Spoon into springform pan and chill for at least 6 hours.

To serve, garnish with additional whipped cream and toasted almonds.

Serves 6–8

Elegant and easy, this silky creation is a luscious denouement to creative continental dining.

Chocolate Coconut Mousse with Caramel Sauce

3 cups semisweet chocolate chips (about 1-1/4 pounds), plus additional to garnish

2 cups heavy cream

1 cup sweetened shredded coconut, plus additional to garnish

4 extra-large egg yolks

8 extra-large egg whites, room temperature

Sauce:

1-1/4 cups sugar

1/4 cup water

1 cup heavy cream

1/2 cup (1 stick) unsalted butter, cut into pieces

1 teaspoon vanilla extract

Melt chocolate chips in a heavy saucepan over very low heat, stirring until smooth. Add 1 cup cream and coconut and stir until smooth. Pour into a large bowl. Cool to room temperature, then whisk in yolks.

In a separate bowl, whip 1 cup cream with an electric mixer until soft peaks form. In another bowl, beat egg whites until stiff but not dry. Fold whipped cream into chocolate mixture. Gently fold in egg whites. Pour all into a 10-inch springform pan. Cover and freeze for 6 hours or overnight.

For sauce: Cook sugar and water in a heavy saucepan over low heat, stirring until sugar dissolves. Boil until syrup turns caramel color. Add cream (mixture will bubble and harden) and stir until smooth. Remove from heat. Add butter and vanilla and stir until smooth.

Soften mousse in refrigerator for 30 minutes, then release from pan. Cut into wedges and spoon warm sauce onto plates. Place mousse on top of sauce, then garnish with chocolate chips and coconut.

Serves 8–10

Must be prepared in advance.

A wonderfully rich dessert, proven to break the best of diets.

1 cup sugar

1/2 cup water

1 (14-ounce) can sweetened condensed milk

1 cup milk

1/3 cup cream of coconut

1/3 cup light corn syrup

1 teaspoon vanilla extract

4 eggs

1 cup toasted shredded coconut, to garnish

In a heavy pan, combine sugar and water. Wet a pastry brush with tap water and brush down sides of pan to remove sugar crystals. Cover pan and bring to a boil over high heat. Do not stir. Boil until sugar is desired caramel color, about 10 minutes. (Watch closely once the sugar begins to caramelize; it can burn quickly.)

Pour caramelized sugar into 6 custard cups and swirl to coat the bottoms. Syrup will harden as it cools, so work fast. If syrup hardens too much to work with before its placed in cups, warm over low heat to liquefy again.

In a blender, thoroughly combine condensed milk, milk, cream of coconut, corn syrup, vanilla and eggs. Pour into caramel-lined cups and place in a shallow baking dish filled with 1/4-inch hot water. Cover baking dish with foil and bake at 350 degrees for 40 minutes or until firm. Remove foil and cool. Place in refrigerator for about 1 hour.

To serve, run knife around outer edges of cups and invert each onto a dessert plate. Garnish with shredded coconut.

Serves 6

Once you get the hang of preparing the caramel for these delectable flans, they'll move onto your list of reliable favorites.

To toast coconut, bake in a shallow pan at 350 degrees for about 15 minutes, or until golden brown. Stir frequently to ensure even browning.

To dry coconut, microwave 1/2 cup of freshly grated coconut on high for 2 to 3 minutes, stirring at 1-minute intervals.

Cold White Chocolate Soufflé

Butter and sugar, for the mold

1/2 pound good-quality white chocolate

2 tablespoons unsalted butter, cold

4 eggs

Pinch of salt

Hot fudge sauce

Fresh raspberries or strawberries, to garnish

Butter a 2-quart soufflé dish and sugar generously, turning so that sides are covered. Chill in refrigerator.

Melt chocolate in a microwave or a double boiler on low heat. Add cold butter and stir until it has melted into chocolate. When chocolate is warm, add egg yolks and mix well. Preheat oven to 350 degrees. Add pinch of salt to egg whites and whisk to firm peaks. Stir 1/3 of the whites into chocolate, then fold in remainder.

Pour mixture into soufflé dish and set dish in a larger pan filled with hot water reaching 2 inches up the sides of the soufflé dish. Sprinkle soufflé with sugar. Bake for about 35 minutes. Insert a knife into the center and remove soufflé from oven if it comes out clean. If not clean, bake for another 5 minutes. (Soufflé will collapse when removed from oven.)

Let rest for 5 minutes on counter. Run a knife around edges and unmold onto a serving dish. Let cool to room temperature. Lightly cover with plastic wrap and refrigerate for 1 to 6 hours. Serve in wedges placed on a pool of chocolate sauce with fresh berries on the side.

Serves 10

You'll want to skip dinner and go straight for dessert after making this white chocolate soufflé. It's moist and light with a cake-like texture.

🍃 *White chocolate, which is not true chocolate, is usually a combination of sugar, cocoa butter, milk solids, lecithin and vanilla. Cocoa butter is the key ingredient to look for in the labeling; without it, the product is confectionary coating, not white chocolate.*

3 tablespoons butter

2 tablespoons sugar, plus additional for coating ramekins

2 tablespoons flour

1 cup milk

3 large egg yolks, beaten

6 ounces bittersweet chocolate

2 teaspoons grated orange zest, plus additional to garnish

2 teaspoons orange extract

4 large egg whites

1/4 teaspoon cream of tartar

Powdered sugar, to garnish

Nectar:

1 tablespoon cornstarch

1 cup apricot nectar

1/3 cup sugar

1/4 cup fresh orange juice

2 teaspoons grated orange zest

Preheat oven to 425 degrees. With 1 tablespoon butter, generously grease 6 ramekins, then sprinkle with sugar to coat.

In medium saucepan over medium-low heat, melt remaining 2 tablespoons butter. Whisk in flour until blended. Cook for 1 minute or until bubbly. Remove from heat. Whisk in milk until blended. Cook, stirring until mixture boils and thickens. Remove pan from heat.

In small bowl, whisk egg yolks and a little of the hot milk mixture until blended. Pour egg mixture into hot milk mixture in pan. Cook, stirring over low heat until mixture thickens, about 1 minute (do not boil). Remove from heat. Stir in chocolate until melted. Stir in orange zest and orange extract. Cool for 15 minutes, stirring occasionally.

In large bowl of electric mixer, at low speed, beat egg whites and cream of tartar until foamy. At high speed, gradually beat in sugar, beating just until stiff. With rubber spatula, fold 1/4 of egg white mixture into cooled chocolate mixture. Fold chocolate mixture into remaining egg white mixture until no white streaks remain. Pour into prepared ramekins. Bake for 12 minutes or until soufflés have risen, edges are firm and center is still slightly wobbly. While baking, prepare apricot nectar.

For nectar: Stir cornstarch into 1/4 cup nectar. In a heavy saucepan, combine sugar, cornstarch mixture and remaining nectar. Bring mixture to a boil, stirring frequently. Cool for 2 minutes. Stir in orange juice and orange zest. Cool for 1 minute.

To serve, place ramckins on serving plates. Punch hole in tops of soufflés and spoon in 2 tablespoons of nectar. Sprinkle with powdered sugar and orange zest.

Serves 6

To vary the presentation, spoon apricot nectar onto serving plates. Carefully turn out soufflés and invert onto plates. Sprinkle soufflés with powdered sugar and sprinkle orange zest onto nectar.

Apricot Mousse

1 (6-ounce) package dried apricots

1 (12-ounce) can apricot nectar

Grated zest of 1 lemon

1/4 cup apricot preserves

4 eggs

3/4 cup sugar

1 teaspoon cornstarch

1-1/2 cups warm milk

1 tablespoon unflavored gelatin

1/2 cup warm water

1 cup heavy cream, whipped

Sauce:

1 cup apricot preserves

2 tablespoons fresh lemon juice

1 teaspoon grated lemon zest

2 tablespoons apricot brandy

2 tablespoons powdered sugar

1/8 cup Kirsch

Combine apricots, nectar and zest and bring to a boil. Cover and reduce heat. Simmer for 30 minutes or until apricots are tender. Add preserves. Puree in blender or food processor.

Beat egg yolks, sugar and cornstarch until fluffy and lemon colored. Combine egg mixture and milk in a double boiler. Cook, stirring constantly, until mixture coats the back of a spoon. Dissolve gelatin in warm water. Stir into custard and add puree. Chill until almost set, at least 1 hour. Fold in whipped cream. Beat egg whites until stiff. Fold in gently. Spoon into 1-1/2-quart soufflé dish.

For sauce: Heat all ingredients except Kirsch in a saucepan. Stir until preserves dissolve. Add Kirsch and chill. Serve over mousse and pool beneath servings.

Serves 8

Capture the hues of sunset in this velvety mousse. Complement with a Chocolate-Filled Pastry Puff.

Orange Custard

1-1/2 cups sugar

5 large eggs

3 egg yolks

1-1/2 cups fresh orange juice

1 cup heavy cream

1/4 teaspoon salt

Grated zest of 2 oranges

Place 3/4 cup sugar in a heavy skillet. Stir with a wooden spoon over medium-high heat until caramelized. Pour immediately into a 2-quart baking dish.

Combine eggs and egg yolks with remaining sugar and beat vigorously with an electric mixer. Stir in orange juice, cream, salt and orange zest. Pour over caramelized sugar into a baking dish and place in a larger pan. Add water to larger pan to reach 2/3 up sides of baking dish. Bake in a 400-degree oven for 1 hour or until a knife inserted in the center comes out clean. Refrigerate until thoroughly chilled.

To serve, spoon into dessert bowls with some of the caramelized syrup in each.

Serves 6

Smooth and delicious! Garnish with twists of candied orange peel and mint leaves.

Peach Kuchen

1-1/4 cups flour

1/4 teaspoon salt

1/2 cup (1 stick) cold
unsalted butter, cut into pieces

2 tablespoons sour cream

Filling:

3 large egg yolks

1/3 cup sour cream

1 cup sugar

1/4 cup flour

1/4 teaspoon salt

1-1/2 pounds fresh ripe peaches,
peeled, pitted and thickly sliced

Combine flour, salt and butter until crumbly. Add sour cream and blend until mixture forms a ball. Gather dough together and shape into a flat disc. Place in a 9-inch tart or springform pan. Press dough onto bottom and sides of the pan evenly. Bake in the center of a 425-degree oven for 18 to 20 minutes until lightly browned. Remove from oven and cool for 15 minutes. Reduce oven temperature to 350 degrees.

For filling: Combine egg yolks, sour cream, sugar, flour and salt. Pour 1/2 cup of mixture over baked crust. Top with sliced peaches in concentric circles. Pour remaining custard mixture evenly over peaches. Bake in a 350-degree oven for 50 to 60 minutes or until custard is set and top is lightly browned. Allow to cool for 10 minutes before removing sides of pan. Serve warm or at room temperature (refrigerate if not serving immediately).

Serves 10–12

A lovely way to enjoy fresh peaches. To peel them easily, blanch in boiling water for about 30 seconds, then place immediately in icy cold water and slip skins off. Refrigerate in a plastic bag for up to 5 days.

Cloaked Apples

6 tart apples (such as
Granny Smith or Jonathan)

1 teaspoon fresh lemon juice

1/2 cup raisins soaked overnight in 1/2
cup brandy (optional), reserve brandy

1/4 cup sugar

3 tablespoons unsalted butter,
thinly sliced

1/4 cup heavy cream

Topping:

1 (3-ounce) package cream cheese,
softened to room temperature

1/2 cup heavy cream

1/4 cup sugar

Reserved brandy from raisins (optional)

For topping: In a food processor fitted with metal blade, process cream cheese for 15 seconds. Scrape sides of bowl. Add cream, sugar, and reserved brandy and process for 15 seconds or until smooth. Refrigerate until serving.

Preheat oven to 400 degrees. Peel and core apples. Cut into 1/8-inch slices and sprinkle with lemon juice. Generously butter a 9-inch ceramic tart dish or pie pan. Arrange apple slices in dish, overlapping them slightly and layering with raisins. Sprinkle evenly with sugar and 3 tablespoons butter. Bake for 30 minutes.

Increase oven temperature to 500 degrees. Add cream and bake for 5 minutes more. Serve warm with cream cheese topping.

Serves 4

The wonderful aroma of these baked apples evokes warm memories.

Blackberry Pinwheels

1/2 cup (1 stick) butter or margarine

1 cup plus 2 tablespoons sugar

1 cup water

2 cups blackberries, fresh or frozen, drained

1/2–1 teaspoon cinnamon

Dough:

1-1/2 cups flour

1/4 teaspoon salt

2-1/4 teaspoons baking powder

1/2 cup butter or margarine

1/3 cup milk, room temperature

In a saucepan over medium heat, melt 5-1/2 tablespoons butter, then add 1 cup sugar and water, stirring until sugar dissolves. Set aside.

For dough: Combine flour, salt and baking powder. Cut in butter until mixture resembles fine crumbs. Add milk and stir with a fork until dough leaves sides of bowl. Turn out onto a floured board and knead 3 to 4 times. Roll out to 11- by 9- by 1/4-inch thick rectangle.

Spread berries over dough, sprinkle with cinnamon and roll up jelly-roll style. Cut into 1-1/4-inch thick slices.

Melt remaining butter and pour into a 10-inch round or oval baking dish. Place dough slices in dish and drizzle syrup carefully over them.

Bake in a 350-degree oven for 1 hour. Fifteen minutes before removing from oven, sprinkle 2 tablespoons sugar over top. Serve warm or at room temperature.

Serves 8

These attractive pinwheels look almost like a pan of cinnamon rolls and are a nice alternative to a cobbler. Serve warm for brunch or as a dessert topped with ice cream.

Gewurztraminer Pears

4 Bartlett pears

1/3 cup Gewurztraminer or other sweet German wine, plus additional for basting

1 tablespoon brown sugar

8 thin strips of lemon zest

4 vanilla beans

French vanilla ice cream, vanilla frozen yogurt or whipped cream

Preheat oven to 400 degrees. Peel, core and halve pears. Spray a 9- by 13- inch baking dish with non-stick cooking spray. Place pears in dish and sprinkle with wine and sugar, followed by strips of lemon zest. Halve vanilla beans and arrange on top of pears. Cover baking dish with foil and seal tightly. Bake pears for about 40 minutes until tender. Spoon liquid over pears occasionally while cooking and add additional wine, if needed.

Remove vanilla beans and transfer pears into 4 serving dishes.

Top each with French vanilla ice cream, frozen yogurt, whipping cream or a soft dessert cheese such as **Mascarpone**.

Serves 4

After removing vanilla beans, rinse them under running water and leave out to dry. Place in original container and store in a cool place. They may be reused 3 to 4 times before losing their flavor.

Fresh Fruit Torte

1 pineapple, cored and peeled

1 small cantaloupe, halved and seeded

1 large papaya, seeded and peeled

6 kiwis, peeled

1 mango, peeled and pitted

3 large bananas, peeled

1/2 lemon

12 strawberries, hulled

1 tablespoon cinnamon

Fresh mint leaves, to garnish

Sauce:

3/4 cup heavy cream

10 ounces semisweet chocolate chips

1 tablespoon cinnamon

2 tablespoons rum (optional)

Thinly slice pineapple, cantaloupe, papaya, kiwi and mango; keep fruits separate. Slice bananas into a bowl. Squeeze lemon over slices and toss bananas to coat.

Place the closed rim of a 9-inch springform pan on a cake stand or serving plate. Arrange pineapple slices in an even layer to completely cover the surface of the plate inside the springform rim. Reserve a few small slices of pineapple for the top. Press firmly to make pineapple layer as compact as possible. Arrange papaya in an even layer on top of pineapple and press firmly. Wipe juices from serving plate. Continue to layer fruit, using kiwi, cantaloupe, bananas and mango. Press between each layer. Top with remaining pineapple slices in concentric circles. Slice strawberries and arrange on top. Carefully pour off or wipe off any juices that have collected on plate. Refrigerate at least 1 hour.

For sauce: Just before serving, prepare chocolate sauce. In a heavy saucepan, bring cream to a boil. Add chocolate and remove saucepan from heat. Allow chocolate mixture to rest for 3 minutes. Stir until smooth, then add cinnamon and rum.

Remove springform rim from torte and wipe juices from serving plate. Dust fruit torte with cinnamon. With a very sharp knife, slice torte. Top with chocolate sauce and mint leaves.

Serves 10–12

These fresh layers of color are beautiful on a glass cake stand. Calorie-watchers will love this without the sauce. Leftovers keep for several days, but prepare the torte the day of serving for best flavor and appearance.

Crème de Menthe Grapes

1/2–1 pound seedless grapes, washed and drained

1/2 cup crème de menthe

1/2 cup powdered sugar

Divide grapes into small clusters. Dip each cluster into crème de menthe, dust generously with powdered sugar, place on a baking sheet and freeze for 25 to 30 minutes. Transfer to refrigerator and keep chilled until ready to serve. Arrange grapes on tray and sprinkle again lightly with powdered sugar.

Serves 4

A wonderful finale. Serve atop a wheel of brie as an edible garnish.

Citrus Blossoms

8 ounces phyllo dough

1/2 cup (1 stick) unsalted butter, melted

1/2 pint blueberries, raspberries or blackberries (or combination)

24 mint leaves

Lime curd:

4 egg yolks

6 eggs

2 cups sugar

1 cup fresh lime juice

2 tablespoons grated lime zest

1 cup (2 sticks) unsalted butter

Brush 1 sheet of phyllo with melted butter. Top with another sheet and brush with butter. Cut into 4-inch squares. Carefully place each square into a muffin tin. Add 2 more squares to each tin, rotating each slightly to make "petals." Repeat to make 24 cups in all. Bake phyllo cups in a 375-degree oven for 8 to 12 minutes or until golden. Remove from pans and cool.

For lime curd: In a heavy saucepan, combine egg yolks, eggs, sugar, lime juice and lime zest. Cook over low heat, stirring constantly with a whisk until thickened (curd coats the back of a spoon). Do not allow curd to boil. Remove from heat and gradually whisk in butter. Cool in a glass or plastic container. Refrigerate until ready to serve.

Spoon 1 rounded teaspoon of lime curd into each phyllo cup. Top with berries and a mint leaf.

Makes 24

A striking centerpiece on a buffet table. Both the phyllo cups and the lime curd may be prepared ahead and assembled just before serving.

Creamy Lemon Sherbet with Marinated Strawberries

4 cups buttermilk

1 cup sugar

2/3 cup fresh lemon juice

2 teaspoons grated lemon zest

Pinch of salt

Mint sprigs or candied lemon peel, to garnish

Strawberries:

1-1/2 pints strawberries

1/4 cup good-quality orange marmalade

2–3 tablespoons Grand Marnier

Combine buttermilk, sugar, lemon juice, lemon zest and salt in a bowl. Transfer to an ice cream freezer and freeze according to manufacturer's instructions.

For strawberries: About 30 minutes before serving sherbet, clean berries, hull and quarter. Place in a bowl and toss with marmalade. Refrigerate for about 20 minutes. Stir in Grand Marnier just before serving.

When ready to serve, scoop sherbet into chilled glasses and top with marinated strawberries. Garnish with mint sprigs and candied lemon peel.

Serves 6

Tart and refreshing. For a seasonal variation, use raspberries or blueberries over orange sherbet.

Champagne Strawberry Sherbet

3 cups fresh strawberries, hulled

2/3 cup sugar

2 tablespoons fresh lemon juice

1/4 cup champagne, bubbly or flat

1/4 cup heavy cream

In a food processor, combine strawberries, sugar, and lemon juice until smooth. Pour in champagne and cream and mix until blended. Freeze in an ice cream maker according to manufacturer's instructions.

Serves 6–8

A simple but elegant ending to any meal. Serve in chilled champagne glasses with pretty iridescent ribbon tied to each stem.

Fresh Ginger Sorbet

1-1/2 cups sugar

2 tablespoons peeled and minced fresh ginger

2 tablespoons finely grated lemon zest

4 cups water

1/2 cup fresh lemon juice

Combine sugar, ginger, lemon zest and 4 cups water in a saucepan. Bring to a boil, stirring often. Boil uncovered over medium heat for 10 minutes. Cool, then stir in lemon juice. Freeze in an ice cream maker according to manufacturer's instructions. When mixture is almost solid, whirl in a food processor until smooth. Freeze 1 hour until firm.

Serves 8–10

A tingling dessert or palate cleanser.

Pink Grapefruit Sorbet

1/2 cup honey

1/2 cup water

2 large pink grapefruits, peeled and sectioned (reserve juice)

1 cup pink grapefruit juice (made up partially from reserved juice)

1 cup half-and-half

1/4 teaspoon salt

Drop of red food coloring (optional)

Mint, to garnish

Pink grapefruit sections dipped in honey, to garnish

In a saucepan, combine honey and water and boil for 2 minutes. Remove from heat and cool. Puree grapefruit sections in a food processor or blender. Add cooled syrup, juice, half-and-half, salt and red food coloring. Blend. Freeze in a metal pan until firm.

Break into chunks and puree in food processor or blender. (To keep sorbet from melting, refrigerate work bowl and blade prior to final processing.) Serve in hollowed grapefruit shells, garnished with sprigs of mint and honey-dipped grapefruit sections.

Serves 6–8

This blushing sorbet is a marvelous addition to a summer brunch. An appealing aspect is that is doesn't require an ice cream maker.

Black coffee is like an empty slate just waiting to be enhanced by spices, sweets and liqueurs. In its virgin form, it's a great A.M. starter; flavored, it becomes a marvelous ending to a memorable meal.

Coffee in bean form may be stored at room temperature for 4 to 5 weeks or frozen for 5 to 6 months. Ground coffee will keep for 7 to 10 days at room temperature, 5 to 6 weeks in the freezer and up to 3 weeks in the refrigerator.

Spicing Things Up

A fun way to experiment with flavored coffees is to allow guests to help themselves from an assortment of ingredients. Provide recipes and proper mixing utensils. Or, tailor your coffee to complement your dessert.

Iced Hazelnut Coffee

12 cups strong, hot coffee

3/4 cup ground hazelnuts

1 large cinnamon stick

Crushed ice

Steep coffee, hazelnuts and cinnamon stick until coffee reaches room temperature. Pour coffee through a strainer lined with 3/4-inch thickness of cheesecloth. Remove cloth and squeeze it over coffee without letting hazelnuts drop in. Chill well, then serve over crushed ice.

Serves 12

Turkish Coffee

4 cups strong, hot coffee

4 tablespoons honey

4 cardamom seeds

Whipped cream, to garnish

Divide honey and cardamom seeds equally between 4 cups of coffee. Top with dollops of whipped cream and serve.

Serves 4

Mexican Coffee

4 cups strong, hot coffee

4 ounces tequila

4 ounces Kahlúa

24 ounces grated semisweet chocolate

Whipped cream, to garnish

Ground cinnamon, to garnish

Divide tequila, Kahlúa and chocolate equally into 4 cups of coffee. Top each with a dollop of whipped cream and a sprinkle of cinnamon.

Serves 4

Chocolate Liqueur Coffee

4 cups strong, hot coffee

4 miniature chocolate cups filled with liqueur

When serving coffee after dinner, pass liqueur-filled chocolate cups on a tray or on the saucer of each cup. Guests may drop the entire cup into their coffee to make an elegant dessert coffee.

Serves 4

Coffee Float

1-1/2 cups strong, hot coffee (French roast or espresso)

2/3 cup heavy cream

4 teaspoons honey

8 scoops coffee ice cream

Grated dark sweet chocolate, to garnish

Whip cream and honey until stiff. Place 2 scoops of ice cream in 4 tall stemmed glasses. Pour on coffee, dividing evenly among servings. Dollop each with whipped cream and a sprinkling of chocolate.

Serves 4

Spiced Coffee

6 cups strong, hot coffee

4 cups water

2 tablespoons firmly packed dark brown sugar

4 (3-inch) cinnamon sticks

4 (2-1/2-inch) strips orange zest

1/2 teaspoon allspice

In a saucepan, combine water, sugar, cinnamon sticks, orange rind and allspice. Over moderate heat, bring mixture to a boil, then remove pan from heat. Let stand for 5 minutes, then strain and divide equally between each cup of coffee.

Serves 6

Raspberry Bars

3/4 cup (1-1/2 sticks) unsalted butter, softened

1-1/2 cups sugar

2 eggs, separated

1-1/2 cups flour, sifted

1 cup raspberry preserves

1/2 cup shredded coconut

1 cup chopped pecans or almond slices

In an electric mixer, beat butter and 1 cup sugar until light and fluffy. Beat in egg yolks and sifted flour. Spread into an ungreased 9-by 13-inch pan. Bake in a 350-degree oven for 25 minutes. Cool and spread with raspberry preserves and sprinkle with coconut.

Beat egg whites until stiff. Gradually beat in 1/2 cup sugar until peaks form. Gently fold in nuts. Spread mixture over baked layer and bake again at 350 degrees for 12 minutes or until golden brown. Cool and cut into bars or squares.

Makes 24–36 small bars

Experiment with other fruit fillings in these chewy, versatile bars.

Lime Almond Squares

2 cups flour

1/2 cup firmly packed brown sugar

1/2 teaspoon salt

3/4 cup (1-1/2 sticks) unsalted butter, chilled

1/2 cup toasted slivered almonds

1-1/2 cups sugar

4 eggs

6 tablespoons fresh lime juice

3 tablespoons grated lime zest

1 teaspoon baking powder

Pinch of salt

Powered sugar, to garnish

In a mixing bowl or food processor, combine flour, sugar and salt. Add butter and almonds until a fine meal forms. Press into the bottom of a 9- by 13-inch baking dish. Bake at 350 degrees until golden brown, about 20 minutes.

Blend sugar, eggs, lime juice, lime zest, baking powder and salt until smooth. Pour onto hot crust. Bake in a 350-degree oven until filling begins to brown, about 20 minutes. Cool completely. Cut into squares and dust with powdered sugar.

Makes 32 small bars

Scrumptious goodies to pack in a picnic basket.

Almonds are the kernel of the fruit of almond trees.

Toasting them intensifies their flavor and adds appealing crunch.

Lily Cookies

1 cup (2 sticks) butter or margarine

1-1/2 (3-ounce) packages cream cheese, softened to room temperature

2 cups sifted flour

Egg wash

6–8 teaspoons orange marmalade

Powdered sugar, to garnish

Cream butter and cream cheese. Add flour, then chill dough for 1 hour.

Roll out dough to 1/8-inch thickness and cut with a 2-inch round cutter. Roll each round into a cornucopia shape (flatten out top portion slightly, to resemble a lily), sealing edges well with egg wash. Fill open end with 1/4 teaspoon marmalade. Bake in a 375-degree oven for about 15 minutes, or until slightly brown. Cool, then dust with powdered sugar until well coated.

Makes 2–2-1/2 dozen

A tender, delicate cookie. Serve on pretty doilies or antique plates.

Irish Lace Sandwich Cookies

1/2 cup (1 stick) butter

1 cup sugar

1 egg

1 teaspoon almond extract

2 tablespoons flour

1/3 teaspoon salt

1 cup quick-cooking oats

Filling:

4 ounces bittersweet or semisweet chocolate

1 tablespoon butter

2 tablespoons orange zest

1 tablespoon Grand Marnier

In a mixing bowl, cream butter and sugar. Add egg and almond extract, mixing well. Add flour, salt and oats. Line a baking sheet with aluminum foil. Use a melon baller (for more uniform shapes) and drop dough by 1/2 teaspoonsful onto foil. (Use only this small amount; dough will spread to give a lacy effect in the finished cookie.) Place only 6 cookies at a time on an average-sized baking sheet.

Bake in a 350-degree oven for 5 to 8 minutes until light browned. Slide foil off sheet and completely cool cookies before removing from foil. (If they resist at all they are not completely cool.)

For filling: In the top of a double boiler or in a microwave at medium power, melt chocolate and butter. Stir in orange zest and Grand Marnier. Cool slightly. Spread mixture on the flat side of 1 cookie and sandwich with a second. Let cool and serve.

Makes 18 sandwich cookies

Serve these light treats with a scoop of vanilla ice cream or orange sherbet and a cup of cinnamon-flavored coffee.

Bittersweet Ravioli

2 ounces bittersweet chocolate

1 cup (2 sticks) butter or margarine, softened

1/2 cup sugar

1 egg

1-1/4 teaspoons chocolate extract

1/4 teaspoon baking soda

Dash of salt

2-1/2 cups flour

1 to 1-1/4 cups seedless raspberry jam

Powdered sugar, to garnish

Melt chocolate in the top of a double boiler or in a microwave at medium power. Remove from heat and cool. In a large bowl, cream butter and sugar until blended. Add egg, chocolate extract, baking soda, salt and melted chocolate. Beat until light. Blend in flour to make a stiff dough. Divide dough in half, cover and refrigerate until firm.

Preheat oven to 350 degrees. Lightly grease baking sheets. Roll out 1/2 the dough to 1/8-inch thick between 2 sheets of waxed paper. Repeat with other 1/2 of dough. If dough becomes too soft, refrigerate until firm again.

Cut dough into 1-1/2-inch squares. Place 1/2 the squares, 2 inches apart, on prepared baking sheets. Spoon about 1/2 teaspoon jam into the center of each square and top with another square. Press edges of squares together with a fork to seal. Bake for 10 minutes or just until edges are browned. Remove and place on wire racks to cool. Dust lightly with powdered sugar when completely cooled.

Makes about 24

A playful ending to an Italian meal. Serve with spumoni and cups of espresso.

Princess Cookies

1 cup (2 sticks) butter or margarine, softened

1 cup firmly packed light brown sugar

2 eggs

1 teaspoon vanilla extract

2 cups old-fashioned oats

2 cups flour

1/2 teaspoon salt

1 teaspoon baking soda

1-1/2 cups dried whole cherries

1-1/4 cups good-quality white chocolate chunks

Cream butter and sugar together with an electric mixer. Add eggs, mixing well, followed by vanilla extract. In a separate bowl, combine oats, flour, salt and baking soda. Add to creamed mixture in several additions. Stir in dried cherries and white chocolate chunks.

Drop by teaspoonsful onto ungreased baking sheets, 1 inch apart. Bake in a 375-degree oven for 10 to 12 minutes or until golden brown.

Makes 2-1/2 dozen

A delightful union of sweet and tart. Nestle these little cookies into a decorative basket or tin.

Chocolate Sherry Cream Brownies

4 ounces unsweetened chocolate

1 cup (2 sticks) butter

4 eggs

2 cups sugar

2 cups flour

1/2 teaspoon salt

1 teaspoon vanilla extract

Filling:

1/2 cup (1 stick) butter

4 cups powdered sugar, sifted

1/4 cup heavy cream

2 tablespoons sherry

1 cup chopped walnuts

Topping:

6 ounces semisweet chocolate chips

3 tablespoons water

3 tablespoons butter

Melt chocolate and butter together in a microwave or a double boiler and cool. Combine eggs and sugar, beat and then add to chocolate mixture. Mix in flour, salt and vanilla. Preheat oven to 350 degrees. Grease and flour a 9- by 13-inch baking pan, then pour mixture into pan. Bake for 25 minutes and cool completely, about 1 to 2 hours.

For filling: Beat together butter, powdered sugar, cream, sherry and walnuts. Spread over cooled crust and chill, about 2 hours.

For topping: In a saucepan, melt chocolate chips, water and butter. Mixture will be thin. Paint onto top of chilled filling with a pastry brush.

With a knife, score the top of bars into desired size. (Without scoring, chocolate topping will break.) Chill for 1 hour, then cut and serve.

Makes 48 small bars

Rich "uptown" brownies with a hint of sherry.

Chocolate-Filled Pastry Puffs

1 (17-ounce) package frozen puff pastry (2 sheets)

6 tablespoons semisweet chocolate chips

2–3 tablespoons Grand Marnier

Preheat oven to 350 degrees. Thaw pastry for about 20 minutes, then cut each sheet into 3 pieces along folds. Thaw until flexible, about 10 minutes more. Sprinkle 1 tablespoon of chocolate chips into the center of each piece. Sprinkle with Grand Marnier. Fold pastry into a triangle to enclose chocolate, pinching edges to seal. Repeat with remaining pastry. (May be prepared 1 day ahead and refrigerated).

Arrange pastries on an ungreased baking sheet and bake until golden brown, about 20 minutes. Serve hot.

Makes 6

Serve these versatile pastry puffs with pureed berries spooned over the top or experiment with different fruit fillings in place of the chocolate chips.

Terrific Truffles

1-1/4 pounds semisweet chocolate

1 cup heavy cream

1 cup (2 sticks) unsalted butter

1/4 cup light corn syrup

2 tablespoons liqueur (crème de menthe, Kahlúa or Amaretto)

1 cup chopped white or dark semisweet chocolate (optional)

8 ounces chopped nuts (optional)

8 ounces semisweet dipping chocolate

Melt chocolate in a microwave or in the top of a double boiler. In a saucepan, heat cream just until boiling. Pour chocolate into cream and stir to mix. Add cubes of butter to chocolate and whisk to incorporate. Add corn syrup and liqueur. Stir well. Pour chocolate into a large bowl and cool in the freezer or over a bowl of ice water.

When mixture has reached about room temperature, stir in optional chocolate or nuts. Chill again for 15 to 30 minutes. Stir frequently until chocolate will hold its shape. Using a small scoop or melon baller, drop truffles onto a waxed paper–lined baking sheet. Cover and chill for at least 2 hours to set truffles for dipping. (Chilling chocolate quickly in freezer will prevent truffles from being grainy.)

Melt dipping chocolate, then cool to 85 to 90 degrees. Dip cold, firm truffles in chocolate, holding with a fork, and coat well. Place on a waxed paper–lined baking sheet to set. Place in an airtight container and store in a cool dry place.

Makes 60

These sinfully good truffles may be refrigerated for 1 week or frozen for 2 months. Place them in miniature muffin tin liners and arrange in a decorative tin for a quick gift.

Coconut Truffles

12 ounces good-quality white chocolate

1/3 cup heavy cream

4 tablespoons unsalted butter

3-1/2 ounces shredded coconut

In a mixing bowl, break chocolate into very small pieces. In a small saucepan, combine cream and butter. Heat just to boiling, then pour immediately over chocolate pieces. Beat until smoothly blended. Chill for at least 1 to 2 hours until firm.

Roll chilled mixture between palms of hands into 1-inch balls and return to refrigerator. Toast coconut and, while coconut is still hot, roll truffles in it. (Hot coconut will fuse to the chocolate.) Chill on a baking sheet before storing in freezer bags.

Makes 24

These sweet little confections will disappear quickly. Make extras to keep in the freezer for spur-of-the-moment special occasions.

Acknowledgments

*The **Above & Beyond Parsley** Development Committee wishes to gratefully acknowledge the many individuals and businesses whose dedication, experience and commitment to quality have made this book possible.*

We must first express our great gratitude to the members of our testing committees. The following individuals spent countless hours and many dollars ensuring that our recipes were outstanding:

Appetizers

Ginny Cerny Beall, *Section Head;* Caroline Hampton McKnight, *Section Head;* Kay Bisagno Bleakley, Marilyn Rockwell Driscoll, Stephanie Brown Harper, Susan Eynatten Hughes, Diane Beaver Johnson, Georgia Quatman Lynch, LaDonna Anderson Marietti, Jo Stewart Riley, Connie Doyle Troutman, DeeDee Davis Warner, Leslie Spurck Whitaker

Breads

Pamela Comer Gray, *Section Head;* Priscilla Gilbert Calkins, Laura Wolff Greenbaum, Jennifer Hurst Gunter, Joanne Copeland Herre, Billie McCormick, Mary Plunkett Reintjes, Katherine Biety Schorgl, Ann Schmidt, Mendy Jacobs Steinwart, Leslie Siemens Stelzer

Brunch

Karen Mance Weltner, *Section Head;* Nancy Ramsey Bethay, Becky Clevenger Hannah, Cynthia Worl Hanson, Ann Rome Hogueland, Laura Springmeier Jones, Constance Helliker Martin, Jill Remsberg McGee, Jill Ericson Oakleaf, Karan Uthoff Rice, Amy Silverman

Salads

Buckie Waller Egerstrom, *Section Head;* Kimberly Kline Aliber, Margie Crossley Austin, Laurie Douglass Barnds, Laura White Bluhm, Denise Austin Dudenhoeffer, Elaine Scarboro Duvall, Mary Ellen Freed Duvall, Marilyn Brunsell Egerstrom, Laura Buercklin Fitzpatrick, Joanna Miranda Glaze, Sherry Callier Hahn, Debbie Dicus Kennedy, Peggy Bunting Lyons, Ellen Benson Merriman, Michele Mayer Orpin, Shelley Allen Preston, Caryn Kenner Ungashick, Alison Wiedeman Ward, Diane Cunningham Zimmer

Soups

Sara Dickerson Bernard, *Section Head;* Julie Sue Bacon, Kathryn Blunk Gustafson, Mary Greaves Hodge, Susan Campbell Heddens, Merrily Thomson Jackson, Elizabeth Beckett James, Victoria Smith Luby, Sharon Murray-Mueller, Lynne Koupal O'Connell, Barbara Brigham Reed, Marya Podrebarac Stallard, Lucy Burch Shelton

Meats

Melinda Kennett DiCarlo, *Section Head;* Nancy A. Arther, Cynthia Cox Batliner, Jennifer Peakes DiCarlo, Patti Castro Gound, Abigail Hayo, K. Darcy Reynolds, Karen Cleveland Thompson, Diane Ball Wilkerson, Karen McNeely Zecy

Poultry

Sara Senter Thompson, *Section Head;* Diane Steinbrueck Andrews, Kay Bisagno Bleakley, Dana Bleakley, Debora Louk Campbell, Cindy Johnson Cook, Teri McClure, Corliss Chandler Miller, Kari Trygg Miller, Marcia Bailey Sabates, Kathryn Lehman Toombs, Mary Schumacher Whitaker, Lori Hansen Hill, Terri Lefholz, Mary Kay Harte Guevel, Marsha Reese, Cindy Campbell Reynolds, Peggy Ludewig Schmidtlein

Seafood

Donna Gerber Missimer, *Section Head;* Terri Lemieux Collier, Cheri Miller Emami, Ann Latimer Harlan, Barbara Reese Joslin, Laura Glover Kaiser, Kathy Sparks Knopke, Pat Warnick Lotz, Susan Hansen Roberts, Meg Robison Smith, Joanie Ferguson Weaver

Pasta

Elizabeth McClintock Allen, *Section Head;* Georgia Quatman Lynch, *Section Head;* Karen Conde Adler, Janice Yukon Benjamin, Laura Peterson Crowe, Maraline Adair Hayob, Sarah Beeks Higdon, Jan Broeg Knopke, Mary Dunlap Lockton, Daphne Nan Muchnic, Jeanne Ryan Sosland, Mina Olander Steen, Katherine Lindeman Wells

Vegetables

Jane Parks Aylward, *Section Head;* Melinda Miller Crowe, Marilyn Krausz Cupples, Vicki Clanton Kinney, Mary Ann Schultz, Janet Olson Taylor, Lannie Haynes Taylor

Desserts

Jennifer Hanna Coen, *Section Head;* Mary Barthelmass, Libby Dallmeyer Blair, Connie Spelts Brouillette, Shirley Stanton Doering, Peggy Massman Freeman, Barbara Jackson Gattermeier, Carol Ann Keller, Jane Nichols Lampo, Luci Whiting Lindwall, Asenath Marie McMorris, Mary Jo Jensen Truog

Special Testing

Julie Sue Bacon, *Section Head;* Siobhan McLaughlin-Lesley, *Section Head;* Cindy Campbell Reynolds, *Section Head;* Nancy Meinershagen Bell, Mary Elizabeth Blackwell, Elizabeth Sprague Brandt, Kay Johnston Campbell, Sarah Menke Curfman, Linda Waters Dro, Mary Kay Harte Guevel, Maureen Mulreany Halter, Lori F. Jabara, Merrily Thomson Jackson, Elizabeth Beckett James, Mary Louise Mead Kilmer, Mitzi D. Martin, Teri McClure, Kimberly Davis O'Dear, Lucy Burch Shelton, Peggy Ludewig Schmidtlein, Connie Skaggs Sowell, Martha M. Steele, Sara Senter Thompson, Karen Massman VanAsdale, Laura Greenbaum Wolff

Our dedicated testing committees had their work cut out for them by the enthusiastic support of the many individuals who contributed recipes and entertaining tips:

Jane Adamson, Karen Adler, Randy Allard, Betsy Allen, Kristin Altice, Martha Anderson, Teresa Anderson, Joan Ansley, Melissa Anthony, Melanie DiCarlo Ausbrook, Mary Axetell, Jane Aylward

Julie Bacon, Cindy Ballard, Sarah D. Bancroft, Stephanie Barnon, Bonnie Bayles, Betsy Beachy, Karen Beal, Linda Beal, Ginny Beall, Betty Beaty, Susan Belger, Nancy Bell, Janice Benjamin, Jennie Bennett, Marjie Bergman, Sara Bernard, Colleen Bjerg, Sarah Blackman, Libby Blair, Laura Bluhm, Lynne Bock, Virginia Boyd, Liz Brandt, Mary Jo Brennan, Sally Bridges, Carmen Briscoe, Ana Maria Brito, Linda Buchner, Lydia Butler

Allison Cahill, Poo Calkins, Donna Callaway, Debbie Campbell, Kay Campbell, Jeff Carter, Sue Carlson, Stephanie Caudill, Blanche Cerney, Karla Champion, Lois Christianson, Don Clabaugh, Wendy Clay, Jennifer Coen, Joni Cohen, Jennifer Collet, Ellen Condron, Becky Connerman, Anne Bolen Connor, Darlene Cooke, Sheri Cook-Cunningham, Lyn Cravens, Mary Lou Cravens, Bill Crooks, Kay Crossman, Diane Crouse, Ken Crouse, Laura Crowe, Sarah Menke Curfman, Lisa Curran

Kathy Davis, Linda Davis, Frances Dean, Janie Dean, Donna Deeter, Susan Delmore, Lynn Devins, Jennifer DiCarlo, Demetra Dickens, Sue Dierks, Kelly Dillman, Martha Doyle, Deborah Dribben, Linda Dro, Mary Duffy, Frances Scott Dunlap, Scotty Dunlap

Martie Eftink, Buckie Egerstrom, Jan Elder, Lynne Elder, Ann Emmerson, Pam Ennis, Susan Erwood, Maureen M. Evans, Susan Everson

Lisa Falconer, Lynn Farrell, Claire Ferris, Jinny McCoy Fickle, Dorothy Flanagan, Jan Flanagan, Jim Flanagan, Julie Flanagan, Pam Fleischer, Mitzi Foster, Beth Fowler, Suzanne Fowler, Peggy Freeman, Diane Frese, Carol Frieirich, Alice Frost, Tammie Frymer

Inez Garr, John Garr II, Linda Geppert, Kate Gibson, Sara Gilson, Joanna Miranda Glaze, Becky Gomerman, Susan Goodman, Pam Gordon, Jan Goss, Patty Gound, Alan Graham, Janet Graham, Karen Graves, Pam Gray, Celeste Greenlee, Lucy Gros, Courtney Grovenberg, Jenny Hurst Gunter, Jane Guthrie

Maureen Halter, Vickie Handy, Cynthia Hanson, Kathy Hardwick, Charlotte Hart, Barbara Hartig, Jim Hartig, Becky Hasfield, Virginia Hassenflu, Danna Deeter Haverty, Norma Hawley, Maraline Hayob, Nancy Hays, Jean Helmers, Maralyn Henbaut, Cheryl Hill, Lori Hill, Mary Boulware Hobbs, Marilyn Hodes, Mary Greaves Hodge, Ann Hogueland, Jennifer Holden, Susan Hornung, Deborah Hosfield, Katherine Hughes, Mary Hunkeler

Ellie Idstrom, M. Ingardia, Barb Innes, Linda Jackson, Lori Jackson, Merrily Jackson, Nancy Jacobs, Betty James, Ann Jandl, Shelle Jensen, Susan Johnson, Rhonda Johnston, Barbara Joslin, Bette Jordan

Sally Kampfe, Frances Kardasz, Carol Keller, Carol Kelly, Tammye Kelly, Debbie Kennedy, Suzanne Kerley, Debbie Kerr, Julie Killion, Mary Lou Kilmer, Peggy Kilroy, Peg Kirk, Mardie Kirkwood, Marilyn Klein, Lynne Knott, Virginia Koenig, Janet Kraft, Alison Kretzinger, Lois Krug, Karen Krumme

Sara Lafferty, Acey Lampe, Jane Lampo, Caroline Langknecht, Jane Lanyro, Lisa Leonard, Martha L. Leonard, Robert O. Lesley, Peg Leslie, Luci Lindwall, Candy Linn, Betsey Locke, Mary Lockton, Florence Loomis, Patricia Warnick Lotz, Vicki Luby, Barbara Luce, David Luce, Mary Luce, Barbara Luhrs, Alice Lund, Marsha Lundy, Georgia Lynch, Ginna Lynd

Patty Mach, Susan Mackey, Dana Mahoney, Linda Male, Jennifer Marino, Gloria Martin, Jeannette Martin, Renée Martin, Ellen McCarthy, Billie McCormick, Sara McElhenny, Ann McElvain, Nancy McGee, Caroline McKnight, Siobhan McLaughlin-Lesley, Eleanor Messmer, June Meinershagen, Blanche Middleton, Annie Miller, Corliss Miller, Donna Missimer, Ann Moore, Jeanie Moore, Nan Muchnic, Alan Myers, Merrill Myers, Yurie Myers

Gail Nason, Dana Nelson, Marty Nichols, Rosann North

Jill Oakleaf, Laura O'Brien, Mary O'Connell, Kimberly O'Dear, Robin O'Hara, Dottie Otis, Cincy Owens

Dee Paone, Linda Patterson, Pam Peffer, Kathy Perry, Vera Pfeifer, Jan Placek-Jones, Betty Poeshel, Debbie Pope, Mary Porto, Carolyn Price, Susan Price, Rhonda Prohaska, Leslie Purdy

Mary Raizman, Lynn Reardon , Barbara Reed, Martha Reed, Marsha Reese, Margaret Reid, Aimee Reif, Mary Reintjes, Julia Reitzes, Cindy Reynolds, Karan Rice, Julie Richardson, Anne Richter, Vicki Riffle, Anne Rinne, Susan Roberts, Dallas Robinson, Patricia Rodina, Lori Rodopoulos, Cristelyn Udouj Roebuck, Helen Rogers, Joyce Romine, Patty Ross, Ann Schupp Royer

Marcia Sabates, Kim Salanski, Leslie Evans Sanchez, Sheila Sanders, Meg Sauer, Melissa Payne Schaffer, Lori Schlotzhauer, Ann Schmidt, Peg Schmidtlein, Katherine Schorgl, Suzie Schradle, Ellen Schreiber, Mary Schust, Leslie Schweitzer, Mindy Scovell, Dorene Shipley, Mary Jane Short, Mary Shortino, Amy Silverman, Jeannette Siminis, Anne Simmons, Mary Beth Simpson, Carol Sindelar, Connie Smith, Joyce Ann Smith, Kim Smith, Susan Smithburg, Catherine Smoot, Jeanne Sosland, Nancy Spangler, Kathleen Donohue Spencer, Linda Baker Spencer, Sarah Stanton, Martha Steele, Mina Steen, Cindy Stehl, Mendy Steinwart, Janet Stevenson, Gay Stewart, Susan Stewart, Una Strauss, Michelle Suter, Laura Sutherland, Sara Sweeney

Jeanne Tapp, Wanda Totty, Mary Frances Taylor, Sheree Thein, Sara Thompson, Joan Titens, Beth Tomlinson, Mary Ann Tornquist, Barbara Travis, Pat Trent, Kay Truitt, Sylvia Tucker

Sally Uhlmann, Jennifer Valentine, Sandie Valentine, Karen VanAsdale, Peggy VanAsdale, Janet Van Cleave, Peggy Van Dyke, Maureen Vaughn, Cindy Vigliaturo, Jana Voth

Judy Walker, Joan Waller, Alison Ward, Lenise P. Ward, DeeDee Warner, Barbara Wasburgh, Mary Ann Wasson, Kay Watkins, Barbara Weatherford, Joanie Weaver, Patricia Weed,

Gail Weinberg, Sally West, Stephanie M. Westwood, Ann White, Hope Wooldridge, Jeanne Williams, Karen Williams, Suzanne Williams, Marti Wills

Karen Zecy, Wendy Zecy, Diane Zimmer, Cathy Zitnik

Our recipe sections also include several special culinary contributions, and we offer our deepest appreciation to the following friends:

Bill Crooks (Corn, Shrimp and Penne Soup, Heartland Pasta, Potato Gnocchi with Fresh Tomato Basil Butter Sauce, Saffron Chicken and Vegetables and White Chocolate Cheesecake); Diane and Ken Crouse (Alpine Torte, Country Manor Breakfast Tart and Terrific Truffles); Linda Davis (Black Bean Salad, Charcoaled Lemon-Lime Chicken, Corn Crêpes with Shrimp and Green Chilies and Zuccotto Frangelico); and Gloria Martin (West Indian Apricot Rice).

We are quite grateful to the following individuals and businesses who lent their unique knowledge of foods and entertaining to our development of special topic boxes, tips and menus:

Cheryl Shields and Heather Jordan of The Better Cheddar, who graciously treated members of the testing committee to a delicious, informative cheese seminar and answered our many follow-up questions; Paula Ann Winchester of The Herb Gathering and Debbie Pope, who both provided much interesting information and many ideas on versatile herbs; and Charlotte Bliss, Susan Cleavenger, Family Features Editorial Services, Carol Keller, Ann Kleb, Val McGrath, Peggy Murray, Mary Porto, Mary Beth Simpson, Evan Walters, and Alison Ward, for kindly offering numerous insights and "special touches."

We wish to sincerely thank the following artists, businesses, League members and community supporters who so generously lent or donated valuable and interesting props for our photography sessions:

Ambience Furs, Lynn Smiser Bowers, Ernie Block Studio, M.L. Briggs Sod Farm, Linda Buchner, Susan Cleavenger/Emma Brown Collectibles, Lisa Curran, Linda Davis, Elephant's Trunk, Halls/Plaza, House of Rocks, Vicki Johnson, Kaplan's Fabrics, Grandma Leierer, Constance Leiter, Chuck Matney and Brian Morley/ Matney Floral Design, Menorah Medical Center, Robyn Nichols, Dixie and Austin Pollard, Debbie Pope, Scandia Down, Anne Simmons, Laura Sutherland, Tile Source, Ann Willoughby and WRK, Inc.

Our thanks also go to the following professionals for so freely sharing their valuable services, support and talents:

Chuck Matney and Brian Morley, for their ongoing advice and exquisite floral donations, especially the glorious roses on the dust jacket; Bill Crooks, Ken and Diane Crouse and Linda Davis, for being such enthusiastic culinary resources; Charles Horner, for always offering a patient ear as well as sound legal counsel; Luke LeTourneau of Image Point, Inc., for generously donating the film processing for the book's photography; Monte Mehring, for many hours of computer programming and cheerful troubleshooting; Calvert Guthrie, for unstintingly sharing both creative talent and a steady mien; Katie Glauber, Brady Myers and Premila Malik Borchardt, for their marketing savvy and services; and Steve Farrell, Roger Rose and Ernst Williams of Digital Equipment Company, for their generous donations of computer equipment to our cookbook operations.

We are deeply indebted to the following employers of our development committee volunteers, who patiently supported our work by permitting countless phone calls, faxes, photocopies and long lunches as well as access to on-site computers:

Freightliner Corporation, The Kansas City Star Co., Menorah Medical Center, University National Bank of Lawrence and Valentine-Radford, Inc.

We also wish to extend warm thanks to those who supported our production efforts in a variety of other ways:

Marilyn Block, Thane Brethour, Linda

Buchner, Steve Gibson and Carlo Pascolini, for always welcoming us and offering their steady expertise in the photo studio; Jim and Kevin Flanagan, for their unflagging patience with all of our agendas; Shelly Rauzi, Nadine Hancock, Betsey Locke and Karen Zecy, for hours of typing and phone calls; Ted Gessler and The Carriage Club, for providing comfortable, convenient meeting areas; Donna Lusten, for sharing her persimmons in the middle of winter; Bernie Eglitis, Sharon Garrett and John Yuelkenbeck of Connell Zeko Type & Graphics, for their consistent generosity, attention to quality and beautiful typesetting; Brian Greenlee of Missouri Engravers, for showcasing our photos through top quality separations; and Dave Plumer, Sallie Buck and Mary Lee Moffitt of Walsworth Publishing, for providing us with so many options and a beautiful end result.

We are indebted to the Junior League administration and Executive Committees of 1990-91, 1991-92 and 1992-93 for their abiding support. Among these special people our particular thanks go to Randy Allard, Betsy Allen, Janice Benjamin, Mary Browne, Linda Cozad, Ginny Curtin, Betsey Locke, Georgia Lynch, Oscar Nelson, Mary Jo Saviano and Mina Steen.

Our heartfelt thanks and appreciation must go to our wonderful families. Their generous amounts of love and endless sacrifices made our efforts possible as well as fruitful.

Finally, we extend a jubilant tip of our toques to our visionary predecessors, the **Beyond Parsley** *development committee, for setting such high standards and showing us what could be done.*

Production Credits

TYPESETTING
Connell Zeko Type & Graphics

FILM PROCESSING
Image Point, Inc.

COLOR SEPARATIONS
Missouri Engravers

PRINTING & BINDING
Walsworth Publishing Company

Tips Index

Almonds, information about, 281
Apricots, information about, 102
Asparagus, peeling French style, 241
Baking stones/tiles, using to bake bread, 76
Beverages, tips for presenting, 59, 190
Bouquet garni, making a, 243
Breads
  adding flavor to while baking, 82
  baking tips for, 76, 82
  thawing, 82
  using hollow loaves of for soup, 133
Butters
  flavoring, 75, 197, 237
  molding, 71
  serving in tortilla cones, 174
Cactus, using edible varieties of, 177
Canape cutters, using to cut peppers, 98
Candles, tips for, 235
Capers, description of, 51
Caviar, types of, 55
Celery, keeping crisp, 98
Centerpieces
  ideas for making, 38, 185
  using herbs in, 113
Cheeses
  accompaniments to, 41
  types of and information about, 41, 44, 223
Chicken
  information on grilling, 173
  precooking, 173
Chilies, information about, 127
Chocolate leaves, how to make, 258
Chocolate molds, using to shape butter, 71
Chocolate, white, information about, 281
Chutney, information about, 145
Citrus peels, grating and freezing, 98
Coconut, drying and toasting, 271
Coffee, flavoring, 280
Containers, for food gifts, 266
Corn husks, serving in, 250
Cream cheese, quick herbed, 48
Crème fraîche
  flavoring with horseradish, 131
  making, 250
Croutons, varieties of, 108
Eggs
  baking in potatoes, 84
  poaching, 84, 89
Fennel, information about, 234
Fish
  judging doneness while grilling, 194
  storing and freezing fresh, 192
  using flavored butters with, 197

Flowers, edible, information about, 103
Focaccia, making sandwiches with, 69
Garlic, freezing, 124
Garnishes
  flaming sugar cube, 85
  for salads, 98, 106
  for soup, 135, 139
  fruit peel, 98, 140
  Mexican blanket pattern for, 46
  pepper flowers, 144
  using a template for, 46
  using chocolate leaves for, 258
Gifts, presenting food as, 266
Ginger
  freezing and grating, 36
  storing in sherry, 251
Goat cheese, storing, 44
Greens, information about, 114, 118
Grilling
  information about, 156, 201
Herbs
  cooking with, 205
  freezing and storing fresh, 205, 216
  use of in centerpieces, 108
  using to flavor vinegars, 205
Honey, flavoring with herbs, 84
Ice cubes, freezing herbs in, 59
Lemongrass, information about, 177
Lemons and limes
  carving designs into peels of, 190
  freezing juice of, 259
  getting more juice from, 259
  grating/zesting, 259
  using in cooking water, 209, 239
Lettuce, storing after tearing, 118
Mayonnaise, information about, 119, 155
Meats
  when to add salt to, 156
  wine vinegar as a tenderizer for, 148
Melon ribbons, making nests of, 265
Mint, growing fresh, 219
Mushrooms, information about, 248
Napkin rings, pasta, 220
Nuts, toasting, 169
Oats, browning, 82
Olive oils, information about, 227
Olives, types of and uses for, 50
Onions
  ridding hands of odor of, 108
  Vidalia, description of, 58
Outdoor entertaining
  chilling beverages in child's pool for, 190
  seaside theme for, 100
Parsley, freezing and flaking fresh, 216
Pasta
  choosing sauces for, 220

cooking, 210, 224
flavoring with lemon juice, 209
making fried snacks of, 96
napkins rings for party, 220
serving large quantities of, 209
storing, 224
Pastry, making applique designs with, 198
Peaches
  peeling easily, 275
  selecting, 78
Pepper flowers, creating, 144
Peppers
  cutting with canape cutters, 98
  how to roast, 52
Pesto, information about, 211
Phyllo, handling and working with, 261
Placecards, ideas for, 141
Potpourri, tying packets of to chairs, 42
Raisins, instructions for plumping, 76
Saffron, information on, 174
Salads
  edible containers for, 96
  garnishes for, 98, 106
  molded, preparation of, 105
  types of greens for, 114
Sandwiches, ideas for, 66, 69
Sauces, techniques for, 148
Sesame seeds, toasting, 97
Setting the table, tips for, 161
Soup containers, baked squash as, 122
Soup
  absorbing fat from, 124
  garnishes for, 135, 139
  crème fraîche garnish for, 131
  muting seasoning of, 124
  nestling bowls of in napkins, 135
  pastry top hat for, 135
  stocks, 124, 131
  thickening, 124
Squash
  information about, 178
  toasting seeds of, 134
Sun-dried tomatoes, making, 171
Sweet potatoes, raw, as crudités, 239
Tortillas
  heating, 171
  making serving cones of, 174
Tuna, information about, 194
Vanilla beans, reusing, 276
Vegetable dippers, suggestions for, 38
Vinegar
  flavoring with herbs, 205
  using as a meat tenderizer, 148
Vodkas, flavoring, 59
Walnuts, information about, 97
White chocolate, description of, 272

Food Index

Adobe Corn with Jalapeño-Lime Butter, 237
Almonds
  Almond Russe, 270
  Alpine Torte, 256
  Broccoli Amandine, 245
  Country Manor Breakfast Tart, 91
  Honey-Almond Coffee Cake, 82
  Lime Almond Squares, 281
Alpine Torte, 256
Amaretto Peach Soup, 141
Ancho Oregano Butter, 237
Angel Hair Pasta with Spicy Sun-Dried
  Tomato Sauce, 217

Anise Seed Bread, 67
Anise Vodka, 59
Appetizers
  Artichokes Athena, 43
  Avocado Mousse, 49
  Basic Bruschetta, 57
  Black and White Spread, 54
  Black-Eyed Peaco de Gallo, 52
  Boursin Blue Cheesecake, 47
  Brie and Pear Bundles, 44
  Caesar Cream, 53
  Carpaccio Dijonnaise, 39
  Caviar Supreme, 55
  Chèvre Pine Nut Toasts with Sun-Dried
    Tomato Pesto, 56
  Crab and Cheese Tarts, 87
  Curried Cauliflower, 54

Farmer's Market Pie, 49
Feta Cheese Parcels, 42
Fontina Grilled in Vine Leaves, 46
Fresh Fruit Salsa, 53
Fruit with Sherried Cheese, 43
Goat Cheese Salad with Nectarines and
  Walnuts, 112
Grilled Pizza with Gorgonzola and
  Prosciutto, 225
Gruyère Cheesecake, 45
Herbed Goat Cheese, 57
Herbed Mozzarella, 45
Jiao Z, 37
Lemon Olive Caviar, 50
Marinated Goat Cheese, 44
Mediterranean Mélange, 51
Mushroom Ravioli in Beef Consommé, 129

New Potatoes with Caviar Cream, 239
Olive Paste, 51
Pâté with Apricots and Pistachios, 38
Peppery Pepitas, 58
Queso Grill, 47
Roasted Red Pepper Garlic Dip, 52
Roquefort Toasts, 56
Santa Fe Cheesecake, 46
Shrimp Cakes, 35
Shrimp and Spinach Phyllo with Mustard
    Cream Sauce, 36
Shrimp in Dijon Vinaigrette, 34
Smoked Salmon and Onion Cheesecake, 48
Smoked Salmon with Salmon Biscuits, 34
Spiced Olives, 57
Stuffed Spinach Crêpes, 42
Sun-Dried Tomato Vinaigrette, 54
Sweet Onion Bites, 58
Tenderloin with Three Sauces, 39
Thai Pies, 37
Toasted Pita Triangles, 40
Tomato and Fennel Spread, 57
Tropical Seviche, 35
Veal Meatballs with Tomato Sauce, 40
White Salsa Dip, 52
Apples
Apple Jack Compote, 87
Apple Pie Cake with Rum Butter Sauce, 267
Carrot and Apple Salad, 111
Cloaked Apples, 275
Fruit with Sherried Cheese, 43
Harvest Brunch Cake, 83
Indian Summer Soup, 140
Minted Spinach and Apple Medley, 112
Roanoke Farm Muffins, 79
Salmon and Apple Salad, 101
Spicy Apple Sausage Patties, 150
Stuffed Cranberry-Pepper Game Hens, 182
Wine-Soaked Apple Lemon Relish, 146
Apricots
Apple Jack Compote, 87
Apricot Butter, 75
Apricot-Honey Baked Ham, 150
Apricot Marzipan Tart, 261
Apricot Mousse, 274
Apricot Nectar, 273
Apricot Sauce, 274
Chocolate Soufflés with Apricot Nectar, 273
Fruit-Glazed Chicken, 167
Harvest Brunch Cake, 83
Pâté with Apricots and Pistachios, 38
Sherried Sweet Potatoes, 239
Shrimp Salad with Apricot Mayonnaise, 102
Stuffed French Toast with Orange Sauce, 84
West Indian Apricot Rice, 251
Arrowhead Veal Chops, 158
Artichokes
Artichoke-Prosciutto Pasta, 215
Artichokes Athena, 43
Basil Scallop and Shrimp Linguine, 218
Classic Creamed Mushrooms and
    Artichokes, 232
Creamy Ham Brioches, 85
Peppered Chicken with Artichoke Hearts,
    176
Queen of Hearts Salad, 116
Asparagus
Chinese Fried Asparagus, 241
Emerald Asparagus Pinwheel, 250
Fresh Asparagus Flans, 241
Autumn River Salad, 97
Avocados
Avocado Mayonnaise, 155
Avocado Mousse, 49

Garden Green Gazpacho, 138
Poached Eggs in Avocado, 89
Tomato Avocado Mold with Creamy
    Horseradish Dressing, 105
Bagel Croutons, 126
Baja Lasagna, 175
Baked Fettuccine, 220
Bananas
Fresh Fruit Torte, 277
Reggae Chicken, 170
Wild Rice with Plantains, 250
Barley
Crunchy Baked Barley, 249
Minted Barley Salad, 110
Basic Bruschetta, 57
Basic Mayonnaise, 155
Basil-Parmesan Butter, 237
Basil Scallop and Shrimp Linguine, 218
Basil Tomatoes with Gorgonzola, 243
Basil Wine Marinade, 204
Beans and legumes See also Peas
Black Bean Pecan Sauce, 173
Black Bean Salad, 111
Black-Eyed Peaco de Gallo, 52
Calypso Black Beans, 247
Chicken in Black Bean Pecan Sauce, 173
Chili String Beans, 236
Cold Herbed Garbanzo Beans, 109
Hearty Lentil Potage, 125
Herbed Black Bean Soup with Smoked
    Chicken, 123
Liberty Green Beans, 236
Ozark Caviar, 248
Tortilla Stacked Pizza, 226
Beef See also Veal
Burgundy Shepherd's Pie, 157
Carpaccio Dijonnaise, 39
Filet Marchand du Vin, 158
Flint Hills Beef Salad, 94
Green Chili Lasagna, 213
Green Chili Stew, 123
Herbed Meat Loaf with Cream Sauce, 153
Mesquite Grilled T-Bones, 152
Orange Fennel Brisket, 156
Pepper-Coated Stuffed Flank Steak, 151
Royal Beef Tenderloin, 154
Savory Steaks, 153
Smoky Brisket, 154
Spinach and Steak Pinwheels, 152
Tenderloin with Three Sauces, 39
Teriyaki-Glazed Flank Steak, 151
Three Pepper Chili, 126
Berried Pork Salad, 95
Beverages
Anise Vodka, 59
Black Tea Vodka, 59
Champagne Fantasy, 59
Champagne and Guava Nectar, 59
Chocolate Liqueur Coffee, 280
Coffee Float, 280
Cranberry Vodka, 59
Herbed Vodka, 59
Iced Hazelnut Coffee, 280
Mexican Coffee, 280
Spiced Coffee, 280
Thoroughly Warming Brew, 59
Turkish Coffee, 280
Bittersweet Ravioli, 283
Black and White Spread, 54
Black Bean Salad, 111
Black-eyed peas. See Beans and legumes
Black Tea Vodka, 59
Blackberry Pinwheels, 276

Blarney Bread, 74
Blue Cheese Potato Salad, 107
Blue Lamb, 160
Blueberries
Berried Pork Salad, 95
"Bleuberry" Spinach Salad, 115
Citrus Berry Muffins, 78
Citrus Blossoms, 278
Cool Blueberry Soup, 140
Boursin Blue Cheesecake, 47
Braised Fennel with Sage Sauce, 234
Bread Pudding, Parmesan, 73
Breads See also Croutons; Muffins
Anise Seed Bread, 67
Basic Bruschetta, 57
Blackberry Pinwheels, 276
Blarney Bread, 74
Caraway Bread, 71
Cheese and Herb Wreath, 68
Citrus Bows, 77
Confetti Loaf, 74
Creamy Ham Brioches, 85
Crescent Moon Sweet Rolls, 76
Deli Rye Bread, 64
Focaccia, 69
Harlequin Loaves, 66
Mustard Wheat Bread, 65
Onion and Corn Spoonbread, 72
Parmesan Bread Pudding, 73
Plaza Popovers, 71
Raisin Spice Bread, 73
Red Bell Pepper Bread, 65
Roma Fennel Bread, 63
Rosemary Breadsticks, 67
Rum Raisin French Toast, 83
Sage Celery Seed Bread, 62
Salmon Biscuits, 34
Savory Olive Nut Bread, 70
Sesame Zucchini Bread, 70
Stonehenge Bread, 62
Stuffed French Toast with Orange Sauce, 84
Swedish Oatmeal Wheat Bread, 63
White Swan Rolls, 72
Brie and Pear Bundles, 44
Broccoli Amandine, 245
Broccoli Blue Soup, 133
Broccoli with Onions and Pine Nuts, 245
Brochettes See also Kabobs
Brochettes of Chicken and Sage, 167
Lamb Brochettes, 163
Broiled Tuna with Provençal Sauce, 193
Brookside Salad, 96
Brownies, Chocolate Sherry Cream, 284
Brunch
Apple Jack Compote, 87
Blackberry Pinwheels, 276
Carriage House Bake, 86
Cheese Soufflé Roll, 88
Country Manor Breakfast Tart, 91
Crab and Cheese Tarts, 87
Creamy Ham Brioches, 85
Crescent Moon Sweet Rolls, 76
Farmer's Market Pie, 49
Gingerbread with Hot Caramel Sauce, 266
Gruyère Cheesecake, 45
Harvest Brunch Cake, 83
Honey-Almond Coffee Cake, 82
Hyde Park Waffles, 85
Italian Strata, 90
Macadamia Nut Coffee Cake, 81
Pecan Muffins, 77
Poached Eggs in Avocado, 89
Puerto Vallarta Crêpes, 89
Rum Raisin French Toast, 83

Salmon Biscuits, 34
Smoked Salmon with Salmon Biscuits, 34
Stuffed French Toast with Orange Sauce, 84
Swiss Custard, 86
Wild Mushroom Quiches in Acorn Squash, 90
Bruschetta
Basic Bruschetta, 57
Bruschetta Salad, 104
Brussels Sprouts, Honeyed, 246
Bulgur
Artichokes Athena, 43
Burgundy Shepherd's Pie, 157
Butterflied Leg of Lamb, 162
Butters
Ancho Oregano Butter, 237
Apricot Butter, 75
Basil-Parmesan Butter, 237
Chili-Cumin Butter, 197
Cranberry Butter, 75
Creamy Dill Butter, 197
Curry Butter, 75
Fiery Pepper Butter, 197
Green Peppercorn Butter, 197
Herb Butter, 183
Jalapeño-Lime Butter, 237
Lemon Dijon Butter, 197
Orange Grand Marnier Butter, 75
Radish Butter, 75
Red Onion Butter, 75
Royal Rosemary Butter, 237
Wasabi Butter, 197
Butterscotch Pumpkin Muffins, 80
Buttons and Bows, 214
Caesar Cream, 53
Cakes See Desserts
Calypso Black Beans, 247
Calzone Napoli, 228-229
Camden County Catfish, 203
Canadian Bacon with Ginger Pineapple Sauce, 149
Caramelized Onions, 180
Caraway Bread, 71
Carpaccio Dijonnaise, 39
Carriage House Bake, 86
Carrots
Carrot and Apple Salad, 111
Lemon Carrot Sheaves, 233
Roanoke Farm Muffins, 79
Spiced Grapes and Carrots, 233
Thyme Veggie Bundles, 244
Zesty Carrot Gratin, 234
Catfish, Camden County, 203
Cauliflower
Cauliflower Stilton Velouté, 135
Curried Cauliflower, 54
Sunburst Florets, 246
Caviar
Caviar Supreme, 55
New Potatoes with Caviar Cream, 239
Champagne and Guava Nectar, 59
Champagne Fantasy, 59
Champagne Strawberry Sherbet, 279
Charcoaled Lemon-Lime Chicken, 172
Cheese
Baked Fettuccine, 220
Basil Tomatoes with Gorgonzola, 243
Black and White Spread, 54
Blue Cheese Potato Salad, 107
Blue Lamb, 160
Boursin Blue Cheesecake, 47
Brie and Pear Bundles, 44
Broccoli Blue Soup, 133
Carriage House Bake, 86

Cauliflower Stilton Velouté, 135
Cheese and Herb Wreath, 68
Cheese Quartet Rigatoni, 219
Cheese Soufflé Roll, 88
Chèvre Pine Nut Toasts with Sun-Dried Tomato Pesto, 56
Crab and Cheese Tarts, 87
Creamy Ham Brioches, 85
Farmer's Market Pie, 49
Fast Lane Bread Topping, 64
Feta Cheese Parcels, 42
Feta Chicken on Couscous, 170
Fontina Grilled in Vine Leaves, 46
Fruit with Sherried Cheese, 43
Goat Cheese Salad with Nectarines and Walnuts, 112
Grilled Pizza with Gorgonzola and Prosciutto, 225
Gruyère Cheesecake, 45
Herbed Goat Cheese, 57
Herbed Mozzarella, 45
Honey-Almond Coffee Cake, 82
Italian Strata, 90
Liberty Green Beans, 236
Marinated Goat Cheese, 44
Mascarpone, 257
Minestrone Parmesan, 129
Mushroom Feta Soup, 137
Parmesan Bread Pudding, 73
Pasta with Herbed Tomatoes and Cheese, 219
Queso Grill, 47
Roquefort Toasts, 56
Santa Fe Cheesecake, 46
Shellfish Gratin, 242
Smoked Salmon and Onion Cheesecake, 48
Swiss Custard, 86
White Cheddar Parsnips and Potatoes, 235
Zesty Carrot Gratin, 234
Cheesecakes
Boursin Blue Cheesecake, 47
Gruyère Cheesecake, 45
Lime Cheesecake, 269
Santa Fe Cheesecake, 46
Smoked Salmon and Onion Cheesecake, 48
White Chocolate Cheesecake, 269
Cherries
Confetti Loaf, 74
Duck with Dried Cherries and Peppercorns, 185
Princess Cookies, 283
Chèvre Pine Nut Toasts with Sun-Dried Tomato Pesto, 56
Chicken
Baja Lasagna, 175
Brochettes of Chicken and Sage, 167
Brookside Salad, 96
Charcoaled Lemon-Lime Chicken, 172
Chicken and Onion Quesadillas, 176
Chicken in Black Bean Pecan Sauce, 173
Chicken in Madeira Cream Sauce, 179
Chicken Medley Stir-Fry, 168
Chicken with Red Pepper Sauce, 171
Chilled Chicken Spiral with Watercress Puree, 169
Chinese Garden Pasta, 210
Cobb Pasta Salad, 109
Dynasty Chicken, 172
Feta Chicken on Couscous, 170
Fruit-Glazed Chicken, 167
Ginger-Lime Chicken, 177
Grilled Hedaki Chicken Sandwich, 181
Herbed Black Bean Soup with Smoked Chicken, 123

Lemon Chicken Turnovers, 181
Lemon Fettuccine with Hickory-Smoked Chicken, 208
Lotus Chicken, 168
Mediterranean Chicken Salad, 95
Orange Chicken with Acorn Squash, 178
Pepper Poulet Pasta, 209
Peppered Chicken with Artichoke Hearts, 176
Pesto Chicken with Basil Cream, 166
Pink Peppercorn Chicken, 175
Poulet Dijon, 179
Rajah Chicken Soup, 130
Reggae Chicken, 170
Saffron Chicken and Vegetables, 174
Spinach Fettuccine with Chicken and Pesto, 208
Szechuan Noodle Salad, 108
Tagliatelle Verde, 211
Taos Tequila Chicken, 180
Thai Pies, 37
Won Ton Chicken Salad, 96
Chili, Three Pepper, 126
Chili-Cumin Butter, 197
Chilies
Baja Lasagna, 175
Chili-Cumin Butter, 197
Chili String Beans, 236
Green Chili Lasagna, 213
Green Chili Mayonnaise, 155
Green Chili Stew, 123
Puerto Vallarta Crêpes, 89
South of the Border Potato Salad, 107
Tortilla Stacked Pizza, 226
Chilled Chicken Spiral with Watercress Puree, 169
Chinese Fried Asparagus, 241
Chinese Garden Pasta, 210
Chocolate See also Chocolate, white
Bittersweet Ravioli, 283
Chocolate Chip Crème Brûlée, 256
Chocolate Coconut Mousse with Caramel Sauce, 270
Chocolate-Filled Pastry Puffs, 284
Chocolate Glaze, 260
Chocolate Liqueur Coffee, 280
Chocolate Mousse Torte, 258
Chocolate Pâté with Crème Anglaise and Raspberry Coulis, 254
Chocolate Raspberry Cream Cake, 267
Chocolate Sherry Cream Brownies, 284
Chocolate Soufflés with Apricot Nectar, 273
Frozen Truffle Loaf, 255
Irish Lace Sandwich Cookies, 282
Mexican Coffee, 280
Pecan Ganache Tart, 262
Terrific Truffles, 285
Zuccotto Frangelico, 268
Chocolate, white
Alpine Torte, 256
Coconut Truffles, 285
Cold White Chocolate Soufflé, 272
Princess Cookies, 283
White Chocolate Buttercream Frosting, 257
White Chocolate Cheesecake, 269
Citrus Berry Muffins, 78
Citrus Blossoms, 278
Citrus Bows, 77
Classic Creamed Mushrooms and Artichokes, 232
Classic Wild Rice Soup, 130
Cloaked Apples, 275
Cobb Pasta Salad, 109

Coconut
    Apple Jack Compote, 87
    Chocolate Coconut Mousse with Caramel
        Sauce, 270
    Coconut Flans, 271
    Coconut Truffles, 285
    Confetti Loaf, 74
    Reggae Chicken, 170
    Roanoke Farm Muffins, 79
Coffee cakes. *See* Brunch
Coffee Float, 280
Coffees. *See* Beverages
Cold Herbed Garbanzo Beans, 109
Cold Roasted Peppers with Mustard Dressing,
    104
Cold White Chocolate Soufflé, 272
Compote, Apple Jack, 87
Confetti Loaf, 74
Cookies and bars. *See* Desserts
Cool Blueberry Soup, 140
Corn *See also* Polenta
    Adobe Corn with Jalapeño-Lime Butter, 237
    Black Bean Salad, 111
    Corn Crêpes with Shrimp and Green
        Chilies, 188
    Corn, Shrimp and Penne Soup, 128
    Grilled Herb Corn on the Cob, 238
    Indian Maize Salad, 105
    Onion and Corn Spoonbread, 72
Cornish hens. *See* Game
Country Manor Breakfast Tart, 91
Country Veal Stew, 125
Couscous, Feta Chicken on, 170
Crab
    Crab and Cheese Tarts, 87
    Crab Tacos with Salsa, 192
    Crusty Crab Burgers, 193
    Madagascar Crab Salad, 99
    Shellfish Gratin, 191
Cranberries
    Champagne Fantasy, 59
    Cranberry Butter, 75
    Cranberry Vodka, 59
    Stuffed Cranberry-Pepper Game Hens, 182
Cream, West Indian, 136
Creamed Zucchini Soup, 134
Creamy Dill Butter, 197
Creamy Ham Brioches, 85
Creamy Lemon Sherbet with Marinated
    Strawberries, 278
Creamy Mustard Sauce, 203
Crème Brûlée, Chocolate Chip, 256
Crème de Menthe Grapes, 277
Crêpes
    Corn Crêpes with Shrimp and Green
        Chilies, 188
    Puerto Vallarta Crêpes, 89
    Stuffed Spinach Crêpes, 42
Crescent Moon Sweet Rolls, 76
Croutons
    Bagel Croutons, 126
    Bruschetta Salad, 104
    Garlic Croutons, 126
Crunchy Baked Barley, 249
Crusty Crab Burgers, 193
Curled Melba Toast, 94
Curried Butternut Squash Soup, 134
Curried Cauliflower, 54
Curried Turkey Breast, 184
Curry Butter, 75
Custards
    Chocolate Chip Crème Brûlée, 256
    Coconut Flans, 271
    Crème Anglaise, 254

Lime Curd, 278
Orange Custard, 274
Swiss Custard, 86
Deli Rye Bread, 64
Desserts
    Almond Russe, 270
    Alpine Torte, 256
    Apple Pie Cake with Rum Butter Sauce, 267
    Apricot Marzipan Tart, 261
    Apricot Mousse, 274
    Bittersweet Ravioli, 283
    Blackberry Pinwheels, 276
    Champagne Strawberry Sherbet, 279
    Chocolate Chip Crème Brûlée, 256
    Chocolate Coconut Mousse with Caramel
        Sauce, 270
    Chocolate-Filled Pastry Puffs, 284
    Chocolate Mousse Torte, 258
    Chocolate Pâté with Crème Anglaise and
        Raspberry Coulis, 254
    Chocolate Raspberry Cream Cake, 267
    Chocolate Sherry Cream Brownies, 284
    Chocolate Soufflés with Apricot Nectar, 273
    Citrus Blossoms, 278
    Cloaked Apples, 275
    Coconut Flans, 271
    Coconut Truffles, 285
    Cold White Chocolate Soufflé, 272
    Crème de Menthe Grapes, 277
    Creamy Lemon Sherbet with Marinated
        Strawberries, 278
    Crescent Moon Sweet Rolls, 76
    Fresh Fruit Torte, 277
    Fresh Ginger Sorbet, 279
    Frozen Truffle Loaf, 255
    Gewurztraminer Pears, 276
    Gingerbread with Hot Caramel Sauce, 266
    Graham Cracker Cake with Praline Glaze,
        265
    Gypsy Torte with Lemon Sauce, 259
    Hazelnut Tart, 263
    Irish Lace Sandwich Cookies, 282
    Lily Cookies, 282
    Lime Almond Squares, 281
    Lime Cheesecake, 269
    Mascarpone, 257
    Orange Custard, 274
    Peach Kuchen, 275
    Pear Tart, 264
    Pecan Ganache Tart, 262
    Pecan Rye Cake, 264
    Phyllo Tortes with Honey Cream, 260
    Pink Grapefruit Sorbet, 279
    Princess Cookies, 283
    Raspberry Bars, 281
    Roanoke Farm Muffins, 79
    Rum Raisin French Toast, 83
    Terrific Truffles, 285
    Trifle St. Croix, 255
    White Chocolate Buttercream Frosting, 257
    White Chocolate Cheesecake, 269
    Zuccotto Frangelico, 268
Dijon Mayonnaise, 155
Dilled Prawns and Melon, 99
Dilled Tomato Soup, 137
Dips and spreads. *See* Appetizers
Duck. *See* Game
Dynasty Chicken, 172
Eggplant
    Eggplant Prosciutto, 242
    Grilled Halibut with Japanese Eggplant, 201
    Ratatouille, 243
Eggs
    Carriage House Bake, 86

Italian Strata, 90
Poached Eggs in Avocado, 89
Wild Mushroom Quiches in Acorn Squash,
    90
Emerald Asparagus Pinwheel, 250
Farmer's Market Pie, 49
Fast Lane Bread Topping, 64
Fennel
    Braised Fennel with Sage Sauce, 234
    Fennel Seed Sauce, 213
    Fennel Soup with Oysters, 124
    Orange Fennel Brisket, 156
    Pork and Penne in Fennel Seed Sauce, 213
    Roma Fennel Bread, 63
    Tomato and Fennel Spread, 57
Festive Pepper Strips, 246
Feta Cheese Parcels, 42
Feta Chicken on Couscous, 170
Fettuccine with Tomato Basil Cream, 220
Fiery Pepper Butter, 197
Figs
    Feta Cheese Parcels, 42
Filet Marchand du Vin, 158
Fish. *See* specific fish
Flans
    Coconut Flans, 271
    Fresh Asparagus Flans, 241
Flint Hills Beef Salad, 94
Focaccia, 69
Fontina Grilled in Vine Leaves, 46
French toast
    Rum Raisin French Toast, 83
    Stuffed French Toast with Orange Sauce, 84
Fresh Asparagus Flans, 241
Fresh Fruit Salsa, 53
Fresh Fruit Torte, 277
Fresh Ginger Sorbet, 279
Fried Rice, Kaleidoscope, 251
Frosting, White Chocolate Buttercream, 257
Frozen Truffle Loaf, 255
Fruit. *See specific fruits*
Fruit-Glazed Chicken, 167
Fruit with Sherried Cheese, 43
Fruited Snow Pea Toss with Poppy Seed
    Dressing, 106
Game
    Autumn River Salad, 97
    Brookside Salad, 96
    Duck with Dried Cherries and Peppercorns,
        185
    Garlic Herbed Hens, 183
    Pheasant au Vin, 184
    Stuffed Cranberry-Pepper Game Hens, 182
Garden Creamy Basil Dressing, 119
Garden Green Gazpacho, 138
Garden Tomato Soup, 132
Garlic Croutons, 126
Garlic Grilled Pork Tenderloin, 144
Garlic Herbed Hens, 183
Gewurztraminer Pears, 276
Ginger-Lime Chicken, 177
Ginger-Lime-Cilantro Swordfish, 195
Gingerbread with Hot Caramel Sauce, 266
Gnocchi, Potato, with Fresh Tomato Basil
    Butter Sauce, 221
Goat Cheese Salad with Nectarines and
    Walnuts, 112
Graham Cracker Cake with Praline Glaze, 265
Grains. *See* specific grains
Grapefruit
    Fruited Snow Pea Toss with Poppy Seed
        Dressing, 106
    Pink Grapefruit Sorbet, 279

Grapes
    Crème de Menthe Grapes, 277
    Fruited Snow Pea Toss with Poppy Seed
        Dressing, 106
    Honeyed Brussels Sprouts, 246
    Poached Trout Sauterne, 202
    Spiced Grapes and Carrots, 233
Green Chili Lasagna, 213
Green Chili Mayonnaise, 155
Green Chili Stew, 123
Green Peppercorn Butter, 197
Grilled Halibut with Japanese Eggplant, 201
Grilled Hedaki Chicken Sandwich, 181
Grilled Herb Corn on the Cob, 238
Grilled Lamb Pita Pockets, 161
Grilled Pizza with Gorgonzola and Prosciutto,
    225
Grilled Potatoes, 238
Grilled Shrimp with Lemon Butter Sauce, 189
Grilled Swordfish with Melon Salsa, 195
Grilled Turkey Breast with Herb Butter, 183
Gruyère Cheesecake, 45
Gypsy Torte with Lemon Sauce, 259
Ham See also Prosciutto
    Apricot-Honey Baked Ham, 150
    Country Manor Breakfast Tart, 91
    Creamy Ham Brioches, 85
    Puerto Vallarta Crêpes, 89
Harlequin Loaves, 66
Halibut, Grilled, with Japanese Eggplant, 201
Harvest Brunch Cake, 83
Harvest Stew in Maple Baked Acorn Squash,
    122
Hazelnuts
    Hazelnut Cognac Dressing, 119
    Hazelnut Tart, 263
    Iced Hazelnut Coffee, 280
    Zuccotto Frangelico, 268
Heartland Pasta, 217
Hearts of palm
    Queen of Hearts Salad, 116
Hearty Lentil Potage, 125
Herbed Black Bean Soup with Smoked
    Chicken, 123
Herbed Goat Cheese, 57
Herbed Meat Loaf with Cream Sauce, 153
Herbed Mozzarella, 45
Herbed Mustard, 204
Herbed Vodka, 59
Honey-Almond Coffee Cake, 82
Honey-Roasted Sesame Pork, 145
Honeyed Brussels Sprouts, 246
Hyde Park Waffles, 85
Iced Hazelnut Coffee, 280
Indian Maize Salad, 105
Indian Summer Soup, 140
Irish Lace Sandwich Cookies, 282
Italian Grilled Tuna, 194
Italian Strata, 90
Jeweled Oat Muffins, 81
Jiao Z, 37
Kabobs See also Brochettes
    Grilled Halibut with Japanese Eggplant, 201
    Shrimp Kabobs and Red Pepper Sauce, 189
Kaleidoscope Fried Rice, 251
Kiwis
    Fresh Fruit Torte, 277
    Minted Kiwi Cream, 139
Kuchen, Peach, 275
Lamb
    Blue Lamb, 160
    Butterflied Leg of Lamb, 162
    Grilled Lamb Pita Pockets, 161
    Lamb Brochettes, 163

Rack of Lamb Dijon, 163
Red Sun Lamb Shanks, 160
Stuffed Leg of Lamb, 162
Lasagna. See Pasta
Leek Timbales, 240
Leeks in Lemon Cream, 240
Lemon(s)
    Charcoaled Lemon-Lime Chicken, 172
    Creamy Lemon Sherbet with Marinated
        Strawberries, 278
    Citrus Berry Muffins, 78
    Gypsy Torte with Lemon Sauce, 259
    Leeks in Lemon Cream, 240
    Lemon Butter Sauce, 189
    Lemon Carrot Sheaves, 233
    Lemon Chicken Turnovers, 181
    Lemon Dijon Butter, 197
    Lemon Fettuccine with Hickory-Smoked
        Chicken, 208
    Lemon Mayonnaise, 155
    Lemon Olive Caviar, 50
    Lemon Sauce, 259
    Lemon and Chive Risotto, 249
    Mediterranean Mélange, 51
    Parsley Pesto, 211
    Wine-Soaked Apple Lemon Relish, 146
Liberty Green Beans, 236
Lily Cookies, 282
Lime(s)
    Charcoaled Lemon-Lime Chicken, 172
    Citrus Blossoms, 278
    Ginger-Lime Chicken, 177
    Ginger-Lime-Cilantro Sauce, 195
    Lime Almond Squares, 281
    Lime Cheesecake, 269
    Lime Cilantro Pesto, 144
    Lime Curd, 278
    Lime Dilled Salmon, 198
    Lime-Red Pepper Hollandaise Sauce, 203
    Shrimp Salad Laced with Limes, 100
Lobster
    Shellfish Gratin, 191
Lotus Chicken, 168
Macadamia Nut Coffee Cake, 81
Madagascar Crab Salad, 99
Mango
    Fresh Fruit Torte, 277
Marinades See also Fish & Seafood, Meats,
    Poultry
    Basil Wine Marinade, 204
    Orange Soy Marinade, 204
Marinated Goat Cheese, 44
Marinated Mushrooms and Romaine Salad,
    115
Martini Scallops with Angel Hair Pasta, 218
Marzipan, Apricot, Tart, 261
Mascarpone, 257
Mayonnaises, 102, 155
Meatballs, Veal, with Tomato Sauce, 40
Meat Loaf, Herbed, with Cream Sauce, 153
Mediterranean Baked Whitefish, 200
Mediterranean Chicken Salad, 95
Mediterranean Mélange, 51
Melons
    Dilled Prawns and Melon, 99
    Fresh Fruit Salsa, 53
    Fresh Fruit Torte, 277
    Grilled Swordfish with Melon Salsa, 195
    Tomato Soup with Basil Cantaloupe Balls,
        138
    Melon Salsa, 195
Mesquite Grilled T-Bones, 152
Mexican Coffee, 280

Minestrone Parmesan, 129
Minted Barley Salad, 110
Minted Kiwi Cream, 139
Minted Peas, 233
Minted Spinach and Apple Medley, 112
Morningside Peach Muffins, 78
Moroccan Ragoût, 200
Mousse
    Apricot Mousse, 274
    Avocado Mousse, 49
    Chocolate Coconut Mousse with Caramel
        Sauce, 270
    Chocolate Mousse Torte, 256
Muffins
    Butterscotch Pumpkin Muffins, 80
    Citrus Berry Muffins, 78
    Jeweled Oat Muffins, 81
    Morningside Peach Muffins, 78
    Nutty Muffins, 79
    Pecan Muffins, 77
    Roanoke Farm Muffins, 79
    Rosy Rhubarb Muffins, 80
Mushrooms
    Classic Creamed Mushrooms and
        Artichokes, 232
    Marinated Mushrooms and Romaine Salad,
        115
    Mushroom Feta Soup, 137
    Mushroom Ravioli in Beef Consommé, 129
    Mushroom and Parsley Sauce, 216
    Pepper-Coated Stuffed Flank Steak, 151
    River Country Pasta, 215
    Spaghettini with Mushroom and Parsley
        Sauce, 216
    Wild Mushroom Quiches in Acorn Squash,
        90
    Wild Mushroom Ragoût, 232
Mustard Wheat Bread, 65
Mustard-Ginger Pork Chops, 147
Nectarines, Goat Cheese Salad with, and
    Walnuts, 112
New Potatoes with Caviar Cream, 239
New Year's Redfish, 202
Noodles. See Pasta
Nuts. See specific nuts
Nutty Muffins, 79
Old-Fashioned Vegetable Soup with
    Homemade Noodles, 131
Olives
    Black and White Spread, 54
    Harlequin Loaves, 66
    Lemon Olive Caviar, 50
    Mediterranean Mélange, 51
    Olive Paste, 51
    Savory Olive Nut Bread, 70
    Seville Salad, 113
    Spiced Olives, 57
Onions
    Broccoli with Onions and Pine Nuts, 245
    Caramelized Onions, 180
    Onion and Corn Spoonbread, 72
    Red Onion Butter, 75
    Red Onion Soup with Apple Cider, 132
    Smoked Salmon and Onion Cheesecake, 48
    Sweet Onion Bites, 58
Orange(s)
    Citrus Bows, 77
    Fruited Snow Pea Toss with Poppy Seed
        Dressing, 106
    Hyde Park Waffles, 85
    Lily Cookies, 282
    Orange Blossom Zucchini, 245
    Orange Chicken with Acorn Squash, 178
    Orange Custard, 274

Orange Fennel Brisket, 156
Orange Grand Marnier Butter, 75
Orange Hollandaise Sauce, 89
Orange Soy Marinade, 204
Pomander Pork, 147
Seville Salad, 113
Stuffed French Toast with Orange Sauce, 84
Summer Palette Salad, 116
Orange roughy
    Mediterranean Baked Whitefish, 200
    Moroccan Ragoût, 200
    Orange Roughy with Pecan Sauce, 199
    Roughy Pepper Packets, 199
Ozark Caviar, 248
Oysters, Fennel Soup with, 124
Pacific Rim Tenderloin, 146
Papaya
    Fresh Fruit Torte, 277
Parmesan Bread Pudding, 73
Parsley Pesto, 211
Parsnips, White Cheddar, and Potatoes, 235
Pasta
    Angel Hair Pasta with Spicy Sun-Dried
        Tomato Sauce, 217
    Artichoke-Prosciutto Pasta, 215
    Baked Fettuccine, 220
    Basil Scallop and Shrimp Linguine, 218
    Buttons and Bows, 214
    Cheese Quartet Rigatoni, 219
    Chinese Garden Pasta, 210
    Cobb Pasta Salad, 109
    Corn, Shrimp and Penne Soup, 128
    Fettuccine with Tomato Basil Cream, 220
    Green Chili Lasagna, 213
    Heartland Pasta, 217
    Lasagna Bolognese, 212
    Lemon Fettuccine with Hickory-Smoked
        Chicken, 208
    Martini Scallops with Angel Hair Pasta, 218
    Mushroom Ravioli in Beef Consommé, 129
    Old-Fashioned Vegetable Soup with
        Homemade Noodles, 131
    Pasta Sauté with Rice and Pine Nuts, 221
    Pasta with Herbed Tomatoes and Cheese,
        219
    Pepper Poulet Pasta, 209
    Pork and Penne in Fennel Seed Sauce, 213
    Potato Gnocchi with Fresh Tomato Basil
        Butter Sauce, 221
    River Country Pasta, 215
    Sesame Pasta Salad, 110
    Sole Primavera Salad, 101
    Spaghettini with Mushroom and Parsley
        Sauce, 216
    Spinach Fettuccine with Chicken and Pesto,
        208
    Summer Bounty Pasta, 216
    Szechuan Noodle Salad, 108
    Tagliatelle Verde, 211
    Tuscan Tortellini Soup, 128
Pâté
    Chocolate Pâté with Crème Anglaise and
        Raspberry Coulis, 254
    Pâté with Apricots and Pistachios, 38
Peaches
    Amaretto Peach Soup, 141
    Morningside Peach Muffins, 78
    Peach Kuchen, 275
    Southern Belle Salad, 113
Pears
    Apple Jack Compote, 87
    Brie and Pear Bundles, 44
    Fruit with Sherried Cheese, 43
    Gewurztraminer Pears, 276

Harvest Brunch Cake, 83
Pear Chutney, 145
Pear Tart, 264
Peas
    Fruited Snow Pea Toss with Poppy Seed
        Dressing, 106
    Minted Peas, 233
Pecans
    Apple Pie Cake with Rum Butter Sauce,
    267
    Black Bean Pecan Sauce, 173
    Butterscotch Pumpkin Muffins, 80
    Chicken in Black Bean Pecan Sauce, 173
    Confetti Loaf, 74
    Nutty Muffins, 79
    Orange Roughy with Pecan Sauce, 199
    Pecan Ganache Tart, 262
    Pecan Muffins, 77
    Pecan Rye Cake, 264
    Pecan Sauce, 199
    Phyllo Tortes with Honey Cream, 260
    Roanoke Farm Muffins, 79
    Rosy Rhubarb Muffins, 80
    Southern Belle Salad, 113
    Stuffed French Toast with Orange Sauce, 84
Pepitas, Peppery, 58
Pepper-Coated Stuffed Flank Steak, 151
Pepper Poulet Pasta, 209
Peppered Chicken with Artichoke Hearts, 176
Peppered Pork Chops with Madeira Glaze,
    148
Peppers
    Chicken with Red Pepper Sauce, 171
    Cold Roasted Peppers with Mustard
        Dressing, 104
    Festive Pepper Strips, 246
    Fiery Pepper Butter, 197
    Garden Green Gazpacho, 138
    Lime-Red Pepper Hollandaise Sauce, 203
    Mediterranean Mélange, 51
    Moroccan Ragoût, 200
    Pepper Poulet Pasta, 209
    Polenta Pepper Soufflés, 247
    Red Bell Pepper Bread, 65
    Red Pepper Sauce, 171
    Red Pepper Soup, 133
    Roasted Red Pepper Garlic Dip, 52
    Roughy Pepper Packets, 199
    Stuffed Cranberry-Pepper Game Hens, 182
    Summer Bounty Pasta, 216
    Tomatillo and Red Pepper Sauce, 180
Peppery Pepitas, 58
Pesto
    Lime Cilantro Pesto, 144
    Parsley Pesto, 211
    Pesto Chicken with Basil Cream, 166
    Pork Tenderloin with Lime Cilantro Pesto,
        144
    Spinach Fettuccine with Chicken and Pesto,
        208
    Sun-Dried Tomato Pesto, 56
Pheasant au Vin, 184
Phyllo
    Brie and Pear Bundles, 44
    Citrus Blossoms, 278
    Feta Cheese Parcels, 42
    Phyllo Tortes with Honey Cream, 260
    Shrimp and Spinach Phyllo with Mustard
        Cream Sauce, 36
    Summer Phyllo Pizza, 223
Pine nuts
    Broccoli with Onions and Pine Nuts, 245
    Chèvre Pine Nut Toasts with Sun-Dried
        Tomato Pesto, 56

Nutty Muffins, 79
Pasta Sauté with Rice and Pine Nuts, 221
Pineapple
    Fresh Fruit Torte, 277
    Ginger Pineapple Sauce, 149
Pink Grapefruit Sorbet, 279
Pink Peppercorn Chicken, 175
Pistachios, Pâté with Apricots and, 38
Pizza
    Calzone Napoli, 228-229
    Grilled Pizza with Gorgonzola and
        Prosciutto, 225
    Pizza Polenta, 224
    Summer Phyllo Pizza, 223
    Tortilla Stacked Pizza, 226
    Upside-Down Pizza Pie, 226
Plantains, Wild Rice with, 250
Plaza Popovers, 71
Poached Eggs in Avocado, 89
Poached Trout Sauterne, 202
Polenta
    Pizza Polenta, 224
    Polenta Pepper Soufflés, 247
Pomander Pork, 147
Popovers, Plaza, 71
Pork See also Ham; Prosciutto; Sausage
    Berried Pork Salad, 95
    Canadian Bacon with Ginger Pineapple
        Sauce, 149
    Garlic Grilled Pork Tenderloin, 144
    Harvest Stew in Maple Baked Acorn
        Squash, 122
    Heartland Pasta, 217
    Honey-Roasted Sesame Pork, 145
    Jiao Z, 37
    Mustard-Ginger Pork Chops, 147
    Pacific Rim Tenderloin, 146
    Peppered Pork Chops with Madeira Glaze,
        148
    Pomander Pork, 147
    Pork Tenderloin with Lime Cilantro Pesto,
        144
    Pork and Penne in Fennel Seed Sauce, 213
    Pork with Dijon Caper Sauce, 149
    River Country Pasta, 215
Potatoes
    Blue Cheese Potato Salad, 107
    Burgundy Shepherd's Pie, 157
    Grilled Potatoes, 238
    New Potatoes with Caviar Cream, 239
    Potato Gnocchi with Fresh Tomato Basil
        Butter Sauce, 221
    Rosemary Potato Tart, 238
    Sherried Sweet Potatoes, 239
    South of the Border Potato Salad, 107
    White Cheddar Parsnips and Potatoes, 235
    White Swan Rolls, 72
Poulet Dijon, 179
Princess Cookies, 283
Prosciutto
    Artichoke-Prosciutto Pasta, 215
    Calzone Napoli, 228-229
    Eggplant Prosciutto, 242
    Grilled Pizza with Gorgonzola and
        Prosciutto, 225
Puerto Vallarta Crêpes, 89
Pumpkin
    Butterscotch Pumpkin Muffins, 80
    Peppery Pepitas, 58
Queen of Hearts Salad, 116
Quesadillas, Chicken and Onion, 176
Queso Grill, 47
Quiche
    Country Manor Breakfast Tart, 91

Wild Mushroom Quiches in Acorn Squash, 90
Rack of Lamb Dijon, 163
Radish Butter, 75
Raisin Spice Bread, 73
Raisin French Toast, Rum, 83
Rajah Chicken Soup, 130
Raspberries
    Berried Pork Salad, 95
    Bittersweet Ravioli, 283
    Chocolate Raspberry Cream Cake, 267
    Raspberry Bars, 281
    Raspberry Coulis, 254
    Summer Palette Salad, 116
Ratatouille, 243
Red Bell Pepper Bread, 65
Red Onion Butter, 75
Red Onion Soup with Apple Cider, 132
Red Pepper Soup, 133
Red Sun Lamb Shanks, 160
Redfish, New Year's, 202
Reggae Chicken, 170
Relish, Wine-Soaked Apple Lemon, 146
Rhubarb, Rosy, Muffins, 80
Rice See also Wild rice
    Emerald Asparagus Pinwheel, 250
    Kaleidoscope Fried Rice, 251
    Lemon and Chive Risotto, 249
    Pasta Sauté with Rice and Pine Nuts, 221
    Sticky Shrimp, 190
    West Indian Apricot Rice, 251
River Country Pasta, 215
Roanoke Farm Muffins, 79
Roasted Red Pepper Garlic Dip, 52
Rolls. See Breads
Roma Fennel Bread, 63
Roquefort Toasts, 56
Rosemary Breadsticks, 67
Rosemary Poached Salmon, 196
Rosemary Potato Tart, 238
Rosy Rhubarb Muffins, 80
Roughy Pepper Packets, 199
Royal Beef Tenderloin, 154
Royal Rosemary Butter, 237
Ruby Cole Slaw, 118
Rum Raisin French Toast, 83
Saffron Chicken and Vegetables, 174
Sage Celery Seed Bread, 62
Salad dressings See also Vinaigrettes
    Apricot Mayonnaise, 102
    Creamy Horseradish Dressing, 105
    Garden Creamy Basil Dressing, 119
    Hazelnut Cognac Dressing, 119
    Mustard Dressing, 104
    Poppy Seed Dressing, 106
    Sour Cream Sherry Dressing, 118
Salads
    Autumn River Salad, 97
    Berried Pork Salad, 95
    Black Bean Salad, 111
    Black-Eyed Peaco de Gallo, 52
    Blue Cheese Potato Salad, 107
    Brookside Salad, 96
    Bruschetta Salad, 104
    Carrot and Apple Salad, 111
    Cobb Pasta Salad, 109
    Cold Herbed Garbanzo Beans, 109
    Cold Roasted Peppers with Mustard
        Dressing, 104
    Dilled Prawns and Melon, 99
    Flint Hills Beef Salad, 94
    Fruited Snow Pea Toss with Poppy Seed
        Dressing, 106

Goat Cheese Salad with Nectarines and
    Walnuts, 112
Indian Maize Salad, 105
Madagascar Crab Salad, 99
Marinated Mushrooms and Romaine Salad,
    115
Mediterranean Chicken Salad, 95
Minted Barley Salad, 110
Minted Spinach and Apple Medley, 112
Queen of Hearts Salad, 116
Ruby Cole Slaw, 118
Salmon and Apple Salad, 101
Sesame Pasta Salad, 110
Seville Salad, 113
Shrimp Salad Laced with Limes, 100
Shrimp Salad with Apricot Mayonnaise, 102
Sole Primavera Salad, 101
South of the Border Potato Salad, 107
Southern Belle Salad, 113
Southwest Turkey Salad, 98
Summer Palette Salad, 116
Szechuan Noodle Salad, 108
Technicolor Toss, 117
Thai Cabbage Salad, 117
Tomato Avocado Mold with Creamy
    Horseradish Dressing, 105
Won Ton Chicken Salad, 96
Salmon
    Lime Dilled Salmon, 198
    Pastry-Wrapped Sole with Salmon, 198
    Rosemary Poached Salmon, 196
    Salmon and Apple Salad, 101
    Smoked Salmon and Onion Cheesecake, 48
    Smoked Salmon with Salmon Biscuits, 34
    Tarragon Mustard Salmon Steaks, 196
Salsas
    Fresh Fruit Salsa, 53
    Melon Salsa, 195
    Salsa, 192
    White Salsa Dip, 52
Santa Fe Cheesecake, 46
Sauces See also Pesto; Sauces, dessert
    Barbecue Sauce, 154
    Basil Cream Sauce, 166
    Béchamel Sauce, 212
    Black Bean Pecan Sauce, 173
    Cognac Sauce, 159
    Cream Sauce, 153
    Creamy Mustard Sauce, 203
    Dijon Caper Sauce, 149
    Dijon Sauce, 39
    Dijon Vinaigrette, 34
    Fennel Seed Sauce, 213
    Fresh Tomato Basil Butter Sauce, 221
    Ginger-Lime-Cilantro Sauce, 195
    Ginger Pineapple Sauce, 149
    Hedaki Sauce, 181
    Herbed Mustard, 204
    Horseradish Sauce, 39
    Lemon Butter Sauce, 189
    Lime Dill Sauce, 198
    Lime-Red Pepper Hollandaise Sauce, 203
    Madeira Cream Sauce, 179
    Marchand du Vin Sauce, 158
    Mushroom and Parsley Sauce, 216
    Mustard Cream Sauce, 36
    Orange Hollandaise Sauce, 89
    Pecan Sauce, 199
    Provençal Sauce, 193
    Red Pepper Sauce, 171, 188
    Spicy Sun-Dried Tomato Sauce, 217
    Tarragon Mustard Sauce, 196
    Thai Sauce, 39
    Tomatillo and Red Pepper Sauce, 180

Tomato Basil Cream, 220
Tomato Basil Sauce, 222
Tomato Sauce, 40
Tomato Sauce Roma, 222
Watercress Puree, 169
Sauces, dessert
    Apricot Nectar, 273
    Apricot Sauce, 274
    Chocolate Sauce, 277
    Chocolate Glaze, 260
    Crème Anglaise, 254
    Honey Cream, 260
    Hot Caramel Sauce, 266
    Lemon Sauce, 259
    Orange Sauce, 84
    Praline Glaze, 265
    Raspberry Coulis, 254
    Rum Butter Sauce, 267
Sausage
    Brochettes of Chicken and Sage, 167
    Buttons and Bows, 214
    Calzone Napoli, 228-229
    Hearty Lentil Potage, 125
    Italian Strata, 90
    Lasagna Bolognese, 212
    Spicy Apple Sausage Patties, 150
    Three Pepper Chili, 126
    Upside-Down Pizza Pie, 226
Savory Olive Nut Bread, 70
Savory Steaks, 153
Scallops
    Basil Scallop and Shrimp Linguine, 218
    Martini Scallops with Angel Hair Pasta, 218
    Scallops Florentine, 191
    Shellfish Gratin, 191
    Tropical Seviche, 35
Sesame Pasta Salad, 110
Sesame Zucchini Bread, 70
Seviche, Tropical, 35
Seville Salad, 113
Shellfish Gratin, 191
Sherbets See Desserts
Sherried Sweet Potatoes, 239
Shrimp
    Basil Scallop and Shrimp Linguine, 218
    Corn Crêpes with Shrimp and Green
        Chilies, 188
    Corn, Shrimp and Penne Soup, 128
    Dilled Prawns and Melon, 99
    Grilled Shrimp with Lemon Butter Sauce,
        189
    Shellfish Gratin, 191
    Shrimp and Spinach Phyllo with Mustard
        Cream Sauce, 36
    Shrimp Cakes, 35
    Shrimp in Dijon Vinaigrette, 34
    Shrimp Kabobs and Red Pepper Sauce, 189
    Shrimp Salad Laced with Limes, 100
    Shrimp Salad with Apricot Mayonnaise, 102
    Sticky Shrimp, 190
Smoked Salmon and Onion Cheesecake, 48
Smoked Salmon with Salmon Biscuits, 34
Smoky Brisket, 154
Sole
    Mediterranean Baked Whitefish, 200
    Moroccan Ragoût, 200
    Pastry-Wrapped Sole with Salmon, 198
    Sole Primavera Salad, 101
Sorbets See Desserts
Soufflés
    Cheese Soufflé Roll, 88
    Chocolate Soufflés with Apricot Nectar, 273
    Cold White Chocolate Soufflé, 272
    Polenta Pepper Soufflés, 247

Soups *See also* Chili; Stews
    Amaretto Peach Soup, 141
    Broccoli Blue Soup, 133
    Cauliflower Stilton Velouté, 135
    Classic Wild Rice Soup, 130
    Cool Blueberry Soup, 140
    Corn, Shrimp and Penne Soup, 128
    Creamed Zucchini Soup, 134
    Curried Butternut Squash Soup, 134
    Dilled Tomato Soup, 137
    Fennel Soup with Oysters, 124
    Garden Green Gazpacho, 138
    Garden Tomato Soup, 132
    Hearty Lentil Potage, 125
    Herbed Black Bean Soup with Smoked
        Chicken, 123
    Indian Summer Soup, 140
    Minestrone Parmesan, 129
    Minted Kiwi Cream, 139
    Mushroom Feta Soup, 137
    Mushroom Ravioli in Beef Consommé, 129
    Old-Fashioned Vegetable Soup with
        Homemade Noodles, 131
    Rajah Chicken Soup, 130
    Red Onion Soup with Apple Cider, 132
    Red Pepper Soup, 133
    Thoroughly Warming Brew, 59
    Tomato Soup with Basil Cantaloupe Balls,
        138
    Tuscan Tortellini Soup, 128
    Vegetable Port Consommé, 136
Sour Cream Sherry Dressing, 118
South of the Border Potato Salad, 107
Southern Belle Salad, 113
Southwest Turkey Salad, 98
Spaghetti Squash with Sun-Dried Tomatoes,
    242
Spaghettini with Mushroom and Parsley
    Sauce, 216
Spiced Coffee, 280
Spiced Grapes and Carrots, 233
Spiced Olives, 57
Spicy Apple Sausage Patties, 150
Spinach
    Calzone Napoli, 228-229
    Cheese Soufflé Roll, 88
    Italian Strata, 90
    Minted Spinach and Apple Medley, 112
    Shrimp and Spinach Phyllo with Mustard
        Cream Sauce, 36
    Spinach and Steak Pinwheels, 152
    Spinach Fettuccine with Chicken and Pesto,
        208
    Tagliatelle Verde, 211
    Stuffed Spinach Crêpes, 42
    Tuscan Tortellini Soup, 128
Spoonbread, Onion and Corn, 72
Stews
    Country Veal Stew, 125
    Green Chili Stew, 123
    Harvest Stew in Maple Baked Acorn
        Squash, 122
Sticky Shrimp, 190
Stonehenge Bread, 62
Strata, Italian, 90
Strawberries
    Berried Pork Salad, 95
    Champagne Strawberry Sherbet, 279
    Creamy Lemon Sherbet with Marinated
        Strawberries, 278
    Fresh Fruit Torte, 277
Stuffed Cranberry-Pepper Game Hens, 182
Stuffed French Toast with Orange Sauce, 84

Stuffed Leg of Lamb, 162
Stuffed Spinach Crêpes, 42
Squash
    Creamed Zucchini Soup, 134
    Curried Butternut Squash Soup, 134
    Harvest Stew in Maple Baked Acorn
        Squash, 122
    Italian Strata, 90
    Orange Blossom Zucchini, 245
    Orange Chicken with Acorn Squash, 178
    Ratatouille, 243
    Sesame Zucchini Bread, 70
    Spaghetti Squash with Sun-Dried Tomatoes,
        242
    Summer Bounty Pasta, 216
    Thai Zucchini, 244
    Thyme Veggie Bundles, 244
    Wild Mushroom Quiches in Acorn Squash,
        90
Summer Bounty Pasta, 216
Summer Palette Salad, 116
Summer Phyllo Pizza, 223
Sunburst Florets, 246
Swedish Oatmeal Wheat Bread, 63
Sweet Onion Bites, 58
Sweet Potatoes, Sherried, 239
Swiss Custard, 86
Swordfish
    Ginger-Lime-Cilantro Swordfish, 195
    Grilled Swordfish with Melon Salsa, 195
Szechuan Noodle Salad, 108
Tacos, Crab, with Salsa, 192
Tagliatelle Verde, 211
Taos Tequila Chicken, 180
Tarragon Mustard Salmon Steaks, 196
Tarts. *See* Brunch; Desserts; Potatoes
Technicolor Toss, 117
Tenderloin with Three Sauces, 39
Teriyaki-Glazed Flank Steak, 151
Terrific Truffles, 285
Thai Cabbage Salad, 117
Thai Pies, 37
Thai Zucchini, 244
Thoroughly Warming Brew, 59
Three Pepper Chili, 126
Thyme Veggie Bundles, 244
Timbales, Leek, 240
Tomatillos
    Fresh Fruit Salsa, 53
    Tomatillo and Red Pepper Sauce, 180
Tomatoes *See also* Tomatoes, sun-dried
    Basil Tomatoes with Gorgonzola, 243
    Bruschetta Salad, 104
    Dilled Tomato Soup, 137
    Fettuccine with Tomato Basil Cream, 220
    Fresh Fruit Salsa, 53
    Garden Green Gazpacho, 138
    Garden Tomato Soup, 132
    Pasta with Herbed Tomatoes and Cheese,
        219
    Potato Gnocchi with Fresh Tomato Basil
        Butter Sauce, 221
    Ratatouille, 243
    Summer Phyllo Pizza, 223
    Thoroughly Warming Brew, 59
    Tomato Avocado Mold with Creamy
        Horseradish Dressing, 105
    Tomato Basil Sauce, 222
    Tomato Sauce Roma, 222
    Tomato Soup with Basil Cantaloupe Balls,
        138
    Tomato and Fennel Spread, 57

Tomatoes, sun-dried
    Angel Hair Pasta with Spicy Sun-Dried
        Tomato Sauce, 217
    Chèvre Pine Nut Toasts with Sun-Dried
        Tomato Pesto, 56
    Orange Fennel Brisket, 156
    Spaghetti Squash with Sun-Dried Tomatoes,
        242
    Spicy Sun-Dried Tomato Sauce, 217
    Sun-Dried Tomato Pesto, 56
    Sun-Dried Tomato Vinaigrette, 54
Tortes. *See* Desserts
Tortilla Stacked Pizza, 226
Trifle St. Croix, 255
Tropical Seviche, 35
Trout, Poached, Sauterne, 202
Truffles
    Coconut Truffles, 285
    Frozen Truffle Loaf, 255
    Terrific Truffles, 285
Tuna
    Broiled Tuna with Provençal Sauce, 193
    Italian Grilled Tuna, 194
Turkey
    Curried Turkey Breast, 184
    Grilled Turkey Breast with Herb Butter, 183
    Southwest Turkey Salad, 98
    Spicy Apple Sausage Patties, 150
Turkish Coffee, 280
Tuscan Tortellini Soup, 128
Upside-Down Pizza Pie, 226
Veal
    Arrowhead Veal Chops, 158
    Country Veal Stew, 125
    Herbed Meat Loaf with Cream Sauce, 153
    Veal Imperial, 159
    Veal Meatballs with Tomato Sauce, 40
    Veal Roast with Cognac Sauce, 159
Vegetable Port Consommé, 136
Vegetables. *See specific vegetables*
Vinaigrettes, 34, 54, 94, 96, 97, 100, 109, 112,
    113, 115, 116, 117
Vodkas. *See* Beverages
Waffles, Hyde Park, 85
Walnuts
    Goat Cheese Salad with Nectarines and
        Walnuts, 112
    Lemon Fettuccine with Hickory-Smoked
        Chicken, 208
    Rum Raisin French Toast, 83
    Savory Olive Nut Bread, 70
Wasabi Butter, 197
West Indian Apricot Rice, 251
West Indian Cream, 136
White Cheddar Parsnips and Potatoes, 235
White chocolate. *See* Chocolate, white
White Salsa Dip, 52
White Swan Rolls, 72
Whitefish, Mediterranean Baked, 200
Wild Mushroom Quiches in Acorn Squash, 90
Wild Mushroom Ragoût, 232
Wild rice
    Classic Wild Rice Soup, 130
    Wild Rice with Plantains, 250
Wine-Soaked Apple Lemon Relish, 146
Won Ton Chicken Salad, 96
Zesty Carrot Gratin, 234
Zucchini. *See* Squash
Zuccotto Frangelico, 268